G000144651

Windows® Remote Access Toolkit

David Angell

WILEY COMPUTER PUBLISHING

JOHN WILEY & SONS, INC.

New York • Chichester • Weinheim • Brisbane • Singapore • Toronto

Publisher: Robert Ipsen

Editor: Cary Sullivan

Assistant Editor: Kathryn A. Malm

Managing Editor: Angela Murphy

Electronic Products, Associate Editor: Mike Green

Text Design & Composition: SunCliff Graphic Productions

Designations used by companies to distinguish their products are often claimed as trademarks. In all instances where John Wiley & Sons, Inc., is aware of a claim, the product names appear in Initial Capital or ALL CAPITAL LETTERS. Readers, however, should contact the appropriate companies for more complete information regarding trademarks and registration.

This text is printed on acid-free paper.

Copyright © 1998 by David Angell
Published by John Wiley & Sons, Inc.

All rights reserved. Published simultaneously in Canada.

This publication is designed to provide accurate and authoritative information in regard to the subject matter covered. It is sold with the understanding that the publisher is not engaged in rendering legal, accounting, or other professional service. If legal advice or other expert assistance is required, the services of a competent professional person should be sought.

Reproduction or translation of any part of this work beyond that permitted by section 107 or 108 of the 1976 United States Copyright Act without the permission of the copyright owner is unlawful. Requests for permission or further information should be addressed to the Permissions Department, John Wiley & Sons, Inc.

Library of Congress Cataloging-in-Publication Data
Angell, David.
    Windows remote access toolkit / David Angell.
        p.   cm.
    Includes index.
    ISBN 0-471-19732-7 (pbk./CD-ROM : alk. paper
    1. Electronic data processing--Distributed processing.
2. Computer networks.   3. Digital communications.   4. Microsoft
Windows (Computer file)
QA76.9.D5A54   1997
004'.368565--dc21   97-13436

Printed in the United States of America
10 9 8 7 6 5 4 3 2 1

Contents

CHAPTER 4

Jacking Into the Net   51

Part Two: Building Your Windows 95 Foundation 69

CHAPTER 5

Windows 95 and Remote Access 71

CHAPTER 6

Remote Access via Dial-Up Networking 85

CHAPTER 7

Assembling a LAN for Remote Access   115

Part Three: 56-Kbps Modems and ISDN 185

CHAPTER 10

The Advent of 56-Kbps Modems 187

CHAPTER 11

Bonding Modem Connections with the WebRamp M3   205

CHAPTER 12

ISDN Essentials   221

CHAPTER 13

ISDN Modems   249

CHAPTER 14

Easy LAN Connectivity with WebRamp   269

CHAPTER 15

Farallon's Netopia Internet Router   299

Part Five: Appendixes   427

APPENDIX A

Windows 95 Remote Access Resources   429

Appendix B
What's on the CD-ROM   455

Acknowledgments

No book is ever a solo project by the author alone. First and foremost, I want to thank Cary Sullivan at John Wiley & Sons, and my agent, Matt Wagner at Waterside Productions, for helping to make this book a reality. A special thanks goes to my technical editor Marc Phillips at ZipNet, and Kathryn Malm and Angela Murphy at John Wiley & Sons for their high quality editorial and production work.

My thanks to the following people and companies for providing essential support for this project. Without them, this book could not have been possible. Alun Junes at Texas Imperial Software; Angie Tucker at Linksys Corporation; Barry Friedman at Earthlink; Ben Reser at Vector Development; Bill Truettner at Hewlett Packard; Brent Heslop at Bookware; Burt Forbes, Steve Kliene at Ascend Communications; Cary Heasley, Mark Persons at Shiva Corporation; Charles Neiman, Rochelle Ross, Ed Harris at Ramp Networks; Charles Sommerhouser, Wayne Luu at Cisco Systems; David Karp at Ipswitch; Fritz Stolzenbhach, Aletha Miller at DirecPC; Gwen Murphy, Barbara Tien at Farallon Communications; Janice McCoy at the Massachusetts Department of Utilities; Jeff Waldhuter at NYNEX; Jens Anderson at Kansman Corporation; John Coffey at White Pine Software; John Foltz at UsefulWare; Jon Jackson at Intel Corporation; Kerry Demke at Hayes Microcomputer Products; Kevin Murray at Symantec Corporation; Mark Gallegos at Pacific Bell; M.B. Fribley at Canyon Software; Mike Beltrano, Robin Porter at U.S. Robotics; Munira Brooks at ZyXEL Communications; Paul Cheng at Ideal Computer Technologies; Paul Corning, Tamara Hanna, Sarah Rades at Diamond Multimedia; Paul Stout at Angia Communications; Paula Giancola at MediaOne; Pavita Howe, Julie Murdoch at Forte Software; Peter Gieger at Eicon Technology; Scott Jackman at Dictaphone; Shannon Clemons at Motorola; and Valerie Motis at Stac.

Last but not least, I want to thank my wife Joanne Angell for supporting me through this entire project.

PART

I

Remote Access Gets Real

1 *Introduction*

Millions of individuals, small businesses, and telecommuters are screaming for more remote access capabilities. Gone is the bucolic era of casual PC communications using slow modems. The PC and the Internet are knocking down the pillars of the centralized workplace and replacing them with smaller interconnected groups of people. Our data communications links are rapidly becoming the links to our livelihoods. This introduction takes a look at the forces driving and shaping the exploding demand for high-speed remote access and provides an overview of this book's coverage of exciting new remote access solutions.

Welcome to the Distributed Workplace

In *The Third Wave* (1980), Alvin Toffler weaves a vision of the future where half-empty office towers testify to a return to cottage industry. This vision hasn't come to pass yet, but as the information age matures, a massive decentralization of the U.S. workplace is taking place. Large organizational structures are unraveling as a convergence of several underlying forces take hold, including:

- The rapid proliferation of powerful and affordable PCs and other technologies for the small office.
- The emergence of the Internet as the global data communications network for linking geographically dispersed locations.
- The personal desire of employees to reduce stress and the time they spend commuting to the corporate life and regain control over their lives.
- Corporate drive to improve productivity and reduce costs.
- Explosive growth in small to medium-sized businesses as large corporations downsize.
- Social policy directives to reduce congestion and pollution.

According to the Gartner Group, more than 80 percent of all organizations will have at least 50 percent of their staff engaged in telecommuting by 1999. This means the number of telecommuters will jump from 10 million in 1995 to 25 million in 1999. Another 24 million people are already self-employed (full-time and part-time) and working in small offices.

The exciting part of working in a "distributed" workplace is what it can do for people's personal lives. People are demanding flexible work arrangements in response to the daily double-digit hours they must spend working in the office and commuting. According to the American Automobile Association (AAA) companies and employees spend 2 billion hours annually commuting to and from their jobs.

More and more professionals want a better way to integrate their home and work life. In a 1994 Hilton Hotels survey of 1,000 professionals, 77 percent said their top priority for the next decade was to spend time with family and friends. Money and prestige came in second. A 1995 survey by AT&T Home Business Resources found that wanting to be near family was one of the primary motivators in people's decision to work at home.

The massive downsizing in corporate America has also contributed to the increasing popularity of small office in two ways. First, employees who have left corporate jobs are starting their own businesses in record numbers. Second, the overworked employees left behind in corporate offices are looking for ways to improve their productivity. In some cases, these workers and their managers have agreed that one way to stay on top of the workload is to do more work outside the office, either by spending more time with clients or in home offices where there are fewer interruptions.

A Booz, Allen & Hamilton study showed that about 25 percent of managers' time in the office is unproductive; for employees, the percentage is even higher. Telecommuters report a minimum of a 15 to 20 percent increase in productivity when they work outside the office, a figure that their managers corroborate.

Remote Access and the Internet

The Internet is the engine driving today's remote access trend. Before the Internet burst on the scene, PC-based communications focused on connecting to an online service or local BBS (computer bulletin board system) or another PC. Remote access was a tiny subset of PC applications. Even in the early days of the Internet, most PC users remained unwired.

Fast forward to 1997. The Internet has become the global infrastructure for the information age. A recent FIND/SVP study entitled *Internet Demographics: Realities & Trends* presents some interesting facts on the Internet and its participants.

- Currently, 31 million people use the Internet; 41 million people have used the Internet in the last 12 months.

- The average Internet user is 38.2 years of age; 70 percent are college graduates, with an average annual income of $61,000.

- Sixty-four percent of Internet users are men; 36 percent are women. The number of women Internet users has jumped from 16 percent in 1994.

- Two-thirds of Internet users view it as indispensable.

- The Internet is displacing other media among Internet users. TV use is down 34 percent among Internet users; long-distance calls are down 34 percent; and newspaper reading is off 17 percent.

The Internet is both a global resource for communications and information gathering, as well as a conduit for remote access to Internet-connected companies. Using the Internet, telecommuters and others can connect to their company's network and work as securely as if they were using a virtual private network (VPN) to exchange data directly with company LANs.

SOHO Islands in the Sun

An important consequence of the unraveling of the centralized workplace and large corporate downsizing is the explosive growth of home offices and small business offices. Link Resources, a New York City-based research firm, estimates that at the end of 1995 there will be slightly more than 40 million people working at home full- or part-time. By the end of 1998, Link predicts that number will jump to 60 million, an increase of 36 percent from 1994.

The small home and business office collectively are referred to as the *SOHO (Small Office/Home Office)* market. Another term for any workplace outside the traditional office in which people still do the work associated with a traditional office is the *virtual office*. The virtual in virtual office implies the use of technology that enables information workers to re-create the support services of the traditional office. The constant stream of new, affordable, and easy-to-use PC and remote access technologies ensure the continued growth of the virtual office in both numbers and capabilities.

The Win-Win of the Distributed Workplace

Distributed work is the practice of working without regard to location by using a combination of communications and computing technologies. To the extent that a job involves the creation, manipulation, storage, or communication of information, it is an increasingly viable option to do that job anywhere that the appropriate computer and data communications infrastructure is in place.

Companies and employees are beginning to appreciate the win-win nature of the distributed workplace. Employers improve their productivity by freeing individuals to work in their own customized work regimens, and at the same time save money by reducing expensive centralized offices. Employers also benefit by being able to recruit the best workers anywhere, without requiring them to move to a central location, and they have the ability to assemble and disassemble teams on an as-needed basis. Employees get to spend more time at home, less time in traffic, and develop the optimal work schedule to suit their individual styles. In short, the distributed workplace enables people to break free from the rigid structure of the corporate office.

For society as a whole, benefits of the distributed workplace may include greater economic efficiency, opportunities for economic growth in underdeveloped areas, expanded employment for individuals with limited mobility, and more efficient use of the transportation infrastructure.

Fear and Loathing for the Distributed Workplace

Like any major upheaval in people's lives, the distributed workplace creates anxieties and fears for many people. Many telecommuters are concerned that working in a home office will make them "invisible" at the corporate office, causing them to be outside the loop for promotions and choice job assignments. And for many people, the workplace is an important social outlet. They see the distributed office as eliminating face-to-face communications in favor of an isolated workplace.

Many potential telecommuters also form unrealistic expectations of what working in a home office will be like. For example, those employees with children mistakenly believe that telecommuting will eliminate the need for child care. In fact, the same focused attention they need in the corporate office is required in the home office. Other issues include managing the distractions unique to working at home. Many telecommuters find it difficult to get family, friends, and neighbors to respect their work time and space.

Beyond the psychological and social issues, there are the tangible problems of home office space requirements and expenses. Although telecommuting will reduce commuting expenses, others will increase. For example, you'll have to heat a house throughout the day, as well as incur higher utility bills. And in the absence of a subsidized corporate cafeteria, your food costs will rise. But the biggest expense is associated with identifying and claiming the necessary space at your home for an office, followed by the tax consequences of such a change. While there are some tax advantages, you need to know what you're doing.

The New Networker

As information technology (telecommunications and computers) improves and becomes more pervasive, more jobs depend on it. It's estimated that about 80 percent of the information workforce could telecommute at least some of the time. That works out to about 48 percent of the workforce. The information workforce comprises those who make substantial portions of their income by creating, manipulating, and transforming, and/or transmitting information, or operating information machines (computers). About 60 percent of the U.S. workforce fit the category.

The people who inhabit these new decentralized workplaces include telecommuters, entrepreneurs, self-employed home workers (full- or part-time), after-hours corporate workers, and small branch office workers. Self-employed entrepreneurs represent a rapidly growing segment of the SOHO market.

Telecommuters by far make up the largest component of people working in the distributed workplace. These are people who divide their time between working at home and working in the traditional corporate office. The typical telecommuter is a part-time employee who works usually no more than two days per week. Full-time telecommuters are employees who routinely work from an at-home office or workstation within the same metropolitan area as the traditional office and travel only once per week or less frequently to the corporate office.

Another specie of telecommuter is the telecenter, or branch office, telecommuter. This is an employee who works for reasons of convenience at a different, but more traditional, office facility provided by the employer. Long-distance telecommuters are those who are allowed to work from a distant residential location because their employer wishes to retain their services. They may report to a more convenient branch office, work from a home office, or do both.

Teleworker is a more encompassing term than telecommuter because it includes anyone who substitutes information technologies to do their job for work-related travel. The teleworker includes such variations as home-based businesses that use telecommunications to interact with their customers, as well as those who use a home-office in addition to commuting to a central office. The number of teleworkers is growing even faster than the number of telecommuters.

There are a number of other types of workers who use remote access as part of their workplace configuration. These include:

- Mobile workers or professionals, who usually report to a traditional office but who are also able to work continuously with location independence because of extensive travel requirements inherent in their job responsibilities. These include traveling salespeople, field auditors, trainers, and maintenance technicians.

- Independent homeworkers, self-employed professionals or business owners who could maintain an office outside the home but who choose to work routinely from an office at home.

- Remote regional field workers, employees assigned to cover a geographic area that is remote from the main office, and are required to work from home, a branch office, a rented office, or some combination.

- Decentralized workgroups, the employees in a workgroup who are reassigned to another employer-provided facility in a different part of the metropolitan or suburban area from the normal office.

- Remote branch/back-office workers, employees staffing a new office in a remote location. The employer transfers current staff to live and work in the new location or else hires new people in the new location.

- Virtual office workers, employees who are provided with home or portable office equipment and relinquish their corporate office because they spend the majority (typically 80 percent or more) of their work time in the field.

Remote Access Is Earth-Friendly

Transportation and telecommunications are increasingly merging into a new paradigm. Remote access technologies have a significant beneficial impact on the environment by reducing automobile use, which cuts down on hazardous emissions and curtails nonrenewable fuel use. Motor vehicles in the United States consume one-eighth of annual global oil production, at the rate of about 8.9 million barrels per day. Motorists use half of all imported oil.

The population in general also benefits from reduced automobile use. Only 60 percent of the $71 billion that it costs annually to operate and maintain the nation's roads and highways is paid by user fees. The remaining $29 billion is paid through property taxes, general funds, and other indirect sources.

Studies of telecommuters have shown clear and dramatic reductions in all aspects of automobile usage.

- A study conducted by Bell Atlantic researchers counted 12 million potential telecommuters in its service region. If just 5 percent (600,000 workers) telecommuted, 73 million gallons of gas would be saved, and 6,443 tons of hydrocarbons, 38,000 tons of carbon monoxide, and 2,300 tons of nitrogen oxide would not be released into the atmosphere.

- A study by Arthur D. Little Associates found that if 10 to 20 percent of traditional commuters switched to telecommuting, savings would total $23 billion annually. These savings would be realized by eliminating 1.8 million tons of regulated pollutants, lowering consumption of gas by 3.5 billion gallons, freeing up of 3.1 billion hours of personal time, and reducing maintenance costs for the transportation infrastructure by $500 million.

- A 1985 study by the Southern California Association of Governments found that a 32 percent reduction in freeway congestion could be achieved if just 12 percent of the regional workforce telecommuted.

Obviously, telecommuting can reduce peak-period commuting travel, and thus help reduce traffic congestion. According to the Federal Highway Administration, congestion now affects more areas, more often, for longer periods, and with greater impact on motorists than at any time in the nation's history. Total market costs of congestion borne by drivers are at least $100 billion per year; the total cost to society in general may be many times that figure. By encouraging telecommuting, local agencies can reduce peak-period freeway congestion for much less than it costs to build carpool lanes or impose peak-period tolls.

Your Remote Access Ecosystem

Enough talk about the big issues swirling around remote access. It's time to get specific about the starring roles those computers and data communication technologies are playing in your remote access future. The remote access "ecosystem" includes three key elements. The computing component includes Windows 95 and the Internet's Transmission Control Protocol and Internet Protocol (TCP/IP), which together create the winning combination for PC-based remote access. On the data communications side, the providers of the data communications links between your site and a remote network complete the remote access ecosystem. These are the telephone companies, cable companies, and others.

TCP/IP: Networking Protocol for the Planet

TCP/IP is the lingua franca of the Internet. It is used for all communication between your computer system, the Internet service provider's system, and every other system connected to the Internet. TCP/IP is not a single protocol but a whole family of protocols for different tasks and functions. As the defining protocol of the Internet, TCP/IP has become the universal language of remote access. It is the great equalizer of computer and network operating systems, and is now taking over as the network protocol of choice for remote access connectivity and even local area networks (LANs). According to Forrester Research, the number of companies with more than half their network traffic on IP will grow from 36 percent in 1996 to 82 percent in 1998. The move is away from proprietary network operating systems, such as NetBEUI (Microsoft) and NetWare (Novell) to full TCP/IP networking. Microsoft saw the writing on the wall and embraced TCP/IP in Windows 95.

The Windows 95 Remote Access Platform

Microsoft Windows 95 is the undisputed operating system of choice for the SOHO market, with an installed base of 66 million. By the year 2000, Microsoft Windows will have an installed base of 300 to 400 million. These numbers provide the critical mass needed for the delivery of affordable, high-speed connectivity products for remote access.

The strength of Windows 95 as viewed by most users is its cornucopia of available office applications, such as Microsoft Office. The lesser-known capabilities of Windows 95 include its impressive support for remote access. Windows 95 also features a collection of built-in remote access tools for connecting a single PC or an entire LAN to the outside world. These features include Windows 95's Plug and Play architecture, simplified LAN setup and use, built-in TCP/IP, Dial-Up Networking for seamless modem communications, a complete suite of Internet tools, and more.

Microsoft continues to push the remote access capabilities of Windows 95. The recent release of the Internet Explorer (IE) 4.0 Suite is both a major upgrade of Microsoft's Web browser, as well as a major facelift of the Windows 95 operating system. This unparalleled integration of the Web interface with the Windows 95 interface seamlessly blends the integration of the Internet into your local computing environment. IE 4.0 delivers a variety of new tools to bring real-time information from the Internet directly to your PC desktop. Office 97, the leading suite of office software, also integrates the Internet directly into applications such as Word97 documents or Excel spreadsheets.

The WAN Ties That Bind

What unites all the SOHO islands is access to the Internet and corporate networks. This is the realm of the wide area network, WAN for short. Wide area networks are the communication systems that interconnect geographically remote computer systems. These WAN links are essential to the decentralized workplace and transparent to the user. They act as the conduit for sending data between computers and networks.

You probably already have experience using the wide area network operated by the telephone companies if you use a modem and a telephone line to make a connection to your Internet service provider. The telephone companies operate the vast global WAN that enables us to make voice or data calls to almost anywhere on the planet. This public network that you connect to routes your calls through a vast infrastructure of switches. Cable and satellite companies also offer wide area networking services, and these public networks typically form the links that most of us use or will use. Large organizations often use their own private WANs.

Bandwidth: The Mantra of Remote Access

"Bandwidth, bandwidth, bandwidth" is the mantra of today's remote access. Bandwidth is the capacity of the data communications link. It's the engine that enables faster and more powerful remote access capabilities. Bandwidth defines which applications can be delivered in a timely manner to a large audience over the Internet. More bandwidth means more content possibilities—audio, video, 3-D virtual reality, Java applets, and so on. More bandwidth is what enables full participation in the benefits of the Internet, from desktop video conferencing to downloading software programs.

More bandwidth also makes it possible for people to work more productively, while having the "look and feel" of being connected to a local network, whether you're around the block or halfway around the globe. A study conducted at West Virginia University found that a data transmission speed of 80 Kbps was the minimum threshold for making remote access users feel as if they were actually connected to a local area network.

Next-generation higher-bandwidth technologies include 56-Kbps modems, Integrated Services Digital Network (ISDN), direct-broadcast satellite, Digital Subscriber Line (DSL), and cable modems, deployed primarily by telephone companies, cable operators, Internet access providers, and satellite companies. The computer industry provides the hardware and software interfaces to these new data communication technologies. However, higher-bandwidth technology is not without its disadvantages, and there is no magic bandwidth solution for all remote access needs.

The Bandwidth Blues

We live, work, and play in the digital age, and digital content is the currency of the information age. The graphical user interface, multimedia, and the World Wide Web have created a bandwidth monster that is eating up today's modems. The Internet is awash in sophisticated, bandwidth-hungry applications, yet it's getting choked in the modem bottleneck. Modems use analog voice grade lines, called POTS (plain old telephone service) in telecommunications circles, a system that was developed almost 100 years ago to handle voice communications.

The Internet has survived up to now by using million instructions per second (MIPS) and bits management as a replacement for bandwidth; faster CPUs and data compression have made up for the constrained bandwidth of public networks. But we're reaching the limitations of this approach, and a growing number of remote access users are becoming more intolerant of being stuck in the bandwidth slow lane. At this stage of high-speed connectivity development, it can be summed up as the best of times and the worst of times. A variety of higher-bandwidth technologies are in varying stages of deployment, and some are more widely available and advanced than others. But at this point, getting a higher-bandwidth connection comes down to the old real estate litany "location, location, location." Case in point: You may be able to get 1.54-Mbps cable modem service for less than $50 a month in your local community, although those in the next town cannot.

The search for a higher-bandwidth connection may take you through several technologies as you determine which is available in your area; if you have more than one choice, you will have to decide which solution is best in terms of price and performance. And don't forget, you'll be dealing with the telephone and cable industries, which have poor customer service records.

Bandwidth Wars

The two most powerful gatekeepers of higher-bandwidth connections are the telephone and cable TV companies. The telephone companies form the mother of all networks on the planet. In the United States, the largest regional telephone companies rule over 600 million telephone lines on a system that has been under construction since Alexander Graham Bell invented the telephone in 1876. Telephone companies are still emerging from 100 years of regulated monopoly.

The second largest network in the United States is that of cable television, which has been under construction since the 1960s and covers 90 percent of U.S. homes. The cable companies sit on a huge source of untapped bandwidth, and have been wiring America for the last 25 years with coaxial cable that can reach 90 percent of American homes. The bad news is that only about 15 percent of cable systems can handle the two-way communications required for high-speed remote access. The cable industry also has financial, technical, marketing, and service problems. Many cable operators see themselves as one-way entertainment companies, not as common carriers of data communications.

Together, the telephone and cable industries control huge reserves of bandwidth potential, and they're battling with each other to deliver it. Both are fighting to capture the big prize, which is to deliver high-speed remote access to the mainstream. This bandwidth war will affect you as a consumer of higher bandwidth.

Note, however, that recent U.S. government changes in the ground rules, which center on the Telecommunication Act of 1996, may promise to open up competition to other players over time. New technologies, such as satellite and wireless, will also generate competition between terrestrial and extraterrestrial players as well.

Look and Feel of High-Speed Remote Access

High-speed access isn't just about changing speeds; it's about doing remote access in a whole new way, and it requires working with new tools, techniques, and terminology. High-bandwidth connections change the way you interact with remote resources, and one of the biggest changes is that these are digital connections. ISDN, cable modems, or xDSL connections operating seamlessly in the background will give you a transparent view of working on the Internet (or other network) or on your local computer. The 20 or more seconds it now takes for a modem to connect to the remote network will drop to two seconds. Clicking on a Web browser on your Windows 95 desktop will bring instant Internet access with stealth. Gone will be the crackling, high-pitched modem connections that can take up to a minute.

About This Book

Metamorphosing into the brave new world of the distributed workplace as a telecommuter, self-employed home worker (full- or part-time), or after-hours corporate worker means you will have to understand the elements of your remote access ecosystem. Entering the realm of high-bandwidth remote access is a learning experience. It requires you to become an educated consumer of bandwidth and gain a working knowledge of the tools and techniques needed to implement your high-speed connectivity solution. This hands-on guide will bridge Windows 95 remote access capabilities with high-speed bandwidth to help you build a holistic remote access ecosystem for your home or small business. This book is organized into five parts.

- Part I, "Remote Access Gets Real," explains the conceptual foundations and underlying technologies driving remote access. It also outlines the key elements that make up the complete remote access ecosystem.
- Part II, "Building Your Windows 95 Foundation," takes you through the process of setting up and managing your Windows 95 PC or LAN for remote access. It covers working with Windows 95 TCP/IP stack, network-

ing, and internetworking features, as well as the essential Windows 95 Internet tools.

- Part III, "56-Kbps Modems and ISDN," begins the hands-on journey up the bandwidth food chain starting with 56-Kbps modem and ISDN (128 Kbps) connectivity options.
- Part IV, "Satellites, Cable Modems, and xDSL," takes you into the brave new world of satellite-based remote access at 400 Kbps; xDSL technologies at 1.54 Mbps; and cable modems at 1.54 Mbps.
- Part V, "Appendixes," includes a comprehensive listing of remote access resources and coverage of the cool remote access software included on this book's CD-ROM.

About the CD-ROM

The accompanying CD-ROM includes a collection of handy Windows 95 remote access tools. I've made a special effort to add tools that allow you to extend and expand your Windows 95 remote access capabilities. All the software on this book's CD-ROM is designed for Windows 95, with most of them 32-bit applications. The software tools on the accompanying CD-ROM will help you:

- Make Windows 95 LAN management easier.
- Enhance Windows 95 Dial-Up Networking capabilities.
- Monitor and control your Windows 95 remote access connections.
- Prevent virus attacks on your local system.
- Improve your communications with new high-bandwidth tools such as desktop video conferencing and group collaboration tools.
- Enhance your Windows remote access toolkit with a Windows FTP server and client program.

Who Should Read This Book

The *Windows Remote Access Toolkit* is about expanding your PC-based communications beyond 28.8/33.6 Kbps modems. Today's GUI computing environment coupled with the explosive data communication requirements of the multimedia Web demand new connectivity options for the Windows 95 user. You'll find this guide serves two distinct yet interrelated purposes. The first is to make you an educated consumer of remote access technologies and equipment. The second is to give you hands-on experience working with different connectivity options within the Windows 95 and real-world context.

In writing this book, I make some assumptions about who you are and what you are seeking. Even if only one of the following describes why you're looking into a faster way to work remotely, you're a candidate for this book.

- You're tired of the World Wide Wait. You're searching for a faster way to work (and play) on the Internet—the mother of all remote access networks.
- You've heard about 56-Kbps modems, ISDN, satellite, cable modems, and DSL but don't have a grasp of what each technology is all about and whether it's an option for you.
- You're working in or plan to work in a SOHO (small office/home office) environment that doesn't have access to the expensive services of professional networking and data communications people.
- You don't have deep pockets to buy dedicated connections that cost hundreds of dollars per month, but you want to have a high-bandwidth connection.
- You're always on the lookout for new ways to gain a competitive advantage in today's business environment and you know a better link to the Internet is an important tool for your business.
- You'd like to leverage a high-bandwidth connection across several PCs connected to a Windows 95 LAN.
- You're using a PC or LAN running Microsoft Windows 95, you know your way around Windows, and you're not afraid of opening up your PC to install an adapter card.

What's Next

This chapter gave you a bird's eye view of the forces shaping the new decentralized workplace and the remote access technologies that enable it to happen. Chapter 2 begins your orientation to the next generation of higher-bandwidth connections. It translates bandwidth lingo, describes the main dishes of the high-bandwidth buffet and how they interface with your PC or LAN.

2   *In Search of More Bandwidth*

Before setting out on the quest for more bandwidth, it is necessary to understand what bandwidth is all about; how different data communications technologies deliver bandwidth; and which bandwidth options support different types of remote access connections. This chapter takes you through these basics and shows you the high-bandwidth terrain in terms of the providers and other forces influencing your connectivity options.

Bandwidth Basics

Bandwidth is the capacity of the communications pipeline to deliver data. The higher the bandwidth, the more data that can flow through it. Understanding bandwidth is more than just knowing about the speed of a connection. You need to understand bandwidth terminology and related concepts in order to become an educated consumer.

Bandwidth Defined

In a communication channel, bandwidth is the difference between the highest and lowest frequencies used within a specific range of frequencies called the *passband*. The range of frequencies is usually specified in hertz (cycles per second, abbreviated Hz). For example, the analog signal used for telephone communications occupies the voice frequency range of 300 to 3300 Hz. The passband for voice telephone communication becomes 3000 Hz, which is the difference between the lowest frequency (300 Hz) and the highest frequency (3300 Hz).

   Electromagnetic radiation is the energy present in all things. The electromagnetic spectrum is the range of electromagnetic radiation in the known universe, which includes radio waves, with large wavelengths, to cosmic rays, with small wavelengths. Within this electromagnetic spectrum, all communication systems function. In the electromagnetic spectrum, sound waves occupy low ranges while microwaves, visible light, ultraviolet, and X rays occupy upper ranges. Various communication technologies occupy different frequencies. The concepts of frequencies is important in understanding how the same telephone line that uses copper wiring can be used for analog voice service and support higher-bandwidth connections.

Note: The Federal Communications Commission (FCC) is in charge of allocating the electromagnetic spectrum in the United States, and thus the bandwidth of various communication systems. As you delve into the world of high bandwidth, the role of the FCC becomes important. Chapter 3 explains the role of the FCC in more detail.

Analog Communications

Sound is an analog waveform. The sounds you hear are transmitted via air pressure to your ears. The changing frequency of the sound waves creates continuously changing air pressure on your eardrums, which your brain interprets as sounds. Most humans can hear sound in the 30 to 20,000 hertz range. An analog signal is one in which the amplitude (wave height) and frequency (number of waves per second) vary over a continuous range. An analog signal is continuous and conveys information by variations in the height and width of its waveform.

The analog signals used in telecommunications are transmitted via electric current over wires that handle waves in a manner similar to the way sound is generated; they then amplify the waves over distances. Telephones turn voice vibrations into electrical vibrations of the same shape, but amplified so they can be carried over distances. Analog lines transmit digital computer information first by converting the digital data to analog signals with a modem. A modem, which is an abbreviation for modulator/demodulator, is required on both ends of the connection. At the receiving end of the connection, a modem is used to change the analog signals back into the digital form used by computers.

The majority of telecommunications systems in use today were originally designed to carry voice. Analog transmission methods have inherent problems that limit their usefulness for high-speed digital data communications because analog lines are subject to transmission impairments that can distort signals. This requires error-correction and -detection mechanisms and data retransmissions that reduce the data-carrying capacity of the connection.

Digital Communications

Digital communication is the exchange of information in binary form rather than analog signals. Unlike sound waves, computer data is transmitted using digital signals. A digital signal doesn't use continuous waves to transmit information the way an analog signal does. Instead, a digital signal transmits information using two discrete signals, or on and off states of electrical current. All computer data can be communicated through patterns of these electrical pulses. A digital channel is a communications path that handles only digital signals, the kind generated by computers. Digital communication not only supports high-speed data communications, it's also a more reliable medium compared to analog. To carry voice over a digital line requires an analog-to-digital conversion.

Note: As you'll learn later, many higher-bandwidth devices are routinely called modems, which is more of a marketing term than a technology-based term.

Changing Channels and Directions

A channel is any pathway used for data transmission. A communications channel is a logical device that is defined separately from the cabling that actually delivers the data communications. Each channel is an independent unit that can transfer data concurrently with other channels. ISDN service, for example, is typically delivered in the form of three channels, one D (data) channel for telephone network control data and two B (bearer) channels, as shown in Figure 2.1. Each of the B channels can support up to 64 Kbps for data communications; the D channel can support 16 Kbps. These three channels are delivered across a single telephone line. The two B channels can be used concurrently to deliver a full 128 Kbps of data communications, or for two completely separate communications—one channel to send a fax and the other to connect to the Internet.

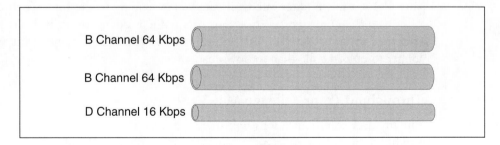

Figure 2.1 *A single ISDN line supports three separate channels.*

Within data communications channels, there can be *bidirectional* or *unidirectional* data flows. A bidirectional channel means that communications can occur in two directions at the same time. A unidirectional channel means that communications can flow in one direction at a time. *Half-duplex* communications can flow in both directions through a channel, but in only one direction at a time. An example of this is two-way radios through which one party can speak at a time while the other party listens. *Full-duplex* communications can flow in both directions simultaneously, by dividing the bandwidth into two frequencies, one for sending and the other for receiving.

Asymmetric or Symmetric Communications

Many forms of data communications have unequal data channel capacities where one data channel supports a larger data communications capacity than the other. This uneven form of data communications is referred to as *asymmetrical*, which means data traveling in one direction moves faster than data moving in the opposite direction. In the case of Internet access, an asymmetrical connection usually means data coming from the Internet to your PC travels at a much higher rate than data going from your PC back to the Internet. In *symmetric* data communications, both channels have equal capacity for uploading or downloading data.

Data Swimming Upstream or Downstream

The terms used to describe the data carrying capacity of asymmetrical links are *upstream* and *downstream*. Downstream refers to data traffic moving from the remote network to your computer; upstream refers to the data moving from your PC to the remote network. For example, a cable modem typically supports a data communications capacity of 1.54 Mbps on the downstream channel and only 300 Kbps on the upstream channel. Likewise, 56-Kbps modems deliver data at 56 Kbps downstream but have an upstream capacity of only 28.8 or 33.6 Kbps.

In terms of Internet access, this means the data from the Internet is coming to your PC at a much faster rate than data you're sending to the Internet. In the case of using a Web browser, most of your data traffic is downstream. If you're transferring files to and from an FTP site, the slower upstream rate means it will take longer to upload a file than to download a file.

Throughput (Your Mileage May Vary)

On any data communications link there are always "bandits of bandwidth." These bandits come from a variety of factors that affect the true throughput of a connection. Throughput is an overall measure of a communication's link performance in terms of its real-world speed. The throughput is the factoring in of impacts on the data speed coming from the entire remote access ecosystem. Factors affecting the throughput of a data communications link can be distance and switching components such as routers, network traffic, and other interference that slow down data transmission.

Think of throughput as equivalent to mileage ratings used for new cars. Claims made by bandwidth providers are like gasoline mileage claims made before the government standardized the methods for setting realistic mileage claims. Having the fastest link to the Internet is only half the story of your real throughput. Remember, the Internet is one giant, shared network. It, too, suffers from rush hour traffic. During peak network traffic periods, downloading a file from a crowded Web server 3,000 miles away can be a slow experience indeed.

You probably have seen for yourself the discrepancy between a modem's capability and the actual rate of a data connection. For example, connecting to the Internet using a 28.8 Kbps modem doesn't mean you'll always get a data transmission rate of 28,800 bits per second. A number of factors affect the connection to make the throughput figure lower, including:

- Internet traffic between your computer and the server. If the Internet is experiencing a heavy volume of data traffic, the entire system slows down.
- The speed of the server in handling your request. In any networking environment, it takes a client and a server to make a connection. If the server is busy, it will slow down in terms of delivering your requested data.
- The quality of your telephone connection to the Internet service provider. A noisy telephone line requires data to be resent more frequently.

Broadband

Broadband is a general term for the more powerful high-speed bandwidth technologies. Technically, broadband refers to using high-frequency transmission over coaxial cable or fiber optics, which is what makes up cable TV systems. This technique allows for the combined transmitting of data, voice, and video using several streams of data transmitted simultaneously over long distances.

Welcome to the Higher-Bandwidth Buffet

For the bandwidth-hungry, higher-bandwidth products are already available or will be in the near future. This buffet of bandwidth options is in different stages of development and deployment. The primary purveyors of remote access bandwidth are the telephone and cable companies; satellite systems are a distant third. The following sections introduce you to the higher-bandwidth technologies that undoubtedly will become part of your remote access future.

Note: Part III covers 56-Kbps modems and ISDN in greater detail, and Part IV covers satellites, cable, and xDSL.

Introducing 56-Kbps Modems

U.S. Robotics, Rockwell Semiconductor Systems, and Lucent Technologies have developed two different implementations of 56-Kbps modem technologies. The U.S. Robotics technology is called x2 and the Rockwell Semiconductor Systems and Lucent Technologies is referred to as 56Flex. Both these solutions are proprietary, and standards are not expected until the U.S. Telecommunications Industry Association ratifies them. However, despite the lack of interoperability between these two technologies, modem manufacturers are releasing 56-Kbps modems.

While some modem vendors are supporting the x2, most are supporting the 56Flex technology. More important, most of the vendors that make equipment for receiving incoming calls for Internet service providers such as Ascend, Cisco, and others, are supporting the 56Flex technology.

The 56-Kbps modems operate differently from earlier modems. They're an asymmetric solution that delivers data downstream at up to 56 Kbps, but have upstream speeds of 28.8 and 33.6 Kbps. There are also a variety of other factors that influence the actual speed you get, which in most cases will be in the mid-40 Kbps range. A 56-Kbps modem requires a good-quality phone line between your home or office and the telephone company's switching facility. Your premises also have to be within a mile or two of the phone company's switch. Furthermore, the host you're calling must have a digital connection to the Internet or corporate network. And at least for the near term, you must make sure the Internet service provider or other remote network is using the same 56-Kbps modem technology—x2 or 56Flex.

The major advantage of 56-Kbps modem technology is that while it can be potentially almost as fast as a single B-channel ISDN connection downstream, it doesn't come with any of the higher installation costs and usage fees associated with ISDN service. These modems, like other modems, use standard telephone service that enables you to make calls within your local calling area with no per-minute charges from the telephone companies.

According to a recent study by Jupiter Communications, 56-Kbps modems will control 50 percent of the remote access market by 1998, and 65 percent by the year 2000. The firm also projects that 23 percent of remote access sites in the SOHO market will have 56 Kbps modems by the end of this year.

Note: Another new development in modem-based remote access is remote access devices that let you combine multiple modem connections and treat them as a single high-bandwidth connection, as well as connect them to a LAN. By combining two or three 56-Kbps modems to work simultaneously, remote access users can get higher-bandwidth connections even if other high-bandwidth options aren't available in their area. These new modem products are covered in Chapter 10.

ISDN

Integrated Services Digital Network (ISDN) is a digital service offered by telephone companies, and was the first digital service offered to the mass market by the telephone companies. For the most part, ISDN as a connectivity option for the SOHO market has proved to be a mixed bag. ISDN service has been around for a few years, but the long road to ISDN deployment, poor packaging, pricing, and marketing of the service by the telephone companies have combined to hamper this technology.

ISDN delivers data communications at speeds up to 128 Kbps without compression (with compression, the rate can reach 512 Kbps—4-to-1 compression). ISDN is delivered to homes and businesses using existing standard telephone wiring, and it is fully integrated with the existing analog telephone network. ISDN is the only symmetric service of the high-bandwidth options.

Several elements of ISDN service make it an attractive option for the SOHO market. First, it's the most widely deployed of the higher-bandwidth solutions after 56-Kbps modems. Approximately 85 percent of U.S. metropolitan areas have access to ISDN service, and many Internet service providers offer ISDN dial-up access to the Internet. Another advantage of ISDN is the cornucopia of powerful and affordable ISDN remote access devices available for connecting a single PC or a LAN. Many of these vendors also provide free ISDN ordering and set-up services.

The biggest drawback to ISDN service in many areas is the cost. ISDN can be expensive—about the same as the price of two analog lines, not including usage charges. Depending on your local phone company tariffs, you may pay a per-call connect charge in addition to per-minute billing on data calls. ISDN service can cost from around $32 month plus usage charges to $185 per month for dial-up 128-Kbps ISDN service. It all depends on your telephone company and the rates being charged in your state.

One important offsetting advantage to using ISDN, even at its higher cost, is that you can easily share a single ISDN line across a small LAN by using an ISDN router. This can be a cheaper option than a modem and separate Internet access accounts for each PC in an office, especially when you consider that your LAN can share a single-user Internet access account as well.

Satellite Access

The satellite option for remote access is in its infancy, but a number of companies are working on satellite systems to deliver high bandwidth for Internet access. Given the long lead times in building land-based high-speed data communications systems, satellites have the capability to ramp up more quickly. A satellite company sends up a satellite, and customers buy or lease a satellite dish to get the bandwidth from the satellite.

Already, satellite TV has been making inroads into the cable TV marketplace, with several companies, such as DirecTV, EchoStar, and PrimeStar, all competing for new customers. Most of these companies have announced plans to add an Internet access component to their packages, which will mean a customer can get both TV and data communications from the same satellite dish.

The most significant advantage of satellite-based systems is that you can access the service from just about anywhere. In the case of land-based high-bandwidth options, your local telephone or cable company must have the infrastructure in place and available in your area in order for you to make the connection. Because most telephone and cable companies are deploying higher-bandwidth solutions in larger urban areas, many other areas won't have access to these services. A satellite or group of satellites can broadcast across the United States or North America, so availability is anywhere there is a clear line of sight to the satellite's location. However, satellite data delivery has its share of drawbacks, including relatively costly start-up and usage fees and technical capacity limitations.

Hughes Network Systems offers a high-speed Internet access service using the same Digital Satellite System (DSS) satellites that bring HBO to your television. The DirecPC system uses a special receiver on an ISA card connected to a 24-inch satellite dish to provide a 400-Kbps downstream link from the Internet. Because the DSS system is a one-way broadcast medium, your outbound data must travel via a modem to an Internet service provider. Besides the up-front expense for the satellite package ($499, plus up to $150 for installation), there are usage costs, and they can quickly add up. Hughes offers a variety of pricing packages starting at $9.95 a month and ranging up to $129.95 per month. Satellite communications have a promising future, but for the time being, they are only an option for SOHO users living in rural areas that don't have access to any higher-bandwidth technologies from the telephone or cable companies.

Cable Service

Cable Internet access service uses your cable television coaxial retrofitted with new networking technology. Cable service is asymmetric, and the specific downstream and upstream capabilities are functions of how your cable operator packages the service and the cable modems it uses for the service. However, if you can get it, cable modem technology is a great high-bandwidth solution both in terms of bandwidth and price,.

Cable modem service delivers an impressive high-bandwidth solution for the SOHO market. For example, the cable company that services my community is MediaOne (formerly Continental Cablevision), and it provides cable modem service for a flat rate of $49.95 a month for a single PC, which includes the cable modem and Internet access account. The service boasts speeds of 1.5 Mbps downstream and 300 Kbps upstream. This is a bandwidth bargain; the same speed using a T1 line from the telephone company would cost you around $1,500 a month! For a modest $100 installation fee, MediaOne installs the system in any location you want. The cable modem connects to a single PC via an Ethernet card.

The biggest drawback is availability. While 90 percent of U.S. households have access to cable television service, only 15 percent of cable-TV systems are ready to deliver two-way Internet data communications. It comes down to being lucky enough to live in an area where your local cable operator is offering cable modem service. The cable companies face a long road to upgrading their systems to handle the two-way traffic needed for Internet access.

Cable modem technology has other limitations. It is set up so that each neighborhood is set up as a LAN, sharing a connection that is split multiple times into each and every household. Right now, with only a few users taking advantage of this service, connections are always speedy; but in the future, when every house in your neighborhood is using cable modems, the network may become seriously bottlenecked. However, the architecture behind the cable system is such that a cable company can divide network nodes to take pressure off the LAN. It remains to be seen how effectively the cable companies will manage bandwidth.

Another limitation of today's cable modems is that they provide only high-speed remote access to the Internet. You can't use a cable modem to connect to other networks, such as a corporate LAN for telecommuting. Perhaps the most frustrating thing about using a cable modem is that it's restricted to a single PC, which means you can't share the high bandwidth with other PCs connected to a LAN. Many of these problems will be ironed out over time.

The xDSL Family

Originally, Digital Subscriber Line (DSL) technologies were designed for use with a video-on-demand system, which would allow users to request what to watch on their televisions. xDSL is a technology that can deliver comparable speeds to cable systems. The x in xDSL is a placeholder for the several members that make up the Digital Subscriber Line family, including ADSL, HDSL, IDSL, RADSL, and SDSL. Table 2.1 describes the capacities of each technology. Digital Subscriber Line doesn't refer to the line, but to the modem technologies that convert a line into a high-speed digital pipeline. The lines being converted via xDSL are standard twisted-pair copper wire used for POTS service today. But instead of the line being linked by analog modems at both ends, the line is linked by an xDSL device at each end of the connection. An important distinction of xDSL technologies is they typically bypass the telephone company's switching infrastructure. This allows the telephone companies to add xDSL services in parallel to their existing switching systems. In theory, this means the telephone companies can roll out xDSL service faster than they did for ISDN, which was an early predecessor of the entire family of DSL technology. ISDN service was linked to the costly telephone-

Table 2.1 The xDSL Family of High-Bandwidth Services

xDSL TYPE	DESCRIPTION
ADSL (Asynchronous Digital Subscriber Line)	Supports 32 Kbps to 9 Mbps downstream, and 32 Kbps to 1.088 Mbps upstream.
HDSL (High data-rate Digital Subscriber Line)	Supports symmetrical service at 1.54 Mbps to 2.048 Mbps.
IDSL (ISDN Digital Subscriber Line)	Supports symmetrical service at 128 Kbps.
RADSL (Rate-Adaptive Digital Subscriber Line)	A rate-adaptive variation of ADSL, which means the telephone company can adjust the bandwidth.
SDSL (Symmetrical Digital Subscriber Line)	Supports symmetrical service at 160 Kbps to 2.048 Mbps.
VDSL (Very-high-rate Digital Subscriber Line)	The high-end member of the xDSL family that supports up to 51 Mbps.

switching infrastructure. This was a major factor in the slow deployment of ISDN by the telephone companies.

Like so many dreams of the media masters and telephone companies, the Internet quickly rearranged priorities. xDSL has become the great high-bandwidth hope for telephone companies entering the Internet access business in a big way. How the telephone companies will handle this technology in terms of packaging, pricing, and marketing is anyone's guess. xDSL in different forms is expected to be deployed in earnest starting in late 1997 through 1998.

The telephone companies will use their existing infrastructure of copper wiring, of which there are an estimated 600 million lines in the United States, as a basis for rolling out xDSL. However, nothing in telecommunications is ever straightforward, and there are an assortment of technical issues that make xDSL deployment more complex than just plugging two xDSL modems into a POTS line.

While xDSL can deliver speeds of up to 8 Mbps, technical and telephone company packaging and pricing practices will ration out bandwidth in considerably smaller chunks for the SOHO market. Like so many things the telephone companies do, there will be a variety of xDSL service offerings and pricing. xDSL will be packaged in bandwidth options at 128 Kbps and up. xDSL is more likely to be marketed as point-to-point connectivity product for data communications only. xDSL uses signal encoding, compression, and special modulation techniques to deliver its high-speed access over unshielded twisted-pair cables. DSL's point-to-point nature makes it ideal for Internet and telecommuting connections. The link is always up, and the service should be very reliable.

Although DSL isn't commercially available yet, several trial installations are up and running. At least two phone companies, US West and GTE, plan to offer DSL service in a few limited markets in 1997. Pacific Bell plans to roll out xDSL products designed for the SOHO market in 1998. Likewise, Bell Atlantic plans a big rollout in 1998; and there are dozens of announced xDSL products from a variety vendors.

Through the Bandwidth Maze

As you work your way through the high-bandwidth maze, you'll have to deal with an entirely new set of challenges to getting connected. As a consumer, you should begin your journey by following a few guiding principles. There are a number of factors to consider before deciding which higher-bandwidth option you should use. Add to this that the decision may be made for you because some of the high-bandwidth solutions won't be available in your area. For the immediate future, the three options are 56-Kbps modems, ISDN, and cable modems. ADSL is a promising bandwidth solution, but implementation is another thing; it is the bandwidth technology that everyone in the SOHO market should keep an eye on as a possible upgrade path.

When comparing different high-bandwidth options, some of the more important features and differences to ask about when comparing these technologies are:

- How long will the technology be around? Will it be out of date in the near future, or will you get at least a few years of good service out of it?

- What is the cost of implementation for you and what is the cost of implementation for the companies providing the service? Is the bandwidth provider making money on the service? If so, chances are the service will be around for awhile; if not, don't expect the provider to continue the service for long.

- What is the compatibility with existing standards and existing equipment? How far along in the development cycle of standards is the technology?

- How easy it is to install and use for end users?

- What is the cost of using the high-bandwidth technology? In some cases, the usage costs can easily outstrip the start-up costs.

- How does the technology really perform in the real world, versus the marketing hype or advertised speeds? Will the technology live up to its high speed over time as more users share the network, or will performance begin to degrade?

Matching Remote Access Needs with Bandwidth Options

Remote access is about connecting to the Internet and/or a corporate network. While the Internet is playing a central role in the development of remote access technologies, a large number of SOHO users will want to connect to the office network as well as the Internet. If your remote access needs require connecting to a corporate network not linked to the Internet, you need to choose a higher-bandwidth option that supports it.

- ISDN and 56-Kbps modems, which are run over the public telephone network, support remote access connections to the Internet as well as to an office network, if the office network or Internet service provider supports 56 Kbps or ISDN connections.

- Satellite-based data communications currently support only Internet access.

- Cable modems currently support only Internet access service.

- xDSL technologies may or may not provide access to an office network over the public telephone network. It depends how the telephone companies are going to handle this new technology.

For at least the immediate future, optimal access for the office network is via the Internet. Many companies are using the Internet as the conduit for remote access in conjunction with firewalls, which add security against intruders to their networks. Other companies, fearful of exposing their networks to the Internet, don't support Internet-based remote access.

Keeping an Eye on the Competition

It's complete chaos out there for the SOHO bandwidth consumer. Telephone companies, cable TV operators, satellite companies, and Internet service providers all are gearing up to capture market share in the expanding connectivity marketplace. The two big players in the delivery of mass-market high-speed data communications are the telephone companies and the cable television companies. Delivering high bandwidth is about building large complex communications systems that form the infrastructure for delivering these higher-bandwidth solutions to consumers. These systems take years to build.

The stakes are high in the multibillion-dollar war of high bandwidth, and each player comes to the table with strengths and weaknesses. No one high-bandwidth provider has the magic bandwidth bullet that will replace all the other options.

The second largest network in the United States is the cable television network, which has been under construction since the 1960s and covers 90 percent of U.S. homes. This industry sits on a huge source of untapped bandwidth, which it delivers using a flat-rate pricing model. You can watch cable TV 24 hours a day, 7 days a week or 1 hour a day, 1 day a week and your bill will stay the same. Exploiting the cable industry's bandwidth for the Internet is touted as the single greatest opportunity for universal, high-speed digital communications at speeds of up to 10 Mbps. The combined pool of millions of 10-Mbps bandwidth cable lines exceeds any capacity the telephone companies have to offer. Unfortunately, the cable industry suffers from inherent technology, marketing, and service problems. The industry as a whole continues to see itself as a provider of one-way entertainment services, not as a common carrier of data. As such, it has upgraded only 15 percent of the cable systems to handle two-way communications.

Injecting More Competition

An unknown factor in the deployment and pricing of digital bandwidth is the Telecommunications Act of 1996. This legislation removed many of the laws and restrictions governing the broadcast, cable, telecommunications, and computer industries. The intent was to leave the future direction of these industries in the hands of the competitive marketplace. The act was designed to open up the regional phone companies to competition even for local dial-tone service. Consequently, jumping into the mix with phone companies are cable operators and satellite services. And you can expect to see Internet service providers (ISPs), alternative local phone service providers (called competitive access providers, or CAPs), wireless data companies, and even utility companies offering high-speed data services.

The act gives the telecommunications industry its first big injection of competition since the government broke up AT&T in 1984. Prior to that, AT&T was the telephone company for most of the United States. Whether the breakup did anything for consumers is questionable. AT&T was replaced by several regional telephone companies, each with its own game plan and local monopoly. This fragmented telecommunications industry continues to plague telecommunications today. To summarize the Telecommunications Act, it:

- Allows RBOCs (Regional Bell Operating Companies) to offer long-distance services; likewise, allows long-distance carriers to offer local service.

- Allows other entities, such as cable service providers, to offer telecommunications services, and allows common carriers to provide video programming in their telephone service areas.

- Allows RBOCs or other companies to jointly market and sell commercial mobile services in conjunction with telephone exchange service and telecommunications services.

- Directs the FCC to regulate pricing of noncompetitive services, and prohibits noncompetitive services from subsidizing competitive services.

- Gives the attorney general several rights over investigation of service monopolies, such as the right to investigate whether an RBOC could impede competition in a local market.

- Provides for FCC oversight of development of blocking technology for video programming.

While the 1996 Telecommunications Act is a legislative attempt to open up the bandwidth marketplace by introducing competition, the force of the Internet itself, along with the emergence of competing technologies, is already driving deployment of high-bandwidth products for the SOHO market.

High Bandwidth Meets the PC and LAN

Remote access is about mixing data communications with computers and local area networks. Many of the new higher-bandwidth technologies interact with your PC via Ethernet instead of the traditional serial communications route. The following sections provide an overview of these two interfaces to high-bandwidth connectivity.

PC Data Communications 101

Your PC can communicate with the outside world in two ways. The first is the serial port, which is the basis of analog modem communications. The major advantage of the serial-based approach is that it is mature and easy to get up and running. The major disadvantage is its inherent limitations on bandwidth capacity because of its reliance on the asynchronous form of serial communications. Asynchronous communication uses a start and stop bit to define each chunk of 8-bit data being sent. This transmission overhead reduces the amount of data actually being transferred by 20 percent.

The second method by which your PC can communicate with the outside world is Ethernet (the basis for local area networking) and synchronous communications. As noted earlier in the chapter, synchronous data transmission is the standard for digital communications; asynchronous is the standard for analog communications. Synchronous communication is faster because it doesn't require the start and stop bits used in asynchronous communication. Synchronous data transmission sends information in larger blocks as a continuous stream using a synchronized timing method.

Both asynchronous and synchronous forms of data communications use the PC's bus as the interface to connectivity. A bus is a digital pathway used by PCs as a channel for allowing attached devices, the processor, memory, and other system components to communicate among themselves. You may already be familiar with buses; the Industry Standard Architecture (ISA), Peripheral Component Interconnect (PCI), Video Electronics Standards Association (VESA), and Personal Computer Memory Card International Association are the most common. This link is a function of connecting your remote access device to an adapter card in your PC.

To get from the internal bus to an external device, data must pass through an I/O (input/output) adapter that works closely with the external device. This I/O control point conveys data to an external device through an adapter device and then the actual external device. For a modem connection, the bus communicates via the serial adapter, which in turn communicates with the modem device. The modem can be an internal card with its built-in serial adapter, or it can connect via a serial adapter card through a serial RS-232 cable to an external modem. Likewise, for a network connection, the bus communicates with the Ethernet-based network using a network adapter card, commonly referred to as an NIC (network interface card). The Ethernet card connects your PC via a cable to other devices on your local area network. Remote access devices that use Ethernet as the medium connect to the LAN as an individual node in the same way you connect PCs to the LAN.

With the exception of 56-Kbps modems and serial-based ISDN modems, most high-bandwidth connections interface with PCs using Ethernet because of its large data transmission capacity. The theoretical capacity of an Ethernet LAN is 10 Mbps, although the real throughput is considerably less due to a variety of factors. Nonetheless, an Ethernet interface has more than enough capacity for linking to a high-bandwidth connection.

Remote Access as Internetworking

Ethernet-based remote access is about connecting your LAN to another network located in a different location. The conduit for connecting two or more physically isolated networks is a wide area network (WAN). This is where the telephone company and cable systems come into play. To communicate among these dispersed networks, you need a data communications link that lets the networking protocols work with each other over long distances. The role of the wide area network is that of a background conduit for connecting client and server computers and networks.

Connecting different networks, such as a Windows 95 LAN to the Internet, is referred to as *internetworking*. The role of internetworking is to connect networks based on different protocols. The combination LANs and WANs defines an internetwork. Windows 95 enables you to communicate in a number of different protocols, including TCP/IP for the Internet, IPX/SPX for Novell NetWare networks, and others.

Internetworking in a Box

A gateway is a functional device that enables two or more dissimilar networks to communicate as a single logical entity. In the case of LAN system software, dissimilar means that the transport protocols and the underlying physical networks are different. The gateway function is built into Ethernet-based remote access devices that connect LANs via WANs to other networks. The two classes of internetworking devices used to communicate via Ethernet over a wide area network to other networks are bridges and routers, which are explained in the next section.

Traditionally, internetworking devices were products designed to meet the needs of large organizations commonly referred to as the enterprise computing market. These devices are expensive and complex and require network gurus to set up and maintain. As the Internet drove internetworking into the mainstream, vendors of internetworking devices saw the opportunities in downsizing and simplifying them for the SOHO market. ISDN, as the first higher-speed, digital connectivity link to the Internet for the SOHO market, spawned a new generation of LAN-based remote access devices. Over time, as other bandwidth options unfold, expect these internetworking devices to follow. The fundamentals of internetworking devices are similar even when the bandwidth links change. This technology is a continuation of the benefits of using a LAN for sharing peripherals.

Internetworking devices also change the dynamics of your remote access connections. Using a bridge or router, you bypass the entire process of dialing up a modem, which can take up to 60 seconds to make a connection. You don't use Windows 95 dial-up networking to use a router. Instead, the movement of TCP/IP protocol traffic generated by opening a Web browser automatically makes the connection over a digital signal that typically takes only two seconds. This on-demand internetworking automatically connects and disconnects the remote access link, based on the flow of data traffic.

Bridges and Routers

A *bridge* is a simple device that has to determine whether a packet of information is intended for the local LAN. It does this by looking at the address in the packet header. If the destination address is on the local network, the bridge leaves it alone. If the packet's destination address is not on the local network, the bridge throws the packet over to the network on the other side of the WAN connection. It does not know where the packet is bound; it only knows that it is not addressed to the device on its own network. Bridges on the remote network will select or reject the packet based on whether it is destined for devices on their networks. One of the major advantages of bridges is that they're protocol-transparent, which means they generally don't make any attempt to distinguish different packet protocol.

A *router* is a more sophisticated device that allows data to be transmitted to different networks based on packet address and protocol information associated with the data. Routers deliver more intelligence than bridges because they can route data by looking at packet addressing and protocol to transmit it accordingly. Bridges are basically "dumb" devices that connect two networks of the same type, routing all information indiscriminately between the two networks. Routers let you read the data passing through and make decisions on where it is sent to, or not sent to, and so on. This decision-making functionality is called *filtering*, which makes it possible for the router to monitor and selectively choose packets as they enter or leave it. With filtering, a router can protect your network from unwanted intrusion, and prevent selected local network traffic from leaving your LAN through the router. This is a powerful feature for managing incoming and outgoing data for your site.

Routers designed for the SOHO market provide a cost-effective way to connect as few as two PCs to the Internet or other network via a WAN. For example, using a router connected to your LAN lets you share an ISDN line across all the PCs connected on the LAN. Acting as a gateway device, the router filters data traffic going across an Ethernet connection and automatically routes data to the specified network by reading address information in the data packets. Internet access appears seamless and instantaneous. Simply double-clicking on the Internet Explorer or Netscape Communicator icon (or any TCP/IP application icon) instantly brings the Internet to any Windows desktop. It's a smoother and quieter experience than you get from modems.

What's Next

The next step to achieving higher-bandwidth enlightenment is to understand the architecture of the two leading wide area networks: the telephone and cable television systems. Chapter 3 takes you into the trenches of wide area networking as a foundation for understanding how it all works. Why should you care? Because these general wide area networking concepts, terminologies, and technologies will permeate down to the installation of these remote access solutions.

3 *Between Here and There*

Remote access is about using wide area networks (WANs) as your data communications link between your PC or LAN and the Internet or any other network. The two largest public access WANs are the telephone system and the cable television system. This chapter presents an overview of these two systems' architecture and the forces shaping them. As a consumer of high-bandwidth services from these bandwidth gatekeepers, knowledge is power.

Wide Area Networking

A wide area network uses dedicated or switched connections to link computers in geographically remote locations. These wide area connections can be made either through the public network or through a private network built by the organization it serves. For the SOHO market, most WAN activities use the public network.

A *cloud* is the common metaphor for any large wide area network that delivers information transparently to the user. Transparency means the operation of the network is hidden from the user. For example, in the case of a Windows 95 user using a modem to access a particular site on the Internet, both the telephone system and Internet networks are invisible conduits to the user. After double-clicking on a Web browser icon, all the user sees is a Web page. Figure 3.1 shows the two network clouds that represent the telephone system and the Internet as the conduit between a client and server.

The Organization of Telephone Service Companies

The telephone system in the United States is made up of telephone companies that act as common carriers. The wide area telecommunications facilities owned by

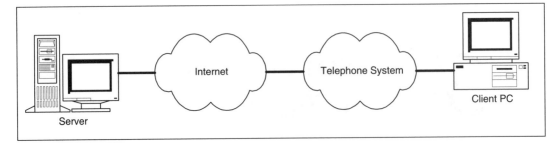

Figure 3.1 *You're in the clouds when you connect to the Internet via the telephone system.*

these common carriers sell their services to the public by subscription. These common carriers are broken down into two main types: local exchange carriers and interexchange carriers. Each type of telephone company offers a wide variety of voice and data services, and they often compete against one another in these markets.

Note: The Telecommunications Act of 1996 allowed LECs to go into the long-distance business; it also allowed IXCs to compete in the local telephone service market. The fruits of this battle may benefit consumers, but it could take years before they see any results.

Local Exchange Carriers

Local exchange carriers (LECs) include the Regional Bell Operating Companies, called RBOCs. These telephone companies include Ameritech, Bell Atlantic, Bell South, NYNEX, Pacific Telesis, Southwestern Bell Corporation, and US West. A recent wave of telephone company mergers in the aftermath of the passage of the Telecommunications Act of 1996 is altering the telephone company landscape. The two largest announced mergers subject to final approval by regulators are between Pacific Telesis and Southwestern Bell Corporation (SBC) and between NYNEX and Bell Atlantic. In addition to the RBOCs are the independent telephone companies (ITCs), which include GTE, Rochester Telephone, Cincinnati Bell, and others.

What is important about local exchange carriers is that they provide the connections to every telephone user in the United States. They deliver the services of the telephone network to the doorstep of homes and businesses. They control what is called the "last mile" in the telecommunication network. The last mile represents the connection of homes and businesses within a given geographical area, which is serviced by a telephone company switching facility, called a central office or CO. The lines between these central offices and customer sites are called *local loops*.

Interexchange Carriers

An interexchange carrier (IEC) is a long-distance telecommunications carrier, such as AT&T, MCI, and US Sprint. These telephone companies use local exchange carrier switches as the gateway for calls into their long-distance telecommunications network. While many IECs use the local facilities that local exchange carriers are required to provide, some have built their own systems to allow customers to bypass the LECs and connect directly into the IECs long-distance services. Unlike local telephone service, customers can choose the long-distance company they want. In other words, there is competition. Interexchange carriers are also referred to as IXCs.

Competitive Local Exchange Carriers

A Competitive Local Exchange Carrier (CLEC) is a new player in the telecommunications industry. A CLEC is a company that buys telecommunications services at a discount from the incumbent LEC to resell to customers. The Telecommunications Act of 1996 allowed CLECs as a way to bring competition into local telephone service. There are a growing number of companies providing CLEC services, including national companies offering services in many local markets. They offer a competitive alternative to both LECs and IECs.

Note: Check out the Web site www.clec.com for more information on CLECs and their services.

Switches, COs, and Local Loops

The integration of all local and long-distance telephone companies forms the global telecommunications network. You enter this network via your local telephone company, which brings telecommunications to your doorstep through standard twisted-pair telephone wiring. The operation of the telephone system revolves around central offices, switches, and local loops.

The Central Office

A central office (CO) is a local telephone company facility that houses telephone company switches. It's a mystical place that is the wiring center, or hub, for all telephone company subscribers. The massive cable plant at the CO provides the path from the switching device to the customer's premises. All kinds of call-management and call-routing activities go on at the CO, including local and long-distance switching. It's the front line of telephone service, taking it from the telephone network to your premises, and vice versa. Large metropolitan areas usually have several COs, each serving a specific geographical area. These central offices connect to others for local calling or to other switching facilities for long-distance calls. There are approximately 19,000 central offices in the United States.

Telephone Company Switching

A switch is a general term referring to facilities that route telephone traffic from one destination to another. Electronic switching software operating on computers provides the basis for the operation of telecommunication switching. These digital switches provide electronic routing for telephone calls, with telephone numbers acting as a routing address system.

The telephone system is a hierarchy of switching. At the local level, calls can often be completed within a single switch. Beyond this, there are switches for long-distance and regional calls. During a long-distance telephone connection, the call goes from your premises to the local CO, which then switches the call to the long-distance carrier. The long-distance call is then routed to the CO that services the premises you're calling. Figure 3.2 shows the path of a long-distance call. Digi-

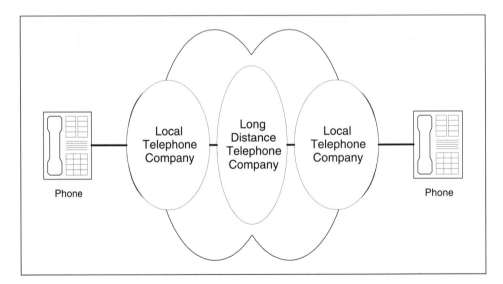

Figure 3.2 The path of a long-distance call from your local telephone company's network to the long-distance telephone company's network and then to another local telephone company's network.

tal circuit switches that control the routing also manage other parts of the telephone system, such as determining toll charges and providing call-management features including call waiting and call forwarding. The leading digital circuit switches used by the telephone companies are AT&T's 5ESS (Electronic Switching System), Nortel's DMS-100 switch, and Siemens EWSD. The AT&T and NT switches dominate the telecommunications industry.

The Local Loop

The term local loop refers to the telephone line comprising the pair of copper wires between your premises and the telephone company's CO. The local loop connects your premises to the CO, which in turn connects you to the telecommunications WAN. There are more than 200 million local loops (lines) in the United States. The wiring for the local loop consists of twisted-pair copper wires. The maximum length of a local loop for different forms of data communications varies. For example, ISDN service has an 18,000-foot limit between the end-user's premises and the CO without the aid of a repeater (a device that amplifies or re-generates the data signal to extend the distance of its transmission).

Teleco Services

Telephone companies offer a variety of bandwidth options for remote access. Traditionally, the telephone companies have focused their higher-bandwidth products on the larger corporate market, and have been slow to respond to the needs of the SOHO market. To date, the main bandwidth products available for the SOHO market are POTS (Plain Old Telephone Service) and ISDN. However, the telephone companies will be rolling out xDSL technologies that will have offerings for the SOHO market. In the meantime, POTS and ISDN are the only viable SOHO solutions for the SOHO market.

Dial-Up or Dedicated

There are two kinds of telecommunication services: dial-up and dedicated. Dial-up service is the most common and least expensive. As the name implies, you must dial up the remote access site to begin an active connection. The communications pathway remains fixed for the duration of the call. At the completion of the session, the telephone connection is terminated. The telephone company charges you usage fees for the time you're connected. Dedicated service is a connection that is available 24 hours a day, 7 days a week. Dedicated service is commonly referred to as 24×7 service. The cost of this service typically starts in the hundreds of dollars per month range. Its target market has traditionally been large companies or Internet service companies that require around-the-clock connectivity. POTS and ISDN service comes in both dial-up and dedicated configurations, although dial-up connections dominate.

Circuit-Switched Services

Circuit-switching services are used as the basis for most telephone communications. POTS and ISDN are circuit-switched services, which means that the communications pathway remains fixed for the duration of the call and is not available to other users. A circuit-switched connection between two users becomes a fixed pathway through the network. When the calling party initiates the call, a set-up procedure tells the network the address of the calling party and sets up the route for the call. The call can be placed for the transmission of data or voice.

Packet-Switched Services

Packet-switched services do away with the concept of the fixed circuit for data communications. Data is transmitted in packets through a network in which each packet has the capability to take a different route through the network. Because there is no predefined circuit, packet switching can increase or decrease bandwidth as required. Taking advantage of the multiple paths of the network, packet-switching services can route packets around failed or congested lines.

Packet-switched services are targeted at large organizations and are designed for dedicated service. As such, they're more expensive than dial-up services. In most cases, SOHO users don't use these services unless their company supplies them. The following are the leading packet-switching services offered by the telephone companies:

- X.25 is used primarily to provide remote terminal connections to host systems. X.25 defines a set of protocols for connecting to a packet-switching network. These networks use extensive error-checking that was required in the days when telephone lines were not as reliable as today. This error-checking overhead reduces the performance and is largely responsible for the growth of Frame Relay. X.25 operates in the 600-bps to 64-Kbps range.

- *Frame Relay.* Frame relay, which began life as a service of ISDN, provides services similar to X.25, but is faster and more efficient. Frame relay doesn't employ the extensive error-checking of X.25, and it's popular with large corporations and other organizations as a way to build fast network connections over public-switching facilities.

- *Asynchronous Transfer Mode (ATM).* ATM is a purely data transmission service. The devices at each end of the connection handle all the error-checking functions. ATM operates in the gigabit-per-second range. ATM is ideal for real-time applications such as video conferencing and voice transmission, as well as data communications.

Dedicated Digital Services

Dedicated digital lines are often used to carry voice, video, and data. Digital circuits provide data transmission speeds up to 45 Mbps. Currently, digital lines are made by "conditioning" normal lines with special equipment to handle higher data rates. The lines are usually leased from the local exchange carrier and installed between two points (point to point) to provide dedicated full-time service. The two leading dedicated digital line services are T1 and fractional T1 lines. These are expensive leased lines that cost in the range of $1,000 and up per month. These lines are used extensively by companies and Internet service providers for around-the-clock connectivity.

- *T1.* The standard and most widely used digital line service is the T1 channel. A T1 provides transmission rates of 1.544 Mbps and can carry both voice and data. The 1.544-Mbps bandwidth is usually divided into 24 64-Kbps channels. This is because a digitized conversation requires 64 Kbps of bandwidth, so when Tls are divided into 64-Kbps channels, voice and data can be carried over the same T1 service.
- *Fractional T1.* Fractional T1 is for those who require channels at 64 Kbps, but don't need a full T1. A customer can start with a number of fractional T1 lines and grow into a full T1 line when necessary When a customer orders fractional T1 service, the carrier sets up a full T1 interface, but makes only the contracted bandwidth available until more is needed. The lines are fractional, meaning that they can be divided into channels for voice or data.

Another more powerful version of the T1 line is the T3 line, which is equivalent to 45 Mbps, or 28 T1 lines, or 672 64-Kbps channels. Large companies and Internet service providers use this service.

Note: Digital Subscriber Line technologies are digital and dedicated services that promise to open up and reduce the price of dedicated digital connections. It remains to be seen how the telephone companies will price and package DSL service so as to not erode their lucrative T1 service business.

The Telecommunications Jungle

For the near term, the shopping experience for high-bandwidth connections from telephone companies will be like the Guns & Roses' song "Welcome to the Jungle." The telecommunications industry is in the throes of a deregulation plan, and this massive unleashing of competitive forces means change and confusion for both providers and consumers. As a consumer of bandwidth, you need to educate yourself by understanding the forces swirling around the delivery of telecommunications services.

The Birth of the FCC

The first comprehensive approach to regulating telecommunications was instituted with the passage of the Communications Act of 1934. Its stated purpose was to protect the public interest based on the assumption that telephone service was an important necessity. The 1934 Act continues to be the bedrock on which all telecommunications regulations are based. The Federal Communications Commission (FCC) was created to regulate the telecommunications industry, and it continues to play a pivotal role in the telecommunications industry. It has the same jurisdiction granted it by the 1934 Act, which is to regulate interstate and foreign telecommunications, but not intrastate telecommunications.

State Telecommunications Regulators

While telecommunications oversight, policy, and regulation at the federal level is the province of the FCC, at the state level, these functions are performed by each state's regulatory agencies. It is at this level where much of the telecommunications policy that affects you is made. These agencies are usually called public utilities commissions (PUCs), and they add different levels of complexity, confusion, and cost to administering an interstate network. A regional telephone company files tariffs in every state in which it offers service. Thus, the same service typically is priced differently depending on a variety of political factors. Your state's regulatory agency determines how the telecommunications business is conducted within its borders. The result is a wide disparity of telecommunications laws reflecting the 50 state regulators.

The Tariff Maze

The United States has seven regional telephone companies, 50 state regulators, and the Federal Communications Commission. Together, they form a complex maze of pricing and service. Prices in the telecommunications industry are called tariffs, which is a published price that sets the allowed rate for telecommunications services and equipment. Tariffs are set by a formal procedure whereby carriers file proposed prices, which are then reviewed, amended, and ultimately either approved or rejected by the appropriate regulator. Tariffs contain the most complete and precise descriptions of carrier offerings, and they cannot be dropped or changed without government approval. Once established, a tariff constitutes a public contract between the user of the product or service and the telecommunications carrier, and it can't be changed except by the express permission of regulators.

Tariffs are filed in each of the 50 states by way of public utility commissions (PUCs) or similar agencies. These governmental agencies are chartered to look after the public interest within the recognized monopoly power of essential utilities. However, a closer look at published tariffs shows that many state regulatory agencies are more telephone company-friendly than consumer-friendly. For example, Bell South in Alabama charges between $221.75 and $228.75 to install an ISDN line, and between $72.35 and $79.35 per month for basic ISDN service. In bordering Tennessee—Al Gore's home state—ISDN installation costs between $24.40 and $31.40, with a charge of $33-$40 per month for basic ISDN service. The telephone companies thrive in this tariff regulation maze because it allows them to extract more revenue.

The Breakup of AT&T

Until 1984, AT&T and the Bell System was the telephone company for most of the United States. It served over 140 million individual telephones, boasted more than $150 billion in assets, and employed over a million people. The rest of the nation, some 40 million people, was served by small independent telephone companies. In 1984, the U.S. Government forced AT&T to divest itself of its local telephone companies.

The Modification of Final Judgment (known as MFJ), approved by U.S. District Court Judge Harold Greene in 1984, ended AT&T's telecommunications monopoly and unleashed the RBOCs. The MFJ broke up AT&T's 24 local telephone companies into 22 Bell Operating Companies (BOCs) that came under the direction of one of seven holding companies, the RBOCs. Today, these RBOCs receive nearly 80 percent of all revenues from local telephone service nationwide.

One of the most significant changes mandated by the MFJ was the redefining of the nation's local exchange carrier (LEC) and interexchange carrier (IXC) system. As stated earlier, a local exchange carrier is any company that provides local telephone service; an interexchange carrier is a long-distance service provider. The

MFJ ruled that providers of long-distance telecommunications services no longer had to be monopolies. This opened up long-distance service to competition, but created local telephone monopolies. When AT&T was divested of the RBOCs, many restrictions were placed upon the RBOCs, because, effectively, they remained monopolies in their regional markets.

In addition to breaking up the Bell System, the MFJ mandated that telecommunications service areas, called local access and transport areas (LATAs) be created to determine which calls were local and which were long-distance. A LATA is one of around 160 geographic areas within the local telephone service provider's territories. Under the MFJ, offering service within a LATA was the sole privilege of the local telecommunications service provider. Between LATAs, long-distance companies, such as MCI and AT&T, compete to offer service. But inside the LATA, the local provider had no competition. The result was that intra-LATA calls became some of the most expensive you could make because there was only one provider.

The MFJ stipulated that all local exchange carriers had to provide equal access to all interexchange carriers. Of course, that left the LECs to charge everyone hefty access fees for local access services to all long-distance companies. The MFJ and its many complex provisions have been constantly under scrutiny, and as a result there have been many revisions. For example, in January 1995, the FCC ruled that intra-LATA traffic should no longer be a monopoly. This meant that long-distance carriers could compete with local exchange carriers for intra-LATA service. And this laid the foundation for the next sweeping change in telecommunications regulation and policy, the Telecommunications Act of 1996.

The Telecommunications Act of 1996

On February 1996, the U.S. Congress passed the Telecommunications Act of 1996. The intent of this sweeping new legislation was to provide telecommunications users with more service and pricing options. The idea was to open up all facets of the telecommunications industry to competition. The result of the Telecommunication Act, in the near term, has been a kind of telecommunications services free-for-all.

Another result of the act has been the merger of several LECs. Pacific Telesis is in the process of merging with SBC communications, and NYNEX is in the process of merging with Bell Atlantic. Other LECs are making far-reaching strategic moves. For example, US West's Media Group began merging with Continental Cablevision, a cable television company. The 1996 Act lets long-distance telephone companies enter local telephone service markets and allows RBOCs to enter the long-distance telephone service market.

The Telecommunications Act requires all telephone companies to allow anyone and everyone to resell their services on a nondiscriminatory basis. This means a telephone company must sell its telephone services at a discount without restrictions on reselling the service. For you, the consumer, this means a lot more companies you never heard of will be cold-calling to offer discounts and special telecommunications services. More important, it enables interexchange carriers including AT&T, MCI, and Sprint to almost immediately offer local exchange services as part of their long-distance services.

The interconnection provisions of the Telecommunications Act of 1996 prevent any LEC from charging other carriers "unreasonable rates" for terminating calls on its network. That means that not only do they have to provide access, they have to charge a fair and reasonable rate for it, which is defined as providing services at enough of a discount to make it a sound business proposition. Who decides what is fair and reasonable falls on the state regulators and the FCC. This is the provision that could give competitors a shot in the local exchange carrier market. It potentially opens up the monopoly of the LEC and makes the LEC share its infrastructure. The interconnection agreements with the LECs are reached through negotiations that sometimes are very complex and incredibly specific. If an LEC wants to make competition difficult, it certainly has the capability to do so. In fact, this has become a major battleground on which long-distance companies and local telephone companies face off, because the last mile (local loops) is still firmly held by the LECs. It may take years for this vast infrastructure to open up.

What This Means to You

It will be some time before anyone really knows the outcome of the provisions of the Telecommunications Act of 1996. As a consumer, the theoretical benefits of competition may offer a cornucopia of new bandwidth services at affordable prices, but there are no guarantees; so although you may know what services you want, you may not know how to get them.

In the best of all possible worlds, the 1996 Act would mean that your telecommunications service providers, rather than relying on their monopolies to make money, would actually start wooing your business—a radical concept given the generally poor customer service record of RBOCs. You could do one-stop shopping for an end-to-end WAN link. The same provider could potentially sell you all your voice and data communications services for both local and long-distance service. Your telecommunications carrier may also sell you remote access equipment as well as configure, manage, and maintain the whole system from end to end. The Telecommunications Act of 1996 offers the potential of new services and products as competition takes hold. For now, it's a wait-and-see situation for everyone.

The Cable Network

As I've said, the cable television industry has been wiring America for the last 25 years with coaxial cable that can reach 90 percent of U.S. homes. This coaxial cable represents a huge, largely untapped pool of bandwidth that exceeds any capacity the telephone companies have to offer. Exploiting the cable industry's bandwidth for Internet access is touted as the single greatest opportunity for universal, high-speed digital communications at speeds up to 10 Mbps.

The cable industry also delivers its bandwidth using a flat-rate pricing model, which I defined previously. Flat-rate pricing is an essential component for Internet access, something the telephone companies have yet to grasp for the SOHO market. Flat-rate pricing translates into the serious use of the Net for electronic commerce, entertainment, and information gathering.

Unfortunately, as I also mentioned earlier, the cable industry suffers from inherent technology, financial, and service problems. How it will ultimately deliver high-bandwidth service is unknown, although optimistic projections show cable modem service will be available to 75 percent of the United States by the year 2000. Early reports on the larger deployments of cable modem service are favorable. Typical cable modem service costs between $100 and $150 for installation, and $34.95 to $59.95 a month for the equivalent of a T1 line! In a play on words, cable modem service delivers the most bits for the buck. From the SOHO consumer perspective, the success of the cable modem option ensures competition for the telephone companies, which is a good thing.

Note: Cable TV is commonly referred to as CATV, which stands for Community Antenna TV. This is the original name for cable TV, which used a single antenna for an entire community.

Cable System Architecture for Internet Access

To offer Internet access, your cable operator must rebuild its network and cable infrastructure. The best cable systems are replacing existing one-way coaxial cable with hybrid fiber/coax (HFC) that supports voice, data, and video services. Recent advances in technology have made it possible for cable operators to cost-effectively push fiber optics deeper and deeper into the cable system, upgrading the wiring out on the street in such a way as to vastly improve signal quality and reliability. This also allows for reliable two-way data transmission. Fiber-optic cable employs light to transmit digital signals through cable made of pure glass. Fiber optics enable large volumes of data to be transmitted over longer distances than can be done using copper cabling.

This infrastructure includes a hybrid fiber/coaxial (HFC) distribution network. This new design, called fiber-to-the-serving area or HFC, subdivides a cable system into neighborhoods of 750 to 1,000 homes, effectively creating several independent cable subsystems within the entire cable system. This HFC design offers a number of advantages over more traditional cable systems. Fewer electronic devices means less noise and cleaner signals; breaking up the system into several smaller systems eliminates a single point of failure and, at the same time, reduces the amount of contention for services requiring upstream capacity. With the advent of affordable, reliable cable modems, upgraded cable systems are now capable of providing a tremendously effective means for transmitting data at high speeds.

Because cable service is broadband, it carries multiple signals, or channels. Your computer is connected to the Internet over the same cable system that delivers your cable TV service. Although your cable video service (to your TV) and your Internet access enter and leave your home over a shared wire, the two services are completely independent of each other, and use of one has no effect on the other. Computers are connected to the cable system using the same coaxial cable that carries video signals.

Data first flows from your home to the cable headend, which is the cable operator's control center. The segment of cable that typically runs from the street or telephone pole to your home is called a *cable drop*. Cable drops connect to the main fiber-optic line at places called *taps* or *nodes*. These nodes act as neighborhood network hubs that can serve between 500 to 2,500 homes. Servers for e-mail, newsgroups, and Web site caching are located within the cable system's fiber network, offering speed and reliability that far exceeds the Internet at large.

Making the cable-to-PC connection requires a cable modem to modulate and demodulate the cable signal into a data stream. Cable modems also include features such as a tuner to separate the data signal from the rest of the broadcast, networking management capabilities, and encryption options. Each cable modem has an Ethernet port that connects to the computer (or network) on one side and to the cable connection on the other side. You install an Ethernet adapter in the PC, then connect it to the cable modem's Ethernet port. As far as your PC is concerned, it's hooked directly to the Internet via an Ethernet network.

Cable Modems

Although a cable modem modulates and demodulates signals, the similarity to analog modems ends there. Cable modems are part modem, part tuner, part encryption/decryption device, part bridge, part router, part NIC card, and part Ethernet hub. Cable modem speeds vary widely. In the downstream direction, speeds can be anywhere up to 36 Mbps. Modems this fast are not currently available but may be by the end of 1997. However, few PCs will be capable of connecting at such high speeds, so the more realistic number is 1.54 to 10 Mbps. In the upstream direction, speeds can be up to 10 Mbps, although most modems will probably be in the range of 300 Kbps to 2 Mbps.

The rising demand for high-speed Internet access and the capabilities of cable service is promising a boom in the production of cable modems for the next few years. According to Dataquest, cable modem shipments are expected to grow from 43,000 unit in 1996 to over 500,000 units annually in 1999. The result is that a growing number of companies are getting in the cable modem business, including 3Com, Bay Networks, Cisco Systems, Com21, General Instrument, Hewlett-Packard, Hybrid Networks, Intel, Motorola, Scientific Atlanta, Sharp Electronics, Terayon, Toshiba, U.S. Robotics, and Zenith.

The new Data Over Cable Service Interface Specification standard should standardize cable modem service by allowing interoperability between cable systems and cable modems. CableLabs is the cable industry's research arm that worked with leading cable TV operators and cable modem vendors to create the Data Over Cable Service Interface Specification. In turn, this interoperability standard should dramatically reduce the price of cable modems.

Note: Cable modems are usually supplied (leased) as part of the Internet service package in the same way a cable box is provided for your cable TV service. Over time, cable modems may be sold directly to consumers in the same way modems are sold.

Location, Location, Location

Cable modem service is deployed on a community-by-community basis because cable TV service is a franchised service. Cable companies must work with local governments to deliver cable services to communities. This process is time-consuming and leads to fragmented deployment of cable modem service.

The major drawback of cable modem service for remote access is availability. While 90 percent of U.S. households have access to cable television service, only 15 percent of cable television systems are ready to deliver the two-way data communications required for Internet access. Even as hardware manufacturers scramble to build cable modems, updating the nation's cable TV infrastructure will take years and cost billions of dollars. And many cable companies are hindered in their plans to upgrade their infrastructure by the huge debt they carry from past excesses. For example, according to *The Economist*, TCI has accumulated $1,000 of debt for each of its 14.5 million subscribers. And converting to digital fiber service, the stuff behind Internet access, will cost around $250 per home. Other cable companies are partnering with telephone companies. US West recently purchased Continental Cablevision, which infused the cash necessary for Continental Cablevision to aggressively roll out its cable modem service.

Currently, there are dozens of U.S. cable systems that have cable modem trials underway or are rolling out cable modem service, including the "big five" cable systems, Time Warner Cable, MediaOne (formerly Continental Cablevision), Tele-Communications Inc. (TCI), Cox Cable Communications, and Comcast Corp. TCI, Comcast, and Cox Cable's @Home Network are providing cable modem service in widening sections of the United States. Time Warner's RoadRunner cable modem service expects to be available to 4.5 million homes by the end of 1997. MediaOne is providing cable modem service to 215 communities in six states in the Northeast.

The Telecommunications Act and the Cable Industry

The Telecommunications Act of 1996 also called for the deregulation of the cable television industry within three years. The cable television companies grew up under a completely different set of regulations from the telephone companies, so deregulation affects them differently, although almost as dramatically. Under the act, telephone companies can enter the cable television business and cable TV operators can enter the telecommunications business. Although the act requires that all public telecommunications companies provide "basic and advanced services" to everyone, private operators like cable television companies have no such mandate.

What's Next

From this chapter's understanding of the two largest wide area networks that deliver data from your office to the outside world, the next stop is the mother of all remote access destinations, the Internet. The Internet has its own dynamics for making remote access connections. And each high-bandwidth option is packaged differently in terms of its Internet access capabilities and services. Chapter 4, "Jacking Into the Net" explains the fundamentals of Internet connections within the high-bandwidth context.

4 *Jacking Into the Net*

The Internet is the mother of all remote access destinations. The Net is both a global resource for communications and information gathering as well as a conduit for remote access to Internet-connected companies. The high-bandwidth access to the Internet only gets you to the Internet; you also need to understand the workings of the Internet to set up and manage your link to the outside world. This chapter will cover the Internet mechanics you'll need to incorporate it into a remote access system.

The Internet and Remote Access

The Internet is a global wide area network that connects millions of computers and networks. Not only is it a destination but a data communications conduit to private intranets. Increasingly, the Internet is being used as a conduit for remote access connections between telecommuters and their company's private intranet. In essence, the company uses the Internet as a virtual private network or VPN. This allows easy connectivity for remote users via the Internet so that, to the user, it is as if he or she were working on the company network. Microsoft's Point-to-Point Tunneling Protocol (PPTP) is designed to facilitate virtual private network connections. Data communication is encrypted to keep the information confidential.

The most common protocol used for remote Internet connectivity is Point-to-Point Protocol (PPP), which is the communications protocol that allows a computer using TCP/IP to connect directly to the Internet. PPP is an official standard that includes support for error detection and data compression. With Windows 95, the preferred method of making dial-up Internet connections is via PPP. Serial Line Internet Protocol (SLIP) is an older protocol that was never an official standard. SLIP ships with UNIX systems, making its usage widespread because that operating system is the dominant one used on the Internet. Most ISPs offer both SLIP and PPP.

Multilink Point-to-Point Protocol (commonly referred to as MPP or MP) is the communications protocol that makes it possible for a computer using TCP/IP and an ISDN connection to use both B channels to connect directly to the Internet. It was developed to extend PPP to handle multiple channel connections to the Internet. Most ISPs that offer ISDN Internet access accounts support MP. Microsoft's support for MP in Windows 95 comes in the form of a free software add-on called the ISDN Accelerator Pack. Most ISDN vendors include this software with their products.

There are two PPP (Point-to-Point Protocol) authentication protocols: PAP (Password Authentication Protocol) and CHAP (Challenge Handshake Authentication Protocol). An authentication protocol requests information to verify a valid user. If PAP is used, a Name and Password is sent unencrypted across the link. If CHAP is used, an encrypted exchange between the local and remote locations occurs. The result is this method of authentication is more secure than PAP, but it's less commonly used.

Packet-Switched Networking

The Internet relies on a technology known as *packet-switched networking*. This technology is a child of the Cold War era; it was designed to survive a nuclear attack on the command structure of the U.S. military and government. The concept behind a packet-switched network is that a large, geographically dispersed network could continue to function even if large parts of it were destroyed. In a packet-based network, data travels across a network in small, independent units that can be routed over various network paths to reach its ultimate destination. These data packets consist of three primary parts.

1. *Header.* This portion of the packet contains information about the intended recipient of the packet, along with an indication of the correct sequence of the packet.

2. *Body.* This portion contains the main information being conveyed. This can either be an entire message (if the message is short) or a part of a larger message.

3. *Trailer.* The trailer simply indicates when the end of the packet has been reached.

As information is broken down into packets, it is transmitted over the network. Each station that encounters a packet examines the header to determine whether the packet is intended for that station. If not, the packet is passed on in a direction closer to the ultimate destination. Eventually, the packets arrive at their destination and are reassembled in the order intended. The benefit of this type of network is that packets in a message do not have to travel to their destination along the same route. In fact, packets can and do travel many different routes but end up at the same destination. This independent routing of packets over a network enables data to be transmitted even if parts of the network are disrupted.

Packets make it possible for information in all sizes to be broken down and mixed with other information to keep traffic moving smoothly. The use of packets relieves congestion and helps smooth the information transfer. Sending packets along differing routes provides three major advantages.

1. Allows for more even use of the network. If you try to cram all the message packets along a given route when other routes are available, you are not using resources wisely.

2. Provides alternate routes, which means it's harder to break down the entire network, even when one segment isn't functioning. Packet traffic is simply rerouted around the malfunctioning area.

3. Error correction is easier when dealing with packets. If, at the receiving end, a packet error is detected, only that packet, not the entire message, must be resent. This saves both time and network resources.

TCP/IP and the Internet

TCP/IP (Transmission Control Protocol and Internet Protocol) is the packet-based networking protocols that unite the Internet. A protocol is a set of rules used to allow interoperability among different systems. TCP/IP is not a single entity, but a group of software protocols that defines how communication between computers takes place, as well as the basis for a variety of network services, such as FTP (File Transfer Protocol) and others. TCP/IP was developed in the early 1970s to create a heterogeneous network environment, meaning that it could be implemented on a wide variety of hardware and operating systems. TCP/IP is built into the UNIX operating system, the dominant operating system on the Internet. With the introduction of Windows 95, TCP/IP was built into the dominant operating system used by PCs.

Understanding IP Addressing

Within any networking protocol, a way must exist to identify individual systems, or nodes, on the network. TCP/IP is no exception. It includes an addressing scheme that pervades everything you do with the Internet. It's helpful to think of the Internet Protocol (IP) addresses as the unique telephone numbers for specific computers or other network devices on a TCP/IP network. Telephone numbers have three parts, recognized by everyone in the United States. The first three numbers represent the area code, which identifies to which region of the country the phone number refers (the region may be a state or a portion of a state). The next three numbers identify the exchange to which the phone belongs. Exchanges can be thought of as neighborhoods; the larger the city, the more neighborhoods and exchanges it has. The final four numbers identify a telephone within the exchange. Thus, every 10-digit phone number uniquely identifies an individual phone in the United States.

Each computer that uses TCP/IP protocols is distinguished from other computers on the Internet by a unique IP address, which is a numeric value that is used by computers. An IP address is organized into four groups of numbers separated by periods (referred to as dots); for example, 199.3.135.8. An IP address is a unique 32-bit address that defines a single location on the network. IP addresses are written as a series of four numbers separated by periods. For instance, the following is a hypothetical example of an IP address:

199.232.255.200

This notation for an IP address is sometimes called a *dotted-decimal notation*, or *dotted-quad notation*. Each of the four numbers in this IP address—199, 232, 255, and 200—is called an *octet* and represents one byte of the full 32-bit address. No octet may have a value above 255. This means that the lowest possible IP address is 0.0.0.0 and the highest is 255.255.255.255.

IP addresses are assigned to networks divided into three classifications: A, B, and C. The breakdown of IP addresses is a simple a way of allocating addresses among the different networks that access the Internet.

- Class A addresses are provided for very large networks. Only 126 Class A addresses are possible in the world, and each Class A network can have in excess of 16 million computers in its individual networks. The first octet of an IP address is between 1 and 126 for Class A network, and all remaining octets identify members of that network.

- In a Class B network, there can be up to approximately 65,000 workstations on the network. In IP addresses, the first octet is a number between 128 and 191, and the second octet further denotes the network address. Thus, there can be approximately 16,000 Class B networks in the world. The last two octets of the IP address denote individual workstations.

- Class C networks have an IP address in which the first octet is between 192 and 223; the second and third octets further define the network, and the final octet identifies the workstation on the network. Several million Class C networks are possible, each with approximately 250 workstations.

Again, the IP address is unique and identifies the workstation within the grand scheme of TCP/IP. The second component, the *subnet mask,* enables the workstation to identify the network of which it is a part. You can think of a subnet as a workgroup within a larger domain or network, or as all of the computers physically connected to a particular network. In reality, the subnet mask is used to mask out the parts of the IP address that are not necessary for the type of network you belong to. For example, if your IP address is for a Class C network (the most common type), then the first three octets of the address are of no importance; only the last octet defines the computers in your network. Thus, a subnet mask of 255.255.255.0 can be used to erase the first three octets in an IP address.

The third component required for successful participation in a TCP/IP environment is the *default gateway address.* This is an IP address of the system to which your workstation should route data packets not destined for computers on the local network. The default gateway address is used in conjunction with the subnet mask. The subnet mask identifies which portions of the IP address are contained within the local network, and is used to route local network mail. The default gateway address identifies the address for packets filtered out by the subnet mask. The system at the default gateway address can then route the packets toward their ultimate destination.

Dwindling Supply of IP Addresses

When the IP addressing specifications were drafted in the early 1970s, the use of a 32-bit address was criticized as wasteful. Early Internet pioneers could not envision a scenario in which all 32 bits would be used. Today, the IP addresses based on the 32-bit addressing system will run out some time in the not-too-distant future. Toward the end of the century, the Internet Architecture Board (IAB) will adopt a new or expanded IP addressing scheme to accommodate the continued growth of the Internet. The IAB will most likely double the 32-bit address to a 64-bit addressing scheme. At the same time, the board will have to make allowances for backward compatibility with 32-bit addresses.

Static and Dynamic IP Addressing

There are two types of IP addressing used for Internet access accounts: static and dynamic. In static IP addressing, an ISP assigns you a unique IP address that you would use to connect to the Internet. For example, if you were connecting a single PC to the Internet, your ISP would assign you an IP address such as

199.3.135.38, which would be your address for as long as you maintain the account. You would use this IP address along with a subnet mask to configure Windows 95 to make your connection. If you were connecting a LAN, each PC on the network would be assigned a unique IP address along with an IP address assigned to a router. Such LAN access packages can cost hundreds of dollars per month because of the high premium on using scarce static IP addresses. This was one of the main barriers for the limited deployment routers in the SOHO market for connecting LANs to the Internet.

To circumvent IP address scarcity, ISPs have begun using *dynamic IP addressing,* which simply means an ISP uses a host system that assigns an IP address from an available pool of IP addresses for use only during the current connection. Once the user ends the connection, the IP address is returned to the pool of available IP addresses for use by others.

In response to the difficulty in getting affordable LAN accounts with multiple static IP addresses, a growing number of router products for the SOHO market now support dynamic IP addressing. Using such a router, you can connect a LAN to the Internet using a dynamic IP addressing scheme that allocates IP addresses from a pool of available IP addresses at the ISP. The result is that you can use the same low-cost, dial-up Internet access accounts used by individuals to connect a LAN. In addition, you don't need assigned IP addresses from your ISP for each machine on your network.

DHCP

DHCP is the acronym for Dynamic Host Configuration Protocol. This set of rules was developed by Internet members (including Microsoft) to allow IP addresses, subnet masks, and default gateway addresses to be assigned to workstations on an as-needed basis. Traditionally, the IP address components necessary for a TCP/IP workstation were statically assigned to workstations.

The DHCP protocol effectively removes the requirement that individual workstations must have static IP addresses. Instead, a network can designate a DHCP server that automatically manages the assignment of IP addresses and routing information to network nodes as they sign in. The server then manages the IP address table, making sure that only one address is assigned to each active workstation. The IP address is leased to the workstation, meaning that it is provided for only a limited time. From a user's perspective, these negotiation and assignment procedures are transparent.

Windows 95 includes a built-in DHCP client as part of the Microsoft TCP/IP stack. Because Windows 95 supports DHCP as a client, there must be a DHCP server in order to use dynamic IP addressing. The ISP's host machine provides the

DHCP functionality for connecting a single PC to the Internet. You can connect a LAN to a dynamic IP Internet access account by using a remote access device that acts as a local DHCP server, which in turn makes the connection to the ISP's host. A growing number of remote access devices, such as ISDN routers, support DHCP. Windows NT Server also provides DHCP server functionality.

WINS

Windows 95 also supports a protocol called Windows Internet Name Service (WINS), which is designed to work with a DHCP server. WINS manages the mapping of information between the symbolic names assigned to PCs and resources in a Windows network and the IP addresses dynamically assigned to those same PCs and resources by a DHCP server. Effectively, it is the responsibility of WINS to handle routing of information to a network device after the IP address has been assigned. Although WINS may sound like one more level of complexity, its purpose is to save you from dealing with otherwise complex issues. Because Windows 95 supports WINS, many addressing tasks that you would need to handle manually are managed automatically by the operating system.

NAT

Network Address Translation (NAT) is an Internet standard that makes it possible for your local network to use IP addresses that are not recognized by users outside your LAN; that is, Internet users. As an example, consider a telephone system with several telephone extensions. Each telephone has its own internal extension number, which it uses to call others in the company. When it calls someone on the outside, however, the outside sees the number of the trunk line that the system uses and not the extension number of the telephone user's telephone. The actual connection between the outside trunk and the inside user is maintained temporarily by the telephone system. NAT-based routers do the same thing for your Internet communication. You assign IP addresses to your internal users, and when they want to connect to the outside Internet, the NAT feature creates a temporary connection, just as the telephone system would. And like the telephone system, the outside doesn't care what sort of internal numbering scheme you create for your users; the only IP Address that matters is the one seen from the outside.

NAT works in conjunction with DHCP to provide a dramatic LAN to Internet access capability that doesn't require a static IP address be assigned to every PC on the LAN. As a result, significant cost savings can be realized because only a single-user Internet access account is required for an entire LAN. Remote access devices designed for the SOHO market include both the DHCP and NAT functionality. NAT also provides increased security because the IP addresses used on the LAN are unrecognizable on the Internet.

What's in a Domain Name?

If IP addresses are the equivalent of telephone numbers on the Internet, then domain names are equivalent to the name of the person or organization to which the telephone number is assigned. In a telephone directory, the name and physical address of the person or company using that telephone number appears. As people move, their telephone numbers change but not their names

Domain names are based on the same concepts. For example, my e-mail address, david@angell.com, is typical. This address is divided into two parts. The part preceding the @ sign is the user ID. It identifies a person within a network system. The portion following the @ sign is referred to as the domain or host name. It identifies the organization or computer network to which the user belongs. When you combine the user ID and the domain name, you get a unique address that identifies any individual on the Internet. This same domain angell.com can appear as part of a Web URL, such as www.angell.com.

When you provide an address for most Internet operations, such as pointing your Web browser to a Web site or sending e-mail, you can use either the IP address or the domain name method. Most people use domain names as their form of addressing simply because it is easier to read and understand. The process of converting domain names to machine-readable IP addresses is called *resolution*. During the resolution process, the domain name is translated automatically into an IP address by a computer called a Domain Name System (DNS) server.

Because name resolution occurs behind the scenes, you generally won't need to be concerned with it. There may be times, however, when you need the full IP address for a host. For example, if you supply a domain name that the DNS server cannot resolve for some reason, you are notified that your action cannot be completed. In such a case, you can try the IP address (assuming you have it) instead of the domain name; for example, you would use the address of david@199.232.255 .200 instead of david@angell.com to send an e-mail message.

Structure of the Domain Name System

Domain naming system, or *DNS*, is the term used for text-based addressing or naming structure. Domain names have a hierarchical structure that is delineated with periods, or dots. Each period within the domain name identifies another level of the overall organization through which the message must pass to arrive at the destination. The order of levels in a domain always proceeds from the most specific to most general when viewed from left to right. Longer domain names simply mean that more organizational levels are necessary to uniquely identify a host system.

There is no common method for decoding the meaning of different levels within a name. The person setting up the address defines the nomenclature used in the address. Therefore, it is not unusual to have different domain levels in a name representing different levels within an organization. For instance, one domain level may refer to an overall organization, while the name to the left of it refers to a department or building. The level to the left of that may represent a specific network within the department or building, and still another level may identify a workgroup within the network. Only the imagination of the individuals assigning the names limit the complexity of a domain address.

Top-Level Domain Names

You may have noticed that at the end of all the Internet addresses is a three-letter domain level such as .com or .edu. These are referred to as top-level domains (TLDs) or organizational domains. These top-level domains indicate the organization that owns the address, and they always appear at the end of the domain name. Their purpose is to provide another level of distinction for a full-domain address. Thus, you could have two addresses that were exactly the same except for the organizational domain, and the messages would be routed to completely different places. Within the United States, you'll find seven different organizational domains, as shown in Table 4.1.

Domain Name Expansion

Domain name registration for .com, .net, and .org domains is currently handled exclusively by Network Solutions Inc. (NSI), which has an agreement with the

Table 4.1 Organizational Domains Used within the United States

ORGANIZATIONAL DOMAIN	ENTITY
com	For-profit commercial organizations
edu	Educational institutions
gov	Nonmilitary government organizations
int	International (NATO) institutions
mil	Military installations
net	Network resources
org	Nonprofit groups

National Science Foundation to award those top-level domains. However, NSI will lose its exclusive right when its contract runs out in 1998. Already there are groups that want to open and manage the fast-growing top-level domain business. The International Ad Hoc Committee (IAHC) is trying to create new domain names to allow more options for domain names. This committee is an informal coalition of international bodies involved in telecommunications, trademark, and Net activities. IAHC has proposed a plan that will allow up to 28 new registrars to administer seven new top-level domains, such as .biz, .rec and .web. Meanwhile, an alternative naming group called the Enhanced Domain Name Service (EDNS) wants to open up the Internet to an unlimited number of top-level domains.

Geographic Domains

Some domain names don't include organizational distinctions, but instead rely on geographic domains. This is particularly true with domain names outside the United States. Geographic domains indicate the country in which the name originates, and in almost all instances, are based on the two-letter country codes specified by the International Standards Organization (ISO), a standards body. Although scores of geographic domains exist, Table 4.2 shows some common geographic domains in use.

How Domain Names Are Assigned

Domain names are chosen by the organization requesting the name, and then registered with the InterNIC, the Internet Network Information Center, which is a

Table 4.2 Common Geographic Domains

GEOGRAPHIC DOMAIN	COUNTRY
Australia	au
Canada	ca
France	fr
Germany	de
Japan	jp
Netherlands	nl
Russia	ru
United Kingdom	gb
United States	us

service provided by three different companies. The information that is compiled, maintained, and distributed by the InterNIC splits into three categories, as follows:

1. *Registration services.* These services relate to registering domain names. Network Solutions Inc. (NSI) manages the InterNIC registration services.

2. *Directory and database services.* These services include information about different databases and resources on the network, as well as a white pages and yellow pages directory of Internet addresses. AT&T provides InterNIC directory and database services.

3. *Information services.* These services include training for and newsletters regarding how to use the Internet more effectively. The information disseminated by this part of the InterNIC is directed toward technical people responsible for organizations and networks connected to the Internet. General Atomics/CERFNet provides InterNIC information services.

The process of getting a domain name is pretty straightforward. Typically, your Internet service provider will register your domain name with InterNIC and charge you a modest fee. Registering a domain name will cost you $100 for the first two years and $50 a year thereafter. You can file for your own domain name, but you'll need to know all the IP addresses you'll be using in conjunction with the domain name; for example, the domain name address of your ISP's mail, network news, DNS servers, and any other services you're linking to that domain name. In most cases, it will be easier for your ISP to do the work for you. After submitting the forms, it takes approximately two weeks for the name to be registered (assuming there are no conflicts or problems).

Getting Your Own Domain Name

In most cases, you'll want to have your own domain name. A domain name is your identity on the Internet. Having your own domain name also allows you to move from one Internet access provider to another without any disruption of your e-mail or other Internet services. Because you own your domain name, not your ISP, you can move it as needed. In most cases, your domain name is the same as your name or your company's name so you can capitalize on any recognition associated with your name. Your business e-mail addresses are tied to your domain name as well as to any Web site URLs.

Creating Your Domain Name

Names are registered on a first-come, first-served basis, and registering a domain name implies no legal ownership of the name. For example, you may be able to

---

Note: Some bandwidth options that bundle Internet access service don't offer domain name registration services, which means you can't use your own domain name as part of their service. If the provider of your data communications link is also providing your Internet access service as part of a bundled package, make sure you ask the bandwidth provider about domain name registration.

---

register a domain name that is the name of another company, but that company can send its lawyers after you for infringing on its trade name.

Domain names are organized in a hierarchical fashion with the most specific (computer name) at the left and the most general top-level domain to the right. For most SOHO users, the name will use the .com top-level domain. Domain names are not case-sensitive, so it doesn't matter whether letters are uppercase or lowercase. No spaces are allowed in a domain name, but you can use the underscore (_) to indicate a space. You can use a combination of the letters A through Z, the digits 0 through 9, and the hyphen. You cannot use the period (.), "at" sign (@), percent sign (%), or exclamation point (!) as part of your domain name. DNS servers and other network systems use these characters to construct e-mail addresses.

Checking Domain Name Availability

After you have decided on your domain name(s), you should check to see whether they are available. Because of the immense popularity of the Internet, finding a domain name that isn't already in use is becoming harder. Do your own checking of domain names before you decide on one and submit it to your ISP. If you don't have Internet access, the easiest way to find out if a specific name is available is to call registration services directly at (703)742-4777. When the registration representative answers, ask to check the status of a domain name.

If you have access to an Internet account, the best way to check out the availability of a domain name is to use your Web browser and point it to http://www.rs.internic.net, which takes you to the InterNIC Web site. You can get all the information you need about how to register your domain name. You can even register a domain name online at this site if you know all the ISP server information.

Clicking on the Registration Service link takes you to the Registration Service page. Click on the Whois hyperlink to access the InterNIC domain name database. Simply type the name you're interested in, including the organization name, into the text field, then press Enter. If the name is available, the database tells you that no match was found. If the name is registered, the public information about the domain name holder appears, including the name and address of the holder, contact information, as well as IP addresses connected with the domain name.

Once you determine your domain name and you decide on your service provider, your Internet service provider will apply for the domain name with In-terNIC registration services. Your ISP usually registers domain names in order to supply the IP addresses that are used to route information to your domain name. These IP addresses include one for the service provider's host computer system and another that is assigned to the host at your end of the connection. To register at the InterNIC, you must have an e-mail address and IP addresses for mapping your domain name. At the time the InterNIC registers your domain name, the mapping to the IP addresses is also entered in the database. As already noted, domain name registration costs $100, which covers the initial registration and updates to the do-main name's database record for a period of two years. The annual domain name renewal fee after the initial two-year period is $50.

Internet Service Providers

An Internet service provider is a company that provides Internet access to cus-tomers. ISPs purchase a bulk bandwidth service to the Internet, and then repack-age and sell it in small quantities to hundreds or thousands of customers, using specialized equipment to connect them to the Internet. Connecting directly to the Internet (bypassing a service provider) is expensive and out of reach for the SOHO market. ISPs deal with different communications links coming in from customers as well as high-bandwidth links to the Internet itself. Providers have different ser-vices, provide various degrees of access, and charge different rates. Most maintain a help desk for customers who are having problems (some are available 24 hours a day, 7 days a week).

Internet access is available from national, regional, and local Internet service providers. In many cases, you may prefer regional or local ISPs to the larger na-tional providers, but it will depend on where you live. The best advice is to con-duct a comparison of services and pricing. Regional and local ISPs are more likely to offer better services and rates than those of the nationals, although there are al-ways exceptions. National Internet access providers use local access points distrib-uted across the country commonly referred to as points of presence, or POPs, to connect users to their network. The use of local POPs is essential for eliminating expensive telephone company usage charges for calls made outside your local call-ing area. Some Internet providers offer toll-free service for nationwide access. This is helpful for the more remote areas and for people who are on the road a great deal. But be aware that toll-free access does not necessarily mean that it is free; most Internet providers with toll-free lines add a surcharge for access via these lines.

A number or resources are available on the Internet for finding an ISP in your area. If you don't have access to the Internet, check your local computer store or the computer section of a bookstore for information on Internet service providers. Also, Appendix A contains a listing of resources for finding Internet service providers.

High Bandwidth and Internet Access

Depending on the high-bandwidth option you end up using, you may or may not need to set up an Internet access account. For example, 56 Kbps and ISDN service is typically à la carte, where you purchase your remote access device, establish service with the telephone company, and then get Internet access service from an ISP. Cable modem service, on the other hand, is an all-inclusive package that comprises the hardware, the connection, and the Internet service account. The following sections explain the ISP interaction for each of the bandwidth options covered in this book.

Using 56-Kbps Modems

You need to make sure 56-Kbps modem service is available in your area before buying a modem. You must check to see what type of equipment an ISP is using and what equipment it requires you to use for 56-Kbps service. Because the 56-Kbps modems lack universal standards, a 56-Kbps modem connection must use equipment from the same vendor or at least support the same chip. Check with the ISP about whether it sells 56-Kbps modems; it may offer a better deal than computer stores. Also, because of certain restrictions of telephone company switches, 56-Kbps service may not be available for your specific location, even though the ISP offers 56-Kbps service. You may need to order a second POTS line for the modem service from your local telephone company.

ISDN Service

If ISDN service is available in your area, typically there will be ISPs that offers dial-up and dedicated ISDN access. As you'll find out, in most cases, dedicated ISDN service is just too expensive—you will typically pay higher telephone line and ISP usage charges. However, ISDN can be a good option if you plan to share the line with several PCs connected to a LAN via an ISDN router.

You order ISDN service from the telephone company according to the specifications of the specific remote access device you're using. Many ISDN equipment vendors offer to establish your ISDN service free of charge as part of purchasing their ISDN equipment. Check them out.

Some telephone companies charge a cheaper tariff for analog calls over an ISDN line than for digital data calls over ISDN. Many ISDN remote access devices let you initiate a call as a voice signal instead of a data signal so that the telephone company switch treats the data call as a voice call. As a result, you're charged the lower analog flat rate instead of the higher digital rates. This can save money because in most cases your Internet service provider is a local call. As such, the cost of connecting to your ISP falls within the flat monthly rate. If you connect to your Internet provider for more than a few hours, the savings can add up. However, for you to use this feature, the Internet service provider side of the connection must support it.

Satellite Service

Currently, the only Internet access service available via satellite is from DirecPC. You buy the satellite dish and PC connection hardware and software. You also get an Internet access account from DirecPC for handling downstream data from the Internet, but you'll need another Internet access account from any ISP to provide the upstream link. For upstream data communications, the data is sent via the Internet to the DirecPC satellite control center.

Cable Modems

Cable modem service is typically sold as a complete package that includes the bandwidth connection, the hardware, and Internet access service. Depending on your cable operator, you may be able to add various services to your Internet account, such as getting your own domain name, Web hosting services, and multiple e-mail accounts. In the case of cable modems, the entire solution is delivered to your site, so you don't need to shop for an ISP.

xDSL

At this early stage in the development and deployment of xDSL, it is still undetermined how Internet access will be handled. Telephone companies like Pacific Telesis and US West may bundle the bandwidth product with Internet access as a one-stop package. Other telephone companies may sell the service through ISPs or require the consumer to order the service from them and then get a separate ISP account.

Acceptable Use Policies

In the early days of the Internet, nearly all providers were either educational institutions or government agencies. These institutions may have received funding from a government agency, and as such were restricted to providing access for only noncommercial traffic. An AUP (Acceptable Use Policy) was used as a way to clarify which types of activities could and could not be conducted using a government-funded ISP. Today, most ISP service no longer have these restrictions, and service commercial accounts. They typically have their own version of an AUP, which is a contract defining what you can and can't do using their service. When you contact an Internet provider, ask for a copy of its AUP to be faxed or e-mailed to you so you can review it completely. An AUP may also be available at the ISP's Web site.

Choosing an ISP

When comparing Internet service providers, typical selection criteria are performance, price, and responsive technical support. Here are general guidelines to keep in mind if you need to shop for a separate ISP account or if you want to check out the Internet access service being bundled with your high-bandwidth connection.

- Make sure that you don't have to pay any telephone usage charges beyond a local call.

- Figure out how much time you spend online and compare charges based on that. Higher-bandwidth users are typically moderate to heavy Internet users.

- Shop around for the best total package-pricing plan for your needs. Some Internet service providers have a higher set-up fee but a lower monthly charge; others have a lower set-up fee but a higher monthly charge. Keep in mind, though, that pricing isn't the only consideration.

- Ask which remote access devices the ISP supports or has experience working with. An ISP may support only one or two or several.

- Analyze your Internet access options. Talk to your friends, associates, and several ISPs.

- Check to see whether the ISP offers compression. Signing up with one that does may be the best deal because this feature means faster data transfer rates.

- If you are using a dial-up service, ask whether the provider has enough dial-up ports to ensure you won't get a busy signal.

- Are the provider's acceptable use policies too restrictive for your intended Internet use? How secure is the provider's system?

- What does the provider charge for the services required? Are there any hidden or up-front charges? What are the payment terms? Is detailed access reporting available?

- Is user support provided at no additional charge? How knowledgeable is the customer support personnel? Can the provider help you with telecommunications consulting, if necessary?

- Is the service provider stable? Find out how long the provider has been in business.

- Can the provider support you across the nation or around the world? If you roll all your locations into a single account, can the provider do better on the pricing?

- Does the provider have toll-free access for your personnel who are on the road? (If you are establishing a dedicated Internet link, this becomes less of an issue, because your mobile workers can call in through your in-house computer system.)

Economize on IP Addresses

A growing number of remote access devices designed for the SOHO market are adding new features to save users money on monthly Internet service provider bills by economizing on IP addresses. In effect, a small office LAN can get Internet access for all its PCs using a single user account instead of expensive, static IP LAN accounts that cost hundreds of dollars per month. Looking after fewer IP addresses also simplifies setting up remote access for a small office LAN. ISDN routers are currently the only SOHO remote access devices using these features; however, expect to see them implemented in all remote access devices in the future.

Getting Additional E-Mail Accounts

If you plan to have more than one user share your Internet access account, make sure your ISP offers additional e-mail boxes for your Internet account. Additional Internet e-mail accounts allow everyone to have private e-mail addresses, yet share the same Internet access account. Typically, an additional e-mail account costs around $10 a month; you may be able to buy multiple accounts for a lower per-unit cost.

You don't have to have additional e-mail boxes for general information requests; for example, info@angell.com, sales@angell.com, and so on. These can be handled using a feature called *e-mail mapping*, which is done by your Internet service provider. E-mail mapping allows any e-mail that is addressed to

@domain_name.com to be considered e-mail for that account. For example, e-mail sent as sales@angell.com gets sent to the angell.com e-mail account. Likewise, david@angell.com gets sent to the angell.com account, as does joanne@angell.com. E-mail that comes into your box on your local PC can be routed to different folders using your local e-mail program. This is a rule-based sorting approach that evaluates information in the incoming message—for example the e-mail address it was sent to—and sorts it to a particular folder associated with the single user e-mail box. This option is useful only if you have all the e-mail managed by a single e-mail box.

What You Need from Your ISP

The information you need from the ISP handing your Internet access depends on the high-bandwidth connection you're using, the Internet service provider, and how your remote access ecosystem is put together. This information is used to configure your remote access devices and Windows 95 to make your Internet connections. Get the answers to some or all of these questions from your ISP after your account is established.

- Which access phone number should I dial with my computer?
- What is my user ID?
- What is my password?
- What is my e-mail address?
- Does the provider use a DHCP server? (If the answer to this question is yes, you can skip the next four questions.)
- What is the IP address of the DNS server used by the provider?
- Which default gateway IP address should I use?
- Which TCP/IP address is assigned to my system?
- Which IP subnet mask should I use?

What's Next

It's time to rock 'n' roll with remote access. The first step is mastering your Windows 95 platform for remote access. Whether you're connecting a single PC via a 56 Kbps dial-up modem or connecting a Windows 95 LAN to the Internet using a router, you need to know how its set up and run using Windows 95 tools. Chapter 5 begins your remote access journey with a tour of the essential Windows 95 tools for setting up your remote access connections.

PART

II

Building Your
Windows 95 Foundation

5 *Windows 95 and Remote Access*

Whether you're connecting a single PC or an entire LAN to the Internet or any other network, Windows 95 provides an impressive collection of remote access features. Together they enable you to easily, quickly, and inexpensively create your remote access connections, and they play a starring role in the remote access ecosystem. This chapter introduces you to the essential Windows 95 remote access tools and draws up a game plan for working with different remote access options within the Windows 95 context.

Remote Access-Friendly Windows 95

Windows 95 is more than just an upgrade of Windows for Workgroups. It is the first operating system from Microsoft that embraced remote access, specifically the Internet as an integral part of PC computing; it has been evolving ever since. Windows 95 is essential to making remote access easy, whether you're connecting a single PC or a LAN, and is the undisputed operating system choice for telecommuters or any SOHO environment. The following sections explain the key components that Windows 95 brings to the remote access system.

Plug-and-Play

Installing new hardware in earlier versions of Windows wasn't user-friendly. PC user who became frustrated working with hardware settings and solving device conflicts, such as Interrupt Requests (IRQs) and Input/Output memory addresses clashes, will find Windows 95 a relief.

In response to earlier PC hardware installation problems, a committee of major hardware and software manufacturers (including Microsoft) created a new standard called Plug-and-Play. Windows 95 uses this standard to support automatic installation of new hardware devices; it does most of the work for users. Management of devices is now done in Windows 95 using a simple control panel window.

Windows 95's Plug-and-Play support has transformed the process of installing new hardware from a complex task to a smooth one. Windows 95 automatically detects Plug-and-Play-compatible devices attached to your system without any manual configuration of jumpers or switches on the adapter cards. This means that communications between the peripheral devices, the BIOS (Basic Input/Output System), and Windows 95 automatically handles resource conflicts. The Plug-and-Play facility in Windows automatically allocates resources such as IRQs and I/O addresses, and loads and unloads dynamically (on-the-fly) any device drivers that your system needs.

Even if you have a problem with IRQs or I/O addresses, you can use the System icon in the Windows 95 Control Panel to make manual changes to the settings. In the System Properties dialog box, the Device Manager tab (Figure 5.1) provides a gateway to all the devices attached to your system so you can manage their settings. For example, you can select an installed network adapter from the Network adapters item and then click on the Properties button to display the network adapter's hardware settings in the Resources tab (Figure 5.2).

Plug-and-Play isn't perfect, however, because it relies on the participation of peripheral devices, the BIOS, and Windows 95. The weakest link in this group is your PC's BIOS. If it's an older version, it may not support Plug-and-Play. To make Plug-and-Play work, the BIOS has to go further by helping Windows 95 recognize which pieces of hardware are present and which are not. The BIOS is also responsible for communicating with those devices and finding out about their needs.

To accomplish this task, a Plug-and-Play BIOS includes a dual-mode resource allocation module. This module provides both 16-bit real- and protected-mode services to the operating system. Its purpose is to help the operating system find the ports, memory addresses, and interrupts that each device can use without conflicting with other devices in the machine. Another module, the event module, alerts the operating system to changes in system configuration. This proactive communication allows the operating system to maintain contact with each device without wasting the CPU processing required to poll them.

This three-way communication process is essential during the initial boot process. Windows 95 finds out what most devices need after it boots; in other words, these devices do not become active until after Windows 95 can "talk" to them. This is because most devices need some type of device driver to activate them. Windows 95 still uses the system BIOS to communicate with these devices, but it takes care of loading and configuring the device drivers that each device

Figure 5.1 *The Device Manager in the System Properties dialog box allows you to view and manually change the settings for a device connected to your system.*

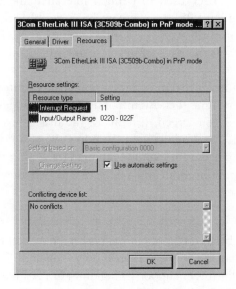

Figure 5.2 *The Resource tab shows the hardware settings and allows you to change them from Windows 95 instead of using settings on the card.*

Microsoft TCP/IP

As I said earlier, TCP/IP is the glue that holds the Internet together. Recall that TCP/IP is actually a collection of networking protocols that together form the basis of Internet communications. In earlier versions of Windows, you had to purchase a third-party program to get TCP/IP compatibility so you could use your PC as a TCP/IP client. One of Windows 95's most significant remote access improvements over Windows 3.11 is the built-in 32-bit TCP/IP stack that provides the TCP/IP networking protocol for connecting your PC to the Internet. It's good, it's easy to install, and it's free, which makes for a very friendly remote access platform. Microsoft TCP/IP is a 32-bit protocol that uses no conventional memory and works in conjunction with other network protocols. Microsoft TCP/IP supports WinSock 1.1, which is a Windows Sockets specification that enables the use of TCP/IP programs with any additional drivers. WinSock is an application program interface (API) that is the basis for all Windows-based communications.

Furthermore, Windows 95 includes support for Dynamic Host Configuration Protocol right out of the box. As you recall, DHCP allows you to connect a Windows 95 LAN to the Internet using dynamic IP addressing. Using a router as a DHCP server, you can save a lot of cash by using a single-user Internet access account and sharing it among several users on your Windows 95 LAN.

Dial-Up Networking

Windows 95 cleaned communications via modem to a remote network with its Dial-Up Networking. Not general-purpose communications software, Dial-Up Networking provides a smooth way to establish a network link over a modem line without leaving your Windows 95 interface. You can use Dial-Up Networking to connect through a modem to a remote LAN, an Internet service provider, another Windows 95 user's PC, or other remote systems.

In a Dial-Up Networking session, one computer acts as a server and another computer acts as a client. If you're connecting to a remote LAN, for example, the computer that you dial into is the server, and your PC is the client. Dial-Up Networking also works in conjunction with Microsoft Exchange's Remote Mail to enable you to send and receive e-mail through remote mail servers.

Using Dial-Up Networking, you can connect to a variety of other systems. The only requirement is that the system you connect to must be capable of supporting one of the connection protocols supported by Windows 95. These include:

- Point-to-point protocol (PPP) for connecting to the Internet
- Serial line Internet protocol (SLIP) for connecting to a UNIX server

- Windows NT and Windows for Workgroups RAS (Remote Access Service)
- Novell NetWare

Note: To add the Dial-Up Networking server capabilities to Windows 95, you'll need the Microsoft Plus add-on program or the Microsoft ISDN Accelerator Pack 1.1 to access the software. The Dial-Up Networking server software turns a PC into a server to enable other users to use Dial-Up Networking clients to dial into your PC and LAN, if your PC is connected to a LAN. The Windows 95 Dial-Up Networking server software supports only NetBEUI and PPP protocols.

Faster Serial Communications Support

Windows 95 eliminated the 19,200-bps limitation for serial communications inherent in Windows for Workgroups. In the age of 56-Kbps analog modems and 115 to 200-Kbps ISDN modems, Windows 95 support for up to 921,600 bps through a serial port is no longer a barrier to high-speed serial communications. Windows 95 support for the higher data transmission rates is based on your PC using at least the 16550A UART (universal ascynchonous receiver/transmitter) chip. UART chips are part of the PC's COM port that handles communications between the CPU and any device connected to the COM port. Most PCs (486s and Pentiums) include the 16550A UART chip.

Easy Networking

Windows 95 makes networking PCs into a local area network about as easy as it gets, with a wide range of improvements over Windows for Workgroups. This includes built-in support for most popular networks. Because the networking components no longer use conventional memory, Windows 95 networking is more robust by up to twice the speed of a Windows for Workgroups network. Another big improvement of Windows 95 networking is its support for simultaneous connections to multiple networks. On the network adapter side of the LAN, Windows 95 dramatically improved the installation process by supporting Plug-and-Play. Network cards are automatically detected by Windows 95 and configured.

Computers belonging to a Windows 95 network can exchange e-mail; share printers, modems, disk drives, and other computer resources. Each copy of Windows 95 is capable of being a client (a user of shared resources) or a server (a giver of resources to others) or a combination of both.

For high-bandwidth remote access, the ability to easily install and work with networking allows you to easily share a remote access connection by way of an Ethernet network, which delivers data at speeds that dwarf the serial port. The sharing of a remote access connection leverages its cost over several PCs to make it an effective way to connect many small offices to the Internet or other networks.

PCMCIA Support

The mobile PC market spawned a new type of bus called PCMCIA, for Personal Computer Memory Card International Association, which uses credit-card-size cards that connect to external slots. This system makes it easy for a portable PC user to change the hardware configuration of a machine without having to open it up, as is the case with desktop PCs. Windows 95 supports PCMCIA and integrates it with Plug-and-Play to allow on-the-fly plugging in and out of PCMCIA cards. Windows 95 will automatically load and unload drivers as necessary in response to changes in any installed or uninstalled cards. Support of these features means you can easily integrate a portable PC into a Windows 95 local area network for sharing high-bandwidth connections across the network. You can also use a PCMCIA modem card with Dial-Up Networking for easy connections on the road. The latest PCMCIA cards include a 56-Kbps modem and a network adapter card for the best of both worlds.

Cornucopia of Remote Access Tools

Windows 95 is indisputably the preferred operating system of the PC world, with an estimated installed base of 62 million (IDC). It should come as no surprise that the available software for Windows 95 is staggering. Hence, you have a cornucopia of software tools to choose from, to do everything you can imagine via remote access. Microsoft offers an ever growing and improving collection of Internet applications that are bundled with Windows 95 or are available free of charge from the Microsoft Web site. In addition to the essential remote access tools such as Web browsers and e-mail programs, there are applications for doing other remote access activities, including:

- Remote control software for operating computers and other devices
- Workgroup software for collaboration over the Internet
- Desktop video conferencing for face-to-face meetings
- Net telephones for voice communications over the Internet

All these applications are enabled and enhanced with a high-bandwidth connection.

Note: See Chapter 9 for information on Microsoft remote access tools, and Appendix A for a comprehensive listing of remote access software, hardware, and services.

The Evolution of Windows 95

Windows 95 continues to evolve into a more powerful and easier-to-use remote access platform. Early releases of Windows 95 Upgrade did not include Internet Explorer, the Internet Wizard for configuring Internet connections, and other remote access features. These programs were available only by purchasing the Microsoft Plus, a Windows 95 add-on package that includes a variety of Windows 95 system utilities and visual enhancements. From a remote access perspective, it was the Internet access tools (called the Internet Jumpstart Kit) and the Dial-Up Networking Server program that were the reasons for getting Microsoft Plus. Now you don't need to purchase this add-on to get these programs because they're both available for free from the Microsoft Web site. And newer versions of Windows 95 Upgrade include the Microsoft Internet Explorer Starter Kit, which has these features.

Earlier OEM (Original Equipment Manufacturer) versions of Windows 95, which are added to new PC systems, included older versions of Internet Explorer and the Internet Wizard. The latest OEM release of Windows 95, called OSR2 (OEM Service Release 2), includes a number of new enhancements to Windows 95. Many dialog boxes contain new settings or different arrangements of settings. Microsoft Exchange, the Windows 95 facility for handing e-mail (local and remote) and faxes, has been replaced with Windows Messaging, which is also included in Windows NT Workstation 4.0. There is a significant update to Windows 95, but you can get it only when you buy a new system or motherboard. Even if you recently purchased a new PC, there's no guarantee you have the latest update. To find out whether you're running OSR2, open the System Properties dialog box in the Control Panel or right-click on the My Computer icon and choose Properties. The OSR2 release identifies itself as version 4.00.950.B. The original retail version of Windows 95 is 4.00.950 (no B).

Internet Explorer 4.0

Microsoft recently released the Internet Explorer 4.0 Suite, which is more than just a new version of Microsoft's Web browser. It represents another big step in

Microsoft's drive to make the Internet a seamless part of the Windows 95 operating system. Internet Explorer 4.0 is actually an interim release of Windows 98 (code named Memphis), which is scheduled for release in late 1997 or early 1998.

Note: Chapter 9 explains the new features of the Internet Explorer 4.0 Suite in more detail.

The installation of IE 4.0 adds new functionality to Windows 95, including the point-and-click interface of the Web. You simply click once on the object, and you are transported to the program or file, whether it's on your PC or on a server on the Internet. Another major enhancement of IE 4.0 is Active Desktop, which transforms your Windows 95 desktop into a customizable "dashboard" for Web-based information. Using desktop components, you can add dynamically updated information directly to your desktop. The Active Desktop allows you to receive Internet or intranet broadcasts and have them appear in real time on your desktop; for example, you can display a stock quote or sports ticker tape that updates itself automatically from a server. This is live Web content displayed on your desktop. Figure 5.3 shows the Internet Explorer 4.0 desktop with various desktop components activated.

There are a number of other Web influences on Windows 95. Standard windows use the point-and-click Web interface and allow you to display HTML documents in a window pane. You can access the Internet from within any window or from the taskbar; or you can place an Internet shortcut on the desktop.

Beyond major enhancements to the Windows 95 interface, the Internet Explorer 4.0 Suite adds an impressive array of new features and programs for working on the Internet. The Internet Explorer Web browser includes a number of new features such as support for Dynamic HTML, automatic updates from Web sites, and offline reading. The IE suite also includes updated Internet mail and newsreader programs that have been integrated into a program called Outlook Express. Other tools that come in the IE 4.0 Suite include: Microsoft NetMeeting for audio and video conferencing; NetShow Player for receiving Web-based broadcasts; and a "lite" version of Microsoft FrontPage97 called FrontPad, which is an HTML authoring program.

Blueprint for Windows 95 Remote Access

Constructing your remote access ecosystem requires a blueprint to help you manage a variety of interrelated components. Windows 95 includes all the remote ac-

Figure 5.3 *Internet Explorer 4.0 lets you add live Web content to your Windows 95 desktop.*

cess tools you'll need, but you must run them on a proper PC platform and match them up with the different high-bandwidth options. The following sections present a blueprint for constructing your remote access ecosystem.

PC Platform Issues

For today's computing and remote access requirements, the operative words are more and faster: more memory, disk space, and multimedia support, along with faster processing and display adapter cards. The Windows 95 minimum PC hardware requirements include the following:

- *Processor:* A 386/486/Pentium processor with a high-density floppy disk and hard disk with approximately 40 MB free disk space for a typical installation
- *Memory:* 4 MB RAM minimum; 8 MB RAM recommended by Microsoft
- *Display:* VGA minimum; SVGA with video card capable of rendering 16-bit TrueColor recommended

Not only should you have more of everything that Microsoft recommends for running Windows 95, you should also think about your PC platform requirements for remote access. Higher-bandwidth options require more capabilities from your PC to keep up with the demands of high-speed data communications. High-bandwidth connectivity requires matching PC power. Using a slow processor, an older graphics adapter, or too little memory—even if supported by Windows 95—will detract from the performance of your remote access capabilities. For example, surfing the Web at speeds of a cable modem or even ISDN with a slower graphics adapter on your PC means that your pages will redraw considerably slower than if you were using an accelerated graphics card. Here is the optimal configuration for working with high-speed remote access. You can get by with less, but you'll pay in terms of performance. Your PC should include the following:

- A Pentium processor (preferably 90 Mhz and higher).
- An accelerated VESA bus or PCI bus graphics card that supports at least SVGA with 800×600×16-bit TrueColor.
- Optimally, 32 MB of RAM (random access memory).
- Empty 16-bit ISA slots or PCI slots, depending on the type of remote access device you're using.
- As a minimum, have a good PC sound system with speakers. One of the coolest benefits of high-speed access to the Internet is the ability to work with multimedia, including sound and video.

For serial-based communications for 56-Kbps or ISDN modems, you must have at least a 16550 UART chip attached either to your motherboard or serial port card. Recall from earlier in the chapter that UART chips are the part of the PC's COM port that handles communications between the CPU and any device connected to the COM port. You can check whether your system has a 16550 UART chip by opening the Modem Properties window from the Control Panel (click on the Modems icon). Click on Diagnostics to display your COM ports. Select the COM port, then click on the More Info button. The UART information appears in the Port Information group.

For Ethernet-based remote access, you'll need at least one network adapter card. If you have a choice, use the newer PCI network cards, which deliver more throughput. If you're building a LAN, you'll need a network adapter.

A new generation of faster COM port cards is available. For example, the Lava Link 650 card can support up to 460.8 Kbps. The only remote access option that could benefit from such a card is an ISDN serial modem, which hits the 115.2-Kbps limit of the 16550A UART chip. However, before you install one, even for an ISDN serial modem, you must make sure the network at the other end of your connection will support the serial data communications rate.

Single-User Remote Access

For 56-Kbps modems and ISDN external modems (those that connect via the serial port), the remote access configuration requires the installation of internal adapter cards or external modems and the Microsoft TCP/IP stack, and setting up Windows 95 Dial-Up Networking. You configure Windows for 56-Kbps and external ISDN modems by using the Modems applet in the Windows 95 Control Panel. You use the Network applet in the Control Panel to install TCP/IP, and the Dial-Up Networking window to set up and manage your dial-up connections. ISDN modems in internal adapter card form are installed as a network adapter card via the Network applet in the Control Panel. Once they're installed, they're managed via the Modems applet in the Windows 95 Control Panel. For these internal ISDN modems, you'll also use Dial-Up Networking to make your connections.

LAN-Based Remote Access

Windows 95 can function as the operating system for a single PC, or you can use it as a peer-to-peer network operating system. Using inexpensive Ethernet cards and a simple network wiring system, the power of networking can be harnessed for any office with two or more PCs. Peer-to-peer networks are the most widely used network system for the SOHO marketplace. The term peer-to-peer means that the computers connected to the LAN all function as both a client and a server for sharing resources across the network. The most common resources shared over a Windows 95 network are drives (to enable file sharing) and printers. And in the case of remote access, peer-to-peer networks enable you to share your bandwidth across multiple PCs on your LAN to leverage your high-bandwidth connections.

Peer-to-peer networks are not designed for running application servers where network versions of applications are centrally stored and accessed by users. An application server is a machine that holds the applications users frequently access, instead of having them reside on their local hard drives. Because applications frequently must load modules or overlays, application servers involve a huge amount of network traffic—more than most peer-to-peer networks can support. Each Windows 95 PC needs to have all or most of its applications running on its local hard drives.

A Windows 95 network is very easy to install and configure. You simply insert a network adapter card in each machine on the network, string a cable between each machine, give each machine a unique name, and select the type of network protocol in a configuration window. Ethernet is the basis for local area networking, and is the connectivity choice for many high-bandwidth options, including ISDN routers, cable modems, and xDSL modems. Ethernet as a remote access connectivity interface uses a network interface card (NIC) in your PC to connect to the remote access device. Depending on the high-bandwidth option and device you're using, the connection can be shared by all the computers on the LAN or be available to only a single PC.

Working with Ethernet-based communications windows involves installing an Ethernet card and using the Network Properties window to set up the protocols and other settings for each PC that is communicating through a network gateway for remote access. This gateway device is a standalone device that can be an ISDN router, a cable modem, or an xDSL modem. They all share the common characteristics of monitoring data traffic going through your Ethernet card and across the LAN. When the device detects packets with addresses or protocols that lie outside your local network, they are routed by the gateway device.

For routers (ISDN, cable, and xDSL), you'll be working with Windows 95 networking features. For these options, you install a network adapter card in every PC you want on a LAN, and configure them for the network protocols you plan to use, such as TCP/IP for the Internet. You then configure the Microsoft TCP/IP properties to support a LAN-based remote access device.

What's Next

Now you know that Windows 95 is full of features ready and waiting for your remote access needs. But now you need to learn which features manage which types of remote access connections. If you want to use a single-user 56-Kbps or an ISDN modem, you'll need to work with Windows 95 Dial-Up Networking, which is covered in Chapter 6. If you want to use a Windows 95 LAN-based remote access solution, you'll need to work with Windows 95 networking features. Chapter 7 and Chapter 8 explain building your network and configuring Windows 95. Whichever router you take, once you get Windows 95 set up for remote access, you can assemble your remote access applications toolkit. Chapter 9 describes working with the Microsoft remote access tools that come bundled with Windows 95.

6 *Remote Access via Dial-Up Networking*

If your remote access plan involves connecting a single PC to the outside world, you're going to use Dial-Up Networking in Windows 95. Dial-Up Networking is a smooth way to connect your PC to the Internet and other networks using a 56-Kbps modem or an ISDN modem. Gone are the days of cryptic PC communication programs; Windows 95 Dial-Up Networking makes the remote network appear transparent as you work with your favorite Internet applications, such as a Web browser or e-mail. This chapter takes you through the process of setting up and using Dial-Up Networking.

What Is Dial-Up Networking?

Dial-Up Networking establishes the communications link with a remote network. Once connected, your computer acts as if it were connected to the network locally. In other words, your computer becomes a client of the remote network. The remote network can be the Internet or any network supported by Windows 95. For establishing a dial-up Internet connection, you use Dial-Up Networking with the PPP (Point-to-Point Protocol) or PPP/MP (Point-to-Point Protocol/Multilink Protocol) for two B channel ISDN connections.

Note: Windows 95 has no built-in provision for sharing a modem or a dial-up networking connection.

Using Dial-Up Networking, you can connect to a variety of other systems. The only requirement is that the system you connect to must be capable of supporting one of the connection protocols supported by Windows 95. The Dial-Up Networking client provided with Windows 95 allows you to connect to a server using any of the following connection protocols.

- Point-to-Point Protocol (PPP)
- Serial Line Internet Protocol (SLIP)
- NetBEUI for Windows NT and Windows for Workgroups
- IPX/SPX-Compatible Novell NetWare

Note: Dial-Up Networking is available as a server in the Microsoft Plus! pack or with the ISDN accelerator pack. The Dial-Up Networking server allows remote users to dial into your computer and access it just as if they were connecting from another computer on the network.

Getting Started

Before you begin working with Dial-Up Networking, you need to do a few things to prepare Windows 95 for using it. You'll need to do the following:

- Install your remote access hardware so Windows 95 knows it's connected.
- Add the Dial-Up Adapter.
- Install the TCP/IP protocol and any other networking protocols you plan to use.
- Install Dial-Up Networking.

Installing a Modem in Windows 95

Windows 95 makes it easy to add any modem to your system thanks to Plug-and-Play. The installation of a specific 56-Kbps or ISDN modem will vary based on the installation software provided by the vendor. However, most devices follow the Windows 95 procedures for installing the device.

To install a modem (internal or external), first make sure your system is turned off. For an external modem, connect the modem using the RS-232 cable's 9-pin or 25-pin serial connector to the back of the unit and the other connector to your PC's serial port, which will be either a 25-pin to 9-pin connector. Installing an internal modem card in your PC involves removing your PC case and inserting the card in an available card slot. You plug in your telephone line to the telephone line port. For an external modem, make sure the power adapter is plugged in and the modem is turned on. You're now ready to install the software in Windows 95.

1. Restart Windows 95. The New Hardware Found dialog box appears.

2. Select Driver from disk provided by the hardware manufacturer and click OK.

3. Insert the driver disk provided by your modem vendor in drive A and then click OK.

4. Select your modem and then click OK. Windows 95 installs the driver software onto your hard drive.

Once the modem driver is installed in Windows 95, you can change any of the configuration settings using the Modems control panel. You can test to make sure your modem works by opening the Modems applet in the Windows 95 Control Panel. The Modems Properties dialog box appears. In the Modems Properties dialog box, select Diagnostics tab, select the COM port connected to the modem, and then click on More Info. A message box appears telling you that Windows 95 is making the connection to your modem. After the connection is made, the More Info dialog box appears indicating your modem is properly installed.

For most internal ISDN modem cards, they appear as network adapters in Windows 95, and their drivers appear in the Network Properties dialog box, which you access from the Network program in the Control Panel. However, these cards are handled through the Modems program for Dial-Up Networking.

Once you have installed the modem in Windows 95, you're ready to use Dial-Up Networking to create your connection profiles for remote access.

Note: More detailed instructions on installing and using specific 56-Kbps or ISDN modems are explained in Part III.

Adding the Dial-Up Adapter

Once you've set up a 56-Kbps or ISDN modem, the first step is to install a logical network adapter in Windows 95. Logical refers to an adapter that is actually a software driver that acts like a network adapter card. Combined with your modem this logical network adapter creates a system that Windows 95 treats as a network-to-network connection. To add the Dial-Up Adapter, do the following:

1. Choose Start | Settings | Control Panel. This displays the Control Panel window.

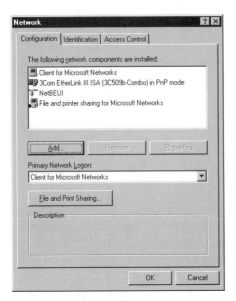

Figure 6.1 *The Network Properties dialog box is where you install the Dial-Up Adapter and add your dial-up networking protocols.*

2. Double-click on the Network icon. This displays the Network dialog box (Figure 6.1). Note that you may have entirely different network components installed on your system from those that appear in the figure. If one of the network components listed is Dial-Up Adapter, then you can skip the rest of these steps because you already have the proper component installed.

3. Click on the Add button. This displays the Select Network Component Type dialog box (Figure 6.2) where you can select the type of network component you are installing.

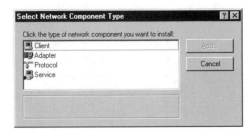

Figure 6.2 *The Select Network Component Type lets you add all the network components for Windows 95.*

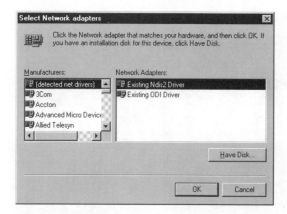

Figure 6.3 *The Select Network adapters dialog box.*

4. Double-click on the Adapter option. The Select Network adapters dialog box appears (Figure 6.3)

5. Scroll through the Manufacturers list until you see the Microsoft option displayed. Select it; the choices in the Network Adapters list change.

6. Select Dial-Up Adapter in the Network Adapters list and click OK, but don't close the Network dialog box yet.

At this stage you've selected the Microsoft Dial-Up Adapter logical network adapter. Next you need to add the TCP/IP protocol, as explained in the next section. After installing the TCP/IP protocol or any other networking protocols you plan to use with dial-up networking, you will install the Dial-Up Networking software.

Installing the TCP/IP Protocol

Recall from previous chapters that a protocol is a common set of rules that any two computers connected via a network and/or communications link must be using in order to communicate. The most widely used protocol is TCP/IP, which is the protocol that drives the Internet. Windows 95 supports other networking protocols, as explained in the next section. Also recall that Windows 95 includes the Microsoft TCP/IP stack, but it's not automatically installed by the Windows 95 Setup program, so for Internet connections, you'll have to do so. The following steps explain how to add the Microsoft TCP/IP protocol to Windows 95.

1. With the Network dialog box open and the Configuration tab displayed, click on the Add button. This again displays the dialog box where you can select the type of network component you are installing.

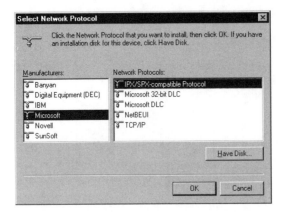

Figure 6.4 *The Select Network Protocol dialog box.*

2. Double-click on the Protocol option. The Select Network Protocol dialog box (Figure 6.4) appears.

3. In the Manufacturers list at the left side of the dialog box, select Microsoft.

4. Select the TCP/IP option, then click OK.

When you return to the Network dialog box, you should be able to scroll through the list of network components and see TCP/IP listed. Notice the component entry for TCP/IP that uses the following notation:

```
TCP/IP -> Dial-Up Adapter
```

This means that TCP/IP has been added to your network component list, and it will be used through the dial-up adapter. This relationship between the protocol and the adapter is referred to as a *binding*. If you have other network adapters installed in your system, Windows 95 may also have bound TCP/IP to them. Unless you need that particular binding, you can delete it. Do this by selecting the protocol binding that you want to delete from the network component list and then click on the Remove button. The binding is immediately removed, and the component list is updated.

Note: For more information on network protocols and binding them to network adapters, see Chapter 8.

When you are through adding your network components and adjusting any bindings, click the OK button. You are informed that for your changes to be implemented, Windows 95 must be restarted. Go ahead and restart the system. Win-

Table 6.1 Networking Protocols Supported by Windows 95

NETWORK VENDOR	DRIVERS
Banyan	Banyan VINES Ethernet Protocol
	Banyan VINES Token Ring
Digital Equipment (DEC)	PATHWORKS v4.1 Ethernet
	PATHWORKS v4.1 Token Ring
	PATHWORKS v5.0 and above Ethernet
	PATHWORKS v5.0 and above Ethernet (ODI)
	PATHWORKS v5.0 and above Token Ring
IBM	Existing IBM DLC Protocol
Microsoft	IPX/SPX-compatible Protocol
	Microsoft 32-bit DLC
	Microsoft DLC
	NetBEUI
	TCP/IP
NetManage*	NetManage TCP/IP v5.0 Dialup Only
	NetManage TCP/IP v5.0 NDIS Dial-up Only
	NetManage TCP/IP v5.0 ODI Dial-up Only
Novell	Novell IPX ODI Protocol
SunSoft	PC-NFS Protocol

* Earlier versions of Microsoft Windows included the NetManage TCP/IP, which later became the basis of Microsoft's TCP/IP stack. Newer versions of Windows 95 have eliminated the NetManage TCP/IP protocol stack.

dows 95 may prompt you for the original distribution CD-ROM or diskettes to complete the installation. Once Windows 95 is restarted, all the settings you added in the Network dialog box are installed.

Using Other Network Protocols with Dial-Up Networking

Windows 95 supports a number of networks from other vendors. Table 6.1 lists the network protocols supported by and included with Windows 95. Installing these network protocols involves the same procedures you used to install the Microsoft TCP/IP protocol, and each one you add with the Microsoft Dial-Up Adapter appears as a dial-up adapter entry in the installed component list of the Network Properties dialog box. For example, adding Microsoft's Novell NetWare IPX/SPX-compatible protocol adds the following entry to the list:

```
IPX/SPX-compatible Protocol -> Dial-Up Adapter
```

You can use additional drivers from other networking vendors for using Dial-Up Networking to connect to their systems, by installing them from a floppy disk or your hard disk. To do so, click on the Have Disk button in the Select Network Protocol dialog box (see Figure 6.4). But before you install any network drivers included in Windows 95 or from other vendors, make sure that you have the original Windows 95 distribution disks or CD-ROM handy. Windows 95 may prompt you for them as part of the protocol installation.

Installing Dial-Up Networking

Like the Microsoft TCP/IP stack, the Windows 95 Setup program doesn't install Dial-Up Networking unless you specify it. If you're not sure that Dial-Up Networking is installed on your system, double-click the My Computer icon on your desktop. Check for a folder labeled Dial-Up Networking. If you don't see it, you need to install the Dial-Up Networking software from your Windows 95 diskettes or CD-ROM, as follows.

1. Choose Start | Settings | Control Panel.
2. Double-click on the Add/Remove Programs icon. This displays the Add/Remove Programs Properties dialog box.
3. Click on the Windows Setup tab and select the Communications component from the list.
4. Click on the Details button. You now see the Communications dialog box (Figure 6.5).
5. Click on the Dial-Up Networking check box, then click OK.
6. Click OK in the Add/Remove Programs Properties dialog box.
7. Follow the Windows 95 prompts for the diskettes or CD-ROM it needs to install Dial-Up Networking. The Dial-Up Networking files are copied from the Windows 95 CD-ROM or disks to your PC.
8. After installing the Dial-Up Networking files, Windows 95 prompts you to restart your computer. Restart Windows 95 by clicking Yes.

Microsoft's ISDN Accelerator Pack

The Microsoft ISDN Accelerator Pack enables you to make Dial-Up Networking connections for ISDN adapter cards. The latest version of the Microsoft ISDN Accelerator Pack (version 1.1) supports Multilink PPP, which allows an ISDN adapter to bind two B channels together for 128-Kbps performance over an ISDN connection. If you're running Windows 95 and using an internal ISDN adapter, you'll

Figure 6.5 *The Communications dialog box.*

need this software. However, for most ISDN adapter cards, you don't need to access this program from the Microsoft Web site because the vendor already supplies it as part of the installation program. External ISDN modems don't require this software.

TIP: One important reason you may want to get the Microsoft ISDN Accelerator Pack 1.1 is that it includes a free copy of the Dial-Up Networking Server program, which is explained later in this chapter.

You can download the Microsoft Accelerator Pack from the Microsoft Web site, point your browser to http://www.microsoft.com/windows/getisdn/dload.htm. The ISDN Accelerator Pack supports PPP, TCP/IP, IPX, and NetBEUI. Note that the ISDN Accelerator Pack 1.1 will not work correctly with 1.0-compatible ISDN card drivers without updated drivers that support 1.1; obtain these from the ISDN modem card vendor. Microsoft maintains a Windows 95 Hardware Compatibility List for ISDN adapter cards at its ISDN site, which is located at http://www.microsoft.com/windows /getisdn/.

Working with Dial-Up Networking Connections

Once you've installed the Dial-Up Adapter, Dial-Up Networking, and any networking protocols you plan to use such as TCP/IP, you're ready to create a dial-up networking connection. You can create as many connection profiles as you need.

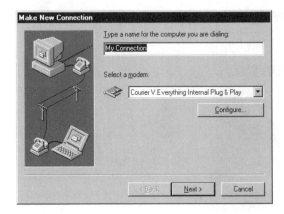

Figure 6.6 *The Make New Connection wizard.*

For example, if you have multiple Internet access accounts, or connect to other networks, you'll create a profile for each connection. Once the profiles are created, making the connection is as simple as double-clicking on the connection icon. The following sections explain creating and managing your Dial-Up Networking connections.

Creating Dial-Up Networking Connections

You create Dial-Up Networking connections using the Make New Connection wizard in the Dial-Up Networking folder, which is located in the My Computer folder on your desktop. Here is how to create a dial-up connection.

1. Choose Start|Programs|Accessories|Dial-Up Networking. The Dial-Up Networking window appears.

2. Double-click on the Make New Connection icon. This starts the Make New Connection wizard (Figure 6.6).

3. Enter the name you want to use for this connection in the field that shows the default value of My Connection. Change the entry to something descriptive about the connection.

4. In the Select a modem field, choose the name of the remote access device you will use for this connection. If you have a single modem installed, it's already the default modem in the field. If not, select the modem you want to use.

5. Click Next. You will see a page asking you for the telephone number information. Enter the area code and phone number for your Internet provider. You should have received this information when you set up your

account. Even if you don't use an area code to dial your Internet service provider, enter it anyway. For the default country code, use United States of America (1).

6. Click Next. The final page of the Make New Connection wizard appears.

7. To complete the connection definition, click Finish. The definition is saved and an icon with the name of your connection appears in the Dial-Up Networking window.

Configuring Your Connection

After you define a Dial-Up Networking connection profile, you need to configure it with information about the network you're connecting to. Before you begin, make sure you have all your Internet access account information, including any assigned IP addresses, DNS server addresses, and your user name and password. The following steps show you how to configure a connection profile you have already created for Internet access.

1. Open the Dial-Up Networking window and right-click on the connection icon you want to configure. This displays a context menu.

2. Choose the Properties option from the menu. A properties dialog box appears with the name you assigned to the connection in the title bar (Figure 6.7). The settings in the General tab should reflect the information you specified when you created the connection.

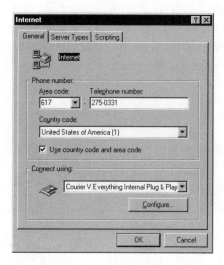

Figure 6.7 *A connection properties dialog box with the name of your connection in the title bar.*

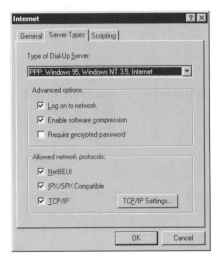

Figure 6.8 *The Server Types properties page lets you specify information about the network you're connecting to.*

Note: The Configure button displays a dialog box that is similar to the Properties dialog box for the modem. Changing any of your modem settings via Windows 95 Dial-Up Networking is explained later.

---

3. Click the Server Types tab to display the Server Types properties page (Figure 6.8).

4. For connecting to the Internet, to another Windows 95, or Windows NT 3.51 networks using PPP, do the following:

  Select the PPP: Windows 95, Windows NT 3.5, Internet from the Type of Dial-Up Server list.

  Check only the TCP/IP item in the Allowed network protocols group.

  Click the TCP/IP Settings button. The TCP/IP Setting dialog box appears (Figure 6.9)

5. In the TCP/IP Settings dialog box, enter the following:

  If your ISP uses dynamic IP addressing, use the default Server assigned IP address setting.

  If your ISP has assigned your computer a specific IP address for your computer, select Specify an IP address and enter the IP address in the IP address field.

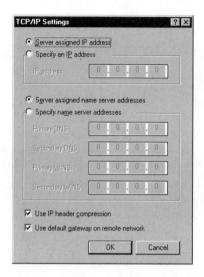

Figure 6.9 *The TCP/IP Settings box is for entering the IP addresses of your Internet service provider's network.*

If your ISP dynamically assigns IP addresses for its DNS (Domain Name System) servers, use the default Server assigned name server addresses.

If your ISP assigns specific IP addresses for its DNS server, select Specify name server addresses. Enter the IP addresses for the Primary and Secondary DNS servers. These IP addresses were provided by your ISP when you opened your Internet access account.

6. Click OK twice and you're finished.

At this point, you're ready to make a connection to your Internet service provider. In most cases, you don't need to make any changes to your modem settings. To use your connection definition to make an Internet connection, go to the "Making the Dial-Up Networking Connection" section.

Making Modem Setting Changes from Dial-Up Networking

If you need different settings from the default Windows 95 modem configuration, you can customize your modem settings for each Dial-Up Networking connection. Right-click on the connection you want and then choose Properties from the context menu. Clicking on the Configure button displays a dialog box that is similar to the Modem properties dialog box in the Windows 95 Control Panel. Figure 6.10 shows a Dial-Up Networking modem properties dialog box. The im-

Figure 6.10 *The Modem Properties dialog box for your Dial-Up Networking connection.*

portant point to keep in mind about making any changes to modem properties via Dial-Up Networking is that the settings aren't applied to the modem unless it's used for this specific connection.

In the General Tab (see Figure 6.10), you can change port settings and specify the maximum speed setting for your remote access device. For a 56-Kbps modem, the setting will be 57600. For an ISDN serial modem, the setting will be 57600 if you're using a single B channel, and 115200 if you're using two B channels. The Only connect at this speed option prevents a modem that supports this feature from making a connection at a lower speed than the one specified in the Maximum speed setting.

The Connection tab (Figure 6.11) includes settings for your modem connections, such as specifying the time for making a connection or disconnecting after a given period of idle time. The Ports Settings button lets you manually specify your COM port setting. In most cases, you don't need to make any changes in this group.

The Advanced button displays the Advanced Connection Settings dialog box for entering any AT commands for making connections. If your remote access device requires AT commands to place a call (see your remote access documentation), do the following.

1. In the Connection tab, click the Advanced button to display the Advanced Connection Settings dialog box (Figure 6.12).

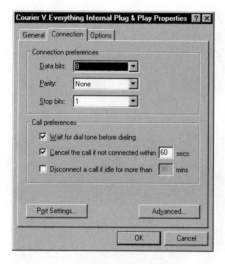

Figure 6.11 *The Connection property page lets you specify connection and call preferences and access port and advanced settings.*

2. In the Extra settings box, type the string of AT commands necessary for your remote access device to place a call.

3. Click OK twice to return to the Connection profile properties window.

The Options tab (Figure 6.13) in the Modem Properties dialog box is used to specify what should happen before or after the connection is made. In most cases, you won't need to make any changes in the Options tab. However, some Internet

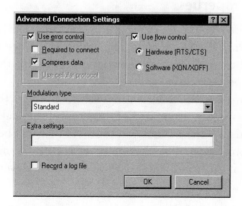

Figure 6.12 *The Advanced Connection Settings dialog box includes a setting for entering any AT Command that your remote access device may need to initiate a call.*

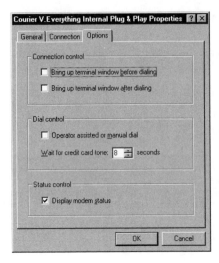

Figure 6.13 *The Options properties page lets you specify actions before or after a connection is made.*

providers require you to manually log in to their systems before the connection protocol is enabled. Thus, using a terminal window after dialing is necessary so that you can follow the steps required by your provider. To enable such a window at the appropriate time, check Bring up terminal window after dialing setting. The Display modem status setting, which is checked, tells Dial-Up Networking to display the status of your connection.

Changing Server-Related Properties

The Server Types dialog box allows you to modify both the protocol used by Windows 95 and what happens during the connection sequence. To change the connection properties related to the server you are contacting, click on the Server Type button in the connection properties dialog box.

In the OSR2 version of Windows 95, these settings are accessed via the Server Types tab in the Connection Properties dialog box. At the top of the dialog box is a pull-down list that is used to define the connection protocol that will be used by the server to which you are connecting. The default value is PPP: Windows 95, Windows NT 3.5, Internet, as it appears in the Type of Dial-Up Server list, but you can change it to any of the following items.

- CSLIP: UNIX Connection with IP Header Compression
- NRN: NetWare Connect

- SLIP: UNIX Connection
- Windows for Workgroups and Windows NT 3.1

Select the connection protocol that is required by your Internet provider. Changing your protocol also modifies the other options available in the Server Types dialog box. This is because different protocols support different capabilities. By definition, PPP supports all six of the options shown in the dialog box. Other options provide only subsets of these options. After you have selected a connection protocol, the only other options that you may need to change are in the Advanced options group area. These options include:

- *Log on to network.* This option is initially checked, because Windows 95 assumes you are connecting with a server that supports this capability. If your provider does not, disable the option.

- *Enable software compression.* This option is available only under PPP. Some systems support PPP with the software compression option, but not all. If you find that your provider does not, turn this option off.

- *Require encrypted password.* This option is available only under PPP. A few systems have a PPP option that supports encrypted passwords. If your provider does this for security purposes, and you have selected Log on to network, then select this option.

Renaming and Deleting Connections

Once you create and configure a connection profile, it's stored in the Dial-Up Networking folder. There may be times after creating a definition that you want to rename it. For instance, you may later decide to use a more descriptive name. To rename a connection definition, point to the text name and click the right mouse button to display a context menu. Choose Rename. The connection definition name becomes a text field. Enter the new name and press Enter. Note: You can't use the Properties item in the context menu to change the name of a Dial-Up Networking connection profile.

At some point, you may also decide that you want to delete a definition. For instance, you may no longer have an account with a particular Internet provider. In such a case, you should delete the definition so that it clears your Dial-Up Networking window and no longer occupies disk space. The easiest way to delete a definition is to select the definition icon (click on it) and then press Delete. Or, instead of pressing Delete, you can choose the Delete option from the context menu, which you display by pointing to the icon and right-clicking.

Making the Dial-Up Networking Connection

After you set up your Internet (or any other network) connection definition, making the connection is easy. To make your first call, open the Dial-Up Networking window. You can initiate the connection in two ways. First, you can double-click on the connection icon. Second, you can select the icon and choose Connections|Connect in the Dial-Up Networking window. Either way, the result is the same. The Connect To dialog box appears (Figure 6.14).

The information at the bottom of the Connect To dialog box indicates where you are calling to and from. The default location specifies where you're calling from relative to the number you're calling. You can change this setting to reflect a different telephone number dialing sequence, as explained later in this chapter. You will typically use this feature when you're traveling, using a laptop, and your temporary location requires you to dial a different number to connect to your Internet provider or other network.

The Dial Properties button displays the Dialing Properties dialog box, as explained later in this chapter. At the top of the dialog box are fields for your user name and password. For most connections (those that don't require a terminal window), you must specify your user ID and password in this dialog box. Your Internet provider should have given this information to you when you set up your account. These entries are usually not the same ones you use to log in to Windows 95 (if you are using a local area network). Replace your name in the User name field with the user ID for your provider. In the Password field, type the password you obtained. As you type the password, asterisks appear in the field instead of the actual characters.

The Save password check box below the Password field, if checked, will tell Dial-Up Networking to remember the password so you won't have to enter it on subsequent dial-up sessions. There is a downside to this, however; if you have an Internet provider for which the login is automated, then anyone can use your machine

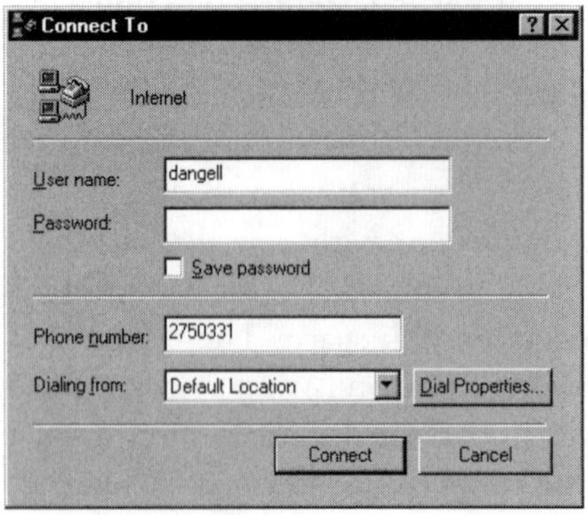

Figure 6.14 *The Connect To dialog box.*

(assuming he or she got past your Windows login), get connected to the Internet with full privileges under your name.

When you are ready to proceed and you have provided any necessary information in the Connect To dialog box, click on the Connect button. Windows 95 immediately tries to make a connection to your provider based on the information in your modem setup and Dial–Up Networking configuration. While a connection is being attempted, a status box appears.

During the first part of the connection process, the modem is dialed and the communications link is negotiated. If you set up your modem correctly and provided the proper phone number and dialing parameters, the connection is made. Dial–Up Networking connects you to the remote system and logs you in with your user name and password. During this phase, you see the status box change. Once your identity has been confirmed and the security system at the remote server is satisfied, you are connected to the Internet.

The information in the Connected to Internet dialog box (Figure 6.15) lets you know that you are connected (and at what speed), as well as how long you have been connected. Two buttons appear on the right side of the status box under the OK button. The Disconnect button will terminate your connection. If you click on the Details button, you will see additional information about your dial-up connection. The information shown in the expanded status box varies based on how you configured your networking. If you want to show the smaller status box, click on the No Details button to again hide the details.

At this point, the status box serves no real purpose, so you can minimize it to the taskbar as you would any other window: Click on the minimize control in the upper right corner of the box. When the status box is minimized, the name used for the task on the taskbar is the same as the name of the Dial-Up Networking connection definition. At this point, you have the entire screen available to do other work.

Working on the Internet

With your Internet connection made using Dial-Up Networking, you can simply open any TCP/IP application on your PC. For example, double-clicking on a

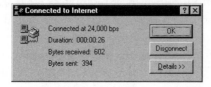

Figure 6.15 *The Connected to Internet dialog box displays the status of your connection.*

Web browser icon on your desktop immediately opens the browser and displays the default home page. Likewise, you can open an e-mail program to retrieve or send messages. As long as you're connected, you can work with any TCP/IP application. Your interface to the Internet is all Windows 95.

Ending Your Session

When you are ready to break your connection, display the by Dial-Up Networking status box by clicking on the small icon showing two connected PCs located on the right side of your taskbar. To terminate your session, click on the Disconnect button. The modem link terminates immediately.

Using the Terminal Window

If you can't get past the login message box, your Internet provider probably does not support an automatic login. This means you'll have to establish a connection using a terminal window and a command line. Once the connection is made using a terminal window and commands, you can use your Windows 95 remote access applications. Here's how to use the terminal window that's included with Dial-Up Networking.

1. Open the Dial-Up Networking window, right-click on the connection for your Internet provider, and then choose Properties from the context menu.
2. Click on the Server Type button.
3. Disable the Log on to network option, then click OK.
4. Click on the Configure button, then click OK.
5. Select the Options tab, and enable the Bring up terminal window after dialing option.
6. Click on OK twice.

When the terminal window appears during login, exactly what you see and what you do in the window depend, for the most part, on your Internet provider. Different providers have different procedures for logging in. When the Post-Dial Terminal Screen window (Figure 6.16) is displayed, it resembles an MS-DOS window. This form of interaction with an Internet service provider is like using a traditional communications software package. Information sent by your ISP is displayed in the terminal window and you type in your responses. At this point, your provider's computer has displayed a welcome message and is asking you to identify yourself. This is where you enter your user ID. After typing it and pressing Enter, you're asked to supply your password and then press Enter. Finally, you click

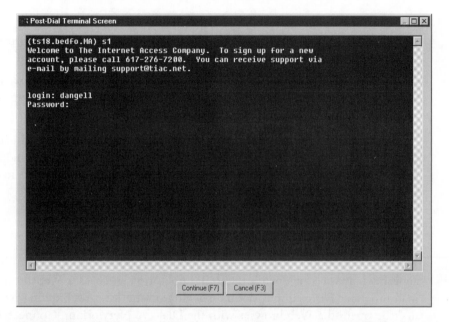

Figure 6.16 *The Post-Dial Terminal Screen lets you log in manually for Internet service providers that don't support automatic login.*

on the Continue button at the bottom of the terminal window. The terminal window then closes, and a status box appears informing you that your user name and password are being verified. The connection is made and you're ready to use your TCP/IP applications.

Streamlining Dial-Up Networking

Dial-Up Networking is a great tool for remote access, and you can make it even better by learning a few tricks. You can create a shortcut for your connection on the desktop, link Dial-Up Networking to work when you open a TCP/IP application, bypass the Connect To dialog box, speed up the dialing initialization process, and share a Dial-Up Networking Connection across a LAN.

Creating a Dial-Up Networking Shortcut

If you're planning to use the Internet on a regular basis, consider adding your Dial-Up Networking connection to the desktop for quicker access. This makes starting your connection as close as your desktop. To create such a shortcut, follow these steps:

1. Open the Dial-Up Networking window.

2. Right-click on the connection icon and choose the Create Shortcut option from the context menu.

3. A message box appears telling you that a shortcut cannot be created in the Dial-Up Networking window and asks if you want the shortcut to be placed on the desktop. Click on the Yes button.

Windows 95 creates a shortcut to your connection definition and places it on the desktop. Now, instead of opening the Dial-Up Networking window every time you want to connect to the Internet, double-click on the icon to take the shortcut you just created.

Linking Dial-Up Networking to TCP/IP Applications

A handy way to use Dial-Up Networking is to have the Connect To dialog box appear whenever you open a TCP/IP application, such as a Web browser or e-mail program. For example, double-clicking on the Internet Explorer icon on the desktop opens the Web browser with the Dial-Up Networking Connect To dialog box. This feature is available from the Internet Properties window. You access the Internet Properties window (Figure 6.17) by clicking on the Internet icon in the Control Panel or by pointing to the Internet icon on the desktop, then right-click-

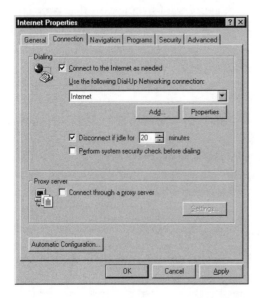

Figure 6.17 *The Connection tab in the Internet Properties dialog box.*

ing to display a context menu, and then choosing Properties. Most of the settings in this Window are for configuring Internet Explorer. However, the Connection tab provides a few helpful features for managing your Internet dial-up connections.

- The Connect to the Internet as needed setting at the top of the Internet Properties box links with one Web browser at a time. If you use more than one browser from your desktop, Windows 95 displays a dialog box whenever you choose a different Web browser from the one used in the previous session, asking whether you want to assign it as the default browser. Clicking Yes does so.

- The Connect to the Internet as needed check box allows you to specify which Dial-Up Networking connection is automatically used whenever you open a TCP/IP application. When this box is selected, a message appears if you try to open any TCP/IP application but have not yet established a connection. The Connect To dialog box appears inside the TCP/IP application window prompting you to make the Dial-Up Networking connection. This saves you the steps of starting the Dial-Up Networking connection and then opening a TCP/IP application.

- The Disconnect if idle setting lets you specify whether to disconnect from the Internet if you have not used your computer for the number of minutes entered in the box. The default is 20 minutes. This feature can save you a lot of money if you accidentally leave a connection on.

- The Perform system security check before dialing setting, if selected, tells Windows 95 to prompt you for your Windows 95 user name and password before enabling you to initiate an Internet connection.

Bypassing the Connect To Dialog Box

Every time you use a Dial-Up Networking connection, the Connect To dialog box appears prompting you for confirmation of your connection before making the call. You can get rid of this box and automatically make the dial-up connection by using a program call Dunce. Vector Development's Dunce Dial-Up Networking Connection enhancement program is available at Web site http://www.vecdev .com/. The Dunce and Dunce Pro programs also add a number of other enhancements to Dial-Up Networking.

Speeding Up Dial-Up Networking Initialization

Dialing up with built-in Dial-Up Networking in Windows 95 is clean and straightforward, but it may seem to take a while to complete the connection. You may notice that a connection is established long before Dial-Up Networking fin-ishes the connection. Here are some tips on how to speed up the process:

1. Open the Dial-Up Networking window, right-click on the desired con-nection, then choose Properties from the context menu.

2. Click Server Type, and turn off support for NetBEUI and IPX/SPX—but make sure TCP/IP is turned on.

3. Turn off Log on to network in the same box.

4. Click OK twice.

5. Double-click on the Network icon in the Control Panel.

6. Highlight the Dial-Up Adapter, and click Properties.

7. Click on the Bindings tab, and uncheck all items in the list other than TCP/IP.

8. Click OK twice.

Going Mobile with Dial-Up Networking

Windows 95 Dial-Up Networking adapts to your needs on the road. It enables you to create new locations for the same dial-up connection as you move around. To create a different location, double-click on the Dial-Up Networking connec-tion you want to change from the Dial-Up Networking folder. This displays the Connect To dialog box. Click the Dial Properties button to display the Dialing Properties dialog box (Figure 6.18).

You create a new calling-from location by clicking on the New button, giving the location a name, then specifying how you want the call to be made from the How I dial from this location group. Select the Dial using Calling Card option if you want to charge your call to a telephone company credit card. You can specify multiple calling cards for a single location entry. Clicking the Change button dis-plays a Change Calling Card dialog box (Figure 6.19). The Calling card to use drop-down list displays telephone calling cards and telephone access numbers to select from. The Calling Card number field is where you enter your PIN number. The Advanced button displays a dialog box for entering any dialing rules for your calling card.

If the location has call waiting, which disrupts modem communications, you can shut it off using the This location has call waiting setting in the Dialing Prop-erties dialog box. The drop-down list includes common codes for shutting off call waiting before making the outbound call. After all your settings are in place, the sequence of numbers appears at the bottom of the Dialing Properties dialog box needs. The system BIOS does contain logic that ensures there is a way to boot the machine. It looks for a boot device (hard or floppy disk drive), the keyboard, and a display device. After Windows 95 boots, it obtains the set-up information for these devices from the system BIOS and performs any protected mode setups required. In most cases, this means that it must load a device driver for each boot device.

Windows 95 automatically detects all the Plug-and-Play components attached to your system. You need to provide only minimal information during installation and nothing at all during subsequent reboots. Every device on your computer needs resources in the form of input/output ports, memory addresses, and interrupts. Windows 95 works with the BIOS and peripheral devices to meet these needs without any intervention.

Windows 95's automatic system configuration updates and detects resource conflicts. All of this communication between peripheral devices, the BIOS, and the operating system allows Windows 95 to create a system configuration without any user intervention. The enhanced level of communication also allows Windows 95 to poll the peripherals for alternate port and interrupt settings when a conflict with another device occurs. This is the providence of the Windows 95 Device Manager.

Device Driver Loading and Unloading

CONFIG.SYS and AUTOEXEC.BAT used to contain line after line of device driver and TSR statements. Windows 95 can maintain or even enhance the performance of a Plug-and-Play-compatible system without using an AUTOEXEC .BAT or CONFIG.SYS, which was the basis of device management in Windows for Workgroups.

Although Plug-and-Play can make system configuration changes automatically, you are not left in the dark. Every time the system configuration changes, it notifies you by displaying a dialog box on-screen. Essentially, the dialog box tells you what has changed. This capability has a side benefit: Windows 95 also notifies you whenever your equipment experiences some kind of failure. Remember that Plug-and-Play requires three-way communication, and a defective device usually fails to communicate.

● ●

CAUTION: Learn the difference between those computers on the market today that claim to possess Plug-and-Play capability but that have only Plug-and-Play peripheral boards. This doesn't mean the BIOS supports Plug-and-Play. A Plug-and-Play system must have BIOS that supports Plug-and-Play. Make sure you ask about this additional feature before you buy a system.

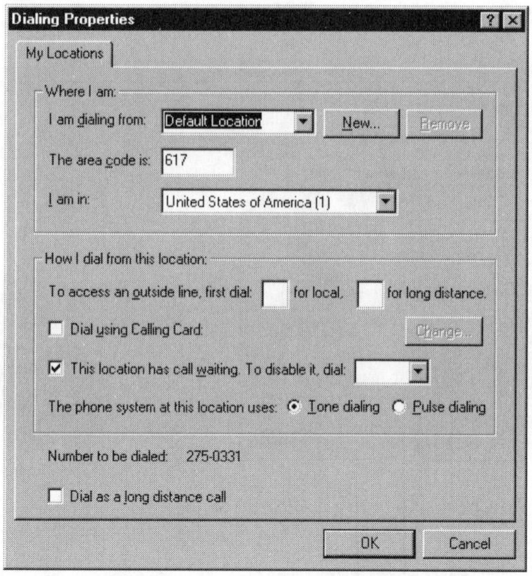

Figure 6.18 *The Dialing Properties dialog box.*

for that location. Click OK. Your new location entry appears in the I am dialing from drop-down list.

The Internet Connection Wizard

The Internet Connection Wizard walks you through setting up a new Dial-Up Networking connection or reconfiguring an existing connection profile for Internet connections. The Internet Connection Wizard on some versions of Windows 95 also lets you set up your own Internet Mail and Internet News programs if

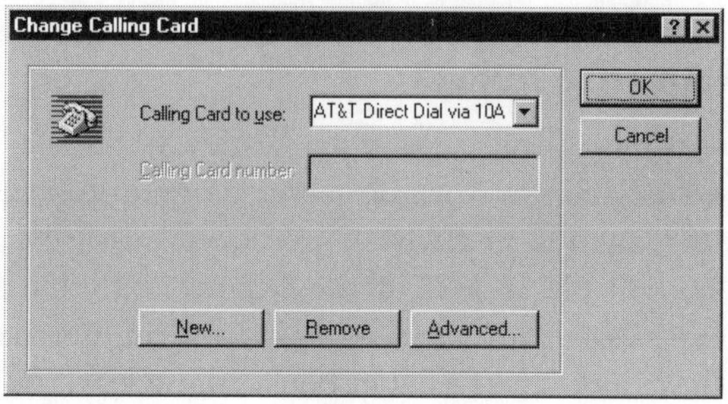

Figure 6.19 *The Change Calling Card dialog box.*

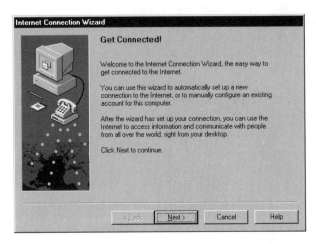

Figure 6.20 *The Internet Connection Wizard's welcome screen.*

they're installed on your system. This wizard will vary in format depending on the version of Windows 95 you're using. The Internet Connection Wizard is also affected by which components you have installed on your system at the time you run it. The earlier versions of the Windows 95 Upgrade package don't include the Internet Wizard. You can get the Internet Connection Wizard for free as part of the Internet Explorer 4.0 Suite. It's also available in the Microsoft Plus add-on package.

Before you run the wizard, make sure you have all your Internet access account information handy. If you haven't installed Internet Explorer, double-clicking on the Internet icon on the desktop can access the Internet Connection wizard. It's also available by choosing Start|Programs|Accessories|Internet Tools. Depending on the version of Windows you're using, the menu item may be named Internet Setup Wizard, Get on the Internet, or Connection Wizard. Figure 6.20 shows the welcome screen for the Internet Connection Wizard.

Setting Up a Dial-Up Networking Server

The Dial-Up Networking facility that comes with Windows 95 is a client program, but you can get the Dial-Up Networking server program to enable remote Windows 95 users access to your PC or LAN. A free copy of the Dial-Up Networking server program is available as part of the Microsoft ISDN Accelerator Pack version 1.1, as explained earlier in this chapter, or you can purchase the Microsoft Plus package, which includes the Dial-Up Networking server software.

The Windows 95 Dial-Up Networking server supports NetBEUI (the native Windows 95 networking protocol) and Novell NetWare's IPX/SPX protocols.

The Windows 95 Dial-Up Networking server doesn't support TCP/IP, so you can't use the Windows 95 server as a TCP/IP gateway. It does support PPP and asynchronous NetBEUI (used by Windows NT 3.1 and Windows for Workgroups).

The Dial-Up Networking server supports two types of security: shared-level and user-level. With share-level security, shared resources are protected using passwords. Any user that has the correct password can access the shared resource. All Windows 95 workstations use share-level security to protect resources they are sharing. User-level security provides greater protection by requiring access to be handled through a Windows NT or NetWare security provider. Using the user-level security scheme requires your Windows 95 Dial-Up Networking server be connected to a LAN running a Windows NT or NetWare server, which acts as a security server.

Installing and Configuring the Dial-Up Networking Server

If you downloaded the Microsoft ISDN Accelerator Pack (1.1), when you installed it using Start|Run, the Dial-Up Networking server is automatically installed. To install the Windows 95 Dial-Up Networking server software from Microsoft Plus! for Windows, run the Setup program. In Setup, choose the Custom option and select the Dial-Up Networking Server from the Options list; then follow the remaining instructions in Setup to complete the installation process.

After you install the Dial-Up Networking server, the only indication that it's installed is displayed by Opening the Dial-Up Networking folder and choosing Connections|Dial-Up Server. The Dial-Up Server dialog box appears (Figure 6.21).

Figure 6.21 *The Dial-Up Server dialog box.*

To allow remote users to dial into your PC, choose the Allow caller access setting. Click on the Change Password button to display the Dial-Up Networking Password dialog box. The first time you enter a password, leave the Old password field blank because no password is the default setting. Enter your new password in the New password field and then enter the confirmation password in the Confirm new password field. Click OK. If later, you want to change your password, you'll need to enter the password in the Old password field.

After you configure the security options, you need to specify the type of connection protocol your Windows 95 Dial-Up Networking server will use. Click the Server Type button to display the Server Types dialog box. If you select the Default server type, your Dial-Up Networking server attempts to use PPP to connect callers; if the PPP connection fails, it attempts asynchronous NetBEUI; if the NetBEUI connection fails, the call terminates. If you want to limit calls specifically to either PPP or NetBEUI, select the desired protocol from the drop-down list. Two other options on the Server Types dialog box let you control the connection.

- *Enable Software Compression*. Enable this check box if you want the server to use software compression to improve data transfer speed. The remote user must also be using software compression. If not, the server connects without compression.
- *Require Encrypted Password*. Enable this check box to require the caller's client to transmit the logon password in encrypted format. If you clear this check box, the password is sent unencrypted.

Choose OK to return to the Dial-Up Server dialog box; then click OK to begin monitoring the port for incoming calls. The message Monitoring appears in the Status field.

The final part of setting up the Dial-Up Networking server is to arrange for the sharing of any local resources that you want other users to access remotely, such as hard drives, printers, and CD-ROM drives.

Setting Up the Dial-Up Networking Client

After the Dial-Up Networking server is set up and ready, you'll need to configure the Dial-Up Networking clients for the users who are to have access to your PC. Here's how to set up a Dial-Up Networking client for connecting to a Dial-Up Networking server.

1. Install the NetBEUI protocol on your system using the Network applet in the Windows 95 Control Panel.
2. Create a new Dial-Up Networking Connection with the telephone number of the modem being used for the Dial-Up Networking server.

3. Use the PPP: Windows 95, Windows NT 3.5, Internet option in the Type of Dial-Up Server setting in the Server Types dialog box.

4. Make sure the Log on to network setting is checked.

5. Be sure to check NetBEUI in the Allowed network protocols group.

6. To make the connection, double-click on the connection icon. In the Connect To dialog box, enter the Dial-Up Networking server's password in the Password field.

Terminating a User

Occasionally, you might need to terminate a user's connection to your Dial-Up Networking server. The user might have forgotten to log off and terminate the connection, for example, which is tying up the line and preventing other callers from connecting. Or, you might need to disconnect a user for security reasons. To disconnect a user, open the Dial-Up Networking folder and choose Connections|Dial-Up Server to open the Dial-Up Server dialog box. Click the Disconnect User button. Dial-Up Networking prompts you to verify that you want to disconnect the current caller.

What's Next

You've learned about working with Windows 95 Dial-Up Networking for single PC remote access connections. Now it's on to the big time: LAN-based remote access. Windows 95 makes local area networking about as easy as it gets for creating a shared remote access connection. And exciting new LAN-based remote access devices now let you connect your small office to the Internet for not much more than it takes to connect a single PC. Chapters 7 and 8 guide you through building your own Windows 95 LAN.

7 Assembling a LAN for Remote Access

What does a Windows 95 local area network have to do with remote access? Plenty. High-bandwidth connections (ISDN, Cable, and xDSL) all share a common interface to the PC—Ethernet. It's the conduit used for most local area networks. Ethernet is the interface of choice for most high-bandwidth options because it delivers more data communications capacity between your PC and the remote access device. Capacity is only part of Ethernet's advantage. New generations of LAN-based remote access devices make sharing a high bandwidth a cost-effective way for small offices to connect to the Internet. And Windows 95 is network-ready, which makes assembling a LAN easy and inexpensive. There are two key parts to building a Windows 95 LAN: hardware and software. This chapter explains the hardware fundamentals.

Ethernet-Based Remote Access

Ethernet can be a high-speed conduit from a single PC or an entire LAN to a remote access device. In most cases, you'll want to use Ethernet as a conduit to share your high-speed connection across two or more PCs. However, some high-speed remote access devices, such as cable modems, allow you to connect only one PC via Ethernet to the remote access device. For the most part, cable companies have decided it should be one PC per cable modem, which no doubt is an extension of their mind-set that determined there should be a cable box on every television set. It's nonsensical, but the reality. For these cable modems, you connect a single PC using a network interface card connected to the remote access device directly.

If your site has two or more PCs, or you have only one PC but anticipate adding other PCs, I recommend connecting them to a local area network as a foundation for sharing your remote access devices. The Windows 95 peer-to-peer networking

115

system is easy to set up and configure; it makes operating a network a breeze. With a Windows 95 LAN, you can leverage the cost of a high-speed connection over multiple PCs and enjoy faster performance than using Dial-Up Networking.

The added cost of building a network is minimal when you compare it to the cost of your PCs or the cost of using a modem for each PC. In general, you can expect to spend around $75 for each network adapter card; and cabling will run around $6 to $9 per computer. In most cases, you'll also need a device called a *hub* which will cost under $100. However, a growing number of remote access devices include a built-in hub so you don't even need that. And assembling your Windows 95 LAN is a do-it-yourself project that will take a few hours from start to finish.

Lay of the LAN

In networking jargon, *topology* refers to the layout of the network components as defined by the type of physical wiring system used to connect PCs and other network devices. For PC-based local area networks, there are two popular topologies: *bus* and *star*. Each is based on its own type of cable and connectors. The type of cabling you use defines your network topology. There are two types of cabling systems used for PC networks: 10Base2 and 10BaseT.

Note: You can buy either of these network cables in a variety of common lengths with connectors already attached from most computer retail stores, such as CompUSA.

Bus Topology and 10Base2 Cabling

The bus topology is based on 10Base2, or coaxial cabling (also referred to as thinnet), which looks like the cabling used for cable television. It consists of a center copper cable surrounded by plastic insulation. On the outside of the insulation material is a copper braid that in turn is surrounded by a thin plastic outer cover.

A 10Base2 network is basically a straight line of cable. Bus topology uses a single cable routed through a work area with PCs connected anywhere along the line with connectors, as shown in Figure 7.1. Although you can route the cable in a twisted and circular arrangement, the two ends of the cable are never connected. Each end is terminated with a small terminator piece. A coaxial bus network is limited to about 600 feet of wire, end to end, with a maximum of 30 computers per leg. Each computer is attached to the coax network via a BNC T (tee) connector. This arrangement lets you attach a single leg of the connector to your

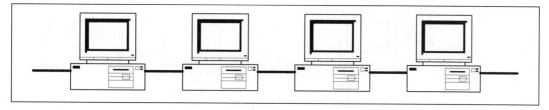

Figure 7.1 *The bus LAN topology uses 10Base2 cabling.*

computer's network adapter card and the two network cable segments to the arms of the connector.

Coaxial cabling is more tolerant of electrical influences and can transmit data over longer distances than 10BaseT. If your network must run in an environment where heavy machinery operates, near fluorescent lighting, or in parallel with other electrical wiring, then coaxial wiring may be a better choice over twisted-pair (discussed in the next section).

Until recently, the bus (or distributed bus) was the most common topology used in the PC world, but it is being replaced with 10BaseT cabling. The weak point in the bus topology is the connecting cable itself. The bus must remain unbroken from one end to the other with special hardware terminators at each end, or the network won't work. Also 10BaseT cabling is less expensive, easier to work with, and used by most remote access devices as the interface to a LAN. Most remote access devices do not include BNC connectors for connecting to 10Base2 cabling, requiring you to purchase a clunky adapter.

Note: If you already have a network setup using 10Base2 cabling, you can use it with remote access devices by connecting a hub device that supports the use of both 10Base2 and 10BaseT networks together.

Star Topology and 10BaseT Cabling

The star topology attaches multiple PCs through a hub and uses 10BaseT cabling (also called twisted-pair), which looks like standard telephone wiring used in business environment with eight-wire RJ-45 connectors on each end of the cable. At the center of this LAN topology is the hub that acts as the network traffic intersection for the LAN. Each computer or other network device connects to the hub via a 10BaseT cable. This is the most popular form of LAN topology in PC networking because it's a more reliable system than 10Base2. The reliability of this topology comes from the fact that each device has its own link to the LAN. If one

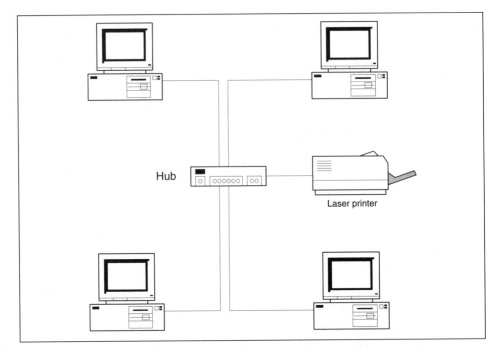

Figure 7.2 A LAN based on the star topology is more reliable than the bus topology.

computer on the LAN goes down, the LAN continues to function, unlike a bus topology network. Figure 7.2 shows a LAN based on the star topology. The 10BaseT cable is easier to work with when laying out your network and is less expensive than 10Base2 cabling. A 10BaseT network is limited to about 300 feet per cable (a 300-foot radius from the hub). For most SOHO sites, this maximum distance won't be a factor in deciding which cable to use for a network. However, you must use a hub, so it will typically cost a little more than a 10Base2 system.

Getting Your Wires Crossed

If you're connecting a remote access device, such as a router or cable modem to a single PC via Ethernet, you'll typically use a special 10BaseT cable where one pair of the eight wires is crossed. Cross-wired cables are usually designated with a different color patch, or connect on one end. If the cable isn't marked, mark it so it doesn't become mixed up with your standard 10BaseT cables. You can check the connectors at each end to determine whether the 10BaseT cable is a cross-connect cable. Check that one pair of the eight color wires is crossed over; if not, it's a standard 10BaseT cable that can be used to connect any network device to your LAN.

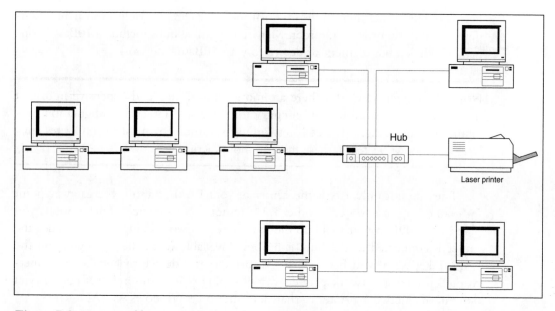

Figure 7.3 *You can add a star network to an existing bus network to create a hybrid LAN topology.*

Combining Bus and Star Networks

The 10Base2 and 10BaseT networks can be combined to work as one network. If you already have a 10Base2 type of Ethernet network in place, you can use an inexpensive hub that includes a BNC connector as well as 10BaseT ports. You can connect the 10Base2 network to the BNC port on the router, then add the ISDN router and other PCs using 10BaseT cables to the hub. Figure 7.3 shows what a combination bus and star topology looks like. One important reason you may want to add a hub and 10BaseT cabling to your existing bus network is for adding remote access devices. Many LAN-based remote devices, such as ISDN routers, include only 10BaseT (RJ-45) ports. While these devices typically include an attachment unit interface (AUI) connector for attaching a 10Base2 connector, this option is less than ideal because you have to purchase an adapter device that can cost about half as much as a hub.

Hub Fundamentals

A hub is an external device that is about the size of a standalone modem. Hubs are relatively simple, passive devices with 4 to 10 10BaseT connection ports; and they're inexpensive, at well under $100. As your network expands, you can connect one hub to another. Hubs for small networks are available from many computer retail stores or by mail order. Many inexpensive hubs include a 10Base2 connector to link a bus segment or device to your 10BaseT network.

Note: For larger networks, there are more sophisticated and expensive hubs that include more ports, protection circuitry for the ports, internal configuration programming, and other advanced networking features. For most SOHO sites running a Windows 95 LAN, these hubs are not practical.

The hub not only acts as the center of your LAN, it also is the gateway point for connecting to a router or other LAN remote access devices. For example, you plug in an ISDN router to a hub the same way you would plug in a PC. Once the router is connected to the hub, it becomes available to all the computers on the LAN. Likewise, if you have a network printer or a device that makes a nonnetworked printer a network printer, you also plug it into the hub. Of course, you don't need a network printer to share a printer on a Windows 95 LAN.

TIP: Before you purchase a router, check out the remote access devices available for the bandwidths option you use because a growing number of LAN-based remote access devices have hubs built in. These products are designed specifically for the SOHO market. For example, there are several ISDN routers that include four or eight port hubs.

Test-Driving a LINKSYS 10-Port Workgroup Hub

LINKSYS makes a number of affordable hubs and other LAN products designed for the PC networking market. The LINKSYS 10-port hub includes one 10Base2 (BNC) port and nine 10BaseT (RJ-45) ports. The single 10Base2 port allows you to connect a bus network to a star (10BaseT) network.

Ports 1 through 8 at the back of the unit are used to connect computers or other network devices to the hub. Port 9 can be used to attach either a computer or another hub. Connecting a hub to another hub is called uplinking. Underneath the hub is a switch that allows you to activate the port for connecting to another hub device. When the uplink switch is turned on, port 9 expects to be joined to another hub. When turned off, port 9 can be connected to a computer or other network device in the same manner as ports 1 through 8.

Before you install the hub, you must have one standard 10BaseT cable for each computer that you plan to connect to the hub. Each cable should have RJ-45 connectors on each end, be wired straight through, and not exceed 328 feet in length.

Installing the LINKSYS 10-Port Workgroup Hub is easy because you don't use any software to get the hub up and running. You place the hub where the LEDs on the front of the unit are visible and there is an electrical outlet. Make sure the hub isn't near any source of electrical interference. Plug the power adapter into the electrical outlet; the hub's green power LED should light up signaling that it is ready to add your computers and other network devices.

At this stage, if you haven't installed your network adapter cards, you need to install them into each PC that you want to connect to your LAN. (See the next section for information on installing network cards.) With your network adapter cards installed in your PCs, attach one connector of the 10BaseT cable into the back of the network card and the other into any available 10BaseT port on the hub. Repeat the process for each computer and network device you want to add to your LAN. If you are connecting a BNC T-connector into the hub's BNC port, then plug a terminator into the other end of the hub's T-connector.

The absence of a power switch on the hub is intentional, to ensure that it is always left on. If the power to the hub is off, your LAN won't work. However, if you need to reset the hub for any reason, which can happen sometimes after a power outage or other electrical interference, use a paper clip or the tip of a pen to press the hub's Reset button, which is located to the right of the LED indicator lights. Table 7.1 explains the functions of the LEDs located at the front of the hub, which provide useful status information.

Network Interface Cards

The network interface card (NIC) provides the network interface to your PC. You must install a network adapter for each PC that you want to connect to the network. A network card, like any adapter card installed in your PC, communicates with your PC using one of several bus standards in use today. A bus is the vehicle the computer uses to transfer data into and out of memory and between the CPU and other components of your PC.

The oldest bus is Industry Standards Association (ISA), a 16-bit bus that originated in early PCs. Two newer bus standards found in today's machines are Video Electronics Standards Association (VESA) and Peripheral Component Interconnect (PCI). These are called local bus connections because they offer direct connections between the CPU, memory, and local bus components. Local buses are 32- or 64-bit connections that operate at much higher speed than the older 16-bit ISA bus.

Table 7.1 The LED Functions on the LINKSYS 10-Port Workgroup Hub

LED	COLOR	STATUS
Power	Green	Solid indicates hub is in working order.
Collision	Red	Blinks when network collisions are detected. Some collisions can be expected on any network. If you receive excessive collisions, double-check your cabling.
Status	Yellow (blinking)	Indicates hub utilization. Blinking rate increases as network traffic increases.
Link/TX	Green	Solid indicates link, blinking indicates data transmitting.
ACTivity/RX	Yellow	Fast blinks indicate network activity is at 5 percent of overall carrier throughput or above. Solid indicates reverse polarity—check network cabling.
Alternating TX/RX	Alternating	Indicates that the port has been partitioned from the rest of the network due to excessive collisions or faulty cabling.

These cards are now widely available, and while they typically cost a little more than ISA cards, the improved performance is worth the extra expense.

The PCI bus is the fastest of the PC buses, and using PCI for your Ethernet card improves the performance of your LAN over slower ISA cards. The benefits of these cards go beyond speeding up your network. The 32-bit PCI data bus also provides a bus-mastering technique that allows processor independence. This technique reduces CPU overhead by taking control of the system bus, which can be important for bandwidth-intensive applications.

Another feature to look for in purchasing a network adapter is that it supports Plug-and-Play. As you recall, Windows 95 support for Plug-and-Play makes instal-

Note: Windows 95 includes the software drivers for most network adapter cards. You can check them out by opening the Network applet in the Control Panel. In the Configuration tab, click on the Add button. In the Select Network Component Type dialog box, select Adapter and click Add. You'll see an extensive list of network adapter card manufacturers and their products listed in a dialog box. Most network adapter cards also come with a disk with the Windows 95 driver software on it.

lation of adapter cards easier than manually configuring the cards. Plug-and-Play network adapter cards are widely available. You also need to make sure the NIC supports the type of network cabling you'll be using for your network (10BaseT or 10Base2). Many network adapter cards include ports for both types, although you can use only one type of cabling at a time.

Installing a Network Card in Your PC

The procedure for installing a Plug-and-Play network card in Windows 95 is to install the adapter card first with the machine turned off. After you install the network adapter card, turn on the machine. Windows 95 detects your network card and prompts you for the software to install it. The following steps explain how to install a Plug-and-Play PCI network adapter card.

1. Turn off your PC and any peripheral equipment attached to it.

2. Remove the case to your PC. Each computer manufacturer has a different case design, but in general you will remove the backside of the computer case and then slide the case away from the chassis.

3. Remove the back panel cover for the free slot you want to use for the NIC.

4. Carefully slide the PCI network card into your PC's slot. Make sure all of its pins are touching the slot's contacts. Then secure its fastening tab to your PC's chassis with a mounting screw.

Note: You must insert a PCI network card in the master slot. Older 486 and 586 PCs may have both master and slave PCI slots. In newer PCs, all the PCI slots are master slots. Check your PC documentation to determine the status of your PCI slots.

---

5. Replace your PC cover.

6. Connect the network cable to the network adapter card.

    If you're using 10BaseT cabling, connect one cable link for each PC with one RJ-45 connector plugged into the network adapter card at the back of your PC and the other connector plugged into an available 10BaseT port on your hub.

    If you're connecting your PCs with 10Base2 cabling, connect each PC with a BNC T-connector. Cabling will run from PC to PC in a linear fashion with the first and last PC having a terminator on one side of the T-connector.

7. Turn on your PC and start up Windows 95. Because the network adapter card is Plug-and-Play-compatible, Windows 95 will automatically detect it when it starts up.

Adding the Network Adapter Card Software

After you install a network card in your PC, you start up Windows 95. Windows 95 will automatically detect the card and display a new hardware dialog box. Just follow the instructions on the screen to install the required software in Windows. If for some reason Windows doesn't detect the card, you need to install it manually. To install the network adapter card manually, do the following.

1. With Windows 95 running, choose Start | Settings | Control Panel to display the Control Panel window.

2. Double-click on the Add New Hardware icon in the control panel to launch the Add New Hardware wizard.

3. Click Next on the wizard's opening screen to start the process. A page appears asking you if you want Windows to detect the hardware.

4. Choose Yes (Recommended) and click Next to continue. Windows begins a routine to detect your new hardware. This will take several minutes or longer depending on your PC's configuration. If the progress indicator stops for a long time, you may need to start over. Let the detection process run its course.

5. After the wizard reports that it is ready to begin installing support for all detected devices, click Finish. You'll see a suggested configuration dialog window. If the setting in the dialog box doesn't appear with an asterisk in front, click OK. You probably will be asked to insert your Windows 95 CD-ROM or a specific floppy disk from the Windows 95 set so the wizard can load the software it needs to complete the installation. You'll see a process dialog window showing the files being copied. You may see a message saying that a file being copied is older than one that already exists on your PC. You should keep the newest file.

Note: If Windows detects a setting conflict, an asterisk precedes the setting. In this case, choose another value to remove the conflict. Use the up and down arrows to choose a new value until the asterisk disappears. Even if you don't fix the setting during the initial installation, you can make any setting changes later using the System applet in the Control Panel, which is explained later in this chapter.

---

6. Finally, click Yes on the final wizard page to restart you computer and finish setting up the new hardware. After Windows loads, you'll probably see the Control Panel window open on your desktop, since that is how you got to the New Hardware wizard.

Adding Multiple Network Cards

Windows 95 supports up to four network adapters in a single computer. Why would you want to add more than one network card? Some Ethernet-based remote access devices connect directly to a single PC and cannot be shared across the LAN. For example, many cable modems work with only one network interface card by accepting data originating from the card's unique Media Access Control (MAC) layer that controls access to the physical transmission medium on a LAN. The use of the MAC layer in this case is to restrict the access of a device beyond the one designated network adapter card. The network card that connects your PC to the cable modem is a direct connection that bypasses the hub; as such, you're disconnected from the LAN. In this scenario, the only way around this limitation is to add another network adapter to the PC that is connected to the cable modem and use the second network card to connect to the LAN.

You connect a second network adapter card in the same way you did the first card. Windows 95 notes the differentiation of the two network cards. You control the data passing through each network adapter by binding the appropriate protocol to each card. For example, for the network card used to connect to the cable modem, you bind only the TCP/IP protocol. For the second network card you're using to connect to your LAN, you bind only the networking protocol used by the local network, which must be different from the networking protocol used by the cable modem, which is TCP/IP. The second network card is connected to the network hub. Binding protocols to network adapter cards is explained in Chapter 8.

One benefit of using two network adapter cards and binding different protocols to each one is that it restricts any data traffic between the two protocols. For example, in the case of a separate card for TCP/IP and another for NetBEUI, access to the local network from the Internet is restricted because the two protocols have no way of communicating with each other. It creates a form of firewall that restricts access to your LAN from the Internet.

Adding a Laptop to Your LAN

You can easily add your laptop to your network by using a PCMCIA (Personal Computer Memory Card International Association) Ethernet card. These credit-card-size cards, introduced in Chapter 5, are typically used on laptops to add modems, memory, and other peripherals. A PCMCIA card is commonly referred to as a PC card, and a growing number of them also include a modem for access on the road. Having both on one card saves a PCMCIA slot on your laptop, and makes it easier to connect to your network or make a modem connection.

Windows 95 supports PCMCIA cards and runs them in an enhanced Plug-and-Play mode to allow *hot swapping,* whereby Windows dynamically loads and unloads the proper drivers from memory when you switch PCMCIA cards. This means you can unplug a modem and plug in a network adapter. Windows 95 recognizes the change automatically, unloads the software required for the previous card, and starts up the software you need for the network adapter.

Note: If Windows 95 is unable to detect your PCMCIA slots, you can use the PCMCIA wizard to install support for the slots. To run the wizard, double-click the PC Card PCMCIA icon in the Control Panel.

Installing the EtherLink III LAN+33.6 Modem PC Card

A leading producer of Ethernet cards is 3Com, and it makes the EtherLink III PC Card, which includes a network adapter card and 33.6-Kbps modem in one PCMCIA card. Installing 3Com's EtherLink III LAN+33.6 Modem PCMCIA card is straightforward. Do the following:

1. With your laptop turned off, slide the card into the PC card slot; don't force it. Press it into the slot until it seats firmly.

2. Connect the network cable, either 10BaseT or 10Base2 using the appropriate connector supplied with the EtherLink III.

3. Start up your laptop. When Windows 95 finds the EtherLink III card installed in your system, it prompts you for the driver software.

4. Insert the EtherDisk diskette in your A: drive, and click OK. Windows 95 installs the card as a modem, as a network adapter, and as a multifunction device. After your card is installed, you can add and modify the settings using the Network window by double-clicking the Network icon in the Control Panel.

Sharing Devices on Your LAN

One of the major advantages of using a network is that it gives you the ability to share expensive resources, such as printers and remote access devices. In Windows 95, you can share drives and printers that are attached to a specific computer.

However, in many busy offices, tying up someone's PC as a print or file server is an expensive and disruptive option. For example, if you have several PCs sharing a printer that is attached to an individual's PC, a moderate to heavy printing load will slow down that person's system enough to impact productivity. To circumvent this dilemma, you can use one of a growing number of network-ready devices as well as adapters to convert a nonnetworked device into a network device, which free your PCs from being servers and make the device a node on the network available to anyone on your Windows 95 network. This enables you to place the device in any location; it doesn't have to be near a PC that it's connected to. Traffic is routed directly to the device instead of a PC for processing and routing to the device.

Printer Sharing

Printers are expensive, and sharing them over a Windows 95 network makes good sense. There are two ways to share a printer over a Windows 95 network. The first is to connect the printer to one of the PCs on the network and share it with other machines using the Windows 95 printer-sharing features. The second method is to make the printer a dedicated network output device that connects to the network like any other device you connect to the Windows 95 LAN.

For small Windows 95 networks with light printing needs, you can use one of the PCs on the network as a printer server. That's the cheapest and easiest way to share a printer. To use this method, you don't need to do anything to the hardware beyond what you do to use the printer on a standalone PC. Simply connect the printer to your computer's parallel port with the proper cable. If the printer was working before you installed the network hardware, you should be able to use it from any PC on the network by sharing it using the Windows 95 Printer applet in the Control Panel.

If, on the other hand, yours is a network where a lot of printing is going on and you're not running a dedicated PC as a server for printing and other functions, there are some very good reasons you may want to convert existing nonnetworked printers to network printers, including:

- You may not be able to attach a printer to a user's PC and still place that printer where it is convenient for everyone to use it.
- When a PC is used as a printer server, that PC must stay up and functional at all times. The user can't turn it off or reboot it without disrupting the printing services for everyone on the network.
- Large print jobs can slow down a PC significantly when it is used as a print server.
- A network interface for a printer is a lot cheaper than a PC, if that PC must be dedicated to printer services.

A solution for converting a nonnetworked printer to a network-ready printer is a print server device that connects to your printer via the parallel port cable and to the network as a standalone network node. A printer server is a box that sits beside your printer or within the length of a parallel cable. Typical configurations of print servers include a single printer device or a print server device that can support up to three printers. Newer print server products support both parallel and high-speed bidirectional printing, used, for example, by the HP DeskJet color printers. You can also add memory to the printer server to speed up printing. This is like adding more memory to your printer, but it may be cheaper. Typically, print servers support multiple networking protocols. You can expect to pay anywhere from $99 to several hundred dollars for print servers, depending on the manufacturer and options.

A good example of a print server that supports up to three printers is the EtherFast 3-Port 10/100 PrintServer from LINKSYS. This device supports both 10BaseT and the newer and faster 10BaseTX networks. Its three printer ports support both parallel and newer bidirectional printers. The EtherFast 3-Port 10/100 PrintServer offers simultaneous printing capabilities for most HP printers, and supports most network protocols. It has a list price of $399. Hewlett-Packard, the leading printer manufacturer, sells the JetDirect EX Plus3 print server. Check out Appendix A for a detailed listing of printer server products and vendors.

If you are using a printer designed for a workgroup environment, the manufacturer probably offers an optional network interface that plugs directly into the printer. When you purchase a printer that you intend to use on a network, ask your dealer about the possibility of adding a network interface. If you're in the market for a new printer, most printer manufacturers such as Hewlett-Packard make network versions of their printers, which typically cost a few hundred dollars more than nonnetworked printers. On most network printers, you still have the standard parallel or serial interfaces, but you also have the additional ports for 10Base2 or 10BaseT networks.

Fax and Modem Sharing

Almost any modem you buy today can send and receive fax transmissions as well as data communications. Once you network your PCs with Windows 95, you can share the faxing capability of your modem using the Microsoft Fax program that comes with Windows 95. If you already have a fax modem installed on one of the machines you are networking with Windows 95, then all you need to do is configure the PC it is connected to as a fax server. Configuring a PC on your Windows 95 LAN as a fax server in explained in Chapter 9.

Windows 95 does not have any built-in support for sharing modems for data communications across a network. However, several vendors are offering LAN-based modem devices. LINKSYS offers the Internet Workgroup Hub, a dual four-port hub with built-in IP routing for sharing modem access to the Internet. It allows up to six users to access the Internet concurrently via an external modem. The Internet Workgroup Hub lists for $229. With the new 56-Kbps modems, sharing a modem for remote access can make sense for small office or for certain types of connections in larger offices, such as for handling e-mail services. Going a step further is a product from Ramp Networks that not only allows you to share multiple modems but combines the modem channels to enable more bandwidth for LAN connections. See Appendix A for a detailed listing of LAN-based modems and modem-sharing products and vendors.

Sharing CD-ROMs and Other Drives

A growing number of vendors are offering CD-ROM and other storage device-sharing products. By sharing external drives, your office can exchange valuable CD-ROM subscription services across the network without tying up or depending on a user's PC that must always be turned on. Axis Communications offers a network storage device that allows you to connect external CD-ROM drives to your LAN. See Appendix A for a detailed listing of LAN-based CD-ROM-sharing products and vendors.

Troubleshooting Network Hardware Problems

In most cases, installing your network adapters and wiring them into your LAN goes off without a hitch. But glitches can occur. The following are some basic hardware troubleshooting tips and tricks in case you're not able to make your LAN connection. If you determine that your LAN connections are functioning correctly at the cabling and network card level, you can use the Windows 95 Device manager to double-check your network card settings to make sure there are no conflicts, as explained at the end of this chapter.

TIP: One important troubleshooting method to use is rebooting one or all of the machines on a Windows 95 LAN. In many cases, this simple procedure can correct networking problems where nothing appears to be out of order at the hardware and cabling level.

Cabling Problems

Cable connection problems appear as random disruption events. Your network may work fine one day, and then the next day a certain machine or machines aren't visible to the rest of the network. Cable problems are often disguised as software or driver problems. If a machine mysteriously disconnects from your system, a cable problem is a possible first suspect. While it is true that memory problems or a bad network driver on an individual machine can cause similar problems, checking the cable should be one of the first things you do.

If your network connection problems persist after you troubleshoot your cabling, you may have either a bad network card or conflicts with card settings in your PC. First check the setting in the Windows 95 Device Manager, as explained shortly. If there are no conflicts, try installing a new adapter card.

On 10Base2 Networks

A 10Base2 network is based on an end-to-end topology that requires cable terminators at either end of the cable. If the network ends are properly terminated but you still have the problem, the next level of troubleshooting is to make sure there are no loose T-connectors on any devices connected to the network. A bad connection at any one device on the network can cause problems for the entire network. If you don't find any loose T-connectors, it's on to cable roulette. To do this troubleshooting, you need two extra T-connectors.

1. Disconnect one side of the network at the T-connector on a computer located midway in your network topology.

2. Attach a terminator to the free end of the network cable you removed from the tee. You'll need to place a T on the cable end, then attach the terminator to the other end of the T. This isolates one network segment from another.

3. Test both segments of the network. One segment should work and the other probably won't. Now you have narrowed the problem to only one-half of the total network length.

4. Repeat the segmentation process on the section of the network that is not functioning. Again, one of the new segments should work and the other should not.

5. Repeat this process until you have identified the machine causing the problems. Once you know where the problem is, you can then take steps to correct it.

6. Replace the cable segment that runs from the T-connector on the machine causing problems to the section of the network that is okay. You should also replace the T-connector just to be safe.

On 10BaseT Networks

Isolating cable problems on a 10BaseT network is easier than on a bus (10Base2) network because the design of the network itself isolates individual computers and other network devices. That is the major benefit of a 10BaseT network. When a computer in a 10BaseT network can't access other network components, the problem must be in one of three places:

1. On the cable segment that connects the PC to the hub.
2. In the port on the hub to which the computer is attached. You can test this by moving the connector to another port. In many hubs, you can reset the hub.
3. In the NIC that attaches the PC to the network. You can test the card by using it in another PC.

If all the machines on your 10BaseT network are not visible, then the problem may be your hub device. Make sure the hub is powered on and that all the LEDs are functioning properly. These LEDs typically appear on the front of the hub. If the hub is attached to another network segment through a 10Base2 link, check that segment's T-connectors and terminators to make sure the link to your hub is functioning. If necessary, replace the hub.

Network Card Problems

If you suspect a network card problem after checking for any conflicts, the best method is to replace the malfunctioning card. Some interface cards include indicator lights to show when network traffic is flowing through the card. If these lights are dark or red, then either the card is bad or you have a bad cable. After troubleshooting the cable, if the lights still don't display properly, then proceed to troubleshoot the card.

TIP: Even in a small network, it's a good idea to have in stock at least one spare NIC card of the same type and configuration as the one deployed on your network. Once a network card goes bad, it's not worth getting it fixed.

Before you swap out the network card, the first thing you should do is check to make sure the card is set for the proper I/O address and interrupt. In most cases, this can be done using the System applet in Windows 95. To do this, choose Start | Settings | Control Panel. In the Control Panel window, double-click on the System icon. The System Properties window appears. Click on the Device Manager tab.

1. Double-click on the Network adapters item in the list. Your network card is displayed by name under the Network adapters heading.

2. Select the network adapter name, then click on the Properties button located below the list. The dialog box with the settings for that network adapter appears.

3. Click on the Resources tab, which displays the I/O and interrupt settings for the network adapter card. If there is a conflict, it's preceded by an asterisk in the Resource settings list. The device the network card is conflicting with is described in the Conflicting device list box at the bottom of the dialog box.

4. If there is a conflict, click on the Use automatic settings check box to deactivate Windows 95 automatic I/O and interrupt settings. The Change Settings button becomes active. In the Settings based on box, the Basic configuration 0000 setting should appear. This is the default group of resource settings the network card and other resources are using.

5. Click on the setting you want to change in the Resource setting list, and then click on the Change Settings button. If you selected the Interrupt Request setting, and click on the Change Settings button, the Edit Interrupt Request dialog box appears (Figure 7.4). If you select the Input/Output Range setting, the Edit Input/Output Range dialog box appears (Figure 7.5).

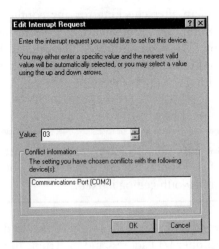

Figure 7.4 The Edit Interrupt Request dialog box.

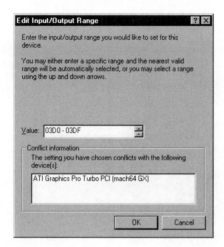

Figure 7.5 *The Edit Input/Output Range dialog box.*

6. Each dialog box operates the same way; you choose an alternative value in the Value drop-down list that does not show any existing conflicts, as indicated in the Conflict information box.

7. Change the settings to remove any conflicts, then click OK three times to exit all the dialog boxes and return to the Control Panel window.

What's Next

Once you've installed the network adapter cards in all your PCs and wired them together, you're ready to configure Windows 95 as your network operating system. This process involves adding network adapter drivers, binding network protocols, identifying each computer and user, and enabling any shared resources. Chapter 8 will take you through these final LAN-building elements to make your network remote access-ready.

8 Setting Up Your Windows 95 LAN for Remote Access

Installing network adapter cards and connecting your PCs using networking cabling takes care of the physical requirements for your LAN. The next step in building your LAN is configuring the logical part of your network, which is the Windows 95 layer. The mechanics of transforming a group of connected PCs into a Windows 95 LAN is straightforward. This chapter guides you through this metamorphosis to complete the Windows 95 foundation for your LAN-based remote access.

Managing Your Network Adapter Drivers

When you installed your Plug-and-Play-compatible network adapter cards, Windows 95 detected the network adapter and installed the driver automatically. However, if for some reason, Windows 95 doesn't detect the adapter card after you start, you'll need to use the Add New Hardware applet in the Control Panel to install it. The Add New Hardware applet provides two ways to install new hardware. The first is to use a wizard that tells Windows to find the adapter card; it then walks you through the installation of the driver software. The second method is to bypass the automatic detection and manually add the driver software.

Using the Add New Hardware Wizard

If for any reason, Windows 95 did not detect your network adapter card, you can use the Add New Hardware Wizard to install it using the following steps:

135

1. Choose Start | Settings | Control Panel to display the Control Panel window, then double-click the Add New Hardware icon to launch the Add New Hardware Wizard.

2. Click Next on the wizard opening screen to start the process.

3. Choose Yes. This tells Windows to automatically detect any new hardware added to your system.

4. Click Next. Windows begins a routine to detect your new hardware. This will take several minutes or longer depending on your PC's configuration. As the message on the screen says, if the progress indicator stops for a long time, then you may need to start over.

5. After the wizard reports that it is ready to begin installing support for all detected devices, click Finish. You'll see a suggested configuration dialog window. Do one of the following:

   If the settings in the dialog box don't appear with an asterisk in front, click OK.

   If Windows detects a setting conflict, an asterisk precedes the setting. In this case, choose another value to remove the conflict. Use the up and down arrows to choose a new value until the asterisk disappears. You may also have to run a separate configuration software utility supplied by the card manufacturer to complete the setup. After you're done, click OK.

6. You'll be asked to insert your Windows 95 CD-ROM or a specific floppy disk from the Windows 95 set so the wizard can load the software it needs to complete the installation. You'll see a process dialog window showing the files being copied. You may also see a message that explains the file being copied is older than one that already exists on your PC. You should keep the newest file.

7. Finally, click Yes to restart your computer and finish setting up the new hardware. After Windows loads, you'll probably see the Control Panel window open on your desktop, since that is how you got to the New Hardware Wizard. Don't close the Control Panel because you need to use another control panel application to continue configuring Windows.

Manually Installing Your Network Card Driver

If the Add New Hardware Wizard could not detect your NIC, then you need to install the network adapter driver software manually using the Add New Hardware applet. This method uses the Add New Hardware Wizard but bypasses the process

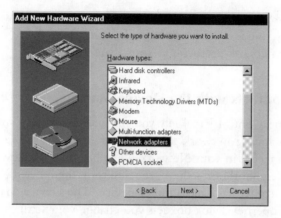

Figure 8.1 *The Hardware types list box lets you choose the specific type of hardware you want to install in Windows.*

of Windows 95 trying to detect the card, and instead lets you add the software drive manually. The following steps explain how:

1. In the Control Panel window, double-click the Add New Hardware icon. The Add New Hardware Wizard appears.

2. Click Next. The screen prompt asks if you want Windows to search for your new hardware.

3. Click on No to manually specify your new hardware, then click Next. A screen appears for specifying the hardware type you want to install (Figure 8.1).

4. In the Hardware types list, double-click on the Network adapters item. The Select Device screen appears.

5. Select the card from the Manufacturers list box, then choose the card model from the Models list box, and click OK. If your Windows 95 driver for your network card is not included with Windows 95 but came on a disk from the manufacturer, click on the Have Disk button. Provide the drive letter or path for the driver and click OK.

6. After installing the driver, Windows 95 displays the hardware settings for the network, including the I/O address range, Interrupt Request (IRQ), or Memory Address settings. If there are conflicts, choose a setting from the appropriate list to change the setting. See the next section "Managing Device Conflicts with the Device Manager."

7. Click OK and then insert your original Windows 95 diskettes or CD-ROM as prompted.

8. When prompted to restart the computer, select Yes. Windows restarts. You're now ready to go to the next phase of setting up your LAN working, which is binding network protocols to your adapter card.

Managing Device Conflicts with the Device Manager

The System applet in the Control Panel lets you manually configure any of your hardware properties, including network adapter cards. If, for some reason, you don't see other PCs connected in your Network Neighborhood window (double-click on the Network Neighborhood icon on the desktop), there may be a conflict between your network adapter card and another device. The Device Manager tab located in the System Properties dialog box lets you change your settings.

Double-clicking on the Network adapters item in the Device Manager list shows any network adapters installed on your system, and double-clicking on a network adapter name displays the hardware and driver software properties for the card. Click on the Resources tab to display the Interrupt Request (IRQ) and Input/Output (I/O) settings. If for some reason there is a clash with the automatic settings, you can manually override the automatic settings.

Click on the Use Automatic settings check box. Select the setting you want to change in the Resource setting list, then click on the Change Settings button. If Windows detects a setting conflict, an asterisk (*) precedes the setting. If the network adapter card can be configured with software (as opposed to one that requires jumper or switch changes), choose another value to remove the conflict. The asterisk disappears. A pound sign (#) indicates that the actual configuration has been tested and set to the current hardware setting.

Note: Older network adapter cards that have jumpers or switches that set IRQ and I/O addresses must be changed on the card; then you need to match the settings in the Device Manager.

Managing Your Network in Windows 95

The Network applet in the Windows 95 Control Panel is your gateway to managing a wide variety of networking functions in Windows 95. Double-clicking on the Network icon in the Control Panel displays the Network dialog box (Figure 8.2). The Network dialog box includes settings for adding and removing network components and identifying computers on your network.

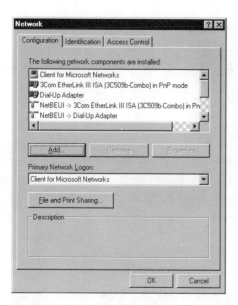

Figure 8.2 *The Network dialog box is the tool*
you'll use to manage a variety of network settings.

The Network Neighborhood icon on your desktop is your window to your
Windows 95 LAN. Double-clicking on this icon displays the Network Neighborhood window (Figure 8.3). This window shows the names of all the computers
that are connected to the LAN and that share resources. The Network Neighborhood window operates in a similar manner to the Windows Explorer, except it

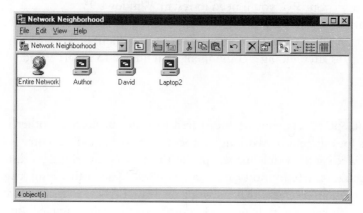

Figure 8.3 *The Network Neighborhood window.*

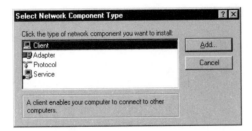

Figure 8.4 *The Select Network Component Type dialog box.*

shows only those folders that are shared. You can browse through any resources that are shared via this window.

Adding and Removing Network Components

Clicking on the Add button in the Network dialog window's Configuration tab accesses the Select Network Component Type dialog box (Figure 8.4). This dialog box includes the links to four types of network components that you can install: Client, Adapter, Protocol, and Service. You access any of these component dialog boxes by selecting the entry and then clicking on the Add button, or simply by double-clicking on the item.

Once a network component is added, it appears in the network components list in the Configuration tab. When you click OK to exit the Network dialog box, Windows 95 may prompt you for Windows 95 diskettes or CD-ROM to complete the installation. After the software for the network component(s) you added are installed on your PC, you'll need to restart Windows 95.

Removing any installed network component is as easy as selecting the component in the installed network components list and then clicking on the Remove button. And, as after adding a component, you'll need to restart Windows 95.

Client

The Client option lets you use the shared files and printers on other networked computers for different networking protocols. The default client entry is Client for Microsoft Networks, which appears in the Primary Network Logon list setting in the Configuration tab. In most cases, you won't need any other login clients unless you're running a server for that network on your LAN; for example, a NetWare server. You can have multiple network protocols and clients installed, but you must specify a primary network login client. If you have other network protocols running, other login client settings are available from the drop-down list if you install

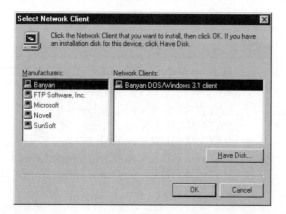

Figure 8.5 *The Select Network Client dialog box.*

them using the Client option in the Select Network Component Type dialog box, which displays the Select Network Client dialog box (Figure 8.5).

Adapter

The Adapter item in the Select Network Component Type dialog box allows you to specify the network card you're adding to your system. Double-clicking on the Adapter item displays the same Select Network adapter dialog box that appears in the Add New Hardware Wizard when you select network adapters. You can use this to see all the network adapter cards supported by drivers that come with Windows 95; and if your network card isn't on the list, you can use the Have Disk button to install the drivers from a disk supplied by the card's manufacturer.

Protocol

Windows 95 supports a number of networking protocols that you can use for your remote access connection. Table 8.1 lists the protocols that are included with Windows 95. Double-clicking on the Protocol item in the Select Network Component Type dialog box displays the Select Network Protocol dialog box (Figure 8.6). Selecting a company name in the Manufacturers list displays the available protocols in the Network Protocols list on the right side of the dialog box.

You can install other networking protocols supplied by the vendor from a floppy disk or your hard disk by clicking on the Have Disk button in the Select Network Protocol dialog box. Before you install any network drivers included in Windows 95 or from other vendors, make sure that you have the original Windows 95 distribution disks or CD-ROM handy. Windows 95 may prompt you for them as part of the protocol installation.

Table 8.1 Networking Protocols Supported by Windows 95

NETWORK VENDOR	DRIVERS
Banyan	Banyan VINES Ethernet Protocol Banyan VINES Token Ring
Digital Equipment (DEC)	PATHWORKS v4.1 Ethernet PATHWORKS v4.1 Token Ring PATHWORKS v5.0 and above Ethernet PATHWORKS v5.0 and above Ethernet (ODI) PATHWORKS v5.0 and above Token Ring
IBM	Existing IBM DLC Protocol
Microsoft	IPX/SPX-compatible Protocol Microsoft 32-bit DLC Microsoft DLC NetBEUI TCP/IP
NetManage*	NetManage TCP/IP v5.0 Dialup Only NetManage TCP/IP v5.0 NDIS Dial-up Only NetManage TCP/IP v5.0 ODI Dial-up Only
Novell	Novell IPX ODI Protocol
SunSoft	PC-NFS Protocol

* Earlier versions of Microsoft Windows included the NetManage TCP/IP, which later became the basis of Microsoft's TCP/IP stack, and was removed from the Manufacturers list in the Select Network Protocol dialog box.

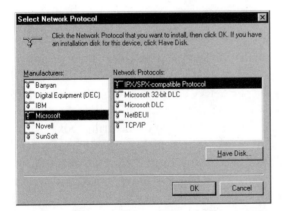

Figure 8.6 The Select Network Protocol dialog box.

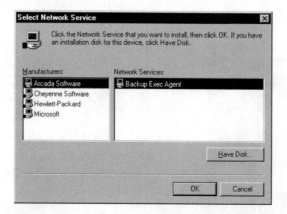

Figure 8.7 *The Select Network Service dialog box.*

Service

The Service item in the Select Network Component Type dialog box allows you add a variety of network services, such as file and printer sharing for Microsoft and NetWare networks. Double-clicking on the Service item displays the Select Network Service dialog box (Figure 8.7). In earlier versions of Windows 95, the only services that came with Windows were file and printer sharing for Microsoft and NetWare networks. The latest version of Windows 95, OSR2, has added support for back-up services, HP network printers, NetWare Directory Services, and other third-party programs. If you install Microsoft IE 4.0, the Personal Web Server appears in the Network Service list.

Note: The file and printer sharing for Microsoft Networks setting, which appears in the Network Service list after you select Microsoft in the Manufacturers list, can be activated by clicking on the File and Print Sharing button on the Configuration tab in the Network dialog box. More on sharing resources later in this chapter.

Network Card Properties

Selecting your network adapter card in the installed components list and clicking on the Properties button displays the Network Card Properties dialog box (Figure 8.8) with the name of your network adapter in the title bar. This dialog box is similar to the one that appears when you use the Windows 95 Device Manager. Depending on the network adapter, there may be up to four tabs in this dialog box:

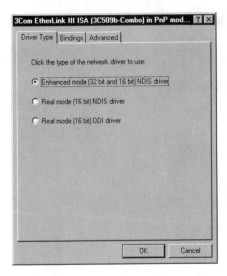

Figure 8.8 *The properties for a network adapter card.*

Driver Type, Bindings, Advanced, and Resources. The following sections describe the functions of these tabs.

Driver Type

The Driver Type tab displays the driver mode Windows 95 assigned for your NIC. The typical setting is Enhanced mode (32-bit and 16-bit) NDIS driver. This is the preferred mode in Windows 95 because it offers the best performance and the best memory management. The real mode (16-bit) NDIS driver is for older network adapter cards. If your system shows this driver being used, you should consider upgrading your Ethernet adapter card. The Real mode (16-bit) ODI driver is for older Novell network adapters.

Bindings

The Bindings tab (Figure 8.9) shows you all the protocols that are bound to the network adapter. When you install your network adapter, typically, Windows 95 automatically installs the NetBEUI and IPX/SPX-compatible Protocol, but there may be other protocols bound to your network adapter card. You can remove bound protocols by clicking on the check box; however, the best way to manage your protocols is from the installed network components list. Managing network protocol bindings is explained later in this chapter.

Figure 8.9 *The Bindings tab shows which network protocols are bound to your network card.*

Advanced

The options in the Advanced tab vary depending on the type of network adapter. It shows you how the card is configured to handle traffic. Depending on your network adapter, the physical medium (cabling used) may also be displayed in the Transceiver Type drop-down list. In most cases, you don't need to make any changes in this tab.

Resources

If Windows 95 detected your network adapter card using the Add New Hardware Wizard, and your network adapter settings can be changed via software (as opposed to using jumpers on the card), then the Resources tab will appear as part of the network adapter's properties. If you are using an older network adapter card, the Resources tab won't appear. However, you can access the Resources tab via the Windows 95 Device Manager.

Managing Your Network Protocol Bindings

Binding a protocol to a network adapter means you're attaching a software network interface to the network adapter. As you recall, protocols are sets of software instructions that determine how data is carried across any networking connection, whether it's a connection to another PC on your LAN or outside your LAN via a remote access device. In order for two computers or networks to communicate with each other, they must both communicate using the same protocol. Windows 95 can support up to four network adapter cards and each of them can have different network protocols bound to them.

For a given protocol to communicate with each network adapter on your computer, the network adapter driver must be bound to the protocol. The binding defines the relationships between networking software components. Whenever you install a new adapter card, Windows 95 automatically binds some protocols to the network adapter. You can and will most likely want to change the bindings.

To change network adapter protocol bindings, you use the Network applet in the Control Panel. Unless you need that particular binding, you can delete it. Do this by selecting the protocol binding to be deleted from the network component list and then click on the Remove button. The binding is immediately removed, and the component list is updated. For example, during installation of your network card, Windows 95 binds the NetBEUI and IPX/SPX protocols. The NetBEUI protocol used in Windows 95 is for compatibility with older Microsoft networks, such as Windows for Workgroups. The IPX/SPX-compatible protocol is a Microsoft protocol operating Windows 95 within a Novell NetWare network. If you're not connecting to either an older Microsoft network or using a Dial-Up Networking server or a Novell NetWare network, you can remove these protocols.

TIP: The general rule for binding protocols is to bind only those you need. Leaving unnecessary protocols bound to your network adapter slows down your network performance and can cause other problems. The bottom line is, if you're not using it, remove it. You can always add a removed protocol at any time.

The following steps show you how to remove a protocol bound to your network adapter.

1. Open the Network properties dialog box.
2. In the Configuration tab, select the protocol that you want to remove. For example, to remove the IPX/SPX protocol, select:

   ```
   IPX/SPX compatible Protocol ->network adapter name
   ```

3. Click on the Remove button.

4. Click on OK. You'll be asked to insert your Windows 95 CD-ROM or a specific floppy disk from the Windows 95 set to complete the protocol removal. You may see a message that tells you a file being copied is older than one that already exists on your PC. You should keep the newest file.

5. Windows displays the System Setting Change dialog box prompting you to restart Windows to make the new settings take effect. Click Yes.

You can also remove a bound protocol by selecting the network adapter in the installed components list, and then clicking on the Properties button. In the Bindings tab, which displays all the bindings currently attached to the network card, uncheck the protocol that you want to remove. Click OK twice. Either way you remove a binding, the protocol is deleted from both the installed components list as well as the network adapter's Bindings tab list.

Windows 95 LAN Set-up Basics

Beyond configuring your network adapter cards, there are several LAN administration tasks you need to perform on every PC to enable them to participate in the local area network. In Windows 95, this involves establishing computer names, naming the workgroup in which devices work, and establishing user names and passwords. The following sections walk you through these essential configuration procedures.

Specifying a Computer and Workgroup Name

Because Windows 95 is a peer-to-peer network, you can configure every computer or a subset of computers on your LAN to share data, programs, and printers. In order for other users connected to the LAN to know your computer, it must be named. This name appears in the Network Neighborhood window and the Windows Explorer.

You can also add an optional computer description that helps users know other information such as which resources you're sharing. This entry is displayed in the Comment column in both the Network Neighborhood and the Windows Explorer windows. For users to see this description text, they must choose View|Details in either window.

Windows 95 also requires you to identify a workgroup that encompasses all the PCs that you want to participate within a specific logical workgroup. You can have a Windows 95 LAN with multiple workgroups, although in most small Windows 95 LANs, you'll only want one workgroup. You must create at least one workgroup. Each PC on your LAN can be connected to only one workgroup at a time. If you have more than one workgroup, the computers attached to each workgroup cannot communicate with computers attached to the other workgroup without changing the workgroup setting on each PC.

The following steps explain how to create a computer name, workgroup, and computer description. You must do this for each PC you connect to your network.

1. Open the Control Panel and double-click the Network icon to display the Network dialog window. Click on the Identification tab to display the Identification properties page (Figure 8.10).

2. Type a name for your PC in the Computer name field. The computer's name may be up to 15 characters long, and be composed only of alphanumeric characters (plus the special characters ! @ # $ % ^ & ( ) - _ ' { } . ~).

3. Type a workgroup name by entering it in the Workgroup field. It, too, may be up to 15 characters long and contain only alphanumeric characters (plus the special characters listed in step 2. Because all the PCs in a single workgroup share the workgroup name, you'll use this name to configure other machines on your LAN. All computers that are part of this workgroup will share the same resources, such as files and a printer.

4. Type any descriptive information about your PC in the Computer Description field. The description entry may contain up to 38 characters.

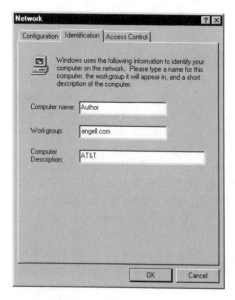

Figure 8.10 *The Identification properties page.*

Setting User Names and Passwords

Each user who will log in to the network needs to be identified with a user name and password. In a network that uses only Windows 95, establishing user names and passwords is easy. The first time you start a networked computer, an Enter Network Password dialog box appears. You must enter a user name, but you don't have to add a password. If you don't want to add a password, simply type in your user name, then click OK. If you enter a password after your user name and then click OK, Windows displays another dialog box to confirm your password.

Your user name and password are stored for future access. If you enter a password, you must use this password each time you use your PC. If you log on without entering a password, Windows lets you work on the local machine but you won't have access to other networked components. If you don't enter a password the first time, you don't need to enter a password each time you log on, only your user name.

You can change your password at any time by using the Passwords applet in the Control Panel. To change a password, double-click on the Passwords icon to display the Passwords Properties dialog box (Figure 8.11). Click on the Change Windows Password button to display the Change Windows Password dialog box. Enter your current (old) password in the Old password field. Enter your new password in the New password field and enter it again in the Confirm new password field. Click OK twice.

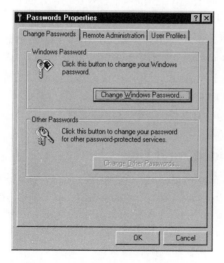

Figure 8.11 *The Passwords Properties dialog box.*

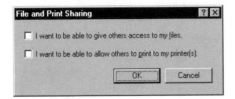

Figure 8.12 *The File and Print Sharing dialog box.*

Sharing Drives and Printers

Because Windows 95 is a peer-to-peer network, any machine on the network can share resources by acting as a server as well as a client. Windows 95 doesn't automatically set up share resources with the rest of the network. It's up to the individual PC users to share specific resources on their PCs.

The first step in sharing resources is to enable file and print sharing. This doesn't automatically give other users on your LAN access to your files or printer connected to your PC, it only enables the ability to allow it. You'll need to perform other tasks to specify what you want to share, as explained later. To turn on the printing and file sharing capabilities for a given computer, do the following:

1. Open the Network dialog window from the Control Panel.
2. Click on the File and Print Sharing icon to display the File and Print Sharing dialog box. (Figure 8.12).
3. Click on the I want to be able to give others access to my files check box to enable file sharing on your PC.
4. Click on the I want to be able to allow others to print to my printer(s) check box to allow other users access to a printer connected to your PC.
5. Click OK twice. You may be asked to insert the Windows 95 CD-ROM or distribution diskettes so that sharing software can be installed. Click Yes when Windows prompts you to restart your computer.

Managing Shared Drives, Folders, and Files

After you enable Windows 95 file and print sharing, you're ready to specify which drives, folders, and files you want to share with others on your LAN. You can allow unrestricted access to all users on your LAN or you can control the access to shared resources by requiring other users to enter a password. The following steps explain how to do this.

1. Double-click on the My Computer icon on your desktop to display all your local resources in the My Computer window (Figure 8.13).

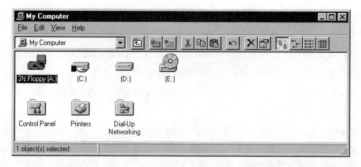

Figure 8.13 *The My Computer window with icons representing all the resources connected to a PC.*

2. Right-click on a drive, for example the C: drive icon, and choose Sharing or Properties from the pop-up menu. The window with the given name of the drive appears.

3. Click on the Sharing tab (Figure 8.14).

4. Click on Shared As. The default name of the shared resource appears in the Share Name field. You can type a description name so that people can easily identify the device; and you can type additional information about the shared resource in the Comment field.

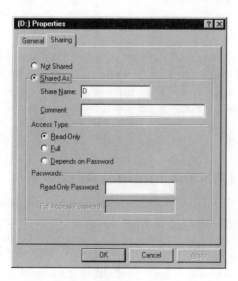

Figure 8.14 *The Sharing tab allows you to enable and control the sharing of a resource on your PC.*

5. Choose a setting in the Access Type group. The three options are as follows:

   Read-Only. This enables other users to open and copy files, but does not allow them to modify or remove any files.

   Full. This enables users to add or remove files. You can also specify a password for Full access.

   Depends on Password. This allows different access privileges depending on the password. You can specify one password that allows the user full access and a different password for read-only access.

6. Click OK to effect the changes and close the Properties dialog box.

Sharing a Printer

The process of sharing a printer connected to any computer on your LAN is similar to that of sharing a disk drive. Before you can share a printer, make sure it's installed and working.

1. Double-click on the My Computer icon on the desktop and then double-click on the Printer icon to display the Printer window.

2. Right-click on the icon for the printer you want to share, and choose Properties or Sharing from the context menu. The Properties dialog box for the printer appears. The contents of this dialog box depend on the printer you're using.

3. Click on the Sharing tab.

4. Click on the Shared As setting to turn on sharing, and enter a Shared Name and Comment. If you want to restrict access to the printer, enter a password in the Password field; users attempting to use your printer will need to know the password.

5. Click OK.

Configuring Your Windows 95 LAN for Internet Access

The Microsoft TCP/IP stack in Windows 95 forms the foundation from which you connect your LAN to the Internet. To connect your Windows LAN to the Internet requires using an IP router. The most likely bandwidth options you'll use to connect your LAN to the Internet using an IP router are ISDN, xDSL, and the aforementioned 56-Kbps IP routers. For more information on routers, see Chapter 2.

The process for configuring your Windows 95 LAN for Internet access via a router assumes you've already performed the following tasks.

- Installed a network adapter in every PC on your LAN, and connected each PC on your LAN to a hub via a 10BaseT cable.
- Configured Windows 95 as a LAN.
- Opened an Internet access account with static IP addresses or a dynamic IP address (see Chapter 4 for more information).

Note: The router you use to configure your Windows 95 LAN does not have to be ready for Internet access. In fact, you should configure your LAN first before installing your router because many router installation programs will check your LAN configuration as part of their set-up routine. The set-up program will then provide different configuration steps depending on which TCP/IP settings it detected on your PCs.

With your LAN up and running and the Internet account set up with the information provided by your ISP in hand, you're ready to configure your Windows 95 LAN for connecting to the Internet. This process involves these two steps.

1. Installing the Microsoft TCP/IP stack on every PC on your LAN.
2. Configuring TCP/IP properties for the type of Internet access account you will be using.

Installing the TCP/IP Protocol

The first step in configuring your Windows 95 LAN for Internet access is to install the Microsoft TCP/IP stack included with Windows 95. You'll need the original Windows 95 distribution diskettes or CD-ROM handy. To install TCP/IP on each PC, do the following.

1. Open the Network dialog box and click on the Add button. The Select Network Component Type dialog box appears.
2. Double-click on the Protocol option. The Select Network Protocol dialog box appears.
3. In the Manufacturers list at the left side of the dialog box, select Microsoft. The Network Protocols list shows four protocol options.
4. Select the TCP/IP option, and click OK. When you return to the Network dialog box, you should be able to scroll through the list of network components and see TCP/IP. Notice the component entry for TCP/IP that uses the following notation: "TCP/IP -> *network adapter name.*" TCP/IP will be bound to your network adapter card.

5. Click the OK button. Windows 95 will prompt you for the original distribution CD-ROM or diskettes to complete the installation. After the software is installed, restart Windows 95.

Setting Up Your LAN for Dynamic IP Internet Access

Recall that dynamic IP addressing is the process by which an ISP uses a host system to assign an IP address from an available pool of IP addresses for use only during the current connection. (For more information on IP addressing, refer back to Chapter 4.) Once the Internet session ends, the IP address is returned to the pool of available IP addresses for use by others as needed. Thanks to dynamic IP addressing, you can now connect your Windows 95 LAN to the Internet using a single-user Internet access account. Using a router that acts as a DHCP (Dynamic Host Configuration Protocol) server enables this capability. Most routers designed for the SOHO market now incorporate this feature. The DHCP server functionality of a router allows IP addresses, subnet masks, and default gateway addresses to be assigned to computers on your LAN as needed. The IP addresses used by the router for your LAN are "fictitious," and not visible to anyone on the Internet.

Each PC on your Windows 95 LAN with the Microsoft TCP/IP stack installed is a DHCP client ready and waiting for a DHCP server, which is built into a router. If you've installed TCP/IP for the first time, you don't need to change any of the default settings to support DHCP. However, if you're unsure of your TCP/IP configuration, you can double-check to make sure the default TCP/IP settings are in place by performing the following steps. You will need do these steps for each PC on you Windows 95 LAN.

TIP: The best strategy for setting up a dynamic IP Internet access system is to make sure you configure all your DHCP clients, if necessary, before installing your router with built-in DHCP server functionality. When you install the router, some installation programs detect your Windows 95 TCP/IP settings and configure the router accordingly.

---

1. In the Network control panel, select the TCP/IP-> [*network adapter name*] in the installed network components list.
2. Click on the Properties button. The TCP/IP Properties dialog box appears (Figure 8.15).
3. The Obtain an IP address automatically setting should be selected in the IP Address tab.

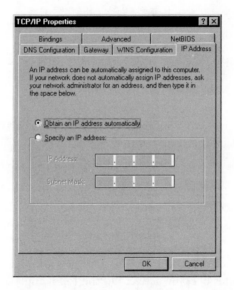

Figure 8.15 *The TCP/IP Properties dialog box.*

4. Click on the WINS Configuration tab and make sure the Disable WINS Resolution setting is selected.

5. Click on the Gateway tab. There should be no entries in the New gateway field.

6. Click on the DNS Configuration tab. Disable DNS should be selected.

7. Click OK to exit the TCP/IP Properties dialog box.

8. Click OK to exit the Network dialog box. Windows 95 may prompt you for your original distribution diskettes or CD-ROM. After installing the necessary information, Windows 95 asks you to restart your computer. Click Yes to restart your PC for the changes to take effect.

At this point, your Windows 95 LAN is ready for a router with built-in DHCP server functionality. When you install your router using the software supplied by the vendor, the router will detect your PCs acting as a DHCP clients.

Setting Up Your LAN for Static IP Internet Access

If you get a LAN Internet access account that uses static IP addresses, you need to configure each PC on your LAN with IP address and DNS information. This means you must configure every TCP/IP stack on your LAN to work with your router. You will need the following information from your ISP to configure your Windows 95 LAN.

- An IP address for each PC on your LAN
- A subnet mask IP address
- An IP address for your router
- A host and domain name
- DNS server IP addresses

The following steps explain how to configure every PC on your LAN for a static IP address Internet access account using a router.

1. Open the Network applet in the Control Panel. This displays the Network dialog box.

2. Select the TCP/IP protocol that is bound to your network adapter card, and click on the Properties button. This displays the TCP/IP Properties dialog box.

3. In the IP Address tab, select the Specify an IP address setting. The IP Address and Subnet Mask fields become active. Do the following:

    In the IP Address field, enter the IP address for the computer you're configuring.

    In the Subnet Mask field, enter the Subnet Mask IP address.

4. Click the DNS Configuration tab and select the Enable DNS setting. All the settings in the Enable DNS group become active, as shown in Figure 8.16. Do the following:

    In the Host field, enter the host name for the PC that was supplied by your ISP and is associated with a specific IP address.

    Enter your organization's domain name in the Domain field. This is the name you registered with InterNIC.

    Enter a DNS server IP address in the DNS Server Search Order field, then click on the Add button. If your ISP provided more than one DNS server address, add it also.

    Enter your domain name in the Domain Suffix Search Order field and click the Add button.

5. Click on the Gateway tab (Figure 8.17). In the New gateway field, enter the IP address your ISP assigned for your router, then click on the Add button.

6. Click OK to exit the TCP/IP Properties dialog box.

7. Click OK to exit the Network dialog box. Windows 95 may prompt you for your original distribution diskettes or CD-ROM. After installing the necessary information, Windows 95 asks you to restart your computer. Click Yes to restart Windows.

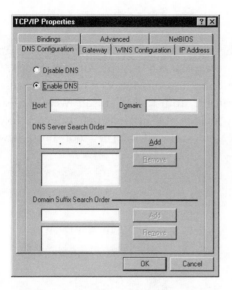

Figure 8.16 *The DNS Configuration tab with the Enable DNS settings active.*

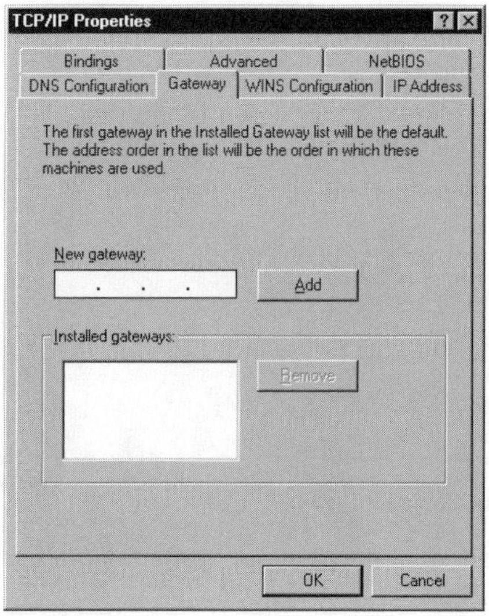

Figure 8.17 *The Gateway tab is for entering the IP address of your router.*

What's Next

You've been working through the mechanics of assembling and configuring your Windows 95 LAN; now it's time to experience the fruits of your efforts. Chapter 9 introduces you to the impressive collection of Microsoft's remote access tools included with Windows 95, or available from the Microsoft Web site—at the best price possible, free. These tools include the just-released Internet Explorer 4.0 Suite, which not only is a full-featured suite of Internet tools but a new Weblike interface to Windows 95.

9   *Windows 95 Remote Access Tools*

Whether you're using the World Wide Web to do research, or e-mail to communicate with geographically dispersed colleagues, remote access can help you implement applications to work smarter. Microsoft bundles an impressive collection of remote access tools with Windows 95 and makes them available for download at no charge from the Microsoft Web site. These core tools include the Internet Explorer 4.0 Suite of Internet applications, TCP/IP utilities, Microsoft Exchange for Workgroup and remote e-mail, and Microsoft Fax for network-based faxing. This chapter introduces you to these tools as a starting point for your Windows 95 remote access adventures.

Microsoft Tools of the Remote Access Trade

Although Microsoft started late in the Internet applications game, it has made dramatic improvements in their quality and availability. Early versions of Internet Explorer left a lot to be desired compared to Netscape Navigator, the leading Web browser. Fast forward to today and it's a whole new ballgame. Netscape and Microsoft are in a battle for dominance of the Web browser market with each new release of their respective Web browsers, both offering more and more capabilities. For Windows 95 users, the latest release of Microsoft Internet Explorer version 4.0 (IE 4.0) goes well beyond just an upgrade to Internet Explorer 3.0. The Internet Explorer 4.0 Suite, which is available for free, is at once a major upgrade of Microsoft's Web browser as well as a dramatic upgrade to Windows 95. As you'll learn later in this chapter, IE 4.0 represents an unparalleled integration of the Internet and Web interface into Windows 95. Internet Explorer 4.0 also comes with a variety of remote access programs, including Outlook Express for Internet e-mail and news.

Note: There is a cornucopia of third-party remote access tools available for Windows 95. For a comprehensive coverage of third-party remote access tools, check out Appendix A, "Windows 95 Remote Access Resources."

Windows 95 Remote Access Utilities

Windows 95 includes a collection of TCP/IP utility and application programs that include an FTP and Telnet client, as well as the Ping and Winipcfig (short for Windows IP Configuration) utility programs. FTP and Ping are DOS programs that work from the MS-DOS window, and Telnet and Winipcfig are Windows-based programs. The most useful of these are the Ping and Winipcfig utility programs.

Ping

Ping is a handy TCP/IP diagnostic utility that made its way from the UNIX world to Windows 95. Ping works like TCP/IP sonar; you send a packet to a remote host, and if the host is functioning properly, it bounces the packet back to you. Ping prints the result of each packet transmission on your screen. Ping sends four packets by default, but you can use it to transmit any number of packets or transmit continuously until you terminate the command. You access Ping from the MS-DOS Prompt window (Start|Programs|MS-DOS prompt). At the DOS prompt and with your Internet connection active, enter the command in the following format: ping *IPaddress*. For example, entering **ping 199.232.240.3** and pressing Enter will ping the host machine with the IP address of 199.232.240.3. The Ping command includes a number of parameters, which you can view by entering **ping** and pressing Enter. The following shows a sample Ping command and its output:

```
C:\WINDOWS>ping 199.232.240.3
Pinging 199.232.240.3 with 32 bytes of data:
Reply from 199.232.240.3: bytes=32 time=36ms TTL=60
Reply from 199.232.240.3: bytes=32 time=36ms TTL=60
Reply from 199.232.240.3: bytes=32 time=36ms TTL=60
Reply from 199.232.240.3: bytes=32 time=36ms TTL=60
```

If the packet doesn't come back after you send it, either the host is not available or there is something wrong with the connection. For troubleshooting the status of any TCP/IP connection, Ping is the single most useful program.

Figure 9.1 *The IP Configuration window displays useful information about your TCP/IP and Ethernet card settings.*

Winipcfg

Winipcfg is a Windows 95 utility that lets you view information about your TCP/IP protocol and network adapter card settings. The Winipcfg program (winipcfg.exe) is located in the Windows folder. To run Winipcfg, choose Start|Run; then enter winipcfg.exe, and click OK. The IP Configuration window appears (Figure 9.1).

The Winipcfg window shows the physical address, IP address, subnet mask, and default gateway settings of your primary TCP/IP adapter. If your PC contains multiple adapters to which TCP/IP is bound, you can select the other adapter(s) from the drop-down list to view their settings. If your PC contains a network adapter and you're also using Dial-Up Networking, for example, you'll be able to choose from the PPP dial-up adapter and the network adapter card.

Clicking on the More Info button displays an expanded dialog box with Ethernet adapter information (Figure 9.2). It displays such information as your computer's host name, the address of a DHCP server (if you're using one), and the adapter's MAC (Media Access Control layer) address.

If you're using a DHCP server on your LAN to receive an IP address from a host, the Winipcfg program is a handy way to know the IP address that has been assigned to your PC for the current connection. The Release and Renew buttons enable you to release and renew the assigned IP address, respectively.

You can copy the data to an application that can print it out for use in troubleshooting. To do this, open the Winipcfg control menu (the small icon in the upper right corner of the dialog box), and choose Copy. Winipcfg copies the information in the Winipcfg window to the Clipboard, enabling you to paste the data into Notepad or another application to print.

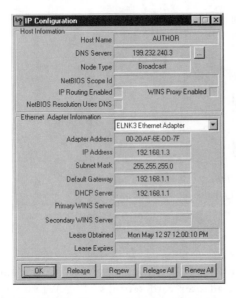

Figure 9.2 *Expanded IP Configuration window displays your Ethernet adapter.*

Telnet

Telnet is a terminal emulator program that enables you to connect to and log on to a remote host, where you can perform tasks, such as running programs. The Telnet program is located in the Windows folder as the file telnet.exe. Open the folder and double-click on telnet.exe to start the program or choose Start|Run, enter **telnet** and then click OK to display the Telnet window. Choosing Connect|Remote System displays the Connect dialog box. In the Host Name field, enter the domain name or IP address of the host to which you want to connect, or choose a previous connection from the drop-down list. You can use the Port field to enter or select a connection port; you can also use the Term Type field to enter or select a terminal type.

TIP: You can create a shortcut to both the Telnet program and a host machine connection using the Properties item in the context menu. In the Target text box, enter the name of the host following the path to the Telnet program file, such as c:\windows\telnet.exe.

The Telnet program supports a number of preferences you can set to control the way the program functions. Choosing Terminal | Preferences displays the Terminal Preferences dialog box. You can also record a log of any Telnet session by choosing Terminal | Start Logging, which creates a file with a .log extension.

FTP

The FTP (File Transfer Protocol) client program that's included with Windows 95 is a DOS program that operates from the MS-DOS Prompt window. It's an older, UNIX-like command line program that lets you send and receive files over the Internet. At the DOS prompt, typing **ftp** and pressing Enter put you in the FTP program. Entering a question mark (?) displays a listing of the commands used for working with FTP. Because Internet Explorer supports FTP, you're not likely to need the command-line version of the FTP program. If you want to use an FTP client program, and there are reasons you might want to, there are several third-party Windows 95 FTP programs that will serve you better. See Appendix A, "Windows 95 Remote Access Resources" for more information on these FTP clients.

Welcome to Internet Explorer 4.0

The Internet Explorer 4.0 Suite is a major upgrade to Microsoft's Web browser, as well as a major face-lift of the Windows 95 operating system. IE 4.0 is actually a preview of new Windows features in Microsoft Windows 98, code-named Memphis. The basic theme of the IE 4.0 enhancements to the Windows 95 shell (Windows 95 interface and controls) is to make browsing your PC much like browsing the Web. Beyond the unparalleled integration of the Web interface and the Windows 95 interface is the seamless integration of the Internet into your local computing environment. IE 4.0 delivers a variety of tools to bring real-time information feeds from the Internet directly to your PC desktop. Many of these features are built on a new generation of Web-based *push* technologies, which means the information is broadcast via the Internet and received by your client PC.

Note: The Internet Explorer Suite of tools for Windows 95 takes full advantage of new high-bandwidth technologies that are Ethernet-based. By using IE 4.0 with ISDN, cable, and xDSL bandwidth options, making connections to the Internet is so quick that the distinction between your local and remote computing resources is negligible.

Internet Explorer 4.0 comes in two forms. The first version is the full suite that includes both IE 4.0 and the Windows 95 shell upgrade. The second version includes only Internet Explorer 4.0. Within these two general categories are three packages that vary according to the number of additional Internet Explorer programs. The following are the three versions of the IE 4.0 suite.

TIP: I strongly recommend the full suite because it offers a number of impressive features for working with Windows 95. Even if you decide you don't want to use the new shell features, you can remove them from the Add/Remove Programs applet in the Control Panel.

- *The Standard package.* Includes the Windows 95 shell upgrade, Internet Explorer 4.0 browser, Microsoft Outlook Express (Internet mail and news client programs), and ActiveMovie. The Standard package is a 11-MB download and requires 43 MB of disk space to install on your system.
- *The Enhanced package.* Includes the Windows 95 shell upgrade, Internet Explorer 4.0 browser, Microsoft Outlook Express (Internet mail and news client programs), FrontPad (Web authoring tool), and ActiveMovie. The Enhanced package is a 15-MB download and requires 50 MB of disk space to install on your system.
- *The Full package.* Includes the Windows 95 shell upgrade Internet Explorer 4.0 browser, Microsoft Outlook Express (Internet mail and news client programs), NetMeeting (conferencing tool) FrontPad (Web authoring tool), NetShow (Internet broadcasting player), Microsoft Wallet (security feature) and ActiveMovie. The Enhanced package is a 20-MB download and requires 59 MB of disk space to install on your system.

Getting the Internet Explorer 4.0 Suite

Internet Explorer is available for free at the Microsoft Web site (http://www.microsoft.com). The following instructions explain how to download it. It's a multiple-step process that is different from the usual way you download software from the Web.

1. Point your Web browser to http://www.microsoft.com/ie/ie40/download.
2. Decide which version of Internet Explorer 4.0 Suite you want to use (Browser Suite Only or Browser Suite with Shell Integration activated).
3. Click the Internet Explorer 4.0 Suite Active Setup link in the gray box on the download page.

4. From the drop–down box on the page that appears, select either Browser Suite Only or Browser + Integrated Shell, then click Next.

5. The final page provides a list of download locations from which you can get the Active Setup Wizard, which guides you through the download process. Find a location near you, and click to download the Active Setup Wizard. When you are prompted, you can either save the Active Setup Wizard to your local hard drive or open it directly.

6. While still connected to the Internet, run the Active Setup Wizard by opening the ie4setupb.exe or ie4setupw.exe file in your Internet Explorer Setup folder. If you choose Open in the previous step, the Active Wizard runs automatically.

7. Choose the configuration of Internet Explorer 4.0 that you would like to install (Standard, Enhanced, or Full), then choose either to install Internet Explorer 4.0 directly or to download the files so you can perform the installation at a later time.

8. The Setup program downloads and installs the items you requested.

Interactive Desktop

The biggest change IE 4.0 brings to Windows 95 is a new desktop functionality aptly named Active Desktop. This is the name given to the combination of the IE 4.0 browser and the Windows 95 desktop. Active Desktops are build on an HTML layer that enables them to transparently display information from the Internet that can be refreshed automatically at any time interval you choose. You can place HTML files, images downloaded from the Web, Java applets, and ActiveX controls directly on the Windows 95 desktop. For example, you can use Active Desktop to create a stock ticker tape that resides in the taskbar. Or you can include a picture from a Web site on your desktop, and then tell your PC to automatically update the picture every day. Figure 9.3 shows an example of a customized desktop that displays interactive components fed by updated data from the Internet.

Weblike Windows Interface

The Web influence on Windows 95 goes way beyond the desktop. Standard windows for the Windows Explorer, Control Panel, My Computer, Network Neighborhood, Recycle Bin, and so on are sporting a new Web-like interface. Figure 9.4 shows the Windows Explorer window. At first glance, it doesn't look that much different from the previous version of Windows Explorer, but there are a number of changes. Folders are now hypertext links, which means you simply click once on the object to access files and executable programs, as you do on the

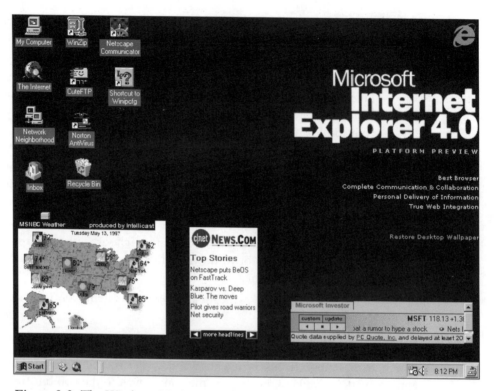

Figure 9.3 *The Windows 95 Active Desktop becomes a rich and customized personal workspace with information feeds coming from the Web at specified intervals.*

Web. Using a feature called Hover Select, icons are automatically selected when the mouse pointer passes over them. The label text turns blue, becomes underlined, and the pointer turns into the standard Web hand with the point index finger. No clicking is necessary to select an icon.

Although the right pane of the window looks similar to the pre-IE 4.0 Explorer window, it's encoded with an HTML layer that supports the display of Web-based documents. Figure 9.5 shows the Windows Explorer window with the right pane displaying a Web document instead of the folder and file icons shown in Figure 9.6. Notice the toolbar has also changed from the standard to a new incarnation called the Internet toolbar.

This toolbar, which enables you to display Web documents in the Explorer windows from the Internet or your local PC or LAN, can be added to any Windows 95 window. Although the Internet toolbar looks like the one in Internet Explorer, it has been extended to work with local files and folders, not just URLs. For example, the backward and forward buttons let you quickly hop back and forth through the nested files you've opened. The Address field on the toolbar lets

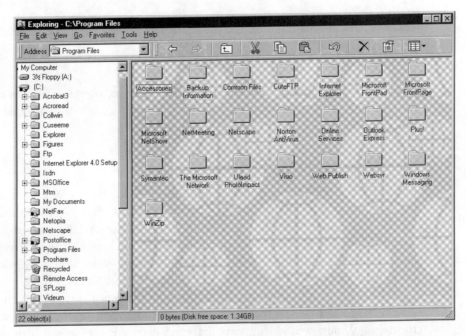

Figure 9.4 *The Windows Explorer window with the new IE 4.0 interface.*

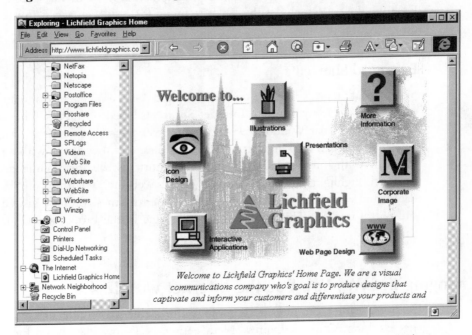

Figure 9.5 *The right pane of the Windows Explorer becomes an instant Web viewer whenever you connect to the Internet via the Windows Explorer.*

Figure 9.6 *A taskbar ready for quick access to the Web.*

you enter or choose a URL address or path. To do so, after entering an address or path, just press Enter and the browser opens to that site but on that same line; you can also type in a folder or filename to open that item.

Web-Savvy Menus and Taskbar

Internet Explorer 4.0 incorporates a number of changes to Windows 95 menus and the taskbar. The taskbar becomes a container for Office 97 style *coolbars*, which can be configured with shortcuts, Web links, and practically anything else you want (including scripts and HTML pages). Right-clicking on the taskbar displays a menu of toolbar options for the taskbar. For example, you can add an Address field for quick access to your favorite Web sites, as shown in Figure 9.6.

The Start menu is expanded to include a new main menu for Favorites, which gives you quick access to specific Internet sites. The Start menu, along with other menus in Windows now supports drag-and-drop editing, so you can drag items between menus or to and from Windows Explorer as if the menus were containers. Each window also includes the Favorite menu for easy Web access from any Windows 95 location.

Enhanced Shortcuts

Shortcuts are icons you place on the desktop to enable quick access to applications or files. IE 4.0 lets you create Internet Shortcuts based on URLs. They are much the same as regular Windows 95 shortcuts except that they point to items on the Internet. You can drag and drop them into files, and they work with any type of browser. With Internet Explorer 4.0, these shortcuts have been enhanced to support rich highlights such as the author of the Web site, when the site was last updated, and what is new on the site. The number of times you have visited the Web site is also tracked. This information is available in the Properties window of the shortcut.

Changing the Way You Use the Internet with IE 4.0

As noted earlier, the Internet Explorer Suite includes a Connection wizard, Internet Explorer, Outlook Express, NetMeeting, NetShow Player, and FrontPad. Together, these tools make a powerful collection of Internet-based remote access tools. When you install IE 4.0 on your system, all these programs are available from the Start menu. You can choose an individual tool from the Programs menu or a menu item from the Internet Explorer Suite menu. You can also access Outlook Express Mail, Outlook Express News, and NetMeeting from Internet Explorer.

Note: The Connection wizard included with the Internet Explorer Suite is the same wizard covered in Chapter 6.

Internet Explorer

The Internet Explorer 4.0 includes dozens of nifty gizmos for making Web browsing a lot more productive. There are so many new features and enhancements to IE 4.0 that they alone could fill a book. Here are the highlights of the most significant changes:

- IE 4.0 delivers a new mode for searching the Web with search engines like Yahoo, AltaVista, and Lycos. Before you conduct your search, Explorer's window splits. On the left side you type your search query and see the list of links. You then click on the link that you want: The right-hand side of the browser jumps to that page. This makes it possible to quickly scan through a bunch of Web sites, looking for what interests you. Figure 9.7 shows the Internet Explorer 4.0 in search mode.

- IE 4.0 implements Dynamic HTML, which is a new extension to the Web's authoring language that makes it possible for Web sites to create animation and Web pages that come alive. It does this with files that are much smaller and take less time to download than the approaches being used today (Java applets and animated GIF images). Extensions to HTML allow you to create dynamic Web pages with little coding and make it possible to update the HTML while users are viewing a page. You can change fonts, colors, insert more text, remove text, and more, all by updating the page you already downloaded. You can move items such as images around a page based on absolute XY coordinates. All the features of Dynamic HTML can be accessed without downloading a new page and without using any ActiveX controls. The result is a snappier, much more engaging Web-surfing experience for everyone.

- IE 4.0 includes built-in support for offline reading of Web-based information. The offline reading feature allows you to download entire Web pages,

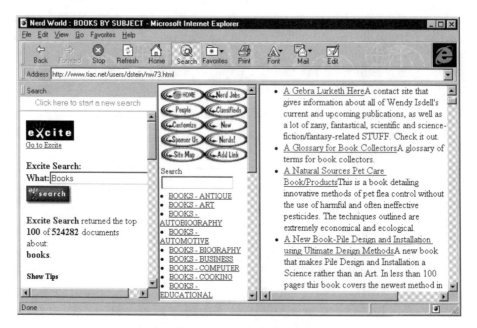

Figure 9.7 *Using windows splits, Internet Explorer 4.0 makes searching easier.*

including graphics and all page components in a fraction of the time it would take to read them. Once they're on your computer, you can read them at your leisure.

- IE 4.0 improves printing significantly, by enabling drag-and-drop printing and enhanced frames and tables printing. You can also do background and selective printing, which allows users to print only portions of a document. Furthermore, IE 4.0 utilizes recursive pages, which means that when you print an HTML page with a table of contents, the browser will automatically print the linked pages in the table of contents.

- The Site Map feature gives you a hierarchical view of a Web site. These maps are not based on the HTML storage built into a site; instead, the Web page author provides the details about the site with an OBJECT tag. Site maps are supported with the use of an SMP file, which is a plain text file created by the Web page author; it contains the description of a site hierarchy and other information, including the document name, URL, size, and date last modified; an index to the associated icon or a URL for the associated icon; and the location of the hierarchy; and the way to display the file. This can be used in conjunction with Internet Shortcuts.

- Smart Favorites enables IE 4.0 to operate in the background to check which of your Favorites links have been updated since you last visited. A red dot appears on the icon of those that have changed. A tooltip tells you what is new and when the page was last updated. Note, however, for this feature to work, the Web document author must add a special META tag.

- Subscriptions allows you to stay current on information by automatically downloading information from your favorite Web sites whenever they change so you don't have to keep checking them. This is handled by a built-in Web-crawling agent that regularly monitors all your favorite Web sites for changes and notifies you when one of them has been updated.

Outlook Express for E-mail and News

E-mail and newsgroups are the two most common means of communicating over the Internet. Outlook Express provides a common interface to work with both Internet e-mail and news. You can access Outlook Express through Internet Explorer 4.0 or as separate programs from the Programs menu.

The Outlook Express Mail program is a fast, friendly, and easy-to-use e-mail package that offers an impressive array of new features. It supports SMTP, POP3, and IAMP e-mail protocols. Outlook Express Mail also includes support for multiple e-mail accounts, which enables Outlook Express to go to your Internet service provider's e-mail server and choose which messages to download while keeping the other messages on the ISP's mail server. If you have several accounts on one server or with several different service providers, you can access and manage them all through the one Outlook Express window. All you have to do is set up each account with its own e-mail name, address, and connection method.

Outlook Express includes full HTML support so you can send e-mail messages that include graphics, text, animation, and even multimedia files. Figure 9.8 shows the Outlook Express Mail program window with an HTML pane for viewing Web documents sent via e-mail. Outlook Express allows you to send encrypted e-mail messages (you digitally sign your messages), as well as encrypt and decrypt messages with certificates. The Outlook Express News program includes comparable enhancements.

Microsoft NetMeeting

The Microsoft NetMeeting program (Figure 9.9) delivers a complete Internet conferencing solution for voice and video as well as for sharing applications, data, and a whiteboard in real time over the Internet. NetMeeting is built on an open,

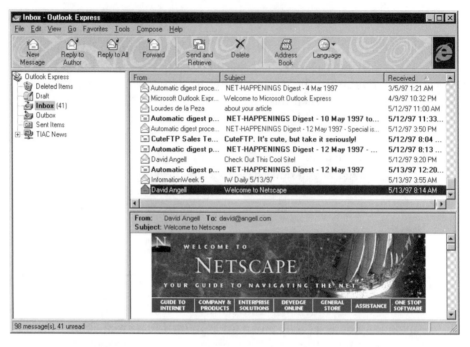

Figure 9.8 *The Outlook Express window includes a convenient HTML pane for viewing Web documents sent via e-mail.*

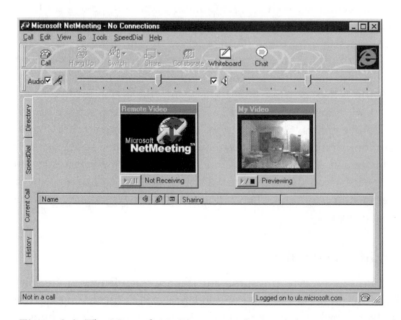

Figure 9.9 *The Microsoft NetMeeting window provides a common interface for data, audio, and video conferencing over the Internet.*

standards–based platform, which means you can use NetMeeting with people who run products from other companies. NetMeeting delivers the following services:

- *Data conferencing among groups.* You can share an application on your computer, exchange graphics or draw diagrams on a shared whiteboard, send messages or take notes via text-based chat, and send files to other meeting members.

- *Audio conferencing that lets you talk with another person in real-time over the Internet and enjoy high-quality audio.* While you're conversing, you can also bring in data or video conferencing.

- *Video conferencing for face-to-face meetings.* When you add a video capture card and camera to your PC, you can conduct high-quality video conferences over the Internet.

NetShow Player

Microsoft NetShow is designed as a multimedia broadcast client that lets you stream audio and video content from Internet sites. The NetShow Player window (Figure 9.10) lets you see and hear the information as it arrives from the server to your PC without having to wait for the file to download in its entirety. It eliminates the download-and-play approach for large sound and video applications. And after a broadcast is played on your system, the data is discarded to save disk space. NetShow uses a new generation of *streaming* technology developed by Microsoft called Active Streaming Format and MPEG compression to deliver high-quality video and audio in this no-wait method.

Web Authoring

FrontPad is a "lite" version of the Microsoft FrontPage 97 Web authoring program. FrontPad takes you step by step through the process of creating Web pages,

Figure 9.10 *The NetShow Player lets you view video or or listen to audio from the Internet.*

plus it lets you edit existing HTML documents. Microsoft FrontPad is a WYSI-WYG HTML editor that lets you insert tables; add multimedia files to your Web pages; and use Java Applets, JavaScript, and ActiveX controls in your Web pages.

Microsoft Exchange for Workgroup E-mail

Windows 95 includes the Microsoft Exchange client, a messaging system that retrieves messages into a user's mailbox from a variety of sources. Microsoft Exchange enables you to send and receive e-mail, faxes, and documents in messages. Information services that can be used with Windows 95 include Microsoft Mail (for LAN e-mail), Microsoft Fax, and Internet mail from an ISP's mail server. Windows 95 includes a workgroup version of Microsoft mail to enable you to create a local e-mail system for your Windows 95 LAN.

Windows Messaging is an updated version of a client program called Microsoft Exchange that was included in earlier versions of Windows 95. The OSR2 release of Windows 95 replaced Microsoft Exchange with Windows Messaging, which was developed for and implemented in Windows NT Workstation 4.0.

Note: You don't need to use Microsoft Exchange or Windows Messaging to use Outlook Express Mail and Outlook Express News. These programs use TCP/IP to handle their communications to the Internet. If you don't want to use a LAN-based e-mail system for communicating locally or use Microsoft Fax, then you don't need to install Microsoft Exchange or Windows Messaging.

Creating a Workgroup Post Office

The Microsoft Mail Server that comes with Windows 95 for creating and managing a post office is a limited version of the full-featured version. It does not allow e-mail exchange between post offices, so you'll only be able to create a single post office for your workgroup. Also, the Microsoft Mail Server that comes with Windows 95 does not act as a gateway for remote e-mail, which means it can't act as a post office for e-mail outside your LAN. However, you can add a remote mail feature to Microsoft Exchange clients to integrate Internet mail service into the Exchange mailbox.

Before you can install Microsoft Exchange, you need to set up a workgroup post office. This post office is set up on one machine on your LAN and acts as a server for your local e-mail services. To create a new workgroup post office, do the following:

1. Select the PC that you want to act as your e-mail server.

2. Double-click the Microsoft Mail Postoffice icon in the Control Panel.

3. In the Microsoft Workgroup Postoffice Admin dialog box, click Create a new Workgroup Postoffice, then click Next.

4. Specify where you want the workgroup post office to be located, then click Next. You can use the default C:\Postoffice\wpo0000 path.

5. Confirm the location of the new post office folder and click Next.

6. In the Administrator Account Details dialog box, type information about the post office administrator, including user's name and mailbox name, and a password to restrict administration of the post office to only the designated administrator.

7. Click Next to finish creating the post office. Before you can add the Exchange client on each PC on your LAN, you need to share the Postoffice folder in the Windows Explorer to allow users to access their LAN e-mail.

8. Open the Windows Explorer and right-click the folder for your workgroup post office.

9. Choose Properties, and then click the Sharing tab.

10. Click on the Shared As setting and verify the name of the post office in the Shared Name field.

11. Click on the Full setting in the Access Type group to allow everyone on your workgroup access to e-mail.

12. Click OK.

Adding Users to the Post Office

After you have created your workgroup post office and shared its folder, you need to set up user accounts for every user LAN e-mail user on the network. This must be done before Microsoft Exchange can be installed on the user's PC because the wizard will ask for the e-mail user account as part of the installation process. The following steps explain how to create e-mail user accounts.

1. Double-click the Microsoft Mail Postoffice icon in the Control Panel to open the Microsoft Mail Postoffice Admin dialog box.

2. Select the Administrator of an existing workgroup post office and click on Next. The next screen will show the path of the post office folder; click Next again. A screen appears prompting you for the mailbox name and password of the post office administrator.

Figure 9.11 *The Postoffice Manager dialog box.*

4. Enter your mailbox name and password, then click Next. The Postoffice Manager dialog box appears (Figure 9.11).

5. Click on Add User to display the Add User dialog box (Figure 9.12).

6. Fill out the form with information for the new user. The three required entries are the Name, Mailbox, and Password fields. After you enter a password, it's a good idea to jot it down on a piece of paper, because you will need it to set up Microsoft Exchange for the user for whom you are creating the account.

7. Click OK to enter the new user and return to the Postoffice Manager dialog box.

8. Repeat steps 5 through 7 for each user on your LAN. After you're finished creating mailboxes, click Close to exit the Postoffice Manager dialog box.

You can remove any mailbox by selecting it from the list in the Postoffice Manager dialog box and clicking on the Remove User button. Selecting a name in

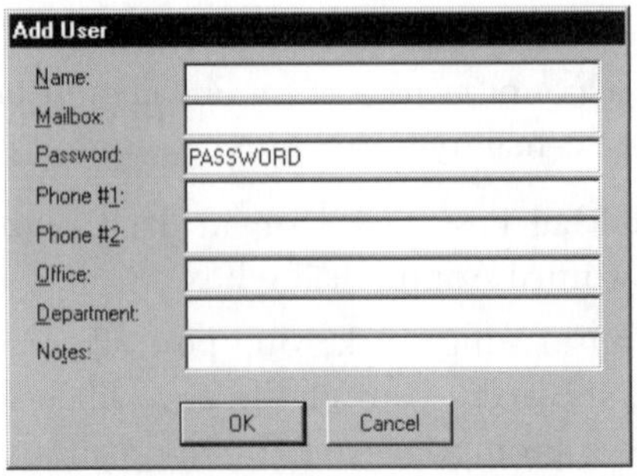

Figure 9.12 *The Add User dialog box.*

the Postoffice manager list and clicking on the Details button lets you edit any information you entered in the user's profile when you added the mailbox by clicking on the Add button. The Shared Folders button in the Postoffice Manager dialog box displays the status of messages in all the shared e-mail folders.

Adding a Microsoft Exchange Client

Once you have created a mailbox for every user on your LAN using the Postoffice Manager, you can install the Microsoft Exchange client. When you install Microsoft Exchange on a PC, a personal folder file is created. The personal folder functions as your universal inbox and outbox for sending messages to and receiving messages from different sources. The following steps show you how to install the Microsoft Exchange client, which must be performed on each PC connected to your LAN that wants access to LAN-based e-mail.

1. Choose Start|Settings|Control Panel to open the Control Panel.

2. Double-click the Add/Remove Programs icon to open the Add/Remove Programs Properties dialog box.

3. Click on the Windows Setup tab.

4. Scroll through the Components list to locate and click on the Microsoft Exchange check box, and then click the Details button. The Microsoft Exchange dialog box appears.

5. In the Microsoft Exchange dialog box, select the Microsoft Exchange and Microsoft Mail Services items and choose OK.

6. Click OK to exit the Add/Remove Properties dialog box. Windows 95 adds the necessary software to your system, prompting you if necessary to supply one or more of the Windows 95 diskettes or Windows 95 CD, if needed.

7. The Inbox Setup wizard appears and asks you if you have used Microsoft Exchange before. Use the default No setting and click Next.

8. In the screen asking which services you want to use with Microsoft Exchange, check Microsoft Mail and Internet mail; click Next.

9. Add the path for your workgroup post office folder, which is a shared folder. Click on the Browse button to display the Browse for Postoffice dialog box. Click on the Network Neighborhood icon, then navigate to the computer and post office folder. If you used the default workgroup folder name, the folder would be named wgpo0000. Click OK and then Next.

10. Select your name from the list. These are the user names entered by the mail administrator using the Microsoft Mail Postoffice icon in the Control Panel. Click Next.

11. In the next screen, your name and mailbox are displayed; you're prompted for your password to gain access to your Microsoft Mail mailbox. This password is the one used to set up the mailbox. Enter your password and click Next.

12. Click the correct method by which you want to connect to the Internet Mail server. Select Network for a network connection, which will be router-connected to the Internet. Click Next.

13. Enter the DNS name or IP address of the mail server used by your Internet service provider, then click Next.

14. Select the Automatic setting and click Next.

15. Enter your Internet e-mail address and your full name in the Full Name field; for example, david@angell.com. Click Next.

16. Enter your mailbox user name and password for gaining access to the ISP's e-mail server; click Next. A screen appears asking you if you want to run Microsoft Exchange when you start.

17. Leave the default Do not add inbox to the StartUp group setting and click Next. The final wizard screen appears. Click Finished.

Network Faxing via Microsoft Fax

Most modems come with built-in faxing capability, and with the enhanced faxing features built into Windows 95, you may want to put your fax modem to good use as a fax service available to your entire LAN. You can send and receive faxes to other fax machines or PCs connected to your LAN, broadcast faxes to groups, or receive faxes that support fax polling.

Microsoft Fax handles faxes as e-mail messages so you must install Microsoft Exchange to use Microsoft Fax. Assuming you already added Microsoft Exchange, do the following steps. And note, these steps must be done on every PC on the LAN for which you plan to have fax service.

1. Choose Start|Settings|Control Panel to open the Control Panel.

2. Double-click the Add/Remove Programs icon to open the Add/Remove Programs Properties sheet.

3. Click on the Windows Setup tab; the Windows Setup page appears.

4. Scroll through the Components list to locate and click on the Microsoft Fax check box; click Next.

5. Choose OK. Windows 95 adds the necessary software to your system, prompting you if necessary to supply one or more of the Windows 95 diskettes or Windows 95 CD.

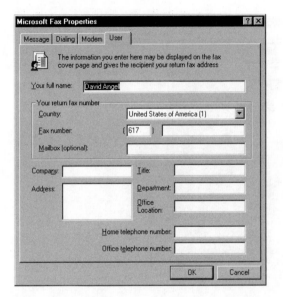

Figure 9.13 *The Microsoft Fax Properties dialog box.*

Setting Up Microsoft Fax for Network Faxing

The modem is attached to a single machine on your LAN; as such, you need to share it to make it available to other users on your LAN. Here's how to set up a shared network fax.

1. Open the Mail and Fax icon in the Control Panel.

2. In the Properties dialog box, click the Add button. The Add Service to Profile dialog box appears.

3. Select Microsoft Fax and click OK. You'll be asked if you want to type your name, fax number, and fax device modem. Click OK to display the Microsoft Fax Properties dialog box (Figure 9.13).

4. In the User tab, enter your fax number (this is a required entry) and any other optional information you want.

5. In the Modem tab (Figure 9.14) do the following:

    Select the modem you plan to use for faxing, if necessary.

    Click on Let other people on the network use my modem to send faxes. The default NETFAX is used.

    Click on the Properties button to display the Fax Modem Properties dialog box (Figure 9.15).

Figure 9.14 The Modem tab in the Microsoft Fax dialog box.

If you want your fax modem to answer the phone and receive a fax, click on the Answer after setting in the Answer mode group and specify the number of rings before the modem answers.

Click OK.

6. Click OK to close the Microsoft Fax Properties dialog box and return to the Properties dialog box.

With the Fax server configured, you're ready to configure one or more client PCs to send faxes over the network through this server.

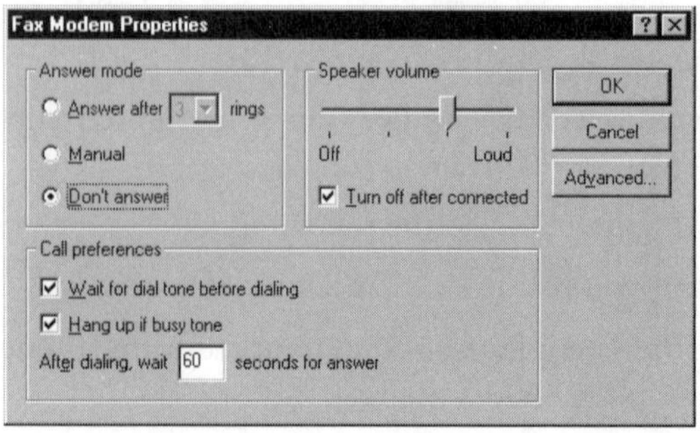

Figure 9.15 The Fax Modem Properties dialog box.

Configuring a Microsoft Fax Client

The following steps show you how to configure each PC on your LAN that you want to enable to use the fax server you configured in the previous section.

1. Double-click on the Inbox icon on the desktop.

2. Choose Tools|Microsoft Fax Tools|Options. The Microsoft Fax Properties dialog box appears.

3. Click the Modem tab; click the Add button to display the Add a Fax Modem dialog box.

4. Select Network fax server and click OK. The Connect to Network Fax Server dialog box appears.

5. Type the path of your fax server. For example, on a server named author, the path would be \\author\NETFAX. NETFAX is the default name used for the fax server.

6. Click OK. Select the server you just specified in the Microsoft Fax Properties dialog box and click the Set as Active Fax Device button.

7. Click on OK to return to the Inbox.

Faxing over the network is straightforward. From the Inbox, you choose Compose|New Fax. A wizard walks you through creating a fax and then sends it. You can also fax from an application, such as Word97. When you receive an incoming fax, a status dialog box appears to alert you that an incoming fax is arriving. The fax appears in the Inbox in the same way as an e-mail message.

Using Remote Mail

You can create a system on your Windows 95 LAN to handle remote access of your e-mail boxes on your local LAN. This feature allows users working off-site to get their e-mail and faxes. These are the steps required to set up a remote mail system.

1. Install the Dial-Up Networking Server on the PC where the post office resides. (See Chapter 6 for instructions on getting and setting up the Microsoft Dial-Up Networking Server.)

2. Install the Dial-Up Networking client on the remote PC that will be calling in to get e-mail from the post office.

3. Configure the remote Microsoft Exchange clients for remote mail access.

Once you set up your remote e-mail system, you can send mail to and receive mail from members of your network. The telephone number will be that of your

Figure 9.16 *The Microsoft Mail dialog box.*

fax modem attached to the PC, which is operating as both your Dial-Up Networking Server and post office. Configuring the Microsoft Exchange client on the remote PC involves the following steps.

1. Open the Mail and Fax icon in the Control Panel.

2. Select Microsoft Mail and click on the Properties button to display the Microsoft Mail Properties dialog box (Figure 9.16).

3. Click on the Dial-Up Networking tab.

4. Click on the Add Entry button to create a Dial-Up Networking connection, which displays the Make New Connection wizard.

5. Create your Dial-Up Networking connection, as explained in Chapter 6. You must use the NetBEUI network protocol for remote mail.

6. Click on the Connection tab, then on Remote using a modem and Dial-Up Networking.

7. Click the Remote Configuration tab. You can accept the default settings in this dialog box, which require that you tell the system to download your mail after you're connected to the remote post office. If you uncheck Use Remote Mail, your e-mail will be automatically downloaded when you're connected to the remote post office.

8. Click on the Remote Session tab. Choose the configuration you want from this tab. You can specify when a dial-up mail session begins and ends.

You can schedule the times you check your e-mail using the Schedule Mail Delivery button in the Remote Session tab of the Microsoft Mail dialog box.

What's Next

Congratulations. You now understand how to transform Windows 95 into your complete remote access platform. From this springboard, you can jump into specific remote access technologies and devices. Part III starts at the low end of the high-bandwidth pool with a discussion of 56-Kbps modems and ISDN service. Both provide remote access connection options for either a single PC or an entire LAN. Part IV takes the plunge into higher-bandwidth connections, including satellite, cable, and xDSL.

PART

III

56-Kbps Modems and ISDN

10 The Advent of 56-Kbps Modems

Analog modems have been the staple of PC data communications since the beginning of PC computing, and 56-Kbps modems are the latest generation of modems that work over POTS. To reach the higher speed, these modems use a different architecture from conventional analog modems. Consequently, an understanding of how they work is essential to determining whether you'll get the higher data communications speed. This chapter educates you on both the potential and pitfalls of 56-Kbps modems. It also looks at some exciting new modem routers that let you share a 56-Kbps modem on a LAN and bond multiple modems into a single high-speed connection.

How 56-Kbps Modems Work

Conventional modems take digital data from a computer, convert it into analog form, and transmit it over the telephone line. On the receiving end, the analog signal is converted back into digital by another modem. In contrast, the new 56K technologies keep the signal digital on the return trip. Eliminating a digital-to-analog conversion is the way 56K modems achieve their higher downstream speeds. The elimination of one conversion is done on the server modem side using a digital connection to the telephone company's switch.

Most analog modem users currently receive data (as well as voice) across the local loop using a modulation process such as V.32bis or V.34. Modulation transforms incoming analog signals into their digital equivalents and determines the data transfer speed. The signal is subject to various types of noise, which distorts the original signal and can significantly reduce the data throughput rate. These modulation protocols limit analog modem users to connection speeds somewhere between 28.8 Kbps or 33.6 Kbps; and this data rate can degrade even further if there is any noise on the line.

In truth, 56K modems are *capable* of delivering 56 Kbps of data communications; what you actually get in practice will vary, depending on a number of factors, most notably the condition of the phone lines between you and the phone company's equipment, the location of your premises relative to the central office (CO), and whether or not your ISP supports a compatible 56K technology. Also, you cannot have more than one switch that converts analog to digital between you and your ISP or the higher speed is negated.

Unlike conventional analog modems, 56K modems operate asymmetrically. The 56 Kbps refers to the downstream (Internet to your PC) data communications capacity, and this capacity is currently restricted by FCC regulations to 53 Kbps because of POTS line voltage restrictions. Modem vendors are petitioning to waive the rule. Upstream capacity (PC to Internet) is between 28.8 Kbps and 33.6 Kbps, although the second-generation modems may provide up to 40-Kbps upstream speeds.

Speed Variations

Estimates fluctuate as to what percentage of the population will be able to enjoy the higher speeds of 56K technology, but the consensus seems to hover around 80 to 90 percent. Field tests conducted by Motorola determined that approximately 20 percent of phone lines can deliver 56-Kbps performance, while an equal percentage will never achieve such speed. The rest will fall somewhere in the 40-Kbps to 50-Kbps range. Others predict typical throughput without using file compression at around 44.8 Kbps.

Shannon's Law and 56K Modems

Shannon's Law is one of physics that governs how fast information can be transferred over twisted-pair copper wire. This law defines why analog modem speeds were limited to 33.6 Kbps, which is the current modem speed standard. But Claude Shannon wrote his law for analog data communications, not digital. The 56K modem technology sidesteps it by converting the information to a digital format instead of the conventional analog format. The catch is, you have to be using a "clean" phone line, one that has minimal electrical interference. If the line is not clean, the 56K modem will reduce speed to that which the line can support. Generally, metropolitan areas have better telecommunications infrastructures, though that is not always the case.

The Telephone System and 56-Kbps Modems

The existing telephone network was originally designed to handle analog voice calls. As digital technology became available, telephone companies have gradually replaced older analog segments with more reliable digital services. This migration process has taken place over the last 20 years—first in the long-distance markets and then in the local telephone service network. It's this migration to digital switches that enables 56K modems to operate because one side of the connection is digital.

Local Loop Segment

The local loop is the last 18,000-foot segment of the carrier network that reaches from a telephone company's central office to an end-user's residence. The 56K technology uses the existing analog wiring infrastructure in the local loop to transport data from a corporate site or the Internet through the telephone network to the end-user's desktop. End users can utilize existing telephone lines with 56-Kbps modems. ISPs and other network service providers can use the local loop to offer 56K services by installing compatible 56K technology at their central site. This lets them cost-effectively offer an additional service option to analog modem users while leveraging their digital lines and switches.

Digital-to-Analog Conversion

Again, 56K technology works only on the downstream portion of the call, where it undergoes a digital-to-analog (D-A) conversion at the CODEC (Coder/DE-Coder) that terminates the analog line. The CODEC is the device that sits between the digital portion of the carrier's network and the analog local loop. It converts the signals back and forth between analog and digital. When the call arrives at the end-user's desktop, this analog signal must be converted back to a digital format.

On the downstream portion of the call, there is a clean digital-to-analog conversion so no throughput is lost. Because there is a direct translation of digital to analog, no throughput is lost during the encoding process. The call is then sent from the CODEC device to the end-user's 56-Kbps modem, where there is a single analog-to-digital (A-D) conversion. On the upstream portion of the call, there is more than one A-D conversion, resulting in a reduced throughput rate. Conversions on the upstream path are not clean, and they are subject to noise, which limits the data rate.

The 56K technology must be installed in the end-user's modem and at the server site. When a connection is made, the modems on both ends send a probing signal back and forth between the central site and the end-user's home. If additional analog-to-digital (A-D) conversions are detected anywhere along the communications path, the connection is established at 33 Kbps or less. Both ends of the connection must use compatible 56K technologies. When the call enters the telephone network from the server side of a 56K connection, it must enter the central office switch on the trunk side via a digital medium, such as ISDN or a T1 line.

Note: Because 56K modems require a digital connection to the telephone network from the server side of any connection, you can't use two 56K modems over POTS to create a 56K connection. For setting up a Windows 95 Dial-Up Networking Server at your site to accept incoming 56K calls, you must have a digital line such as ISDN.

The server located at the ISP sends a stream of digital bytes through the telephone network on a digital trunk line. The call goes through the trunk side of the carrier's CO switch where it is processed as purely a digital connection and possibly forwarded to another CO switch or a tandem switch. The data is processed on the trunk side while continuing to remain purely a digital connection. The call leaves the network via a CODEC device, where a digital-to-analog conversion takes place. The analog call arrives at the end-user's desktop, where it is converted to a digital format. This is the only A-D conversion performed in the connection.

The Bumpy Road to 56K Standards

The technical issues surrounding 56K modems are only part of the confusion, the lack of a universal 56K standard is the other. Two 56-Kbps technologies are vying for dominance in the marketplace: x2 and K56flex (also called K56). x2 is the brand name of U.S. Robotics (USR) implementation of 56-Kbps technology, and K56flex is Rockwell Semiconductor Systems and Lucent Technologies'. U.S. Robotics is the leading modem manufacturer and the only major modem vendor that has its own custom designed and manufactured chip sets; Rockwell makes the semiconductor chips and chip sets for 80 percent of the world's fax modems and 65 percent of the world's PC data modems.

Although Rockwell and Lucent developed separate 56-Kbps modem technologies, they decided to join forces. Their K56flex is a combination of Rockwell's K56Plus and Lucent's V.flex technology. Since teaming up, Rockwell

Semiconductor Systems and Lucent Technologies have gained support from leading personal computer and internetworking manufacturers. For example, Motorola, which has its own 56-Kbps modem technology called 56K Plus, is supporting K56flex.

Note: Lucent Technologies has not yet shipped the K56flex software to make its chips communicate at 56K; the Rockwell chips already support the full 56K. Unlike x2 and K56flex, Lucent's technology is capable of both sending and receiving data in the 45-Kbps range.

The problem for consumers is that these two 56-Kbps modem technologies are incompatible. Until an official standard is in place, consumers who purchase 56-Kbps modems will have to search for an Internet service provider that supports the same type of technology. The 56K war between USR and the troika of Rockwell, Motorola, and Lucent regarding proposed standards is likely to sustain a proprietary fractionalization of the 56-Kbps modem market until formal standards bodies focus on a single standard. The worldwide International Telecommunications Union (ITU; the recognized global arbitrator of modem standards) standard isn't expected until early to mid-1998.

In the meantime, 56-Kbps consumers and service providers must wade through an added layer of complexity brought on by the two proprietary modem technologies. The Lucent-Rockwell team's K56flex is gaining support from most modem vendors, but U.S. Robotics' x2 technology will remain a force because of the company's dominance in the end-user modem market. Both camps claim that once a standard is approved, 56-Kbps modems will be easily upgradeable via flash ROM. However, there's no guarantee of that, since there's no predicting what the ultimate standard will require.

There are also conflicts on standards for upstream data communications. One group advocates the use of V.34 (28.8 Kbps and 33.6 Kbps) technology for the return path from the end user back to the service provider. The reasoning is that this technology is already a well-known standard and its use will expedite the standards-setting process for 56K. The other major school of thought recommends the use of a new technology that can provide a 42-Kbps to 48-Kbps return path. This approach will provide end users greater performance and open the possibility of additional applications.

The Open 56K Forum

The Open 56K Forum is a coalition of 28 companies from key segments of the communications and computer industry promoting the implementation of K56flex modem technology. The Open 56K Forum claims to represent more than 70 percent of the modem communications industry, reaching more than 12 million Internet subscribers worldwide. It includes Ascend Communications, BBN, Bay Networks, Best Data, Cisco Systems, Compaq, Diamond Multimedia, EarthLink, Hayes, Hewlett-Packard, Livingston Enterprises, Lucent Technologies, Motorola, PSINet, Rockwell Semiconductor Systems, Shiva Corporation, Toshiba, UUNet, Xircom, and Zoom. Of course, noticeably absent from the impressive roster of the Open 56K Forum is U.S. Robotics. USR claims a market share at the service provider end of the connection that represents some 18 million users.

Using 56K Modems in the Real World

The best applications for the new 56K modems are those that demand the highest possible downstream bandwidth. Web browsing, for instance, is ideal for the new 56K modems, because a large amount of data (text, graphics, audio, video, etc.) travels downstream from the server to the client. On the other hand, comparatively little data travels upstream, and consists mostly of text-based HTTP requests. Other technologies, such as Internet phones, document and video conferencing, and file transfer, generally require equal amounts of bandwidth both ways, and thus the value of 56K modems for those applications is less clear.

The 56-Kbps modems will not provide enough bandwidth to allow content providers to radically alter the nature of their online presentations; however, the 400 percent improvement over 14.4-Kbps modems allows content providers to move beyond static pages with animation and interactivity. Moreover, 56-Kbps and other dial-up solutions will be capable of greater performance as compression becomes more commonplace.

The main benefit of 56K modem technology is price. Compared to other connection methods that provide comparable bandwidth, purchasing a 56K modem should prove to be one of the cheapest. The fact that 56K modems can deliver the look and feel of a single B-channel ISDN connection (64 Kbps) promises some relief for millions of Internet users.

Despite some of the technological drawbacks, the 56-Kbps data rate seems likely to establish itself as the next modem standard, and 56K modems may be the only viable option for many SOHO sites that lack access to ISDN, cable, or xDSL service or face expensive ISDN and xDSL tariffs. A new market study by Jupiter Communications estimates that 56-Kbps modems will control 50 percent of the access market by 1998 and 65 percent by the year 2000.

Most major ISPs and online services have announced that they will upgrade their services to support 56 Kbps. At this stage, ISPs may support both technologies until a standard has emerged; or they will follow the 56K modem technology that end users are buying. Like users, ISPs are also wrestling with concerns about 56 Kbps. Rates for 56-Kbps service may be higher at first than the standard $19.95 per month to which users have grown accustomed because ISPs and other network providers must swap out large numbers of modems to upgrade their systems to handle 56-Kbps modems—an operation that will take time. In the beginning, users may see prices jump to the mid-$30 range for 56-Kbps accounts.

Choosing a 56K Modem

The battle between USR's x2 and Rockwell and Lucent's K56flex technologies has divided the modem makers into two camps. U.S. Robotics and some other modem manufacturers such as Cardinal Technologies are offering x2 modems. Other modem manufacturers are supporting K56flex, including Practical Peripherals, Hayes, Diamond Multimedia, Motorola, Zoom, Best Data, Boca Research, Global Village, Microcom, and others. The modems range in price from as low as $99 to $395. As is the case with any modem, internal modem cards are cheaper than external modems. PCMCIA 56K modem cards are typically more expensive than external 56K modems.

You can also get 56K voice modems that include software and ports for connecting speakers and microphones for managing voice communications from your computer. Voice modems require stereo-to-stereo cable and a microphone. If your computer already has speakers connected to a sound card, you can connect your voice modem and the sound card to the same speakers. You need a microphone you can plug into the MIC connector at the back of the modem for use with external voice modems. You can purchase a stereo-to-stereo cable and microphone at an electronic or computer store.

TIP: Before you run out and buy a 56K modem, check with the manufacturer of your 28.8-Kbps or 33.6-Kbps modem to learn whether it provides an upgrade program. For example, U.S. Robotics allows users to upgrade Sportster and Courier modems.

Which 56K-capable modem should you buy? Use the following guidelines to help you choose the right 56K modem:

- Check with the ISP or other network you plan to connect with to find out which 56K technology it is supporting. In the short term, which 56K-modem technology you use will be dictated by the technology that is supported at the server side of the connection. The best course of action for now is to find out which 56K technology your ISP supports and buy a modem compatible with it.

- Don't commit to a 56-Kbps Internet access account with an ISP or online service unless you know you'll actually get the higher speed from your POTS line. Many modem vendors include a 56K server site to test the speed you'll get using their modem.

- Make sure the modem supports firmware upgrades from software that is made available on the Internet. This helps protect your modem investment. The X2 technology supports easier firmware upgrades than the K56flex technology.

- Find out whether the modem manufacturer offers an investment protection program to protect your modem investment when standards are enacted. For example, Hayes and Practical Peripherals guarantee free upgrades to the final 56K ITU standard for any of their 56K-modem customers, whether they're a software upgrade or modem replacement.

- Buy your modem at a computer store that makes product returns easy. Because 56K modems are dependent on the quality of your telephone line, you may find that your connection doesn't support the higher capacity of a 56-Kbps modem.

- At this stage in the life cycle of 56-Kbps modems, don't rule out either the x2 or K56flex technologies, because both are viable competitors in the short term and will most likely work with each other once standards are in place.

Internal versus External

Internal 56-Kbps modems are easy to install and generally less expensive than external modems. Internal 56K modems also come with their own high-speed UART chip built in to ensure you get the maximum speed. If you simply want to connect a single PC to a 56-Kbps modem, an internal modem may be fine. However, external modems offer more flexibility in your remote access configuration. A new genre of modem routers is becoming available that allow you to share a 56K modem over a LAN, as well as combine up to three external modems to join their bandwidths. The WebRamp M3 is such as a device; it is covered in Chapter 11.

Setting Up a 56K Modem in Windows 95

Windows 95 makes installing and using 56K modems (internal or external) easy. Windows 95's Plug-and-Play support has dramatically reduced the hassle of installing modems. Windows 95 automatically detects Plug-and-Play-compatible devices attached to your system without any manual configuration of jumpers or switches on the adapter cards. This means that communications between the peripheral devices, the Basic Input/Output System (BIOS), and Windows 95 automatically handle resource conflicts.

Windows 95 also eliminated the 19,200-bps limitation for serial communications inherent in Windows for Workgroups; it supports up to 921,600 bps through a serial port. This support for the higher data transmission rates is based on your PC using at least the 16550A UART (universal asynchronous receiver/transmitter) chip in its COM port for external modems. UART chips are part of the PC's COM port that handle communications between the CPU and any device connected to the COM port. Most PCs (486 and Pentiums) include the 16550A UART chip.

Using 56K modems is also easy thanks to Windows 95 Dial-Up Networking, which eliminates the need for learning a communications package to connect to the Internet. For traditional PC communications to BBS or other PCs, you can use the Windows 95 HyperTerminal program.

The following sections explain how to install and configure an internal and external modem in Windows 95. For the external modem example, I used the Hayes ACCURA 56K, which employs the K56Flex technology. For the internal modem, I used the U.S. Robotics Courier V.Everything, which employs the x2 technology.

Installing and Configuring the Hayes ACCURA 56K

The Hayes ACCURA 56K is a good example of an external modem. It includes all the standard 56K modem features as well as a free ITU upgrade policy. While not the fastest 56K modem, it's one of the most reliable in terms of providing high-speed connections over poor POTS lines.

To connect the Hayes ACCURA 56K modem to your PC, first make sure your system is turned off. The ACCURA uses a 9-pin serial connector at the back of the unit and includes a 25-pin to 9-pin adapter if your RS-232 cable is 25-pin on both ends. Plug in your telephone line to the LINE port, then plug the modem adapter into a power outlet. Turn on the ACCURA 56K using a power switch at the back of the unit. You're now ready to install the software in Windows 95.

1. Restart Windows 95. The New Hardware Found dialog box appears.

2. Select Driver from disk provided by hardware manufacturer and click OK.

3. Insert the Driver and Utilities disk in drive A, then click OK.

4. Select Hayes ACCURA 56K Ext Fax Modem from the Models list; click OK. Windows 95 installs the driver software onto your hard drive.

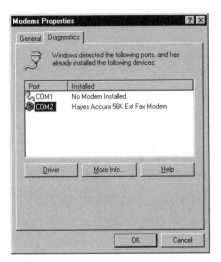

Figure 10.1 *The Modems Properties dialog box with the Diagnostics tab selected.*

Once the Hayes ACCURA 56K Ext Fax Modem driver is installed in Windows 95, you can change any of the configuration settings using the Modems control panel. You can test to make sure your modem is installed by opening the Modems applet in the Windows 95 Control Panel. The Modems Properties dialog box appears (Figure 10.1). In the Modems Properties dialog box, select Diagnostics tab, then the COM port connected to the Hayes ACCURA 56K modem, and click on More Info. A message box appears telling you that Windows 95 is making the connection to your modem. After the connection is made, the More Info dialog box appears indicating your modem is properly installed.

Once you have installed the Hayes ACCURA 56K Ext Fax Modem in Windows 95, you're ready to use Dial-Up Networking to create your connection profiles for remote access. Chapter 6, "Remote Access via Dial-Up Networking" explains how to work with Windows 95's Dial-Up Networking.

Installing and Configuring the U.S. Robotics Courier V.EveryThing

The U.S. Robotics Courier V.Everything is an internal 56K modem based on the X2 technology. This Plug-and-Play modem card is easy to install in Windows 95, and can be upgraded just as easily because it incorporates flash ROM.

To install the card in your PC, do the following:

1. With your PC turned off, unplug your PC, then take off the computer cover.

2. Find an empty slot; remove the slot cover and install the Courier card into the slot. Secure the Courier in your computer.

● ●

CAUTION: The Courier is Plug-and-Play-compatible but it is shipped with settings for COM2 and IRQ3. To prepare the courier for Plug-and-Play installation for any other COM port, you need to change a jumper on the card and change a DIP switch setting as explained in the documentation.

---

3. Replace the computer cover.

4. Connect the phone cable from a wall jack to the TELCO RJ-11 port on the card. If you have a telephone that you want to connect to the Courier, connect it to the RJ-11 port labeled PHONE.

You are now ready to install the Courier in Windows 95.

1. Restart Windows 95. The New Hardware Found dialog box appears.

2. Select Driver from disk provided by hardware manufacturer and click OK.

3. Insert the Connections CD in your CD-ROM drive; type D:\, then click OK.

4. Select Courier V.Everything from the Internal Models list and click OK. Windows 95 installs the driver software onto your hard drive.

Once the Courier V.Everything driver is installed in Windows 95, you can change any of the configuration settings using the Modems control panel. You can test to make sure your modem is properly installed by opening the Modems applet in the Windows 95 Control Panel. The Modems Properties dialog box appears (see Figure 10.1). In the Modems Properties dialog box, select Diagnostics tab, then the COM port connected to the Courier V.Everything modem; click on More Info. A message box appears telling you that Windows 95 is making the connection to your modem. After the connection is made, the More Info dialog box appears indicating your modem is properly installed.

Once you have installed the Courier V.Everything Fax Modem in Windows 95, you're ready to use Dial-Up Networking to create your connection profiles for remote access. Chapter 6 "Remote Access via Dial-Up Networking" explains how to work with Windows 95's Dial-Up Networking.

Working with the Supra PC Card for Laptops

Diamond Multimedia's Supra PC Card is an affordable PCMCIA 56-Kbps fax modem based on K56flex. The Supra PC Card lists for $199.95 and is designed to be upgradeable to the prospective ITU standard for 56-Kbps technology. The Supra Card features a sleep mode that conserves laptop battery life. Installing the Supra PC Card is straightforward as follows:

1. Turn on your laptop.
2. Insert your Supra PC Card into the PCMCIA slot. You're asked to install a driver for your modem.
3. Connect the POTS adapter to the Supra PC Card and plug in the RJ-11 connector to your POTS wall jack.
4. Click on the Driver from disk provided by hardware manufacturer and then click OK.
5. Insert the Windows 95 Driver diskette in the appropriate drive and click OK. Windows automatically installs your modem driver. Your modem is now installed.

Once the Supra PC Card is installed in Windows 95, you can change any of the configuration settings using the Modems control panel. You can test to make sure your modem is properly installed by opening the Modems applet in the Windows 95 Control Panel. The Modems Properties dialog box appears (see Figure 10.1). In the Modems Properties dialog box, select Diagnostics tab, then the COM port connected to the Supra PC Card modem; click on More Info. A message box appears telling you that Windows 95 is making the connection to your modem. After the connection is made, the More Info dialog box appears indicating your modem is properly installed.

Once you have installed the Supra PC Card, you're ready to use Dial-Up Networking to create your connection profiles for remote access. Chapter 6, "Remote Access via Dial-Up Networking," explains how to work with Windows 95's Dial-Up Networking.

Next-Generation 56K Modem Routers/Concentrators

A new generation of sophisticated LAN-based modem routers and concentrators are coming online. There are LAN-based 56-Kbps routers that combine an external 56-Kbps modem with a network hub and router to allow anyone on the LAN to share the 56-Kbps modem connection. The LINKSYS Internet Workgroup Hub is an example of this type of product. This device lets you share an external 56-Kbps modem across a small Windows 95 LAN. With a list price of $229, you can share a faster modem link to the Internet. It works with a single-user, dynamic IP address Internet access account, and acts as a four-port 10BaseT network hub.

Note: Windows 95 does not have any built-in support for modem sharing. Also, using a modem router bypasses Windows 95 Dial-Up Networking. Instead, the connection is handled in the background via the network once the user opens any TCP/IP application.

An even more promising modem-based technology is called an analog multiplexor or concentrator, which enables the combining of modem connections to act as a single bandwidth connection. For example, using a modem concentrator, you can join two 56K modems to connect to the Internet at speeds up to 112K, a speed that approaches ISDN. Although, your true speed for two 56-Kbps modems will most likely be in the 80+ Kbps range. The main reasons for combining modems is that POTS service is widely available, and in many cases it can be cheaper than using ISDN. Two companies are currently working on POTS bonding devices: Ramp Networks and U.S. Robotics. As of this writing, only the former's WebRamp M3 was available.

Ramp Networks' WebRamp M3 is an analog router, 4-port Ethernet hub, and multiplexor that supports up to three external modems (which you must supply) from 14 Kbps to 56 Kbps to produce an Internet connection of up to 168 Kbps downstream. Although, your true speed for three 56 Kbps modems will most likely be in the 120+ Kbps range. The WebRamp M3 sells for $439. The WebRamp M3 will work with either x2 or K56flex modems. The M3 includes a four-port hub. If two or three modems are called into play, they call the Internet service provider simultaneously, attack Web pages as a team, and share in the downloading, resulting in throughput of up to 156 Kbps. Chapter 11 explains working with the WebRamp M3.

USR's LANLinker Dual Analog modem/router will integrate two x2 56-Kbps modems that can be bonded for as much as 112 Kbps. The device is expected to sell for $795. At the time this book was written, U.S. Robotics had announced that it would offer a router that will enable users to download data at uncompressed speeds as fast as 112 Kbps aggregated over two regular telephone lines. U.S. Robotics' LANLinker Dual Analog integrates two x2 modems and allows simultaneous x2 connections to two different locations, so users can connect to the Internet and their remote network at the same time.

Working with the LINKSYS Internet Workgroup Hub

The Internet Workgroup Hub (IWH) lets you connect up to six computers while giving your entire network easy access to the Internet. You can uplink the IWH to expand the workgroup. The Internet Workgroup Hub functions like a regular hub but comes equipped with a high-speed serial port. It allows multiple users to access the Internet through a local dial-up Internet service provider. The IWH requires a single modem, telephone line, and ISP account. The Internet Workgroup Hub is ready to run with a Windows 95 LAN, supports any TCP/IP application, and is fully compatible with 56-Kbps modems.

The Internet Workgroup Hub is a reasonable solution for a small LAN with low Internet traffic demands. Its speed will change noticeably as the number of users sharing the connection increases. At any given time, the IWH's Internet speed will be approximately equal to the speed of the modem divided by the number of users. For example, using a 56-Kbps modem, with three users connecting to the Internet simultaneously, each user's speed will be approximately 18.6 Kbps. E-mail connections are good candidates for the use of the IWH; conversely, FTP isn't a very good use of the IWH.

The IWH includes an easy-to-use dialer program that lets network users connect to an ISP, thus bypassing Windows 95's Dial-Up Networking. When users want to access the Internet, they use the IWH's Login program. The program asks for the user name, password, ISP access phone number, and the desired communication speed. When users are ready, they click on the Connect button, and Login begins communicating with the hub. When the IWH detects a user's request for Internet access, it checks whether the modem is online. If it is, the user is connected to the modem, which in turn is already connected to the ISP, and the Internet packets begin flowing. If the modem is not yet connected to the Internet, the hub commands it to dial the ISP, establish a connection, and then allows the Internet packets to begin moving to and from the user's computer.

When the time comes to disconnect from the Internet, users tell the Login program to end the connection with the hub. If the user is the only one currently attached to the hub, the hub hangs up the modem and waits for the next Internet request from the network. If other users are currently on the connection, the hub doesn't hang up the modem; it simply disconnects from the user who wants to end his or her session, and allows remaining users to continue working uninterrupted on the Internet.

To use the Internet Workgroup Hub, you'll need a single-user, dial-up IP account as well as the following information from your ISP to configure Windows 95 TCP/IP.

- ISP's PPP dial-up phone number
- User name and password
- ISP's gateway and DNS IP addresses

Hardware Setup

Every computer should have an installed network adapter card, and each PC will require its own 10BaseT network cable in order to connect to the hub. Make sure it's the standard straight-through 10BaseT twisted-pair cabling with RJ-45 connectors. You'll need an external modem, serial cable, and standard analog telephone line. The serial cable is a nine-pin going into the IWH.

1. With network adapter cards installed and 10BaseT cabling in place, power off all of your PCs and any other computer devices.

2. Place the IWH near a telephone line and a power outlet.

3. Connect your external modem to the IWH's serial port with a serial cable.

4. Connect your modem to your telephone line, plug in your modem's power adapter, then turn on your modem.

5. Plug in the IWH; turn the unit on by pressing the Power button on the back. The IWH will power up. The LED indicators on the front of the IWH will cycle through a series of diagnostic tests, then remain in a ready state.

6. Connect your computer to the hub with your 10BaseT cables.

7. After connecting your cables to the hub, power up your computers. As each computer powers up, you'll see the IWH-appropriate port LED light up to indicate that a PC has been detected on the port's network cable. At this stage, your hardware setup is complete.

Configuring TCP/IP in Windows 95 for IWH

To use the IWH, you must install the Microsoft TCP/IP stack on each machine you connect to the unit that you want to access the Internet. With the TCP/IP entry in the Network dialog box Components list, you're ready to configure your TCP/IP protocol to work with the IWH. Do the following for each PC on your LAN to configure the TCP/IP stack in Windows 95 to work with the IWH.

1. Select the TCP/IP protocol bound to your Ethernet card in the Network dialog box Components list; click on Properties. The TCP/IP Properties dialog box appears.

2. Click on the IP Address tab and select the Specify an IP Address setting.

3. Enter a private IP address for your computer. The IP address must include the prefix 168.254.X.Y, where X and Y are any number you choose. For example, you might use 168.254.123.10, 168.254.123.11, and 168.254 .123.12 for computers on your LAN.

Any other PC on the network must not use the X and Y values you enter for a computer. And every computer on your LAN will use the 168.254 prefix, because this is the Internet Workgroup Hub's network address and it never changes. Also, don't use 128, 255, or 0 (by itself) for any of your IP values.

4. Enter the Subnet Mask Address of 255.255.0.0.

5. Click on the Gateway tab and enter your ISP's gateway IP address. After entering the IP address, click on the Add button.

6. Click on the DNS tab, and do the following:

   Click on the Enable DNS setting.

   Enter the name of your computer in the host field. Use a single name or word.

   Enter the Domain name of your ISP.

   Enter the DNS server IP addresses for your ISP in the DNS Server Search Order field and click on the Add button.

7. Click OK to close the TCP/IP dialog box, then click OK again to close the Network dialog box. When prompted by Windows 95 to restart your computer, click Yes. Your TCP/IP setting become active.

Setting Up the IWH Software

Installing and setting up the IWH software is done using a friendly wizard. Make sure you install and configure TCP/IP in Windows 95 before running the IWH's Setup program.

1. Insert the Internet Workgroup Hub disk into drive A, then choose Start|Run. Type in A:\SETUP and click OK.

2. Click Next twice to begin copying files to the default directory. Files are copied to the directory.

3. Choose Start|Programs|Internet Hub to display the Internet Workgroup Hub window (Figure 10.2).

4. Enter the telephone number to access your ISP, your user name, your password, and the baud rate of your modem in the appropriate fields.

When you click on the Connect button in the Internet Workgroup Hub window, the Login program dials your ISP, sends the user name and password, and the connection is made. You're now ready to execute any TCP/IP program to begin

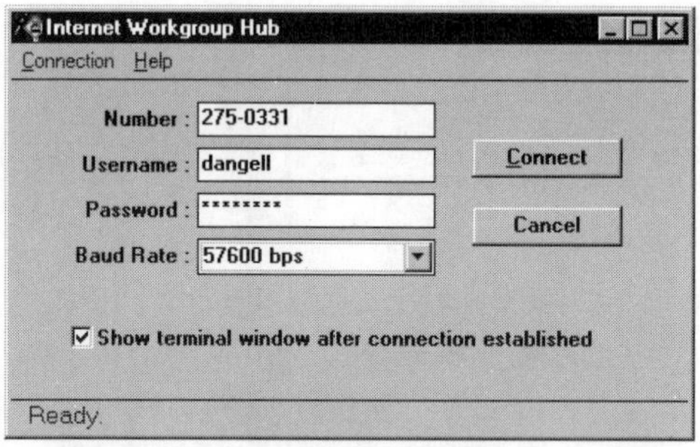

Figure 10.2 *The Internet Workgroup Hub window.*

working on the Internet. The Internet Workgroup Hub window is minimized to the taskbar.

• •

CAUTION: Do not close the Login program window during your Internet session or you will lose your Internet connection. Minimize the window to get it out of the way for working with your TCP/IP applications.

In most cases, you don't need to activate the Show terminal window after connection established setting in the Internet Workgroup window. However, if your ISP doesn't support automatic login, you should activate this setting to display a terminal window (Figure 10.3) to manually enter your user name and password at the prompts. After you have logged in, press the F7 key, which notifies the Login program that you have logged in successfully.

To end a session, click on the Disconnect button or choose Connect|Disconnect. A dialog box prompts you to confirm the disconnection; click OK.

Upgrading the IWH's Firmware

The Internet Workgroup Hub uses firmware based on Flash Memory EEPROM (Electrically Erasable Programmable Read-Only Memory), which means its features can be upgraded with software. Using special software, the information in the IWH's chip can be upgraded or revised as new features are added to the hub. These software upgrades are available via the LINKSYS Web site. You can update your IWH in a few minutes following the instructions included with the firmware upgrades as they are made available. Check the LINKSYS site from time to time for new updates.

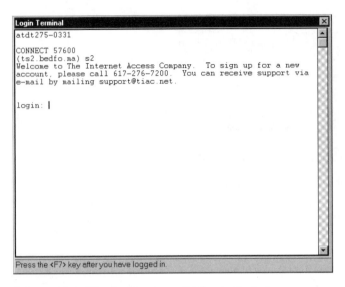

Figure 10.3 *The Login program's Terminal window.*

What's Next

Certainly, 56-Kbps modems are nice, but combining three of them is even better. The next chapter takes you into the world of new modem bonding technology embodied in a product from Ramp Networks called the WebRamp M3.

11 *Bonding Modem Connections with the WebRamp M3*

I magine harnessing the combined power of three 56-Kbps modems into a single high-bandwidth connection that can achieve downstream speeds of up to 168 Kbps. This is exactly what the WebRamp M3 can do for your Windows 95 LAN-to-Internet connections. The WebRamp M3 also includes a router and four-port hub to make this high-bandwidth link to a Windows 95 LAN. This chapter explains this exciting connectivity option.

About the WebRamp M3

Ramp Networks' WebRamp M3 is an analog router and multiplexor device that supports up to three external modems from 14 Kbps to 56 Kbps. The WebRamp M3 sells for $439. For the maximum bandwidth, the WebRamp M3 can combine up to three 56-Kbps modems to produce an Internet connection up to the theoretical bandwidth capacity of 168 Kbps downstream. In reality, you're connection speed will most likely be in the 120+ range. You can connect either x2 or K56flex modems; you can even recycle your older 28.8/33.6-Kbps modems with newer 56-Kbps modems to bring them back into the connectivity fold.

The WebRamp M3 integrates a router, a four-port hub and three serial ports for modem connections using standard analog telephone lines to the Internet. Using a technology called *multiplexing*, the M3 can combine the bandwidths of up to three modems to deliver a single high-speed connection. You need one external modem, one POTS line, and one Internet access account for each modem that you want to connect to the WebRamp M3. However, it's not necessary to have three different dial-up Internet accounts. One account can be used but it requires a different billing plan from your ISP, which many don't offer at this stage. If your office already is using two or three modems for individual PCs, you can consolidate them into a higher-bandwidth solution for your entire office. This allows you to leverage the cost of the connection over all the PCs on your LAN. The Web-Ramp M3 manages your bandwidth more effectively; and you can automatically add more modem connections on the fly as your LANs Internet traffic increases.

The WebRamp M3's built-in router incorporates DHCP and NAT functionality to allow your LAN to share dynamic IP Internet access accounts. The Web-Ramp M3 can also be implemented in a Windows 95 LAN using static IP addresses, whereby an IP address is assigned to each PC on your LAN. Using the WebRamp M3 bypasses the Windows 95 Dial-Up Networking facility. Instead, when a user on your LAN double-clicks on any TCP/IP application, the Web-Ramp M3 router function detects the TCP/IP packets and automatically makes the Internet connection.

Note, however, that in many areas, three POTS Internet access accounts will still be a cheaper alternative than using ISDN service. The standard telephone line access to the Internet is the cheapest way to connect to the Internet. Each additional line typically costs around $20 a month and each additional ISP dial-up account costs around $20 a month. That's $40 a month. Combining three modems translates to around $120 a month for a potential bandwidth of 168 Kbps downstream. For local Internet access, there are usually no additional telephone company usage charges. An ISDN line—in many areas—with its higher telephone usage can easily add up to a $100 a month just for telephone line usage costs. On top of the ISDN line cost is the higher-priced ISDN Internet access account that typically runs in the $40 a month range. Of course, you need to do your own economic analysis with other available bandwidth options to determine whether the WebRamp M3 solution is justified for your location.

Note: Using third-party Internet faxing software and the WebRamp M3, you can fax documents directly from your desktop without using a fax/modem. Ramp Networks recommends using either FaxStorm from NetCentric (http://www.faxstorm.com/) or FaxLauncher from faxSAV (http://www.faxsav.com/).

Getting Started with the WebRamp M3

Before you begin working with the WebRamp M3, you'll need to do the following:

- Order three dial-up PPP Internet access accounts, or have at least one account established to use the WebRamp M3.

- Make sure you have three external modems and their corresponding POTS lines; or have at least one modem from 14.4 Kbps to 56 Kbps. Remember, each modem must be attached to a separate POTS line.

- Set up the WebRamp M3 as your LAN hub and connect your external modem(s) to the unit.

- Set up your Windows 95 LAN for dynamic IP addressing by configuring the Windows 95 TCP/IP Properties for each PC.

Ordering Internet Service

The WebRamp M3 works with dynamic IP Internet access accounts as well as static IP accounts or mixed dynamic and static IP accounts. The dynamic IP addressing scheme is used by most ISPs for analog dial-up accounts. You need only one modem and Internet access account to get started. Just remember: For every modem you connect to the WebRamp M3, you need a single-user PPP Internet access account and separate POTS line. After you establish your Internet access account(s), you'll need the following information from your ISP for each account:

- ISP's dial-in telephone number
- User name and password for logging in
- Domain name
- Domain Name Server (DNS) IP addresses

Choosing Modems

The WebRamp M3 supports the use of most popular modems (14.4 Kbps, 28.8 Kbps, 33.6 Kbps, and 56 Kbps) from these leading modem manufacturers.

Boca Research
Diamond Multimedia
Global Village
Hayes
Maxtech
Motorola
Multi-Tech
U.S. Robotics
Zoom

If your modem manufacturer is not one of those listed, you can choose the Standard option in the WebRamp M3 configuration program to use the modem; for example, if you're using a Cardinal modem.

Setting Up the WebRamp M3

The WebRamp M3 can be installed in any convenient location, such as on a table or mounted on a wall. Connect the 10BaseT Ethernet cables from each PC on your LAN to the 10BaseT ports on the back of the M3. Plug in the power adapter. Because the M3 acts as your LAN's hub, it doesn't have a power switch; this prevents it from being turned off, which would disable your LAN. The 10BaseT hub function of the WebRamp M3 operates without any configuration. Once you get the hub running, you can add your external modems to the M3 using standard RS-232 cables.

You can convert the 10BaseT port labeled 1 to accept an uplink from another hub to expand your LAN. Underneath the WebRamp unit is a switch for changing the port to an uplink port. You'll need a small screwdriver or paper clip to change the switch.

Connecting external modems to the WebRamp M3 is easy. Connect the serial modem cable from the first modem to the Modem 1 port on the M3. Modems 2 and 3 are connected to the Modem 2 and Modem 3 ports. The modem ports at the back of the WebRamp M3 are nine-pin females, so make sure you have the right RS-232 cables for each modem. You connect the telephone line from the wall jack for each modem.

Setting Up Your Windows 95 LAN for a Dynamic IP

Before you configure the WebRamp M3 software, you must set up your LAN by configuring each Windows 95 PC. On the Windows 95 side of your LAN, make sure you have TCP/IP installed on each PC and bound to the network adapter card used for your TCP/IP connection to the Internet. For using the WebRamp with a dynamic IP address Internet access account, make sure to use the default TCP/IP settings. In the Network control panel, select the TCP/IP-> [*network adapter name*] in the installed network components list, then click Properties. The Obtain an IP address automatically setting should be selected in the IP Address tab. Every computer on your Windows 95 LAN should be configured this way.

Note: The Chapter 8 section titled "Configuring Your Windows 95 LAN for Internet Access" explains this configuration process in more detail, if you need more help.

Configuring the WebRamp M3

Before you can configure the WebRamp M3, select the PC on your LAN that you intend to use to configure the unit. For this computer, you need to specify an IP address of 192.168.1.254 and a subnet mask of 255.255.255.0 in the TCP/IP Properties dialog box IP Address tab. In the Gateway tab, enter the IP address for the WebRamp M3 IP address 192.168.1.1. Click OK twice to exit the Network dialog box and restart Windows 95. You need to do this whenever you want to configure the WebRamp M3. After you're finished, choose the Obtain an address automatically setting.

You configure the WebRamp M3 using a Web browser via your Windows 95 LAN. You can use any Web browser. (The WebRamp M3 comes with an older version of Microsoft's Internet Explorer in case you don't have one.) You first configure the modem connected to the Modem 1 port, and then configure each additional modem along with the WebRamp M3's multiplexing features.

Configuring the First Modem

Configuring the first modem is performed using a Web-based wizard that walks you through several Web page forms. Here's how to configure the WebRamp M3 for the first modem.

1. Launch your Web browser; enter **http://192.168.1.1** in the URL address field, then press Enter. The M3 Configuration page appears (Figure 11.1).

TIP: You may want to save the M3 Configuration page as a bookmark for future access.

---

2. Click on the Wizard link to display the opening WebRamp Wiz page; verify your modem is turned on and connected to the WebRamp, then click Next. The Modem Connection page appears (Figure 11.2).
3. Select the modem manufacturer and maximum modem speed. If your modem is not listed, select Other and enter the modem initialization string from your modem user's guide. Click Next. The Enable DHCP page appears (Figure 11.3).
4. Click the check box to enable DHCP; click Next. The next page confirms the DHCP configuration. Click Next. The Internet Account page appears.
5. Click Next. The ISP Configuration page appears (Figure 11.4).

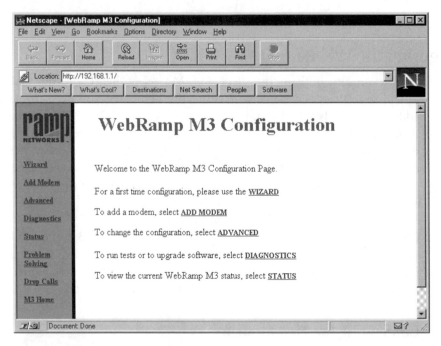

Figure 11.1 *The M3 Configuration page.*

Figure 11.2 *The Modem Connection page.*

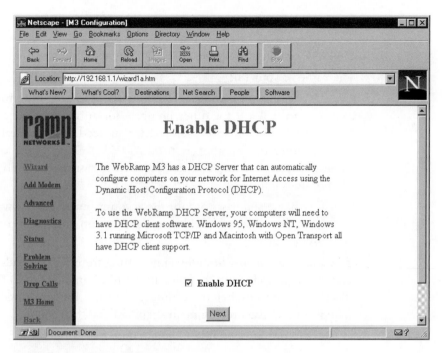

Figure 11.3 *The Enable DHCP page.*

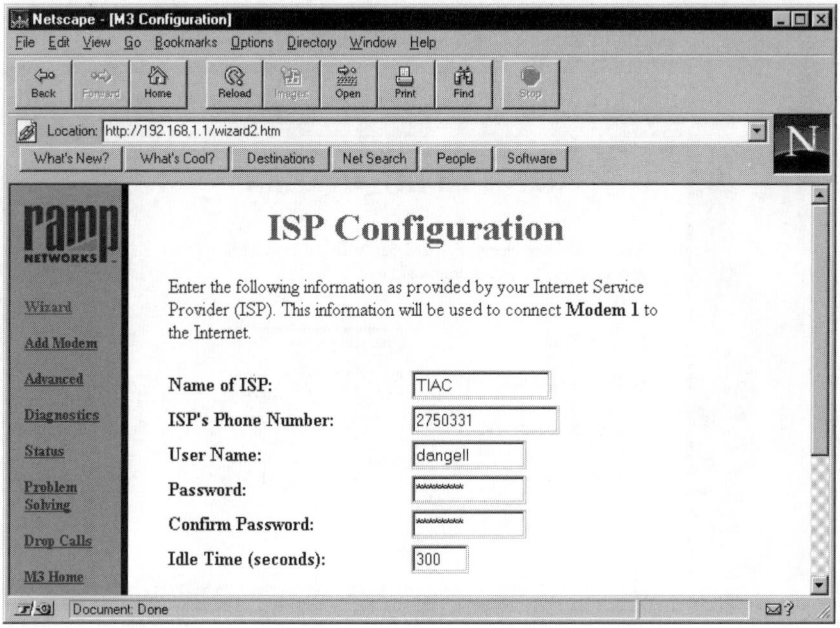

Figure 11.4 *The ISP Configuration page.*

6. In the ISP Configuration page, enter the following information.

The name of your ISP.

The ISP's phone number, exactly as you dial it to access the Internet. If you need to dial a 9 (or other number) for an outside line, enter the number as 9,275-0331, for example. If you need to disable call-waiting features, enter the number as ★70,275-0331. Check with your telephone company for the sequence required to disable call waiting if ★70 or 1170 does not work.

Your user name and password for the account. Enter the password again in the Confirm Password field to make sure you entered it correctly in the Password field.

If you want to change the Idle Time setting from 300 seconds to a different time period, enter the value in the Idle Time (seconds) field. The idle time is the number of seconds before the modem disconnects if there is no activity. I recommend keeping the default value.

7. Click Next to display the DNS Configuration page (Figure 11.5).

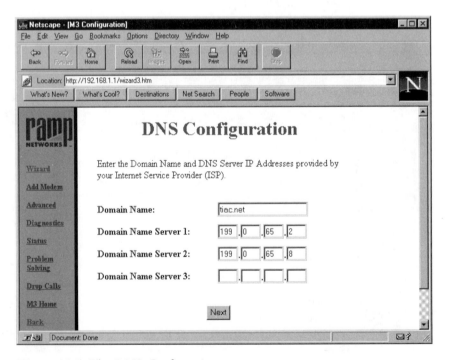

Figure 11.5 *The DNS Configuration page.*

8. Enter the Domain Name and Domain Name Server IP addresses provided by your ISP. The only required field is Domain Name Server 1. Domain Name and Domain Name Server 2 and 3 are optional.

9. Click Next. The next page confirms the DNS configuration.

10. Click Next. The final configuration page appears. Do one of the following:

   Click Register Now to access the Ramp Networks Web site and register your WebRamp M3; follow the instructions on the registration page, then reboot your computer.

   Click Finish to end your configuration session and reboot your system.

• •

CAUTION: You must reboot your PC before the changes will take effect.

Adding Other Modems

To add additional modems to the WebRamp M3, attach each modem to the back of the M3. Configure the WebRamp M3 for each modem and to handle multiplexing. You can instruct M3 to dynamically activate the second and third modems as network traffic demands or have the M3 automatically activate all the modems anytime a user activates a TCP/IP application. The following steps explain adding other modems to the M3 and configuring them for multiplexing.

1. Launch your Web browser, then enter **http://192.168.1.1** in the URL address field; press Enter to access the M3 Configuration page (see Figure 11.1).

2. Click on Add Modem. The Add a New Modem page appears (Figure 11.6).

3. Click on Modem 2. The Modem Connection page appears (see Figure 11.2).

4. Select the modem manufacturer and maximum modem speed. If your modem is not listed, select Other and enter the modem initialization string from your modem user's guide. Click Next. The ISP Configuration page appears (see Figure 11.4).

5. In the ISP Configuration page, enter the following information:

   The name of your ISP.

   The ISP's phone number, exactly as you dial it to access the Internet. If you need to dial a 9 (or other number) for an outside line, enter the number as 9,275-0331, for example. If you need to disable call-waiting

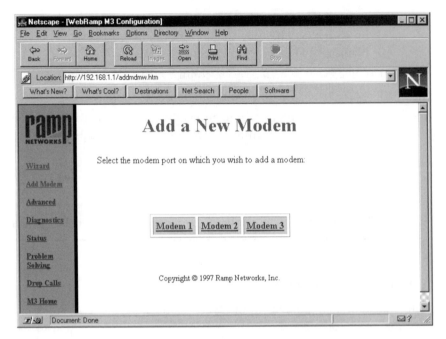

Figure 11.6 *The Add a New Modem page.*

features, enter the number as ★70,275-0331. Check with your telephone company for the sequence to use to disable call waiting if ★70 or 1170 does not work.

Your user name and password for the account. Enter the password again in the Confirm Password field to make sure you entered it correctly in the Password field.

If you want to change the Idle Time setting from 300 seconds to a different time period, enter the value in the Idle Time (seconds) field. The idle time is the number of seconds before the modem disconnects if there is no activity. I recommend keeping the default value.

6. Click Next to display the Modem Multiplexing page (Figure 11.7).

7. In the Modem Multiplexing page, choose either the Always use all Modems or the Dynamically use second and third modems when required setting; click Next.

The Use Only One Modem setting is for those using the Modem 1 port only.

The Always use all Modems setting tells the WebRamp M3 to automatically dial all the modems simultaneously.

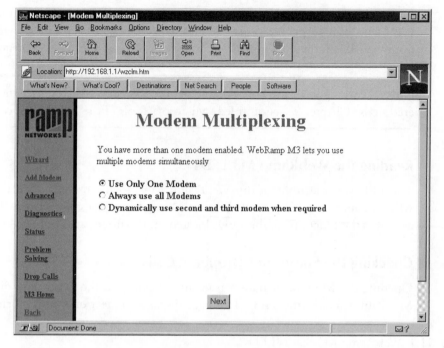

Figure 11.7 *The Modem Multiplexing page.*

The Dynamically use second and third modems when required setting tells the WebRamp M3 to use the second and third modem dynamically as Internet traffic increases on your LAN.

8. When your additional modem has been successfully configured, click Finish to return to the WebRamp M3 Configuration page.

9. Repeat Steps 2 through 8 for the third modem.

Making the Internet Connection

As noted earlier, using the WebRamp M3 bypasses setting up each modem in Windows 95 and using Dial-Up Networking. Once the WebRamp M3 is set up, you're ready to access the Internet using any TCP/IP application on any computer connected to your Windows 95 LAN. To surf the Web from any computer connected to the WebRamp, simply double-click on the Web browser icon. For example, clicking on Internet Explorer on your Windows 95 desktop automatically makes the Internet connection and then displays your starting page.

To use e-mail or network news, you need to configure your e-mail and network newsreader programs. This involves specifying the e-mail and network news server addresses supplied by your ISP. For each Internet e-mail user on your local LAN who wants a private e-mail address, you will need a separate e-mail account from your ISP. Individual e-mail accounts typically cost about $10 per month.

Note: Working with the core complement of Windows 95 Internet tools is covered in the Chapter 9 section titled "Microsoft Tools of the Remote Access Trade."

Reading the WebRamp M3 LEDs

The LEDs on the front of the WebRamp M3 provide useful information about what is going on with your WebRamp M3 and Internet connections. Table 11.1 describes the functions of the LEDs located on the front panel of the M3.

Checking the Status and Dropping Calls

Opening the M3 Configuration page and clicking on the Status link displays the M3 Status page (Figure 11.8). This page displays connection status information for

Table 11.1 WebRamp M3 Status LEDs

LED	STATUS INFORMATION
Power	Solid green if on. Dark indicates power off.
DIAG	Solid amber if hardware diagnostics fail. Solid green if system is okay (should appear 20 seconds after startup). During startup, Amber is normal.
Ethernet Ports	Solid green if properly connected to a computer or hub that is on. Dark if not connected.
Collisions	Amber flash indicates Ethernet packet collision. Collisions indicate that amount of data traffic on your network is very heavy. A computer on your network with a bad Ethernet card can also cause collisions.
Modem 1, Modem 2, Modem 3	Solid green if modem has a live connection to remote. Solid amber if modem initialization failed on the last attempt. Amber flash if sending/receiving data. Dark if modem is not in use. Amber flashing in a sequence indicates that Internet access has been set to block.

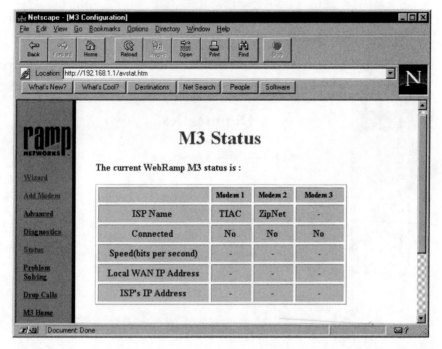

Figure 11.8 *The M3 Status page.*

every modem. Clicking on the Drop Calls link displays the Drop Calls page. Clicking on the Apply button disconnects any modem connections.

WebRamp M3 Diagnostics

Clicking on the Diagnostics link in the WebRamp M3 Configuration displays the Diagnostics page (Figure 11.9). The options on this page are used to test common functions and to reset the WebRamp M3. The following describes each of these diagnostic tools.

- *Problem Solving.* This page displays an event log that describes the most recent actions of the WebRamp. You can print the log from your Web browser.

- *Test Modems.* This page lets you do an internal loopback to check the initialization strings for your modems. If the modem is working properly, the M3 displays a message telling you the initialization works for the specified modem.

- *Run Ping Test.* The Ping Test page allows you to check the status of any Internet server by sending "sonar" packets to the IP address. You can use Ping

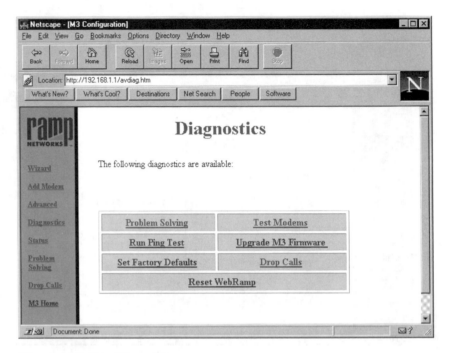

Figure 11.9 *The Diagnostics page.*

to check an ISPs gateway host machine. Enter an IP address and click on the Ping button.

- *Upgrade M3 Firmware.* Use this page to upgrade the WebRamp M3 firmware after a new release of the software is released on the Ramp Networks Web site. All the settings are already in place so you can quickly make the connection and load the software into the WebRamp M3.

- *Set Factory Defaults.* Resets all the WebRamp M3 settings to their original out-of-the-box settings. If you reset your M3 to factory defaults, you must use the Wizard to configure your WebRamp.

- *Drop Calls.* Use this page to disconnect all modem connections.

- *Reset WebRamp.* Use this page to reboot the WebRamp M3.

Advanced Configuration Options

Clicking on the Advanced Configuration link in the WebRamp M3 Configuration page displays the Advanced Configuration page (Figure 11.10). This page is used to add or change modems or ISP information; enable or disable modem mul-

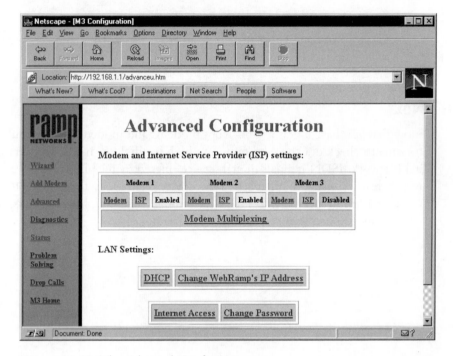

Figure 11.10 *The Advanced Configuration page.*

tiplexing; or modify any selections relating to DHCP. This page is also used for changing the WebRamp's IP address, disabling or enabling Internet access, and changing the password used for configuration.

- *Modem and Internet Service Provider (ISP) settings.* This group of settings lets you make changes to your modem and ISP settings that you specified using the Wizard and the Add Modem pages.

- *Modem Multiplexing.* Lets you change Modem Multiplexing settings with two additional settings. These threshold settings let you specify the time before an additional modem is activated for dynamic connections. The default time is 5 seconds.

- *DHCP.* This page accesses the DHCP Setup page that acts as a gateway to a variety of DHCP management settings. These settings include enabling or disabling DHCP, defining a new range of private IP addresses from the default range, changing DNS server IP addresses, showing the status of current entries in the DHCP table, and changing the default IP address of the WebRamp M3.

- *Change WebRamp's IP Address.* This page lets you change the IP address of the WebRamp M3.

- *Internet Access.* This page lets you block or allow Internet access.
- *Change Password.* This page lets you define a user name and password used to access the WebRamp M3 to configure it.

What's Next

Now that you have a grasp of 56-Kbps modems and modem routers/multiplexors, it's time to check out the next option in high bandwidth, Integrated Services Digital Network. ISDN is an all-digital service offered by telephone companies that in many areas is a viable high-speed connectivity technology for the SOHO market. Chapter 12 introduces you to ISDN technology, including how it works, how you get it, how you configure it, and how you use it.

12 *ISDN Essentials*

ISDN, the Integrated Services Digital Network, is a digital communications service offered by the telephone companies, whose record for delivering this service to the SOHO market has been mixed. Some telephone companies, such as Pacific Bell, have been more aggressive in marketing ISDN service, while others such as US West and NYNEX have been unresponsive to demand for more bandwidth. Overall, telephone companies have been slowly deploying ISDN for the last several years.

In spite of this erratic availability, ISDN enjoys the distinction of being the most widely deployed digital communications link available to the SOHO market. The biggest barrier to ISDN today continues to be pricing. This chapter introduces you to the ISDN realm, including how it works, and the factors involved in getting and using the service. It provides the foundation for the remaining chapters in this part on working with specific ISDN remote access devices.

ISDN Executive Summary

ISDN is the early digital connectivity product from the local telephone companies designed for the SOHO market. Its full name, Integrated Services Digital Network, refers to the fact that various data and voice services can be combined to travel over an ISDN line simultaneously. For example, voice and digital data can travel over the same ISDN line. Because ISDN is part of the ubiquitous telephone system used for regular voice, you can communicate with other ISDN users as well as to people connected to POTS. ISDN enables you to use existing analog devices, such as telephones, faxes, and modems, as well as ISDN equipment for high-speed data connections.

ISDN delivers data communications at a speed of up to 128 Kbps over two B (bearer) channels, each delivering 64 Kbps. With compression, ISDN can deliver up to 512 Kbps. ISDN uses the same telephone wiring as voice-grade service; the difference is the devices at each end of the connection. ISDN is the only symmetrical high-bandwidth option that allows you to download or upload at the full 128 Kbps. As such, it is an attractive bandwidth option for desktop video conferencing and other two-way communications. And because ISDN is a digital connection, it offers better reliability and performance over voice-grade telecommunications.

As just noted, the biggest stumbling block to ISDN use has been the confusing and unreasonably high costs imposed by the telephone companies. ISDN pricing, called tariffs in telephone company lingo, is based on the application of complex cost allocation and recovery rules established by both federal and state regulators. The result is that ISDN tariffs vary from one telephone company to another and from one state to another. For example, Bell South in Alabama charges between $221.75 to $228.75 to install an ISDN line, with a monthly usage charge of $72.35 to $79.35. In bordering Tennessee—Al Gore's home state—ISDN installation costs between $24.40 and $31.40, with a monthly charge of $33 to $40.

The telephone companies thrive in this tariff regulation maze because it allows them to extract more revenue. Your final cost for ISDN service depends on a variety of configuration and usage factors. Although progress is being made in standardizing prices and service packages, ordering the right package of services still remains the most difficult part of establishing an ISDN connection.

Telephone company customer service for ISDN also varies. As mentioned, some telephone companies have been aggressively marketing ISDN services, while others have been slow to implement ISDN service. Your ISDN service experience will be good or bad depending on where you are located and your local telephone company.

ISDN availability also varies from one telephone company to another. ISDN service is dependent on digital switches located at telephone company facilities that service a given area. Because these switches are not deployed, many locales outside metropolitan areas don't offer ISDN service. But even in areas that have digital switches, there are inherent technological barriers to ISDN deployment based on the proximity of your premises to the telephone company's central office facility. Still, ISDN is the most widely deployed digital form of data communications available to the SOHO market. And given the long lead times for deploying more powerful bandwidth options, such as cable and xDSL service, ISDN may be a viable option for at least the next few years.

In spite of ISDN's warts, it's still a serious option for many SOHO users. Because ISDN is a relatively mature data communications medium, it has a number of standards in place. Many of the early incompatibility problems of ISDN service and equipment have been solved. The result has been a cornucopia of affordable and powerful ISDN remote access devices designed for the SOHO market. ISDN equipment vendors from the ranks of the PC industry have had a tremendous impact on ISDN remote access options and service delivery. Many ISDN equipment vendors offer free customer assistance; they will order your ISDN service for you and provide help through the entire process of getting your ISDN connection via your local telephone company. The latest generation of ISDN remote access devices (called customer premises equipment in telco lingo) are easier to use, less expensive, and more powerful than their predecessors. ISDN remote access products range from $149 for ISDN adapter cards to $899 for a full-featured router for connecting a LAN to the Net.

Microsoft has also made working with ISDN in Windows 95 easier with support for the Multilink Protocol (MP) standard, which allows Internet access via ISDN at the full 128 Kbps. And because Windows 95 makes networking easy, it provides a great platform for connecting a LAN via ISDN to the Internet or other networks.

Meet the ISDN System

Using ISDN as a dial-up service uses the same telecommunications network used for analog communications. While ISDN uses the same public-switched network used for POTS, there are a number of unique elements associated with the delivery of ISDN service. If you are going to use ISDN service, it is essential to understand the architecture of the ISDN system because it defines the what, where, and how of ISDN service. The following sections explain the working of the ISDN network from the telephone company side.

COs and Local Loops

The central office (CO) of a local telephone company facility is the hub of switches and wiring for all telephone system subscribers. The wiring for ISDN from the CO to your home or business, the local loop, is of the same copper wires used for POTS. The maximum length of a local loop for ISDN is approximately 18,000 feet, using standard POTS lines without any repeaters. A repeater is a device that amplifies or regenerates the data signal to extend the distance of its transmission. This limitation is one of the main reasons why ISDN service may not be available to your specific location, even if your local CO is equipped with switches that can handle ISDN service. If your telephone company employs repeaters on the line, the limit can be extended well beyond 18,000 feet. Some telephone companies offer an extended reach for a price, while others don't.

Teleco Switches and ISDN

ISDN service is a circuit-switching system, which means that the communications pathway remains fixed and is not available to other users for the duration of the call. This is the same type of system used for POTS connections. When the calling party initiates the call, a set-up procedure tells the network the address (telephone number) of the calling party and sets up the route for the call to the recipient's telephone number.

A switch in telecommunications refers to facilities that route telephone traffic from one destination to another. Electronic switching software operating on computers provides the basis for today's telecommunications infrastructure. These digital switches provide the routing for telecommunications services as well as manage other parts of the telephone system, such as metering toll charges and providing call management features including call waiting and call forwarding. The telephone companies operate a hierarchy of switching links depending on the call. At the local level, a call can be completed within a single switch at the CO. Beyond the local exchange calls, there are switches for routing calls locally through different exchanges and switches for long-distance connections.

The leading digital circuit switches used by the telephone companies are AT&T's 5ESS (Electronic Switching System), Nortel's DMS-100, and Siemmens' EWSD. The AT&T and Nortel switches dominate the telecommunications industry. For ISDN service, the AT&T 5ESS and Nortel DMS-100 switches use either their own custom software or a standards-based software referred to as National ISDN (NI), which was developed to standardize the services.

Note: You'll see references to telephone switches in all ISDN equipment documentation because different switches support different services and capabilities. Your ISDN equipment will include specific configuration settings for each type of switch platform.

You Need Your Own Power

Your regular telephone line requires electrical power to operate. For POTS service, the telephone company provides the power for the line as part of the service. Even when a storm knocks out your electrical power, for example, in most cases, your telephone service remains active. An ISDN line is not powered by the telephone company, so subscribers are responsible for providing the power for the line when in use. Fortunately, the power demands of an ISDN line between the CO and your premises are minimal and are maintained on your line only when you're using it. The power for an ISDN is typically provided as part of your ISDN remote access device, which can be an adapter card in your PC.

The Basic Rate Interface

In the lingo of networking, an access interface is the physical connection between you and the network. There are two forms of ISDN access: *basic rate interface* (BRI) and *primary rate interface* (PRI). PRI is the wholesale version of ISDN service. It delivers 23 64-Kbps B (bearer) channels and one 64-Kbps D (data) channel. PRI is referred to as 23B+D. PRI service is typically used by an ISP or large organization to handle incoming BRI connections.

The BRI is the retail version of ISDN service. For BRI service, the telephone company divides the standard twisted-pair copper wiring between the CO and your premises into three separate channels. The three channels of a BRI connection include two 64-Kbps B channels and one 16-Kbps D channel. This standard BRI configuration is commonly referred to as 2B+D. The B channels deliver the voice and data communications. These two B channels combined define the maximum ISDN connection speed of 128 Kbps (without compression). You can use each B channel as a separate channel or combine them for full-speed data communications.

The D channel is primarily used for the signaling information, to manage what's going on in the B channels. It delivers the instructions that tell what to do with the data that's being delivered on the B channels to the telephone company switches and equipment at your end. This signaling also opens and closes circuit switches to route calls. The expanded capacity of the D channel in ISDN allows for more powerful voice communication capabilities than POTS.

Note: A new technology called Always On/Dynamic ISDN (AO/DI) enables the D channel to become a permanent connection between an ISDN user and the telephone company. This 9.6-Kbps channel can be used to send low bandwidth data, such as e-mail, without making a B channel connection, which can save usage charges. However, it remains to be seen whether the telephone companies will embrace this technology. In the meantime, many ISDN equipment vendors plan to add AO/DI as a feature to their products.

An analog line must send the instruction in the same channel you use for voice; thus the reason for touch-tone signals. All the intelligence for extra calling services, such as call waiting, call forwarding, and other services are operated from the telephone company switch in POTS. With ISDN, the functionality of these types of service is offloaded from the telephone switch (with configuration set up at the time of ordering your ISDN service) to a device at your premises designed to handle these calling features. An ISDN telephone is such a device.

Signaling and Your True Bandwidth

In ISDN service, the use of the D channel for handling the signaling is referred to as *out-of-band signaling;* that is, the information used to control the connection is sent on a channel separate from the one used to deliver the actual data being transmitted. Because most local telephone companies have not implemented out-of-band signaling connections to and from the long-distance company switches, many long-distance ISDN calls combine the D-channel signaling into the B channels. The result is that each B channel is robbed of 8 Kbps (one-half of the 16-Kbps D channel) as the D channel is combined with the B channels. The result is a real capacity of 56 Kbps for each B channel, or a combined 112 Kbps. Because a B channel can potentially be transmitting data at either 56 Kbps or 64 Kbps, most ISDN equipment supports both levels of data transmission automatically.

Note: Most ISDN remote access devices support data communications at either 56K or 64K.

ISDN Functions and Reference Points

There is a core group of protocols that defines the functional components that combine to make a fully operational ISDN connection. These protocols specify the types of logical devices used in an ISDN connection. The communications between these functional devices are called *reference points* or *interfaces.* The important thing to remember about functional devices and interfaces is that they are protocol definitions that specify the functionality a particular piece of ISDN equipment can handle. These protocols become embodied in ISDN equipment in a variety of configurations.

As a consumer of ISDN remote access equipment, you need to understand the role of functional devices and interfaces to make sure you're getting the right equipment for your needs. Figure 12.1 shows the complete layout of an ISDN connection's functional devices and reference points.

End of the Line with NT1

The network terminator 1 device called NT1 represents the boundary between the ISDN system and the end-user's equipment. NT1 includes the physical and

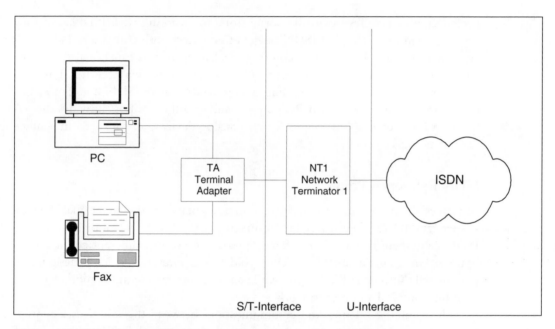

Figure 12.1 The functional devices and reference points of an ISDN connection.

electrical termination point of the ISDN service coming from the telephone company into your premises. The NT1 is also the functional device that provides an interface between the twisted-pair wires used by the telephone company in delivering BRI service and the four-wire (two-pair) cables used by ISDN equipment. The NT1 also includes the function for powering the ISDN line between your premises and the CO.

Each BRI connection has only one NT1 device that terminates it. The NT1 device is typically embodied in the ISDN remote access device. However, the NT1 function can also be embodied in a standalone device for purposes of working with more than one ISDN device. In the United States, the FCC mandates that the consumer is responsible for supplying the NT1 device, not the telephone company. In most of the world, the NT1 function, in the form of a small device at the termination of the ISDN line, is provided and maintained by the telephone company.

Terminal Adapters

The functional device called a terminal adapter (TA) allows any non-ISDN-ready device to work over an ISDN connection. Because most computers and networking systems as well as analog devices are not ISDN-ready, they need to be connected via the TA. TAs form the cornerstone for working with ISDN, and they are embodied in a variety of ISDN devices to connect both computers and analog equipment to ISDN. The most common packaging of this functional device for remote access is a TA to handle your PC communications via Ethernet, bus, or a serial port, as well as TAs for handling analog devices on an ISDN line. For example, an ISDN router with two POTS ports and an Ethernet port provides the TA function for your LAN as well as for two analog devices, all packaged in a single unit along with the NT1.

ISDN Reference Points

Interfaces define the communication functions between the functional devices. Understanding the key interfaces connected with ISDN is important because ISDN equipment is offered in different interface flavors for different configuration options. For example, an ISDN device sold as a U interface device is designed to plug directly into your ISDN line, while an S/T interface requires another device with built-in NT1 in order to work.

The S interface defines the communications between the ISDN user's equipment functional devices (TAs) and the network terminator 1 (NT1) device. The T interface is an interface between a local ISDN switching device and the local loop NT1 device. The T interface isn't used in the SOHO market because it's implemented in conjunction with Private Branch eXchange (PBX) systems, which are in-house telephone switching devices for large-enterprise telephone networks. Most ISDN vendors package both the S and T interfaces as a single functional device. As such, ISDN equipment designed to work with separate NT1 devices are referred to as S/T interface devices.

The U interface is the point at which the local telephone company network arrives at your doorstep, up to and including the NT1 functional device. ISDN devices that terminate the U interface with network termination can be plugged directly into an ISDN line. A U interface device can include ports for S/T-interface devices and analog ports. Many ISDN vendors offer equipment in S/T-interface or U-interface models, although the U-interface models are the most common. Just remember that an S/T-interface model will require an NT1 device to work with your ISDN line, while the U-interface device does not. As you'll learn later, there are reasons for using an S/T-interface remote access device instead of a U-interface device.

ISDN Standards

Interoperability means related devices from different vendors can work together. In the analog communications world, using a modem from one vendor to connect to a modem from another works because of standards that all the modem manufacturers follow. There are several ISDN-related protocols that establish interoperability across different vendors' ISDN equipment.

Multilink Protocol for Internet Access

In the Internet access area, the Multilink Protocol (MP) supports PPP over two B channels and allows different vendors' remote access products to work with each other. The MP standard has been universally adopted by ISDN equipment vendors. MP has been adopted by the Internet Engineering Task Force (IETF), a worldwide group that has responsibility for developing the technical protocols for the Internet.

Note: The Microsoft ISDN Accelerator Pack 1.1 enables Windows 95 to use MP.

Rate Adaptation

V.120 is a standard of the ITU (International Telecommunications Union) that governs what a system should do when the data rates offered by ISDN can't be matched by the device. To make this happen, bits must be added to the transmission to make a lower stream of say 19.2 Kbps from your PV serial port fit into a 64-Kbps B channel. V.120 allows multiplexing of B channels on ISDN. It's widely used in North America as the method of adapting the rate of an asynchronous serial port on a computer to ISDN.

Bandwidth-on-Demand Power

Bonding stands for Bandwidth ON Demand INteroperability Group, which is a method for combining multiple channels to form a single channel. For ISDN, bonding allows the two B channels to be combined into a 128-Kbps transmission for the same application. Combining multiple B channels allows more data to flow over an ISDN connection. Applications such as file transfers and video conferencing depend on bonding. Bonding is embodied in remote access devices.

H.320 and T.120 for Video Conferencing

Desktop video conferencing products are also based on two key standards. The ITU's H.320 standard provides the basis for interoperation of different video conferencing systems. The ITU's T.120 general multimedia conferencing standard is designed for interoperability that enables real-time annotation, file transfers, share applications, and fax exchange within the context of video conferencing systems. For video conferencing over TCP/IP (the Internet) and LANs, the ITU H.323 and H.324 standards will most likely be implemented in ISDN video conferencing systems in the near future.

Getting Started with ISDN

Establishing an ISDN connection doesn't follow the same approach you typically use in getting a POTS connection. For ISDN, you need to figure out specifically which devices you plan to use on your line before you actually order your ISDN service. You'll also need to know the type of switch used by the telephone company, which configurations you need for the B channels, and other ISDN line configuration options. The following sections explain the essential ISDN service configuration requirements.

Checking ISDN Availability

Before you can start down the ISDN road, make sure there is an ISDN path to your door. If there isn't a switch at the local central office that supports ISDN service, or your premises are outside the radius of ISDN service from a CO, you're out of luck. One way or another, you must check with your local telephone company to confirm that ISDN service is available to your premises. Some telephone companies have this information available in databases and can tell you right away. Others must perform a loop qualification, whereby the telephone company checks your local loop to see whether it supports ISDN; this process can take days to complete.

TIP: Many ISDN remote access device manufacturers offer free ISDN ordering services that will check the availability of ISDN service in your area. See "Using Third-Party ISDN Ordering Services" later in this chapter.

Getting information about ISDN service availability from telephone companies has improved, but it can still be a hit-or-miss proposition. Most telephone companies now offer ISDN service centers, automated voice systems for checking ISDN availability, and Web sites for checking availability and other information, such as tariffs and provisioning options. Table 12.1 lists telephone numbers and Web URLs for obtaining ISDN information from telephone companies.

Table 12.1 Telephone Company ISDN Service Centers

TELEPHONE COMPANY	INFORMATION SOURCE
Ameritech	24-hour voice and fax-back system: 800-832-6328 Home ISDN service: 800-419-5400 Business ISDN service: 800-417-9888 Web: www.ameritech.com
Bell Atlantic	ISDN InfoSpeed Solutions Center: 800-204-7332 Small businesses: 800-843-2255 TeleProducts: 800-221-0845 Web: www.bell-atl.com
BellSouth	ISDN individual line service: 800-858-9413 Web: www.bell.bellsouth.com
GTE	24-hour, menu-driven voice and fax-back system: 800-888-8799 Voice: 214-718-5608 Web: www.gte.com
NYNEX New England	24-hour, menu-driven voice and fax-back system: 800-438-4736 ISDN Service Center: 800-650-4736 Web: www.nynex.com
NYNEX New York	24-hour, menu-driven voice and fax-back system: 800-438-4736 Voice: 914-644-5152 Web: www.nynex.com
Pacific Bell	24-hour voice and fax-back system: 800-995-0345 ISDN Service Center: 800-472-4736 Web: www.pacbell.com
Southwestern Bell Corporation (SBC)	Austin: 800-792-4736 Dallas: 214-268-1403 South Houston: 713-567-4300 North Houston: 713-537-3930 ISDN DigiLine Service: 800-792-4736, ext 500 Web: www.sbc.com
US West	24-hour voice and fax-back system: 800-728-4929 Voice: 800-246-5226 Web: www.uswest.com

Note: Some RBOCs offer a virtual ISDN service that enables a telephone company to offer ISDN service from a CO that doesn't have the switches to handle ISDN service. The telephone company routes the local loop termination at your local CO to another CO via an internal high-speed data link. Telephone companies may charge you extra for this service.

What Kind of Switch Is Running at the CO?

Most telephone companies have three main types of ISDN switch software options: AT&T 5ESS Custom, AT&T 5ESS NI-1 (National ISDN-1), and NT DMS-100. These switches have different capabilities for handling multiple ISDN devices and other configuration options. Most ISDN remote access devices will work with all ISDN switches, and they include specific configuration information for each of these switches in their documentation.

The importance of the type of switch to which your ISDN line is connected has an impact if you're planning on adding multiple devices to your line. In the case of remote access, this may come into play if you want to use the POTS ports in an ISDN device for a fax machine with its own telephone number. Another example of multiple devices sharing an ISDN line is a desktop video conferencing system with a remote access device. Most ISDN devices support all the leading telco switches and software. The following lists the number of devices supported by each type of switch:

AT&T 5ESS NI-1	8 devices
AT&T Custom	8 devices
NT DMS-100	2 devices

B-Channel Configuration Options

BRI is typically packaged as two B channels and one D channel. However, many telephone companies offer a menu of BRI channel configurations. Your specific ISDN equipment and applications will dictate the configuration of the B channels. BRI channel configuration determines the type of information that is transmitted through each B channel. You determine the channel configurations when you order your ISDN service. If you make any changes, your telephone company will probably charge you a change-order fee. The following are the available channel configuration options:

- *Circuit-switched voice (CSV) only.* This option allows only voice traffic for the B channel. This is a restrictive option that doesn't allow the full bandwidth of the BRI connection because it ties up a B channel for just voice.

- *Circuit-switched data (CSD) only.* This option allows circuit data only for data transmission speeds of up to 64 Kbps, uncompressed for each B channel.
- *Alternate circuit-switched voice/circuit-switched data (CSV/CSD).* This option allows either circuit data or voice communications to be carried over the channel. This channel configuration allows for the most versatile use of an ISDN line.
- *Packet data only.* This option allows for only X.25 packet data. In most cases, you won't use this provisioning option for your BRI configuration.

As you'll learn later in this chapter, most ISDN remote access devices use configuration templates that take care of specific configuration requirements. These ordering codes streamline the ordering process.

Note: Before you order the 2B+D configuration, make sure your Internet service provider or other network can support two B channels. In some areas, you may only be able to connect to the Internet using a single B channel.

What's the Point?

An ISDN line can be configured either as a point-to-point or multipoint line. Point-to-point configuration refers to the operation of one device on an ISDN line. With a point-to-point configuration you get only one phone number, which means you can't add unique calling features to each B channel. You must apply services to the entire line without unique phone numbers assigned to specific devices. Point-to-point on the AT&T Custom switch is the easiest for the telephone company to provide and in many cases is less expensive than a multipoint configuration.

Multipoint configuration refers to the operation of multiple devices on the ISDN line. For example, if you have a telephone and a fax on a multipoint line, the switch delivers the called number as part of the call setup. The correct telephone or fax machine will answer the number because the switch knows which device the number is associated with. Within a multipoint configuration, each switch allows a certain number of devices to be connected to the line, with a maximum of eight. If you're working with multiple ISDN devices that will share your ISDN line, you'll need the multipoint configuration. For example, your PC might have an ISDN adapter card that includes one or two analog ports, or you might want to add another device at a later time. An important criterion for ISDN equipment is to make sure it supports the multipoint protocol, which most do. For a multipoint configuration, you need to use Service Profile IDentifiers (SPIDs) so the device knows its ID in the switch. More on SPIDS later in this chapter.

Supplementary Services

The collection of voice communications features supported by ISDN is referred to as *supplementary services*. These services are an extensive set of defined call-management features you can implement as part of your BRI service. You're already familiar with many of these features from the analog world—call waiting, call forwarding, and conference calling, for example. The total set of supplementary services available at your premises depends on your telephone company and the services available from the central office serving your area. In most cases, your ISDN device will specify any supplementary service the device needs to use for its POTS ports.

ISDN Costs

The total cost of your BRI line depends on a variety of fixed and variable charges, many of which are similar in structure to those of a POTS connection. They include a one-time installation charge, monthly charges, and usage charges. One thing is certain about ISDN service: It typically costs roughly twice as much as POTS; but because ISDN service lets you perform both analog and digital communications on the same line, you may be able to leverage the cost of ISDN service by adding a fax machine to the ISDN line and canceling the POTS line.

• •

CAUTION: Unless your telephone company offers standard POTS calling plans for your ISDN line, be careful about moving outgoing voice and modem communications to your ISDN line. Otherwise, you may find you're paying more to use your ISDN line for analog communications than if you were using a POTS line.

Business or Residential Tariff

As is the case for analog telephone service, ISDN service can be based on a business or a residential tariff. The cost of business telephone service is higher than residential service. Many telephone companies, such as Pacific Telesis, offer residential ISDN telephone rates; others don't. Without a residential tariff rate, the telephone company charges you the more expensive business rate. The residential rate is cheaper not only for installing an ISDN line but also for recurring charges and usage charges.

Installation Costs

It costs an average of about $150 to install an ISDN line. Your exact installation charge depends on your channel configurations, whether you're installing a new line or converting an existing POTS line for ISDN, and any wiring work performed at your premises. Keep in mind that specific costs break down on a state-by-state basis. If the telephone company wires your home or business from the point at which the telephone wire comes into your premises, it will charge you extra. One alternative is to use independent contractors or do the wiring yourself. Remember that ISDN uses the same wiring as for POTS lines. Getting wired for ISDN is explained later in this chapter.

The U interface, or the line the telephone company terminates at your premises, is a two-wire interface, so it uses an RJ-11 jack and cord. This is the standard cabling used by analog telephones. The S/T interface, on the user's side of the NT1, uses the RJ-45 (eight-pin) jack. Most ISDN remote access devices provide a short RJ-45 cord to extend from the NT1 to the equipment. You can plug an RJ-11 connector into an RJ-45 jack.

TIP: Don't let the telephone company installers sell you an RJ-45 jack for ISDN service; you don't need it. All you need is the standard RJ-11 jack, which you can probably install yourself.

Recurring and Usage Charges

ISDN service has a monthly charge, which depends on your BRI configuration. This charge doesn't reflect a variety of other charges that can be added to your monthly bill for other features. In addition to the monthly cost of ISDN service, there are the usage charges. These are the charges that can easily dwarf your monthly cost, depending on where you call on a regular basis. The local telephone company charges you for local calls and the long-distance telephone company bills you for those calls.

ISDN toll charges generally follow the formula used for POTS service, which breaks down the charges according to the time the call is made and the distance of the call. The three standard calling time categories are day, evening, and night. The day rate is the most expensive and the night rate is the least expensive. The toll rates for ISDN are just as complex to figure out as POTS charges; plus, ISDN has additional charges. For example, if you're using both B channels during a connection, you'll be charged twice the published tariff because the two B channels are treated as separate lines.

Internet Access Charges

Getting connected to the Internet requires an ISDN account with an Internet service provider. The cost of the ISP connection is an addition to all the charges for your ISDN line from the telephone company. ISDN Internet access accounts typically cost more than POTS-based accounts. A typical ISDN, single-user access account costs anywhere from $17.95 to $99 a month for a block of free hours (often around 100 hours). Many ISPs also charge a one-time set-up fee. As is the case with POTS accounts, a variety of plans are offered by ISPs. Shop around.

Digital Calls or Data over Voice

Telephone company tariffs are usually cheaper for analog calls than for digital data calls. In some telephone company service areas, you may be charged a flat rate for analog local calls, while digital calls are billed by usage at a higher metered rate. Some ISDN remote access devices let you initiate a call as a voice signal instead of a data signal so that the telephone company switch treats it as a voice call, when in fact it's a data call. The result is that you're charged the lower analog flat rate instead of the higher digital rates. This can save money because, in most cases, your Internet service provider is a local call. As such, the cost of connecting to your ISP falls within the lower POTS pricing. This toll-saver feature is referred to as *data over voice*. If you connect to your Internet provider for more than a few hours, the savings can add up.

Note, however, that this toll-saver feature works only where there are two separate tariffs for analog and ISDN and the service is supported by your ISP. In the case of Pacific Telesis, it charges one metered rate for all calls over ISDN, regardless of the type of call. NYNEX, on the other hand, charges a lower analog rate so that initiating a call as voice will get you the lower rate. However, NYNEX reduces the value of initiating a data call as a voice call by allowing only one B channel to be configured for both voice and data. You must have a B channel configured for both data and voice for this feature to work.

Ordering Your ISDN Service

Order your ISDN service only after you've assembled the information on the devices you plan to use, the BRI channel configurations you want, and any other specifications. Ordering an ISDN connection involves exchanging information with your ISDN provider, and there are several routes you can take to establish your ISDN service.

A growing number of ISDN equipment vendors offer ISDN customer service groups that coordinate the entire process of getting your ISDN service. Likewise, many Internet service providers offer similar services. You can also take the do-it-yourself route by dealing directly with the telephone company using your ISDN equipment documentation as your guide. But no matter who handles your ISDN ordering, only your local telephone company can actually establish your ISDN line and bill you for the service.

Streamlining ISDN Service Ordering

To simplify the process of ordering and configuring your ISDN connection, there are ISDN ordering codes that represent a preestablished set of commonly used ISDN services. A widely used series of ISDN ordering codes are referred to as *Compatibility Packages.* Bellcore, which was the RBOCs research and development organization that developed many of the standards used by ISDN today, developed these codes. Compatibility Package M is one of the most commonly used provisioning templates, and is similar to the Intel Blue product code described in the next paragraph.

Another widely used collection of ordering codes is based on defining the provisioning of an ISDN line around a unique ISDN device. For example, the product code for the Intel ProShare Personal Video Conferencing System 200 is Intel Blue. When you order your ISDN service, you simply tell the telephone company representative Intel Blue or other code name supplied by your vendor, and he or she will know exactly how to provision the line based on that product. This code includes provisioning for voice and data communications.

National ISDN Users' Forum (NIUF) has introduced EZ-ISDN codes designed to make ordering ISDN service easier. These four configuration templates provide preconfigured packages of ISDN services that are very useful for end users or the mass market. The four codes are named EZ-ISDN 1, EZ-ISDN 1A, EZ-ISDN 2, and EZ-ISDN 2A. ISDN equipment vendors can register their equipment as compliant or compatible with these codes.

Note: Most vendors provide detailed configuration information in their documentation, including specific ordering codes. They also provide specific provisioning information for each switch type, in case your telephone company doesn't use any ordering codes.

Using Third-Party ISDN Ordering Services

Many ISDN equipment vendors have set up customer service groups to help customers get up and running with ISDN service. These services typically provide information on setting up ISDN service for your locality, along with information on installation charges and ISDN provisioning. These groups work with the local telephone and long-distance companies on a routine basis.

An example of an ISDN ordering service is U.S Robotics' I-Team. By calling its toll-free number, 888-USR-ISDN, the I-Team will order ISDN service for you through the local telephone company and arrange the scheduling and installation of ISDN service. U.S. Robotics doesn't charge for these services. Many other vendors, including Motorola, 3Com, Diamond Multimedia, and others provide similar services. Check with the vendors of any ISDN remote access device before you buy to see if they provide free ISDN ordering services. Appendix A provides a comprehensive listing of ISDN equipment vendor contact information.

A number of ISDN Internet service providers will also help you set up your ISDN service. Many also sell ISDN remote access devices at discounted prices. Two advantages of going this route is that the ISP will establish your ISDN line and set up your Internet account.

Contacting the Telephone Company Directly

Contacting the telephone company to order ISDN service yourself can be a good or a bad experience, depending on your telephone company—although most telephone companies now have separate ISDN ordering centers staffed with ISDN-literate representatives. One of the best places to start your quest for ISDN service is to check out your telephone company's Web site. More on contacting telephone companies for ISDN service later.

SPIDs

As mentioned briefly earlier, ISDN can support up to eight devices on the same B channel, but no two devices can use a single B channel at the same time. To allow multiple devices to share B channels, the telephone companies use Service Profile IDentifiers (SPIDs). Your telephone company may assign a SPID to each device connected to the ISDN line. One SPID can be assigned to different devices as long as the service type is different. Most notably a data device and an analog device can have the same SPID since they each are looking for a different service, one for data and one for voice. SPIDs let the telephone company switch know which ISDN services a given device can access. A unique SPID is required for every device on a multipoint ISDN line, or for each B channel. The SPIDs for two B channels, for example, might be 50862890210000 and 50862809620000. Typically, a SPID is a telephone number with several digits after it.

Usually, you need to configure the software for an ISDN device to tell it the SPID assigned to it. Multipoint ISDN lines can handle multiple SPIDs. The AT&T 5ESS Custom switch and the AT&T 5ESS National ISDN switch support up to eight SPIDs. The Nortel DMS-100 National ISDN 1 supports only two SPIDs.

Note: All the telephone companies have adopted standards established by the National ISDN Council (NIC) that will totally automate SPID capabilities in network switches by 1998.

Directory Numbers

A directory number (DN) is the telephone number for the ISDN line assigned by the telephone company. Each ISDN line receives at least one directory number, although you may have several directory numbers for each B channel, depending on the switch being used by your telephone company. If the CO switch is an AT&T 5ESS Custom, for instance, you can have one DN for each device; a fax machine, a telephone, and a PC could all use one B channel, but each with a different number. If the CO switch is an NT DMS-100 NI-1, you must have two DNs, one for each B channel.

A typical ISDN remote access device includes POTS ports for connecting analog devices such as telephones, fax machines, and modems. To provision this type of device involves using a multipoint configuration and separate directory numbers for each B channel. These telephone numbers are then shared by the B channel for digital communications, as well as one directory number for each of the two analog devices attached to the POTS ports on the remote access device.

Getting Wired for ISDN

Although ISDN uses the same wiring as that used for POTS, the configurations operate differently. Depending on the type (business or residence) or the location of your premises, there may be certain restrictions on adding a new telephone line. In most cases, business sites don't have any restrictions for bringing in additional lines, but residences located outside metropolitan areas may be restricted to the two lines (most homes in metropolitan areas can install an additional number of lines). The standard single four-wire cable allows for two lines. One line uses the red and green wires and the other line uses the yellow and black wires. Check with your telephone company to see if you can bring in an additional line before deciding whether to convert an existing analog line.

If you have a choice, bring in your ISDN line as a separate line and use just one of the wire pairs; then use a separate wall just for the ISDN line—it makes it easier to install and set up ISDN equipment. If you can't bring in another line at your home, you'll need to convert an existing POTS line to ISDN. Typically, the conversion will involve the telephone company canceling your POTS line and number and replacing it with an ISDN line.

• •

CAUTION: You don't want to convert your primary analog voice line to ISDN service because ISDN tariffs can be more expensive than POTS for outgoing calls, and you don't want to tie up your ISDN line with incoming voice calls.

Wiring from the Telephone Company to Your Premises

The U interface covers the wiring from the telephone company's CO to your premises and your site's internal wiring to the NT1. In the United States, the telephone company is responsible for any wiring to your doorstep, but from that point it's your responsibility. The *demarcation point* is the dividing line between the telephone company's wiring and the premises wiring. The physical device that provides the means to connect the telephone company's wire to the premises wire is a Network Interface box. The demarcation point and Network Interface box are the same for POTS and ISDN service. However, if your building is an older structure, you may not have a Network Interface box. Instead, the incoming telephone line connects directly to a device called a *Protector Block.* If your house doesn't have a Network Interface box, you need to have the telephone company install one. Only the telephone company can install the Network Interface device or any device directly wired to the telephone line.

Wiring Your Premises for ISDN

Again, from the demarcation point, the telephone wiring is your responsibility. You can choose to have the telephone company or an independent contractor do the inside wiring for a new line; or you can do it yourself. If you're using one of two pairs of wires in a line, you need to know which pair is used for which line. Chances are, if your existing wiring has worked properly for analog service, it will continue to work for ISDN service. You may, however, run into problems if the existing wiring is complex, such as office wiring originally installed for older key-based telephone systems. If this is the case, consult your telephone company or wiring contractor.

The standard for wiring analog and ISDN service requires an unshielded twisted-pair (UTP) cable of category 3 or above, 24-gauge for new residential wiring. The designation "unshielded" refers to the fact that the sheath does not include an electrical shield. You can get this wiring at most hardware or electronics stores.

RJ-11 and RJ-45 Connectors

At the end of your wiring are the connectors. Standard analog wiring uses the RJ-11 modular connectors that snap into a surface-mounted or flush-mounted jack.

ISDN uses the same RJ-11 connectors and cabling. RJ-11 connectors are four-wire connectors used for analog equipment. ISDN devices use eight-wire RJ-45 connectors to link to the NT1 device. These are S/T-interface devices (ISDN devices without built-in NT1). The RJ-45 is an eight-position jack commonly used in business telephone systems but not usually used in residential wiring. The NT1 device typically has an RJ-45 jack, to which you can plug in the RJ-11 cable from your inside wiring.

ISDN Wiring Configurations

For POTS service, you normally add a new telephone or other analog device simply by splitting the RJ-11 jack or tapping into an existing line and adding a jack. Your ISDN service comes in as a single line and terminates at the Network Termination device (NT1). You can't add an ISDN device to the line before it gets to the NT1. Once the ISDN line terminates at the NT1, you can add multiple ISDN devices—if you have an NT1 device that supports multiple devices. The wiring arrangement for ISDN is a star configuration, where the wiring to any individual piece of terminal equipment comes from a central point, which is the NT1 or NT1 Plus device, and goes to the terminal equipment.

The normal wiring scheme for connecting ISDN devices to the NT1 device via RJ-45 wiring is called a *passive bus configuration*. Typically, most small businesses and individuals can use this ISDN device configuration. The passive bus arrangement allows the connection of multiple S/T interfaces or analog devices to share an ISDN line without the need for repeaters to boost the digital signal.

ISDN Remote Access Devices

Because ISDN is one of the most widely available digital communication services, there are a variety of ISDN remote access devices on the market. ISDN remote access devices fall into three categories.

- Standalone serial-based devices that connect to your PC via the serial port using a standard RS-232 cable. These devices look like standard analog modems.
- ISDN bus adapter cards that fit into an expansion slot in your PC. Bus cards use the PC bus configuration to communicate to the PC.
- Ethernet-based devices that use Ethernet networking to facilitate communications between a LAN and the Internet via ISDN.

In most cases, you'll use an ISDN remote access device that includes the built-in NT1 device (U interface). However, if you plan to use an ISDN video conferencing system, you'll need to use an S/T-interface remote access device. This ISDN video conferencing system uses the ISDN network to make calls, as opposed to using an Internet-based video conferencing system, which uses your ISDN remote access device. ISDN desktop video systems, such Intel ProShare, come as S/T-interface devices. ISDN equipment made for the S/T interface requires the NT1 function to connect to ISDN. Because most remote access devices with built-in NT1 don't include an S/T-interface port, both the desktop video conferencing system and remote access device must connect to an external NT1 device. Figure 12.2 shows the configuration for using both a remote access device and an ISDN video conferencing system.

Note: A typical NT1 device looks like a small modem. It usually has two or three LEDs on the front, with one U-interface port for the ISDN line and two S/T-interface ports at the back of the unit. An NT1 device plugs into an AC power outlet to provide the power necessary to operate the ISDN line. A standalone NT1 device costs approximately $100 to $150. A number of vendors offer NT1 devices. See Appendix A for a listing of NT1 vendors and products.

Serial-Based ISDN Modems

The first category of ISDN remote access hardware is the serial-based external terminal adapters. These standalone units look like modems and are commonly referred to as ISDN modems, which is more a marketing term than a technical term. A serial ISDN device typically includes its own power supply and connects to your PC's serial port via a standard RS-232 cable. Because it works via your serial port, these ISDN devices make use of the AT Command set. The Hayes Standard AT Command set is used by all modems. This means the ISDN device works with your existing modem-based Internet and PC communication programs. Serial-based devices are built around the V.120 standard that adapts the rate of an asynchronous serial port on a computer to ISDN.

The major advantage of using serial ISDN modems is they are typically easier to set up and operate than other ISDN remote access devices. In Windows 95, these ISDN devices are treated like modems when you set up and use them. Windows 95 has made working with ISDN serial devices even easier with its support of serial data rates of up to 921,600 bps and Dial-Up Networking.

The major disadvantage of the serial ISDN modem is the reduced data communications speed resulting from the reliance on the asynchronous form of serial communications. PCs can communicate via two forms of serial communication:

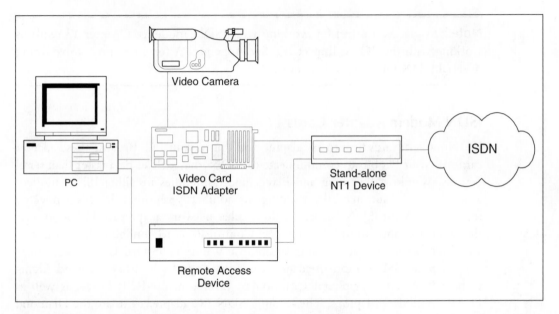

Figure 12.2 *The configuration for using an ISDN line for both remote access and ISDN-based video conferencing requires an external NT1.*

asynchronous and synchronous. ISDN can support both forms of serial communication. Synchronous communication is the faster method of data communication because it doesn't require the start-/stop-bit overhead used in asynchronous communication. Asynchronous uses a start/stop bit to define each chunk of eight-bit data being sent, which reduces the amount of data actually transferred by 20 percent. So, while asynchronous communications can transfer data at speeds up to 115.2 Kbps via ISDN, or 57.6 Kbps for each B channel, the extra start/stop bits result in a true data transfer rate of about 92 Kbps for both B channels.

Using synchronous communications with the MP protocol lets you transfer data at the full 128 Kbps. Synchronous data transmission sends information in larger blocks as a continuous stream using a synchronized timing method. Synchronous data transmission is the standard for digital communication; asynchronous is the standard for analog communication.

The leading serial ISDN modems are the 3Com Impact IQ, the Farallon Netopia, the Motorola BitSURFR, and the U.S. Robotics Courier I modem. The U.S. Robotics Courier I modem (and some other ISDN modems) includes both an analog modem and an ISDN modem in one box. Most of these ISDN modems include one or two RJ-11 ports for connecting analog devices (faxes, modems, telephones) to your ISDN line.

Note: To give you a feel for working with ISDN modems, Chapter 13 explains working with the 3Com Impact IQ. See Appendix A for a comprehensive listing of serial ISDN modems and vendors.

ISDN Modem Adapter Cards

ISDN modem cards fit into an adapter card slot in your PC. Because these adapter cards use your PC bus to communicate to ISDN, they deliver data faster than serial devices. Windows 95's Plug-and-Play support simplifies installing ISDN modem adapter cards by automatically avoiding any conflicts with other devices connected to your PC. Most ISDN adapter cards install as network adapter cards, but you use the Modems applet in the Windows 95 Control Panel to configure them if necessary. To make remote access connections, use Windows 95 Dial-Up Networking.

There are ISDN modem adapter cards that support Industry Standard Architecture (ISA) and Peripheral Component Interconnect (PCI) buses, as well as PCMCIA cards for laptops. The leading ISDN PC adapter cards are the Diamond Multimedia NetCommander, the U.S. Robotics Sportster ISDN 128 Kbps, and the Cardinal IDC100i. Most ISDN modem adapter cards include a single POTS port for connecting an analog device (fax, modem, or telephone) to your ISDN line.

Note: To give you a feel for installing and using an internal ISDN modem, Chapter 13 explains working with Diamond Multimedia's NetCommander. See Appendix A for a comprehensive listing of serial ISDN modems and vendors.

LAN-Based Remote Access

Connecting a Windows 95 LAN to the Internet (or any other network) via ISDN involves using a router. Routers cost more than ISDN modems, but they allow you to leverage your ISDN connection across all the PCs connected to your Windows 95 LAN. ISDN routers link to LANs using 10BaseT connectors, and many include built-in hubs so you can build your LAN and LAN-to-Internet connection using a single device.

The latest generation of ISDN routers are more affordable, and they're also surprisingly easy to set up and use. Windows 95 wizards, Web interfaces, and text-based menu systems make installation and configuration a breeze. Another benefit of using an ISDN router is that it seamlessly and instantaneously makes a remote access connection. All a user on your Windows 95 LAN has to do is double-click on Internet Explorer or Netscape Communicator (or any TCP/IP) application), and the Internet is delivered instantly to his or her desktop. It typically takes less than two seconds for an ISDN router connection. Using an ISDN router bypasses Windows 95 Dial-up Networking completely.

Until recently, routers and internetworking were the exclusive domain of large organizations with deep pockets and in-house expertise. And connecting a LAN to the Internet required an expensive LAN access package whereby the ISP assigned static IP addresses to the router and every PC on your LAN. These accounts typically cost hundreds of dollars per month just for the Internet access. The latest generation of ISDN routers use Dynamic Host Configuration Protocol (DHCP) and NAT (Network Address Translation) capabilities that let you connect an entire LAN via a single user ISDN Internet access account. This saves thousands of dollars per year.

ISDN router prices have fallen rapidly, in the $599 to $895 range, making them an affordable option for even the smallest of networks. ISDN routers can support all kinds of different networking protocols, but IP routers for Internet access comprise the largest market for ISDN routers. A number of companies manufacture ISDN routers, including Ascend, Ramp Networks, Farallon, ZyXEL, and others. Traditional enterprise-networking vendors including Cisco Systems, 3Com, Bay Networks, and Cabletron also offer ISDN routers.

Note: Chapters 14 through 16 explain working with the leading ISDN routers designed for the SOHO market. See Appendix A for a comprehensive listing of ISDN routers and vendors.

How ISDN Routers Work

Routers form the basis of internetworking, which is the connecting of different networks over wide area networks (WANs). In the case of ISDN access to the Internet, the router sends data from your local network via the ISDN to the Internet. Routers deliver more intelligence than bridges because they can route data by looking at the packet address and protocol. Bridges are basically "dumb" devices that connect two networks of the same type, routing all information indiscriminately between the two networks. Bridges also have an inherent limitation that can cause internetworking problems, whereas routers let you define routing tables for handling connections to different types of networks at different locations, all based on information in the data packets.

Furthermore, routers support filtering, which allows the router to monitor and choose packets as they enter or leave. With filtering, a router can protect your network from undesired intrusion and prevent selected local network traffic from leaving your LAN through the router. This is a powerful feature for managing incoming and outgoing data for your site. The aforementioned routing tables also allow you to create multiple data communication paths for your data depending where particular data needs to go.

ISDN Routers, IP Addresses, and Internet Access

Until recently, using an ISDN router required a LAN Internet access account. For connecting a LAN to the Internet, an ISP assigned IP addresses for every machine on the local area network, including one for the router itself. This required an ISP to relinquish IP addresses and a subnet mask for each LAN. Because of the growing scarcity of IP addresses, many ISPs charge a lot more for static IP accounts. These LAN access packages can run into the hundreds of dollars per month. The high cost of static IP accounts for LAN-to-Internet connectivity was the main reason for the limited deployment of ISDN routers in the SOHO market.

As a workaround, ISPs began using dynamic IP addressing for single-user accounts. Simply, in dynamic IP addressing, an ISP uses a host system that assigns an IP address from a pool of IP addresses available for use only during the current connection. Once the user ends the connection, the IP address used for the connection is returned to the pool for use as needed.

An ISDN router that supports DHCP and NAT enables you to connect an entire LAN to the Internet using a single-user, dynamic IP address account. The result is that you can use the same low-cost, dial-up Internet access accounts used by individuals to connect a LAN.

DHCP and NAT Support

ISDN routers designed for the SOHO market support DHCP and NAT together. The ISDN router acts as a DHCP server for a Windows 95 LAN. Windows 95 supports DHCP to automatically obtain IP addresses from a DHCP server for each PC on a Windows 95 LAN. But DHCP is only half of the solution; NAT is the other half. Network Address Translation (NAT) is an Internet standard that allows your LAN to use "private" IP addresses, which aren't recognizable outside your local area network but are by your ISDN router.

Combining DHCP with NAT creates a low-cost means of connecting small Windows 95 LANs to the Internet or any TCP/IP network. As with most computing technologies, there are advantages and disadvantages to this combined approach. Here are the advantages.

- You save a lot on Internet access costs by not requiring assigned IP addresses.
- Configuring your Windows 95 LAN is a lot easier because you don't need to enter TCP/IP information for each computer on your LAN.
- Security from the Internet into your network is good because your private IP addresses are not available to anyone on the Internet.

The disadvantage of using the DHCP/NAT combo ISDN routers is that none of the PCs on your Windows LAN has an IP address that is recognized on the Internet; thus, it may not be possible to provide any server functions for incoming access of your LAN via the Internet—for example, running an FTP server.

What's Next

With the ground rules established for establishing your ISDN service, it's time to roll up your sleeves and try out different ISDN remote access devices, starting with ISDN modems. The next chapter orients you to working with ISDN modems, then takes you on a test drive of the leading internal and external ISDN modems.

13 *ISDN Modems*

ISDN modems connect a single PC to the Internet or other network via an ISDN line. Like analog modems, they come in both internal and external flavors. For a single PC, they offer an easy and inexpensive way to get connected. This chapter takes you through the process of installing and working with two leading ISDN modems: the 3ComImpact IQ (external) and Diamond Multimedia's Supra NetCommander (internal) ISDN modems.

External ISDN Modems

Serial ISDN devices connect to your PC via a serial port using a standard RS-232 cable. Setting up and using serial modems usually is easier than setting up an internal ISDN modem. Prices for external ISDN modems run in the range of $299 to $499. External ISDN modems typically come with a built-in NT1 (U interface) as well as POTS ports for connecting a telephone, a modem, or a fax.

The major disadvantage of serial ISDN modems is their reduced data communications speed caused by inherent limitations of the asynchronous form of serial communications. As described earlier, asynchronous communications use a start-and stop-bit to define each chunk of 8-bit data being sent, which reduces the amount of data actually transferred by 20 percent. The result is that a 115,200-bps rate is actually moving data at about a 92,000-bps rate.

To take advantage of the 115,200-bps rate for ISDN modems, your serial port must be using the 16550A UART (universal asynchronous receiver/transmitter) chip. Most of today's PC include this chip. Several vendors also sell serial adapter cards that support even higher rates. For example, the Lava Link 650 supports up to 460 Kbps. However, the ISDN device at the server must also support the higher data communications rate, which many ISPs do not.

A number of vendors offer external ISDN modems. The 3ComImpact IQ is one of the most popular. Farallon's Netopia ISDN modem is an OEM (original equipment manufacturer) version of the 3ComImpact IQ. Other leading external ISDN modems include the Motorola BitSURFR Pro EZ, the ZyXEL Omni TA 128, and the Adtran Express XRT. The U.S. Robotics Courier I modem is a combination ISDN and 56K modem.

Note: See Appendix A, " Windows 95 Remote Access Resources," for a comprehensive listing of external ISDN modem vendors and products.

Internal ISDN Modems

Because ISDN modem cards use your PC's bus to communicate with ISDN, they deliver data faster than serial devices. Most ISDN modem cards are Plug-and-Play-compatible for easy installation in Windows 95. Prices of ISDN modem cards are considerably cheaper than external ISDN modems, with prices ranging from around $149 to $299. ISDN PCMCIA cards for laptops are more expensive, and some include an analog modem to give the mobile user the option of a POTS connection.

Most ISDN modem cards come with a built-in NT1 (U interface) as well as an RJ-11 port for connecting a telephone, a modem, or a fax. ISDN adapter cards install as network adapter cards, but you use the Modems applet in the Windows 95 Control Panel to configure them. To make remote access connections, you use Windows 95 Dial-Up Networking.

Like external ISDN modems, there are a number of internal ISDN modem cards. The leading ISDN modem cards include Diamond Multimedia's Supra Net-Commander, the U.S. Robotics Sportster ISDN 128K, the Cardinal IDC 100I, and the Eicon Diva Series. For PCMCIA ISDN modem cards, the leading products are Angia's I-Bahn Combo Card, Eicon's DIVA TA and DIVA Pro PC Cards, and Farallon's Netopia ISDN PC Card.

Note: See Appendix A, "Windows 95 Remote Access Resources," for a comprehensive listing of ISDN modem card vendors and products.

3ComImpact IQ External ISDN Modem

The 3ComImpact IQ External ISDN Modem ($250 street price) is the company's second-generation external ISDN modem that combines good performance, two analog ports, and painless installation. The IQ also includes a six-foot RS-232 cable, an ISDN line cable, and installation software for Windows and Macintosh computers. The 3ComImpact IQ has an impressive collection of features, some of which are highlighted here.

- Easy-to-use set-up wizard that automatically detects your telephone company switch type and configures the SPIDs for you.
- Multilink PPP support for two B-channel bonding.
- Toll-saving data over voice support.
- Compression support for the PPP Compression Control Protocol and PPP Stacker US Compression Protocol.
- PAP security support.
- Two analog (RJ-11) ports.
- Dynamic bandwidth allocation.
- Flash memory for easy firmware updates.

• •

CAUTION: The 3Com Impact IQ can do CHAP (Challenge Handshake Authentication Protocol) only on one B channel. CHAP is one of two Point-to-Point Protocol authentication protocols used for connecting to the Internet. You should make certain that your ISP is not using this authentication method before buying the IQ.

Ordering ISDN Service

You can either let 3Com order ISDN service for you, or you can call your telephone company and order it yourself. To place your order for ISDN service using 3Com, call 1-800-572-3COM. 3Com will provide the appropriate line parameters to your telephone company and schedule installation of your ISDN line.

If you're ordering ISDN service for the IQ from your telephone company, there are two ISDN codes that work with the Impact IQ modem: the Compatibility Package K and the Compatibility Package U. The U package supports two telephone numbers and the K package supports only one. Having two telephone numbers assigned to an ISDN line enables both analog ports to be used simultaneously. If only one telephone number is assigned, the ISDN line can place or receive only one call at a time.

Setting Up and Configuring IQ

Installing the Impact IQ is easy. With your PC turned off, connect one end of the serial cable to the RS-232 port on the IQ (25-pin connector) and the other end to your PC (9-pin connector). Next connect your ISDN line to the ISDN U port (RJ-45) on the IQ and connect any analog devices to the RJ-11 ports on the IQ. Connect the power adapter to the unit and plug it in.

Before you start the configuration process, make sure that the TCP/IP dial-up adapter and Dial-Up Networking are installed, as explained in Chapter 6, "Remote Access via Dial-Up Networking." You also need the following information from your Internet service provider to set up Windows Dial-Up Networking:

- If your ISP is using a static IP address, an IP address for your PC. If your ISP uses dynamic IP addressing, an IP address is assigned every time you log on.
- IP addresses for the domain name system servers. Typically, two are provided.
- Your user name (host name) and password.
- Your domain name or the domain name of your ISP.

Follow these steps to install the 3ComImpact IQ in Windows 95:

1. Reboot your PC with the IQ modem powered up and connected to your PC. The New Hardware dialog box appears.
2. Click the Select the Driver from disk provided by hardware manufacturer option; click OK. The Install From Disk dialog box appears.
3. Insert the 3ComImpact IQ Windows & DOS Installation Diagnostic Utilities disk in your floppy drive; click OK. The Select Device dialog box appears.
4. With the 3ComImpact IQ device selected, click OK. The 3ComImpact IQ driver is installed.
5. With the 3ComImpact IQ Windows & DOS Installation Diagnostic Utilities disk in your floppy drive, choose Start|Run; type **A:\SETUP**, then click OK.
6. Click Continue to begin the IQ configuration. A dialog box appears prompting you for the directory path on which you want to store the IQ files. To use the default directory, click Continue. The IQ files are copied to your system; then a Readme file appears in a Notepad window.
7. Review the information in the Readme file and then close the Notepad window. A message box tells you that the setup is completed. Click OK.
8. Double-click the 3ComImpact IQ icon in the 3ComImpact IQ window. The wizard starts, then displays a dialog box for entering your first telephone number.
9. Type your first ISDN phone number, including area code; click Next. The wizard verifies the number and the SPID, and displays the dialog box for the second directory number.

10. Type the second ISDN phone directory number; click Next. The wizard verifies the number and SPID, and the Finish dialog box appears.

11. Click Finish. The User Registration window appears.

12. Click Skip Registration (stop reminding) for now. A message appears telling you that the IQ is correctly configured.

13. Click Yes. The wizard closes. You're now ready to set up Windows 95 Dial-Up Networking for the IQ.

Making Connections

Once you have installed and configured the Impact IQ, you're ready to use Dial-Up Networking to create your connection profiles for remote access. Chapter 6, "Remote Access via Dial-Up Networking," explains how to work with Windows 95's Dial-Up Networking. You can change the Impact IQ's configuration settings for all connections using the Modems applet in the Windows 95 Control Panel. During your connections, you can use the eight status LEDs on the front panel of the IQ to monitor the status of the IQ and your connections. Table 13.1 describes the functions of the IQ LEDs.

Table 13.1 Front Panel LED Status Definitions

LED	COLOR	DESCRIPTION
PWR	Green	*Power Indicator.* Lit when power is on and remains lit as long as power is supplied to the unit.
TEST	Green	*Self-Test/Status.* Flashes when the IQ is executing its power-up self-test or a user-initiated reset. If the results of the self-test or reset are normal, the LED goes off. If the result of the self-test is abnormal and a fault is detected, the LED remains lit but does not flash.
D	Green	*D-channel Status.* Indicates the ISDN physical network interface and D-channel status: Goes off once the physical and D-channel signaling are synchronized. Flashes if the physical interface establishes synchronization and the ISDN D-channel signaling procedures are not properly established. Remains lit if the physical ISDN interface is not synchronized or is disconnected.
B1	Amber or Green	B1-channel Activity. Green indicates a circuit-switched data or call in progress. Amber indicates a circuit-switched voice call in progress. If a call is in a dialing state, the LED flashes. When the call is disconnected, the LED goes off.

(continues)

Table 13.1 (*Continued*)

LED	COLOR	DESCRIPTION
B2	Amber or Green	*B2-channel Activity.* Green indicates a circuit-switched data or call in progress. Amber indicates a circuit-switched voice call in progress. If a call is in a dialing state, the LED flashes. When the call is disconnected, the LED goes off.
SD	Green	*Send Data.* Indicates that information is being transmitted over the serial data port from the computer to the ISDN modem.
RD	Green	*Receive Data.* Indicates that information is being transmitted over the serial data port to the computer from the ISDN modem.
DTR	Green	*Data Terminal Ready.* Indicates that communication between the ISDN modem and computer has been established.

The 3ComImpact IQ Window

The 3ComImpact IQ window (Figure 13.1) enables you to make changes to your IQ settings. Choose Start | Programs | ComImpactIQ | 3ComImpactIQ to open the window. This window provides the tools you need to manage the IQ and your

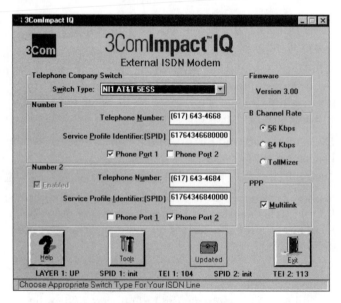

Figure 13.1 *The 3ComImpact IQ window.*

ISDN line. The window displays your ISDN line settings and a few buttons at the bottom of the window. The following describes the setting in the 3ComImpact IQ window:

- The Switch Type setting in the Telephone Company Switch group lets you specify the switch used by your telephone company.

- The Telephone Number and Service Profile Identifier (SPID) settings in the Number 1 and Number 2 setting groups define the respective telephone numbers and SPIDs for each B channel.

- The Phone Port 1 and Phone Port 2 settings in both the Number 1 and Number 2 groups let you specify which telephone number is connected to which POTS port on the Impact IQ. Only one of these settings should be selected for each Number group. For example, if Phone Port 1 is checked in the Number 1 group, then Phone Port 2 should be selected in the Number 2 group.

- The B Channel group lets you choose the way you want to initiate a call. You can choose 56 Kbps, 64 Kbps, or the TollMizer setting for data over voice.

- The PPP group's Multilink setting specifies using PPP/MP for bonding the two B channels.

- The Updated button becomes active any time you make a change in the 3ComImpact IQ window. Click on this button to save your changes to the Impact IQ. When you click on the Updated button, a message box appears informing you that the Impact settings will be changed. Click Yes and the changes are saved.

- Clicking on the Tools button at the bottom of the window displays a button bar that includes buttons for updating the IQ's firmware and running diagnostics on your ISDN line. The Test button in the tool button bar displays the 3ComImpact IQ Protocol Trace window (Figure 13.2) and the 3ComImpact IQ Diagnostics window (Figure 13.3). These windows let you test your ISDN line and incoming and outgoing calls.

- The Exit button exits the 3ComImpact IQ window.

- The Help button displays a help window for the 3ComImpact IQ.

Advanced Configuration

To change advanced configuration parameter values, you need to use the Windows 95 HyperTerminal terminal emulation software and AT commands. The advanced configuration parameters and their default settings are as follows:

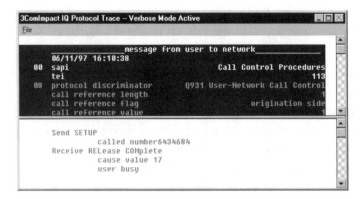

Figure 13.2 *The 3ComImpact IQ Protocol Trace window.*

- Auto Answer. When Auto Answer is disabled (the default), a RING message is delivered to the RS-232 port upon reception of an incoming data call to the IQ. If Auto Answer is enabled, the call is automatically answered after the number of rings you specify.

- *Baud Rate (automatic detection of rates up to 115.2 Kbps).* By default, the baud rate is set using Autobaud, which automatically detects the maximum data rate of your computer's COM port. Rates up to 115.2 Kbps can be detected automatically. Leave Autobaud enabled unless you want to set the baud rate to 230.4 Kbps.

- *Compression.* Compression is a method of reducing the size of data without losing any information. By default, the Impact IQ automatically compresses data to improve data transfer times using the Stac compression method. The IQ compression is automatically invoked unless you are running compression on your computer. If you are, that compression method will be used instead of IQ compression even if IQ compression is enabled.

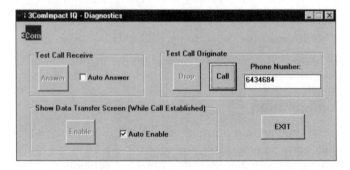

Figure 13.3 *The 3ComImpact IQ Diagnostics window.*

- *Dynamic Bandwidth Allocation.* Allows you to place or receive a voice call while a Multilink PPP call is active. When a voice call comes in, or if you lift the handset to place a call while you have both B channels in use because of Multilink PPP, one of the B channels is temporarily removed from the Multilink PPP call and is used for the voice call. Once the voice call ends, that B channel is automatically returned to the Multilink PPP call. Although throughput is reduced while the voice call is active, the reliability of the Multilink PPP call is not affected. If you are on the receiving end of a Multilink PPP call and you place a voice call, one of the B channels will be used for the voice call; but once the voice call ends, the B channel cannot be returned to the Multilink PPP call. The B channel can be returned to the Multilink PPP call only if you placed the call.

- *QuickSelect.* Automatically detects and uses the protocol required for each digital call, either V.1 20 or Async-Sync PPP. Typically, V.1 20 is used for communication between two computers, while PPP is used for communication between a computer and an Internet service provider.

Changing the Parameter Settings

To change the IQ Advanced Parameters, use the Windows 95 HyperTerminal with the unit attached to a PC via the supplied RS-232 cable. The following steps explain how to create a HyperTerminal connection to the Impact IQ using the HyperTerminal program in Windows 95. Once you create the connection, you can save it to use again.

1. Choose Start|Accessories|HyperTerminal. The HyperTerminal window appears.

2. Double-click on the Hypertm icon. The Connection Description dialog box appears.

3. Type a name for your connection (such as Impact IQ), choose an icon, and click OK. The Phone Number dialog box appears.

4. In the Connect using list, choose the Direct to Com port for the serial port you're using to connect the PC to the Impact IQ, then click OK. The COM Properties dialog box appears.

5. Change the Bits per second setting to 9600, and choose None for the Flow control setting. The Data bits, Parity, and Stop bits use the default values of 8, None, and 1, respectively.

6. Click OK. The HyperTerminal window appears. You're ready to configure the Impact IQ.

Table 13.2 Changing the Impact IQ Default Settings

PARAMETER	TO CHANGE THE DEFAULT
QuickSelect	Send the command ATS71=1 to use Asynch-Synch PPP exclusively, or ATS71=2 to use V.120 exclusively.
Dynamic Bandwidth Allocation	Send the command ATS70=0 to disable Dynamic Bandwidth Allocation.
Auto Answer	Send the command ATS0= (number of rings before the ISDN modem answers the call) to enable Auto Answer.
Compression	Send the command AT%C0 to disable compression.
Autobaud	Send the command AT$B (rate) to set a specific baud rate. Send the command AT$B0 to return to Autobaud. The command AT$B (baud rate) is used to set a specific baud rate, such as 230.4 Kbps.

To change the IQ Advanced Parameter settings, follow these steps:

1. Launch the HyperTerminal connection for the Impact IQ.

2. Be sure the IQ is in command mode (called local mode or terminal mode) so that it interprets your commands. When your computer is powered on, the IQ automatically starts in command mode. If you recently used the IQ to make a call and have not yet disconnected, type **+++** to switch to command mode.

3. Type: **AT <command>** then press Enter. Table 13.2 lists the appropriate commands. For example, to disable compression, type **AT%C0**, then press Enter. An AT command line starts with the characters AT. The command line accepts up to 40 command characters in the line (not including the two AT characters, or spaces). After completing its tasks, the IQ sends a message to the screen followed by a result code.

4. To change another parameter setting, repeat steps 1 through 4.

The NetCommander Internal ISDN Modem

The NetCommander is representative of a good internal ISDN modem. It offers Windows 95 Plug-and-Play support, a full-featured analog port, excellent performance, and easy-to-use installation and management software. Diamond Multimedia's Supra NetCommander lists for $249, with a street price of $230. Diamond also offers an ISDN line-ordering service called ISDN Now!

The Plug-and-Play-compatible NetCommander installs easily, and a rear-panel LED provides visual confirmation that the ISDN line is working. The simple software installation sets up Microsoft's ISDN Accelerator Pack 1.1 and the NetCommander's own AutoISDN program to manage your ISDN line.

One of the most significant benefits of the NetCommander is its support of true dynamic bandwidth allocation. The NetCommander determines the bandwidth it needs for a particular session and adjusts the channel allocation accordingly. In low-traffic sessions, such as surfing the Web without downloading large graphics files, it uses only one B channel. When you go into file download mode, it kicks in both B channels for overdrive speed. This feature saves you money in connection charges. Additionally, the NetCommander works with all the leading bandwidth allocation protocols, so it is compatible with most Internet service providers.

The Supra NetCommander provides full ringing support, which means your regular telephone will ring on the ISDN line. You can assign a Distinctive Ring capability for up to three analog devices connected to your line. NetCommander includes PPP/MP and user-programmable bandwidth on demand. It also includes built-in NTI and voice and data capability on both B channels. You can upgrade the NetCommander by software, and it supports Stac and Microsoft compression.

The NetCommander's single analog port lets you connect up to three devices. It supplies ring voltage to the analog jack on incoming calls, which lets you use answering machines, fax machines, and analog modems. Voice quality on the NetCommander's analog port is excellent. Finally, the NetCommander can add or remove the second B channel as needed, without user intervention. This feature switches dynamically between single and dual B-channel operation, saving on telephone and ISP charges.

Ordering ISDN Service for the NetCommander

With most telephone companies, you can simply request the Intel Blue ordering code or Capability Package M, which has configuration characteristics nearly identical to Intel Blue. Either package provides 128-Kbps transmission potential, which enables you to take full advantage of the NetCommander MPPP and analog voice communications features. What you need from the telephone company are the switch type, the directory number or numbers, and any SPIDs.

Installing the NetCommander Card

The following steps explain how to install the Supra NetCommander in an ISA slot in your PC. Note that the Windows 95 TCP/IP stack and Dial-Up Networking must be installed before you can install NetCommander.

1. Turn off the power to the computer and any related equipment.

2. Remove the cover from your computer and touch the power supply box on your computer with one hand while the computer is plugged in. This grounds you and discharges any static electricity, allowing you to safely handle your Supra NetCommander card.

3. Unscrew and remove the slot cover from the 16-bit ISA expansion slot you have chosen for the NetCommander card.

4. Insert the NetCommander card into the ISA expansion slot. Replace the screw that originally held the slot cover in place, then put the cover back on your computer.

5. Plug your ISDN phone line into the ISDN port on your NetCommander—RJ-45 on the back of the NetCommander board, labeled ISDN to Wall.

6. Plug in any analog device you want to connect to your ISDN line by connecting the RJ-11 jack into the port labeled Analog Phone on your NetCommander.

Diamond recommends connecting analog devices in the following order: analog modem, fax machine, and then telephone. There are two connections on your modem: one marked phone and the other marked line or wall. Use the included phone cable to connect your fax machine or modem to the analog phone port on NetCommander.

• •

CAUTION: If your computer is turned off, analog devices will not work on the ISDN line.

Installing the NetCommander Software

After you've installed your Supra NetCommander adapter card, you need to install the supporting software. It includes the AutoISDN program for configuring and managing your ISDN connection, as well as the Microsoft Accelerator Pack. The following steps explain how to install and configure the NetCommander. Make sure that you have all your ISDN line-provisioning information available before you install the software.

1. Restart your PC and Windows 95. The New Hardware Found dialog box is displayed.

2. Choose Drivers from disk provided by the hardware manufacturer (the default), and click OK.

3. Insert the NetCommander ISDN CD in your CD-ROM drive, enter **D:\Win95**, then click OK. The NetCommander software drivers are copied to a new directory, and the NetCommander ISDN Installation Setup Wizard appears.

4. Click Next. The Select Destination Directory dialog box appears.

5. To accept the default directory, click Next. If you want to use a different directory, type the path, then click Next. The Select Switch Type dialog box appears.

6. Select the Switch Type used by your telephone company at the central office that is providing your ISDN service; click Next. The SPID dialog box appears.

7. Type one SPID in each of the spaces provided. Or, if your telephone company didn't provide any SPIDs, select the No SPID Required check box. Click Next. The Phone Numbers dialog box appears.

8. Enter your 10-digit ISDN phone numbers. You must include the area code of the ISDN phone numbers (directory numbers). Click Next. The Save Configuration dialog box appears.

9. Click Next. The NetCommander Setup program completes the installation and then displays a Hints dialog box. Click Next. A Setup Complete dialog box appears.

10. Click Finish. A dialog box appears, prompting you to restart Windows 95; click OK to restart Windows 95.

Making Connections

Once you've installed the NetCommander in Windows 95, you can create a Dial-Up Networking connection profile. This is done in the same way as for any modem, as explained in Chapter 6, "Remote Access via Dial-Up Networking."

The NetCommander appears in the Select a modem setting in the Make New Connection Wizard. After creating a connection profile for the NetCommander, right-click on the Connection Profile icon and choose Properties from the context menu. The standard Dial-Up Networking profile dialog box appears. Clicking on the Configure button displays the Connection dialog box. The Speed preference list has the following three entries.

- *64K Data.* This setting is for full digital data communications.

- *56K Data.* This setting is for ISDN data communications over ISDN connections that have in-band signaling.

- *56K Voice.* This setting allows you to use data over voice to save on usage charges if your telephone company and ISP support it.

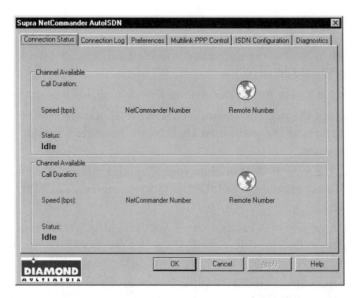

Figure 13.4 *The Supra NetCommander AutoISDN dialog box.*

The Set additional settings in the Dial–Up Networking Profile dialog box for a NetCommander connection lets you specify which ISDN B channel and telephone number you want to use for an analog device attached to the NetCommander.

NetCommander's AutoISDN Program

The AutoISDN program (Figure 13.4) provides a collection of tools for managing the NetCommander and your ISDN connection. You can open the AutoISDN window by clicking the Diamond AutoISDN icon on the Windows 95 taskbar. You can also open the program by choosing Start|Programs|NetCommander|AutoISDN.

The following describe the tabs in the AutoISDN dialog box:

- The Connection Status tab shows the status of your ISDN connection. When you're connected, it provides status information for each B channel.

- The Connection Log tab provides a listing of your ISDN calls. Entries can be sorted, and you can produce a printout.

- The Preferences tab (Figure 13.5) is where you control how incoming calls are handled; determine whether the connection log is enabled or disabled, and whether the AutoISDN icon is always displayed on the taskbar or only when the ISDN line is active; and adjust phone volume control.

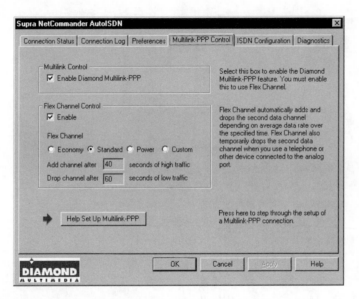

Figure 13.5 *The Preferences tab.*

- The Multilink-PPP Control tab (Figure 13.6) lets you enable Multilink PPP for two B-channel connections and *flexing*, which is the capability to use both B channels to aggregate data to handle larger data transfers. To ac-

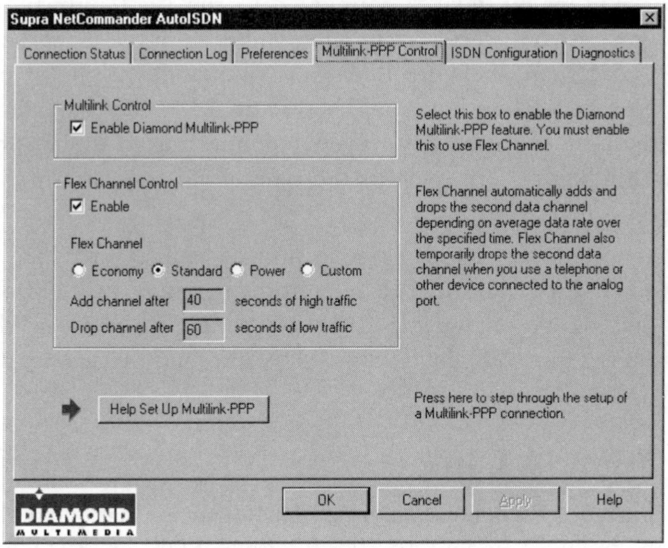

Figure 13.6 *The Multilink-PPP Control tab.*

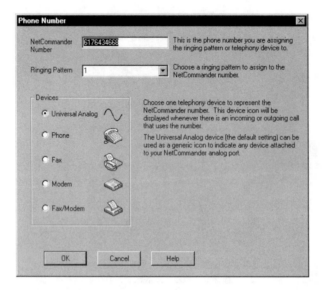

Figure 13.7 *The Phone Number dialog box.*

tivate the Multilink PPP protocol, check the Enable Diamond Multilink-PPP option.

• The ISDN Configuration tab includes the settings for the telephone company side of your ISDN connections, including SPIDs, switch types, and settings for any analog devices connected to the NetCommander's analog (RJ-11) port. If you select a telephone number from the list at the bottom of the page and then click the Edit NetCommander Number button, the Phone Number dialog box appears (Figure 13.7). This window lets you specify the type of analog device you're connecting to the telephone number. The ringing pattern specifies the type of ringing pattern you want for the line.

• The Diagnostics tab provides a collection of tools with which to test the NetCommander card and the telephone ringing. In addition, a troubleshooting log file can keep track of your activities and record them, along with responses from Windows, your ISDN line, and the adapter card.

Using the I-Bahn PCMCIA Card

Angia Communications' I-Bahn is the little PCMCIA card that could. The I-Bahn can connect the mobile Windows 95 user to either ISDN or POTS with a combined ISDN modem and V.34 (28.8 Kbps) modem on one PC card. The I-Bahn comes in either U-interface or S/T-interface models and supports V.110, V.120, PPP, and PPP/MP. You can use it almost anywhere in the world because it supports most telephone switch protocols, including all telephone switches in the United States, Japan, and Europe.

Angia Communications has made installation of the I-Bahn easy with a Windows 95 Configuration Manager program. It also features a pair of LEDs that provide line-status information for both ISDN and POTS lines. The POTS adapter provides dual RJ-11 jacks to attach both a telephone and the phone line from a wall jack to the card. Another cool mobile user feature is the I-Bahn's capability to work with digital PBX phone systems, which are commonly found in hotels and offices.

Setting Up and Configuring the I-Bahn

Setting up the I-Bahn is easy. Insert the card into a PCMCIA slot in your laptop. With your laptop turned off, connect the U-interface *podule* (an Angia term for the U-interface connector) to the card. Connect the RJ-45 connector from the supplied ISDN cable into the U-interface port (RJ-45) on the U-interface podule. You're ready to configure the I-Bahn as follows:

1. Restart Windows 95. The New Hardware Found dialog box appears.

2. Insert the Angia Install disk and choose the default option, Driver from disk provided by hardware manufacturer; click OK. The I-Bahn drivers are installed on your system.

   You can check to see that the I-Bahn card was installed in Windows 95 by opening the PC Card (PCMCIA) applet in the Control Panel, which displays the PC Card (PCMCIA) Properties dialog box (Figure 13.8).

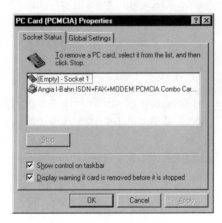

Figure 13.8 The PC Card (PCMCIA) Properties dialog box.

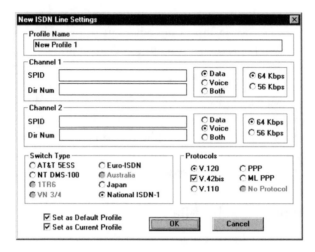

Figure 13.9 *The New ISDN Line Settings dialog box.*

3. With the Install disk still in your disk drive, choose Start|Run, and type **A:\SETUP**, then click OK. After copying files to a temporary directory, the Installation Menu dialog box appears.

4. Use the default Express Installation, then click OK. After the installation is completed, the Installation Menu dialog box appears again.

5. Select the Exit Installation option, then click OK. A dialog box appears telling you the installation was completed successfully. Click OK.

6. Choose Start|Programs|Angia I-Bahn ISDN|Angia I-Bahn ISDN Configuration Manager. The first time you run the Configuration Manager, a warning message appears. Just click OK. The New ISDN Line Settings dialog box appears (Figure 13.9).

7. In the New ISDN Line Settings dialog box do the following (use the Tab key to move between fields):

Enter a Profile Name.

Enter SPID Number 1 and Directory Number 1 (enter only numbers), then select the channel type and speed for your Channel 1 directory and SPID numbers.

Enter SPID Number 2 and Directory Number 2 (enter only numbers), then select the channel type and speed for your Channel 2 directory and SPID numbers.

Select the switch type.

Table 13.3 I-Bahn Protocol Options

PROTOCOL	DESCRIPTION
V.120	ITU asynchronous rate adaption protocol for a single B channel with error control.
V.42bis	ITU standard for the compression of asynchronous data. The I-Bahn POTS modem uses this protocol.
V.110	ITU rate-adaption protocol for a single B channel without error control.
PPP	Standard point-to-point protocol for TCP/IP connectivity.
MLPPP	Special PPP protocol to enable both B channels to bond together into a single channel.

Choose the protocols you want to use for the connection profile. Table 13.3 describes the available protocol options.

Set the profile as either Current or Default.

8. Click OK. The ISDN Configuration Manager window (Figure 13.10) appears with your settings displayed. If you need to make changes, choose Profile|Modify to return to the New ISDN Line Settings to make your changes.

Figure 13.10 *The ISDN Configuration Manager window.*

Table 13.4 The I-Bahn's LED Functions

LED	FUNCTION
LS (Line Synchronization) ISDN	No light. Not connected. Red. Has power but not synchronized. Green. Has power, is synchronized.
DTE (Data Terminal Equipment rate) ISDN	No light. Not connected and on hook. Blinking red. Off hook and not connected. Blinking red. Ring detected. Green. Connected.
OH (Off Hook) POTS	Green. Off hook. In between dialing, while the modem is answering a call, and while the receiver is off the hook, this LED is green.
CD (Carrier Detect) POTS	Yellow. Carrier detect. Lights up only when there is an active connection.

9. Click on Submit Settings to send your configuration to the I-Bahn card. Once the settings have been downloaded and your ISDN line connection is synchronized, the LS LED turns green.

Making Connections

Once you've installed and configured the I-Bahn, you're ready to use Dial-Up Networking to create your connection profiles for remote access. Again, Chapter 6, "Remote Access via Dial-Up Networking," explains how to work with Windows 95's Dial-Up Networking. To help you monitor your connections, the I-Bahn includes two LEDs on the ISDN podule and two LEDs on the SafeJack analog modem adapter, as described in Table 13.4.

What's Next

The next stop on your ISDN remote access journey is connecting your Windows 95 LAN to the Internet via ISDN. ISDN routers offer powerful reasons for using a Windows 95 LAN with ISDN for your remote access needs. The next chapter begins your ISDN router adventures with one of the easiest to set up, Ramp Networks' WebRamp Entré.

14 *Easy LAN Connectivity with WebRamp*

R amp Networks makes connecting your Windows 95 LAN to the Internet via ISDN an easy and affordable process. The WebRamp family of ISDN routers includes built-in hubs and a friendly Windows 95 interface to deliver a complete Internet connectivity solution. This chapter takes you on a tour through the setup and use of a WebRamp ISDN router.

About the WebRamp Family

Ramp Networks (formally Trancell Systems) isn't one of those big internetworking companies that doesn't "get it" when it comes to making router technology inexpensive and easy to use. Its entire focus is on products designed exclusively for the SOHO market, which means making them easy to use and affordable.

The WebRamp family of ISDN routers currently includes two dial-up, IP router products: WebRamp IP and WebRamp Entré. WebRamp IP is an ISDN router and eight-port 10BaseT hub. The WebRamp Entré is an ISDN router with a four-port 10BaseT hub and two POTS ports for connecting a telephone or fax machine to your ISDN line. The WebRamp IP suggested list price is $899, but it can be had on the street for around $629. The WebRamp Entré has a list price of $849 with a street price of around $599. The WebRamp family also includes a product that supports Novell's IPX. For more information, check out the Ramp Networks site at http://www.rampnet.com/.

TIP: You may be able to purchase the WebRamp products from an ISP as part of your ISDN Internet access account at a much lower price. Check with your ISP first before buying one of these products.

Both WebRamp models allow you to expand your LAN beyond the number of ports built into the unit. One of the Ethernet ports can be used as an input port from another hub simply by turning on a switch at the back of the unit. All Web-Ramps also include built-in NT1 for terminating your ISDN line. Configuration of either WebRamp is simple; you just use the WebRampWiz program, and the Internet/ISDN Worksheet guides you through the process of assembling all the ISP and ISDN information you need to start. Both models support do-it-yourself firmware upgrades, as well as a collection of useful diagnostic utilities for troubleshooting your Internet and ISDN connections.

One disadvantage of the WebRamps is that they don't include a toll-saver feature (also called data over voice) found on other ISDN routers, such as the Netopia Internet router. If you're an ISDN customer in Ameritech and NYNEX service areas, not having this feature can increase the cost of your telephone connection charges. The toll-saver feature "fools" the telephone company switch into treating the call as a voice call, which is billed at the lower POTS rate. Typically, your local telephone company allows unlimited call usage within your local calling area for a flat monthly rate. The data-over-voice feature allows data to be sent at 56 Kbps instead of the ISDN 64-Kbps rate. To use data-over-voice service, your ISP must also support it at its end of the connection.

Both the Entré and IP models include what Ramp Networks calls EasyIP, a feature that enables you to share a single-user ISDN Internet access account for your Windows 95 LAN. EasyIP combines the DHCP (Dynamic Host Configuration Protocol) server and NAT (Name Address Translation) capabilities of the WebRamp to support dynamic IP addressing on your LAN. Windows 95's TCP/IP stack automatically configures a PC to be a DHCP client. The EasyIP features of the WebRamp deliver big benefits that include:

- Dramatically lower Internet access costs. Using dynamic IP means you don't need to use an expensive LAN account, whereby an ISP assigns you specific IP addresses for your router and every computer on your network. These accounts can cost a few hundred dollars a month compared to around $30 a month for a single-user ISDN Internet access account.

- Easier configuration of a Windows 95 LAN for remote access. The DHCP server feature of the WebRamp means you don't need to configure each computer on your network for a unique set of IP addresses as you do using a static IP Internet access account. Windows 95's default TCP/IP settings are ready-made for working with a DHCP server.

- The WebRamp provides built-in security for your LAN from Internet intruders using dynamic IP addressing, which means there are no static IP addresses on your LAN that can be accessed from the Internet. This creates a firewall that prevents Internet intruders from gaining access to your Windows 95 LAN through your gateway. Your LAN uses private IP addresses that are not recognizable outside your local network.

Even if you already have a static IP Internet access account, the WebRamp ISDN router can double as a traditional router. For these LAN access accounts, you need an IP address for each computer connected to your network and one for the WebRamp. Thus, if you have three computers, you'll need a range of four IP addresses. The smallest LAN access package typically consists of five IP addresses.

Getting Started with the WebRamp Entré

Because of the inherent cost-saving benefits of going the EasyIP route for most SOHO sites, the remaining instructions in this chapter cover working with the WebRamp Entré as a dynamic IP router. Before you begin working with the WebRamp, do the following:

- Order ISDN service and provision it for the WebRamp.
- Order your ISDN Internet access account.
- Set up the WebRamp unit by connecting it to your ISDN line, all your networked PCs, and any analog devices that you want to share your ISDN line.
- Install Windows 95's TCP/IP Properties for each PC.

As you establish your ISDN and Internet access service, use the ISDN/Internet Worksheet provided with your WebRamp unit to keep track of your information. You'll need this information when you run the WebRampWiz program to configure the Entré. The following sections explain how to get these components together.

Ordering ISDN Service for the WebRamp Entré

When you order ISDN service, you need to tell the ISDN provider what type of equipment you'll be using on the line. Most telephone companies use ordering codes for ISDN CPE. The WebRamp Entré supports the Intel Blue (with voice and data) or the EZ-ISDN-1. The manual includes specific provisioning parameters for the Entré in case your ISDN provider doesn't support ordering codes.

If you want to add any supplementary voice services, such as Conference Calling, you can use the information found at the back of the Entré manual. However, the higher tariffs for most ISDN services may preclude you from using your ISDN line as your primary voice communications link; as such, you probably will not order additional calling features over the basic voice features. In most cases, you'll use your POTS ports to connect a fax machine or possibly a back-up modem.

Your ISDN provider must supply you with the following information so that you can configure your WebRamp Entré.

- Switch type
- ISDN phone number 1
- SPID number 1
- ISDN phone number 2
- SPID number 2

The Entré will work with all the main telephone company switches and software. It supports the AT&T 5ESS, Nortel DMS-100, and Siemens switches running National ISDN-1, Custom (DMS only), Custom Point-to-Point (AT&T only), and Custom Multipoint (AT&T only). An AT&T 5ESS Custom Point-to-Point switch will have one phone number and no SPIDs, so don't use this option if you plan to add any analog equipment to your Entré; you will need two phone numbers to use any POTS device. For example, if you add a fax machine, you need a designated telephone number for it.

Ordering Internet Service

The WebRamp Entré will work with either a LAN access package or a single-user Internet access account that uses dynamic IP addressing. The single-user account based on dynamic IP addressing will be a lot cheaper than getting a LAN access package in which several static IP addresses are assigned. In most cases, this is the option you'll want in order to keep your Internet access costs low.

After you establish your Internet access account, obtain the following information from your ISP. Record all information on the ISDN/Internet Worksheet included with the Entré.

- ISP's ISDN phone number
- ISP's IP gateway address, if any
- ISP's IP subnet mask, if any
- Authentication type (PAP or CHAP)
- Authentication name and password
- Domain Name Server (DNS) IP addresses
- Domain Name

If the ISP is using dynamic IP addressing, it will not supply an IP address for its side of the Internet connection. In this case, The Entré uses the following addresses in the ISP data screen during installation:

- IP address: 127.0.0.2
- Subnet mask: 255.0.0.0

Navigating the Entré Box

Before installing the WebRamp Entré, you should familiarize yourself with the ports and LEDs on the Entré unit. All the ports are at the rear of the unit, and the status LEDs are at the front of the unit. Table 14.1 explains the LED functions and Table 14.2 explains the functions of the Entré ports.

Plugging Everything into the Entré

The following steps show you how to set up your Entré and connect all your LAN and analog devices to it:

Table 14.1 Entré LED Functions

LED	FUNCTION
Power On LED (Red)	When on, it indicates that there is power to the unit.
Power-up Diagnostics LED (Green)	Indicates that all internal diagnostic tests have been completed at power-up and that the hardware is functioning properly. It should turn on and should stay on within 10 seconds after power is applied.
Hub Traffic LED (Yellow)	A flashing LED indicates traffic on any Ethernet port.
Connected Port LEDs (Green)	Any Ethernet port that is connected to a network device (PCs, printers, or other devices) will cause the corresponding LED to turn on (up to four).
B1 Active LED (Green)	When on, it indicates that the ISDN B1 channel is active.
B2 Active LED (Green)	When on, it indicates that the ISDN B2 channel is active.
WAN Error LED (Red)	When on, it indicates that there is an error on the ISDN line connection or configuration.

Table 14.2 Entré Port Functions

PORT	FUNCTION
ISDN port	Connector for the ISDN line.
POTS ports	Two RJ-11 POTS ports for adding analog devices to your ISDN line.
MDI switch	Switch for turning the number 1 Ethernet port into an input port from another hub. This allows you to expand the network beyond the four 10BaseT ports. Default is in the OFF position.
Ethernet ports	Four 10BaseT Ethernet ports, or three ports for computers and one port for connecting another hub to the WebRamp.
Serial port	Used for firmware upgrades done via a COM port connected to the PC running the WebRamp configuration program.
Power connector	The Entré uses a 12V DC IA wall-plug power supply. The center pin is positive (+) and the outer ring is negative (-) polarity.

1. Place the Entré on a desktop or mount it on a wall where you can see the LEDs and near your ISDN wall outlet and a power outlet.

2. Connect the power supply and leave the unit powered on because the Entré also acts as your network's hub. Also, your analog devices will not work on an ISDN line if the Entré is not powered on, because an ISDN line does not have its own power. For these reasons, the Entrée does not include a power switch.

3. Use the supplied RJ-11 cable to connect the WebRamp to the ISDN line. The RJ-11 cable will adapt to an RJ-45 connector.

4. Connect your PCs and any other networked devices, such as a printer, to the Entré using 10BaseT cables. One connector of the 10BaseT cable connects to the PC's network adapter card and the other plugs into the 10BaseT port at the back of the Entré.

   If you want to connect more than four network devices to your WebRamp Entré, turn the MDI switch located at the back of the unit to the ON position. Connect the other 10BaseT hub into the Ethernet port labeled 1. Make sure your other hub is connected to the WebRamp using its uplink port, which is specifically used for connecting one hub to another.

5. Connect any analog devices you want to use into the RJ-11 POTS ports. Any device that plugs into a modular RJ-11 telephone jack can be plugged into either the line 1 or line 2 port on the back of the Entré.

Setting Up Your Windows 95 LAN for a Dynamic IP

With the Entré hardware installed, you're ready to move on to software installation. The hub function of the Entré is ready to use and does not require any software setup for the unit itself. However, before you install the WebRampWiz software, you must set up your LAN by configuring each Windows 95 PC.

On the Windows 95 side of your LAN, make sure you have TCP/IP installed on each PC and bound to the network adapter card used for your TCP/IP connection to the Internet. For using the WebRamp with a dynamic IP address Internet access account, make sure the default TCP/IP settings are implemented. In the Network control panel, select the TCP/IP-> [*network adapter name*] in the Installed Network Components list, then click Properties. The Obtain an IP address automatically setting should be selected in the IP Address tab. Configure every computer on your Windows 95 LAN this way.

The WebRampWiz installation and configuration program detects your current TCP/IP configuration before proceeding with your installation process. If it's not properly set up, the configuration process will be different from the one described in this chapter. Chapter 8, the section titled "Configuring Your Windows 95 LAN for Internet Access," explains this configuration process in more detail.

Setting Up the Entré

With your Windows 95 LAN properly configured for dynamic IP addressing and each PC connected to the Entré, you're ready to use the WebRampWiz installation software. Make sure you have the ISDN/Internet Worksheet filled out and handy because you'll need to enter information from it into the WebRampWiz software as you go through the installation process.

Note: If you have a problem with the installation of the WebRampWiz software, you can use the Windows Explorer to delete the WebRamp directory. You don't need to run an uninstall program or use Add/Remove Programs in the Windows 95 ControlPanel.

Here's how to install and configure the WebRamp for a dynamic IP Internet account.

1. Select the PC on which you want to install the WebRampWiz software. You install WebRampWiz on only one PC, which will be the PC you use to configure and manage the WebRamp. For this computer, specify an IP address of 192.168.1.254 and a subnet mask of 255.255.255.0 in the

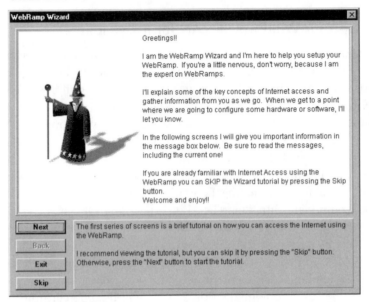

Figure 14.1 *The WebRamp Wizard welcome screen.*

TCP/IP Properties dialog box. You only need to do this the first time to initially configure the Entré. After you're finished configuring the Web-Ramp, choose the Obtain an address automatically setting again.

2. After configuring the PC you're using for configuring the WebRamp, insert the WebRampWiz disk in your floppy disk drive, then choose Start|Run. Type **A:\SETUP** and click OK. The WebRamp Wizard welcome screen appears (Figure 14.1)

3. Click the Next button until you access the screen shown in Figure 14.2. The screens you're bypassing are informational screens. This is the first configuration screen for the WebRampWiz. It's used for specifying whether you're using the WebRamp to create a new LAN with the Web-Ramp acting as a hub or adding the WebRamp as just an ISDN router to an existing network.

4. Choose the New option, which is the default setting. Click Next. A screen appears with a checklist of items that you should have in place before proceeding with the installation.

5. Click Next. The WebRamp Wizard gets configuration information from your Entré and displays another informational screen. Click Next again. The screen for specifying dynamic or static IP addressing appears (Figure 14.3).

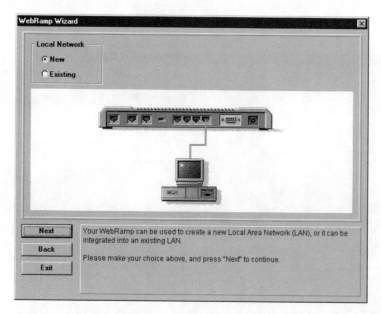

Figure 14.2 The WebRamp Wizard screen for specifying whether you're using the WebRamp to create a new LAN with the WebRamp acting as a hub or adding the WebRamp as only an ISDN router to an existing network.

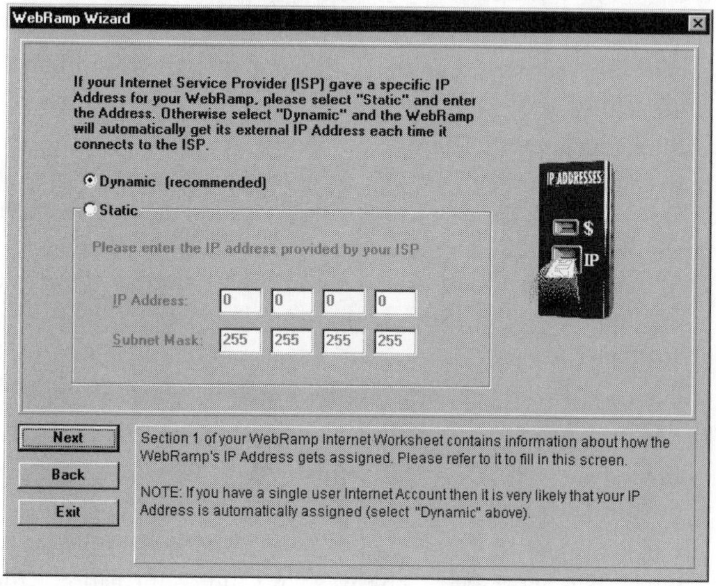

Figure 14.3 This screen is for specifying whether you'll be using a dynamic or static IP address Internet access account.

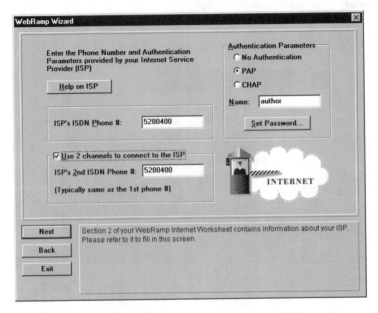

Figure 14.4 *This screen is for entering ISP account information.*

6. Choose the Dynamic (recommended) setting, and click Next. A screen appears for entering ISP account information (Figure 14.4).

7. In the ISP screen, enter the following information; click Next when you're finished. All this information should have come from your ISP.

Enter the ISDN telephone number(s) you'll use to connect to the ISP. If you don't require an area code to get to your ISP, don't enter one. Don't use any dashes or parentheses in these fields, just the numbers. If you have two B–channel access, click on the Use 2 channels to connect to the ISP check box, and enter an ISDN number if different from the first number. Most ISPs use the same ISDN access numbers for both B channels.

Choose the type of authentication used by your ISP, which typically is PAP or CHAP.

Enter your user ID in the Name field. This is the name used to log on to your ISP's host computer.

Click on the Set Password button. A Password dialog box appears where you enter your logon password and confirmation. Click OK.

8. In the screen used for entering your ISDN line information (Figure 14.5), enter the following information; click Next when you're finished. All this information should have come from your ISDN service provider. The

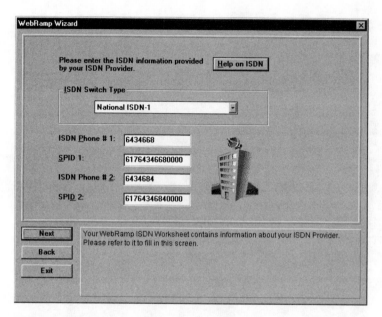

Figure 14.5 *The screen for entering information about your ISDN service, including switch type, phone numbers, and SPIDs.*

Help on ISDN button provides more detailed information on these setting, if you need it.

Select the ISDN switch type from the ISDN Switch Type drop-down list.

Enter your primary ISDN telephone number in the ISDN Phone #1 field and its SPID number (if one was assigned) in the SPID 1 field.

Enter your second ISDN telephone number in the ISDN Phone #2 field and its SPID number (if one was assigned) in the SPID 2 field.

9. In the POTS port screen (Figure 14.6), select the analog devices you plan to connect to each line port on your Entré. The default setting is Phone for Line 1 and Fax or Modem for Line 2, but you can change these assignments. You don't have to use any analog devices with your Entré. Click Next.

10. In the DHCP configuration screen (Figure 14.7), do the following; click Next when you're finished.

Click on the Yes check box to enable DHCP.

Enter the IP addresses for your ISP's Domain Name Server(s) in the Primary DNS Server IP Address and Alternate DNS Server IP Address fields.

If you have a domain name, enter it in the Domain Name field.

11. In the screen showing your DHCP settings, click Next.

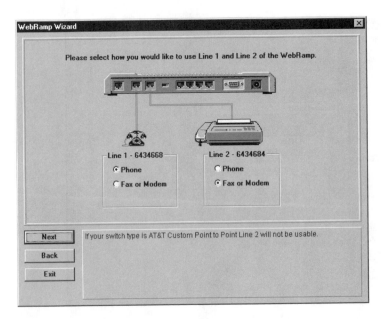

Figure 14.6 *The POTS ports configuration screen.*

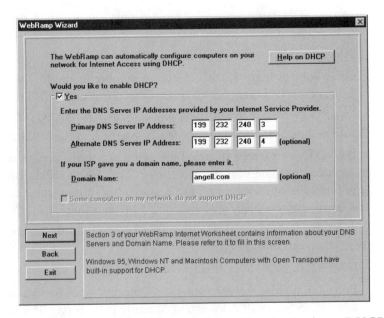

Figure 14.7 *The DHCP screen is for enabling the Entré as a DHCP server.*

Figure 14.8 *The WebRampWiz window.*

12. In the final WebRamp Wizard screen, click Next to send your settings to Entré for configuration. After the configuration is complete, a screen appears telling you the Entré will run a series of tests to make sure your ISDN line and Internet access connections are working properly.

13. Click on the Next button to begin the tests. The WebRampWiz program runs diagnostic programs to check your ISDN line and ISP settings. If a problem is detected, the WebRampWiz will return you to the screen on which the setting in question appears for you to double-check.

14. After all the tests are successfully completed, click Next.

15. In the final wizard screen, click the Finish button. The WebRamp Wizard prompts you to respond whether you want to display the WebRampWiz application; click the WebRampWiz button to display the WebRampWiz window (see Figure 14.8). Congratulations! You have successfully installed the WebRamp.

16. On the PC you used to configure the WebRamp, reconfigure the TCP/IP properties from the specified IP address of 192.168.1.254 and subnet mask of 255.255.255.0 to return to the Obtain an address automatically setting to make the computer a DHCP client.

You don't need to be running the WebRampWiz program to use WebRamp. The WebRampWiz window is the manager program for the Entré, and it also displays ISDN and Internet connection status information. You can keep it available by minimizing it to your taskbar.

You can always run the WebRampWiz Wizard at any time to reconfigure your settings by choosing Configure|Wizard in the WebRampWiz window. You can also use the Advanced Configuration dialog box, as explained later in this chapter.

Making the Internet Connection

Once the WebRamp is set up, you're ready to access the Internet using any TCP/IP application on any computer connected to your Windows 95 LAN. To surf the Web from any computer connected to the WebRamp, simply double-click on the Web browser icon. For example, clicking on Internet Explorer on your Windows 95 desktop automatically makes the Internet connection and then displays your starting page. It's fast because ISDN connections via Ethernet take only a few seconds to complete instead of the 30 seconds (or more) it takes using Windows 95 Dial-Up Networking with a modem or ISDN adapter card or modem.

To use e-mail or network news, you need to configure your e-mail and network newsreader programs. This involves specifying the e-mail and network news server addresses supplied by your ISP. For each Internet user on your local LAN who wants a private e-mail address, you will need a separate e-mail account from your ISP, which typically costs about $10 per month.

Note: Working with the core complement of Internet and other remote access tools is covered in Chapter 9, in the section titled "Microsoft Tools of the Remote Access Trade."

A Tour of the WebRampWiz Manager

The WebRampWiz application is the software for the Entré that lets you monitor your connection status and make any configuration changes to your WebRamp configuration. A number of configuration options are available from the WebRampWiz window (Figure 14.8) beyond those that are essential for setting up the WebRamp. Through the WebRampWiz window, you can access all the features and controls of the WebRamp. Also, the main window displays two control panels for displaying the condition and status of your ISDN line and your analog calls.

The Configure and Actions menus provide the access to the nuts and bolts of the WebRampWiz program. Table 14.3 describes the commands in the Configure menu, and Table 14.4 describes the commands in the Actions menu. The File

Table 14.3 Configure Menu Commands

COMMAND	DESCRIPTION
Wizard	Lets you reenter the wizard you used the first time you configured the WebRamp, from which you can change settings at any time.
Advanced	Accesses a dialog box for changing configuration values entered using the wizard, as well as advanced setting that aren't available from the wizard.
Print	Prints a copy of the current WebRamp configuration settings.
Factory Defaults	Resets all the parameters back to the factory defaults. Once set to Factory Defaults, the WebRamp appears as an unconfigured unit with no IP address.
Set IP Address	Sets the LAN IP address of the WebRamp. A WebRamp that is new or that has been set to Factory Defaults will not have a LAN IP address. Set IP Address locates the WebRamp on your LAN without a valid IP address and allows you to set a new IP address.
Select WebRamp	In networks that contain multiple WebRamp units, Select WebRamp will search for and list unconfigured and configured units with valid IP addresses.

Table 14.4 Actions Menu Commands

COMMAND	DESCRIPTION
View Log	Allows viewing of WebRamp system events for diagnostics.
Diagnostics	Provides access to several diagnostic programs for checking your ISDN line and ISP connection.
Setup Monitor	Allows you to set start and stop times for the display of channel usage and traffic statistics for the WebRamp.
Show Monitor	Displays the WebRamp Monitor panel that shows channel usage and traffic statistics for the WebRamp.
Show Phone/Fax	Shows Line 1 and Line 2 on-hook and off-hook activity.
Firmware Upgrade	Allows the upgrading of the WebRamp firmware.
Drop ISDN Connections	Hangs up both channels of the ISDN line.
Reset	Reinitializes the WebRamp; does not affect save parameters. This is like a warm reboot for the WebRamp.
Switch to IP Router mode	Allows you to switch the WebRamp functionality to a static IP address router.

menu includes the Exit command, and the Help menu includes the standard Windows 95 online help system for the WebRamp. The Help menu also includes access to a listing of ISDN service providers and Internet providers offering ISDN Internet access.

Entré Advanced Configuration Options

Once the WebRampWiz is installed and the WebRamp has been configured, the Advanced Configuration dialog box (Figure 14.9) can be used to perform a variety of configuration changes to your WebRamp. You access the Advanced Configuration dialog window by choosing Configure|Advanced Configuration from the WebRampWiz window.

The Advanced Configuration dialog box has several tabs for organizing different types of Entré settings. Some of the settings in the Advanced Configuration dialog box are the same as those in which you entered data while using the wizard to configure the WebRamp. There are also a number of other settings that can be accessed only by using the Advanced Configuration dialog box. As the name of the dialog box implies, many of these are advanced settings. The following sections describe the functions covered by each tab in the Advanced Configuration dialog box.

The ISP Tab

The ISP tab (see Figure 14.9) includes the standard ISP settings you used in the wizard, including the ISP's ISDN telephone number and authentication type settings, but there are additional settings here that weren't available in the wizard.

If checked, the ISP's IP Address not given setting means the ISP did not supply an IP address for its side of the Internet connection. In this case, the WebRamp uses the IP address 127.0.0.2 and subnet mask 255.0.0.0. If this changes, you can specify the IP addresses provided by your ISP.

If you want to prevent anyone from accessing your WebRamp from the Internet, you can define a user name and password for accessing the WebRamp. To do this, select Incoming in the Authentication Parameters group. Enter a user name in the Name field, click on the Set Password button, and enter your password.

The Options button displays the ISP Options dialog box (Figure 14.10). This lets you specify a variety of settings.

- The Disconnect After setting tells the WebRamp to disconnect after the specified amount of time, measured in seconds.

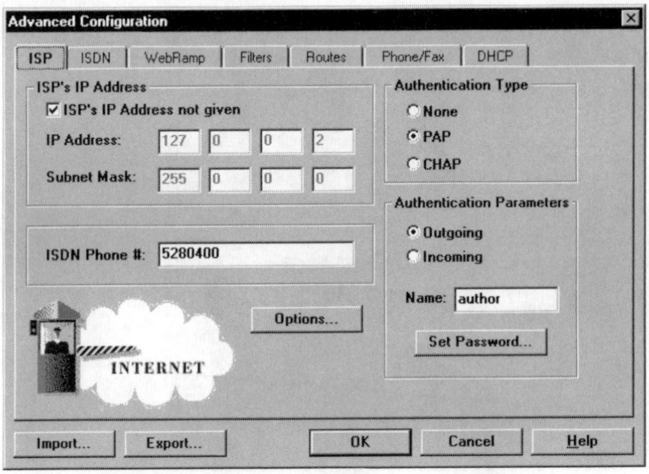

Figure 14.9 *The Advanced Configuration dialog box.*

- The Active Filter Set option is the Default, which is the one you'll use the most, as explained later in this chapter.
- The Multilink PPP group lets you specify the use of the second B channel. The Dynamically setting lets the WebRamp automatically adjust the number of B channels used in a connection with the amount of traffic. The 2nd Channel setting specifies the telephone number of the ISP for the second B channel.

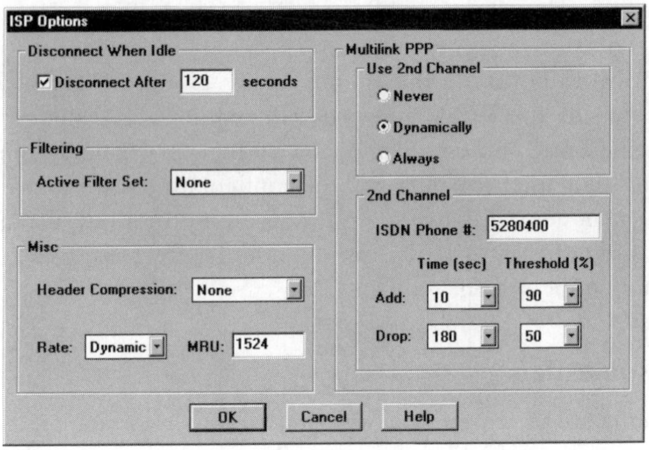

Figure 14.10 *The ISP Options dialog box.*

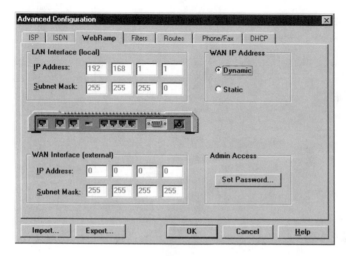

Figure 14.11 *The WebRamp tab in the Advanced Configuration dialog box.*

ISDN and WebRamp Tabs

The ISDN tab includes the same settings that you used in the wizard to tell the WebRamp the type of telephone switch used at central office, ISDN telephone number, and SPIDs. The WebRamp tab (Figure 14.11) includes settings for specifying LAN and WAN IP addresses. The IP address and subnet mask in the LAN Interface group are the default WebRamp IP address of 192.168.1.1 and the subnet mask of 255.255.255.0. The WAN Interface IP addresses aren't used when you have an ISP that doesn't assign you a gateway IP address, which is the case for most dynamic IP accounts.

The Set Password button in the Admin Access group lets you add your own password for accessing the WebRamp for configuration via Telnet. Using Telnet, you can access the Entré and use a command prompt for changing the configuration. The commands used for this form of configuration are listed in the Entré manual. The default administrative login for accessing the Entré is the user name *wradmin;* the password is *trancell.* This setting doesn't affect using the WebRamp-Wiz program for configuration.

Filters and Routes Tabs

Filters and routing are the core elements behind internetworking and routers. The WebRamp is designed to shield you from working with these complex configuration parameters for most SOHO remote access users. However, the WebRamp does include tools to enable MIS professionals to work with filters and routing tables to configure WebRamps.

The Filters tab, which you'll see later in this chapter, lets you create custom filters for the WebRamp. These filters can be used to control and selectively filter different data packets as they enter or leave the WebRamp. The Default filter that appears in the Filter Set list is premade, and designed to provide the necessary filtering for working with the WebRamp out of the box. It prevents Internet intruders from gaining access to your LAN, along with other features to support your Internet connection. For more information on the WebRamp's default and custom filters, see the "Entré Filter Fundamentals" section later in this chapter.

The Entré provides a default routing mechanism that automatically handles the routing table requirements needed by most SOHO sites. And like filters, the Entré includes features to enable professionals to add customized routing table entries. The Routes tab, which you'll see later in this chapter, is for adding and editing routes different from the default system routes for delivering data. For more information on the WebRamp's routing table features, see the "Which Route?" section later in this chapter.

The Phone/Fax Tab

The Phone/Fax tab (Figure 14.12) lets you configure options for your analog equipment (telephone, fax, or modem) attached to your ISDN line via the Web-

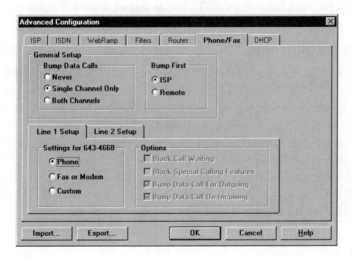

Figure 14.12 *The Phone/Fax tab lets you configure how WebRamp handles analog equipment connected to your ISDN line.*

Ramp. The Bump Data Calls setting lets you specify whether you want the Entré to bump data transmission from two to one B channel in the event of an incoming analog call. The Line 1 and Line 2 Setup options are used to specify the type of device you're connecting to the WebRamp. Choosing the Custom option lets you specify different settings, which appear in the Options group. All these settings are active as the default Custom setting.

The DHCP Tab

The DHCP tab (shown later in the chapter) lets you customize the DHCP functions of the WebRamp, which is the server functionality that lets you use dynamic IP addressing. The settings here enable you to change the IP address range for your LAN, as well as other settings that are required for every PC on your LAN to connect to the Internet. These settings include DNS server addresses, domain name, and any excluded IP addresses from DHCP server functions. More on the DHCP server functions in the "DHCP for Fun and Profit" section later in this chapter.

Entré Monitoring and Diagnostics Tools

The WebRampWiz manager program includes several tools for monitoring your remote access connection, such as checking the status of your ISDN connection and data traffic. The Entré also includes tools for performing diagnostics on your ISDN line and Internet connection. The following sections explain these tools.

Monitoring the Situation

The WebRampWiz includes a status monitor, which is always active to keep track of the status of your ISDN line and other helpful data. It tells you the condition of your ISDN line and the MAC address (unique hardware address) of the Web-Ramp; it also provides a message log for your ISDN connection.

The Monitor, which you display by choosing Actions|Show Monitor, lets you track ISDN activity within specified time periods. The Monitor panel appears below the WebRamp status panel (Figure 14.13). Choosing Actions|Phone/Fax Lines displays the Phone/Fax Lines monitor panel (see Figure 14.8), which appears below the WebRamp status panel replacing the monitor panel.

View the Log

The View Log displays the most recent message that appeared in the Entré. These messages inform you of background connectivity activities, including ISDN and ISP connections. Figure 14.14 shows the View Log dialog box. You can access the

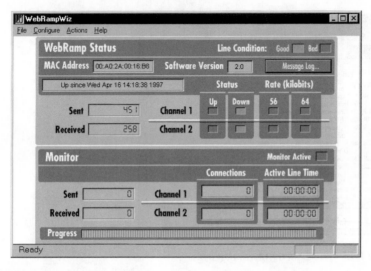

Figure 14.13 *The WebRamp Status and Monitor panels.*

View Log by choosing Actions | View Log or by clicking the Message Log button in the WebRamp Status panel. The View Log dialog box includes several buttons for managing the log.

Diagnostics for Troubleshooting

Choosing Actions | Diagnostics displays the Diagnostics dialog box (Figure 14.15). Diagnostics runs three different tests that verify connectivity between the Entré, the ISDN provider, and the Internet service provider. A key diagnostics tool is the event log, which appears in the Diagnostics dialog box. It shows what is happening

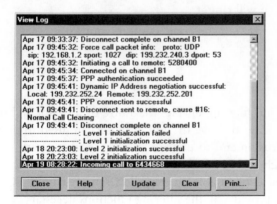

Figure 14.14 *The View Log dialog box.*

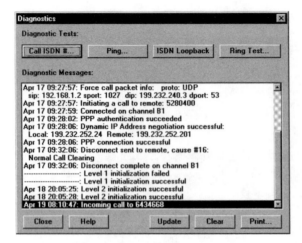

Figure 14.15 *The Diagnostics dialog box.*

when a test is executed. Information in this event dialog box is useful to ISDN or Internet providers in solving connectivity problems. The following are the tests that can be run from Diagnostics dialog box.

- The Call ISDN # button tests a specific ISDN number to make sure it can be reached. The test establishes a connection to the remote host and then disconnects.

- The ISDN Loopback button runs an ISDN loopback test between the Web-Ramp and the local switch. This test verifies that the ISDN numbers and SPIDs were properly entered.

- The Ring Test button checks the phone line connection from the analog devices (fax or phone) to the WebRamp. You select the phone line you want to test, and the device will ring it.

- The Ping button lets you test the connection to your ISP.

Entré Filter Fundamentals

As mentioned briefly earlier, filtering enables the Entré to monitor and selectively filter data packets as they enter or leave the router. Filters are used to protect your LAN from unwanted intrusion and to prevent selected local network traffic from leaving your LAN through the Entré. The Entré filtering module comprises one default filter set and three configurable custom filter sets. For most SOHO sites, the Entré default filter set provides all the filtering functions necessary.

The Default Filter

The default filter set was designed to prevent an attack technique known as *IP spoofing,* where an attacker from the outside pretends to be a user on one of the computers on the local LAN, thus allowing the intruder to have complete freedom to roam your local network if you're using a static IP account. The default filter works by implementing the following filtering rules:

- Any incoming packets that have the same source address as any address on your LAN will be dropped. This is the reject IP spoofing feature that prevents outside intruders from gaining access to your LAN. The local address is determined when the Entré LAN address is configured.

- All incoming connection requests to TCP port 25 (used by SMTP mail servers) will be allowed. All other TCP port requests will be denied for purposes of connecting to a server on your LAN (such as Telnet, FTP, and HTTP).

- Any other incoming TCP/IP traffic will pass the default filter from servers on the Internet to computers on your LAN.

The Filter Configuration Dialog Box

The Filters tab in the Advanced Configuration dialog box (Figure 14.16), which you access by choosing Configure|Advanced, is the gateway to creating and editing custom filters. Each filter set is a complete filter package and can be applied to either the ISP or the remote office connections. Only one filter set at a time can

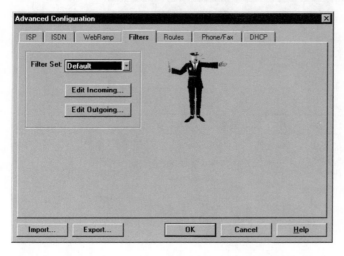

Figure 14.16 *The Filters tab in the Advanced Configuration dialog box.*

be used for either connection. Each filter set has two (groups) strings of filters: One string examines incoming IP packets, and the second examines outgoing IP packets. Each string consists of 16 separate filters that can examine protocol, source IP and destination IP addresses, and source and destination ports.

● ●

CAUTION: Don't create your own filters unless you know what you're doing, because filter mistakes can be difficult to troubleshoot.

To create a filter, you first choose the custom filter set (custom1, custom2, or custom3) you want from the Filter Set drop-down list. You cannot edit the Default filter. After selecting a custom filter, if you want to make changes to packets coming into your LAN from the WAN, click on the Edit Incoming button. Selecting Edit Outgoing will affect packets leaving your LAN. Figure 14.17 shows the default custom1 Incoming Filters dialog box. The default custom1 Outgoing Filters dialog box looks the same.

In the Incoming Filters and Outgoing Filters dialog boxes, the Source IP and Destination IP groups are referenced by which filter direction you are working with. Source for outgoing packets is referenced from the LAN side; source for incoming packets is referenced from the WAN side of the Entré. And note, even though the 16 filters are in a series, any number can be configured without regard to sequence. These filters are specified in the Filter field.

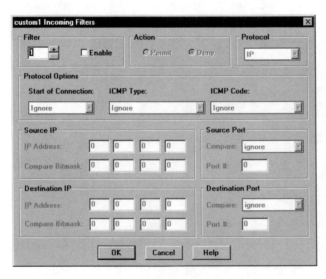

Figure 14.17 *The custom1 Incoming Filters dialog box.*

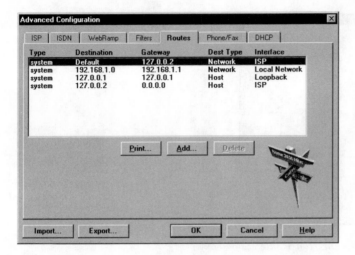

Figure 14.18 The Routes tab in the Advanced Configuration dialog box.

Which Route?

The Routes tab in the Advanced Configuration dialog box (Figure 14.18), which you access by choosing Configure|Advanced, displays the routes used by the Entré. Routes are instructions that tell the Entré acting as a gateway which path or route to take when sending data across the Internet (or any TCP/IP network). A gateway is a device that connects two networks and allows data to be transferred between networks. There is always a default system route, which the Entré uses for your ISP's gateway. System routes are created automatically based on information you supplied in the WebRampWiz software; these cannot be deleted. However, you can add routes to access other gateways.

• •

CAUTION: Like working with filters, I don't recommend that you add your own routes unless you know what you're doing.

Clicking on the Add button brings up the Add Route dialog box (Figure 14.19). This lets you add a route for packets based on three different types of routes: Static, Permanent, and Metric. The destination specifies the end point of the message, either the recipient's host or network. The Network destination is a specific network and the Host destination is an individual PC or device. You enter the address of either the destination network or host in the IP Address field.

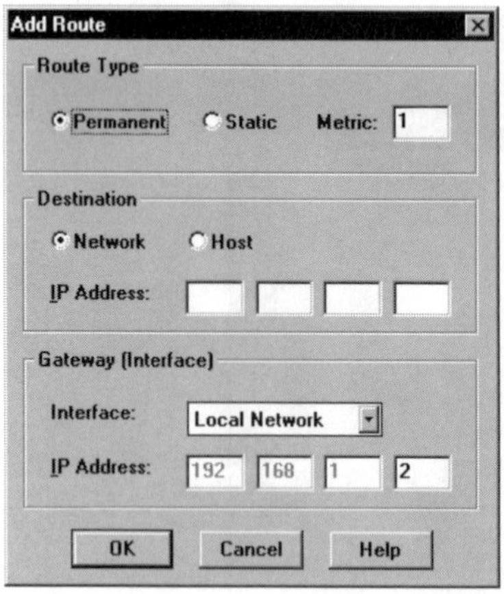

Figure 14.19 *The Add Route dialog box.*

DHCP for Fun and Profit

The Entré has a built-in Dynamic Host Configuration Protocol (DHCP) server. As a DHCP server, the WebRamp can assign the following parameters to any computer running as a DHCP client (of which Windows 95 is one):

IP address from the available pool of IP addresses

Subnet mask

Domain Name Service (DNS) server addresses (primary and alternate)

Gateway address (typically the IP address of the WebRamp)

Domain name for the network

Whenever a Windows 95 computer with the DHCP client functionality enabled is started, it sends a query on the network to a DHCP server for the preceding information. The DHCP server will assign one of the IP addresses from the available pool of addresses. In the case of using the WebRamp as a router for a single-user ISDN Internet access account, the IP addresses are private and not recognized by the Internet. The default range of IP addresses used by the WebRamp's DHCP server is 192.168.1.1 to 192.168.1.254.

Using DHCP eliminates configuring the preceding five parameters for every computer on your Windows 95 LAN. If there is a need to change any of these parameters, all you have to do is change the setting in the DHCP server and restart the computers; they will be reassigned with new information. This is done using the WebRampWiz program.

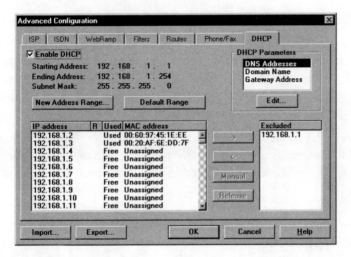

Figure 14.20 *The DHCP tab lets you make changes to your WebRamp's DHCP server.*

In most cases for dynamic IP Internet access accounts, you won't need to make any changes to the WebRamp's DHCP server. However, as is the case for other features, Entré includes tools for more advanced configuration. The DHCP tab (Figure 14.20) in the Advanced Configuration dialog box includes settings for making such changes. The settings in the DHCP tab include:

- The Enable DHCP box enables the DHCP server on the WebRamp. Thereafter, the dialog box shows the starting and ending IP addresses, which will be the range of private IP addresses for your LAN available from the DHCP Address Pool. The default range of IP addresses used by the DHCP server is 192.168.1.1 to 192.168.1.254.

- The New Address Range button allows you to modify the existing range of addresses to be assigned to computers on the network. You can change the starting address range and the number of addresses.

- The Default Range button will recalculate the DHCP address range based on the Entré IP address and Subnet mask. The Entré IP address will be automatically excluded for use by other computers.

- The address lists show the IP addresses in the range and their current status. The list includes the IP address, a reserved indicator, a free or used status for the address, and the MAC address if the IP address is assigned or reserved.

- The Excluded list lets you specify computers on a network that don't support DHCP or that should maintain fixed IP addresses. The right and left arrow buttons let you add or remove computers to and from the Excluded list.

- The Manual button is used to ensure that certain computers always get the same IP address. You have to enter the MAC address of the computer.

- The Release button lets you release an assigned IP address from a specific computer. You have to enter the MAC address of the computer.

- The DHCP Parameters setting lets you define three other parameters that the DHCP server can assign: DNS Addresses, Domain Name, and Gateway Address. To configure or modify them, select the item and click on the Edit button.

Making Firmware Upgrades

Technology changes so fast that most router vendors, including Ramp Networks, allow do-it-yourself firmware upgrades. Firmware is a category of chips, such as EPROM chips, used in computer hardware devices that hold their content without electrical power. The Entré firmware upgrade feature allows you to download new firmware from the Internet and send it to the WebRamp unit via a port at the back of the unit. This feature allows you to periodically update the capabilities of the Entré. To perform a firmware upgrade, follow these steps:

1. Connect the Entré to your PC serial port using a 9-pin connector for the Entré and either a 9- or 25-pin connector for your PC. Make sure the serial port is connected to an open COM port in Windows 95.

2. Download the firmware upgrade file from the Ramp Networks Web site at http://www.rampnet.com/ using any Web browser. Copy the file to the Webramp directory.

3. Open the WebRampWiz program and choose Actions|Firmware Upgrade. A message appears asking you to confirm the upgrade; click Yes.

4. In the Open dialog box, locate your WebRamp directory and select the .bin file that you downloaded from the Ramp Networks Web site; click OK.

5. In the COM Port Options dialog box, choose the appropriate COM port setting, and click OK. A dialog box appears telling you to unplug the Entré.

6. Unplug the Entré for three seconds then plug it back in. The Entré begins immediately transferring the firmware from your PC to the unit. Downloading the firmware takes several minutes, after which you'll see an Upgrade Successful message.

7. Once the upgrade is completed, reset the Entré by removing and reapplying power by unplugging and replugging the unit.

8. Choose Configure | Select WebRamp from the WebRampWiz program to reestablish connection with the Entré.

What's Next

The WebRamp Entré is one of the easiest ISDN routers to set up. Another is the Netopia So-Smart ISDN router from Farallon Communications. The next chapter walks you through the latest incarnation of this popular router.

15   *Farallon's Netopia Internet Router*

The latest generation of Farallon's Netopia ISDN routers offer an impressive collection of features specifically designed for the SOHO market. The Netopia So-Smart Internet Router series includes the DHCP and NAT combination for low-cost LAN connections to the Internet as well as a host of other useful features. This chapter takes you on a hands-on tour of the Netopia So-Smart Internet Router.

About the Netopia ISDN Router

Farallon's So-Smart ISDN router (model 635) is the latest addition to the Netopia Internet Router family. It builds on an already outstanding line of ISDN routers designed for the SOHO market. The Netopia ISDN router is full-featured and looks good too. Although its street price is $849, you can get it at an even cheaper price if you buy it as part of your Internet access service from an authorized ISP. The Netopia So-Smart ISDN router includes the following key features:

- Easy configuration. A friendly, step-by-step menu system walks you through the process. You can also use a Web interface version of the configuration program.

- Smart IP, which allows you to connect a LAN to the Internet via ISDN using a single-user access account. The Netopia includes built-in DHCP server and NAT functionality to enable these big cost-saving features. You can also use the Netopia as a static IP router.

- Data over voice, which allows data calls to be placed or answered using ISDN speech grade capabilities instead of circuit-switched data-grade capabilities. In many areas, this feature enables Netopia customers to avoid paying higher ISDN per-minute charges.

- Firmware upgrade and configuration via software downloads from the Farallon Web site.

- IP and IPX routing support. Model 435 includes IP, IPX, and AppleTalk routing support.

- Built-in firewall filter for security. The preconfigured firewall blocks undesirable traffic originating from the Internet (for static IP connections). You can also deploy more customized filters using Netopia's extensive custom filtering capabilities.

- Scheduled connections based on preset times. The Netopia enables you to schedule connections at specific times. This feature is great for SOHO sites that want outsiders to have access to their LANs during specific times.

- Two PCMCIA card slots for remote configuration over POTS as a backup to ISDN or Internet-based remote configurations.

- Two analog ports with advanced calling features for sharing your ISDN line with analog devices (telephone, fax, and modem).

- An integrated two-port 10BaseT Ethernet hub; or you can connect the Netopia to your existing hub.

- Support for up to 12 computers.

• •

CAUTION: Earlier releases of the Netopia So-Smart router firmware didn't include support for the Web interface configuration. Make sure you're using version 2.0.2 , which you can download for free from the Farallon Web site. Upgrading the Netopia firmware is explained later in this chapter.

Getting Started with the Netopia

Before you begin working with the Netopia 635, do the following:

- Order ISDN service and provision it for the Netopia.

- Order your ISDN Internet access account.

- Set up the Netopia router by connecting it to your ISDN line, to all your networked PCs, and any analog devices you want to share your ISDN line.

- Set up your Windows 95 LAN for dynamic IP addressing by configuring the Windows 95 TCP/IP Properties for each PC.

Ordering ISDN Service

Your telephone company may have the Netopia ISDN router on a list of supported products that has been tested with a particular ISDN line configuration. If your telephone company confirms that Netopia ISDN Router is on that list, then it will know how to set up your line. If your ISDN telephone company is familiar with NIUF Capability Packages, request the following for your Netopia: Capability Package P (2B+D), which includes alternate voice/circuit-switched data on two B channels, and basic D-channel packet. This package provides non-EKTS voice features, including Flexible Calling, Additional Call Offering, and Calling Number Identification. Data capabilities include Calling Number Identification. You can also specify the Intel Blue configuration package, which is widely known by most telephone companies.

Note: Make sure you inform the telephone company that your Netopia has two POTS ports because earlier versions of the Netopia did not.

To configure the Netopia ISDN Router, your telephone company must provide you with the type of switch configuration used on your ISDN line. The Netopia ISDN Router supports all the leading telephone company switches and software, and the product's documentation contains a reference table summarizing the recommended provisioning parameters offered by various North American ISDN switches, in case your telephone company doesn't support the NIUF Compatibility Packages.

An ISDN line requires one or more directory numbers (DN) and usually one or more service profile identifier (SPID) numbers. Your telephone company provides this information when you order your ISDN line or after your ISDN line is set up. If the switch on your line is an AT&T 5ESS custom point-to-point, you won't have any SPIDs or be able to use the POTS ports for analog communications.

Ordering Internet Service

The Netopia will work with either a LAN access package that uses static IP addresses or a single-user Internet access account that uses dynamic IP addressing. The single-user account based on dynamic IP addressing will be a lot cheaper than getting a LAN access package in which several static IP addresses are assigned. This is the option you'll probably use for affordable LAN-based Internet access.

After you establish your Internet access account, you'll need the following information from your ISP:

- ISP's ISDN phone number
- ISP's IP gateway address, if any
- ISP's IP subnet mask, if any
- Authentication type (PAP or CHAP)
- Authentication name and password
- Domain Name Server (DNS) IP addresses
- Domain Name

Setting Up the Netopia Hardware

The Netopia ISDN router's back panel has a connector labeled Config Console for attaching the router to a PC COM port. To make this connection, use one of the supplied cables. Connect one end of the supplied ISDN phone cable to the RJ-45 ISDN port labeled U on the Netopia ISDN router back panel. Connect the other end of the ISDN phone cable to the ISDN wall jack. The Netopia ISDN Router back panel has three RJ-45 ports, so be sure you connect the ISDN cable to the correct one. Connect the Netopia ISDN router to a hub using 10BaseT cabling with one end plugged into one of the two RJ-45 ports on the back of the Netopia and the other plugged into your hub.

Note: You can use the Netopia with two PCs without using a hub. Simply plug in the 10BaseT cables from each PC directly into the back of the unit. If you want to use the Netopia as a hub for more than two PCs, you'll need to use Farallon's daisy-chain Ethernet connectors.

Setting Up Your Windows 95 LAN for a Dynamic IP

With the Netopia hardware installed, you're ready to move on to software installation. Before you configure the Netopia, make sure each Windows 95 PC on your LAN is properly configured. On the Windows 95 side of your LAN, make sure you have TCP/IP installed on each PC and bound to the network adapter card used for your TCP/IP connection to the Internet. For using the Netopia with a dynamic IP address Internet access account, make sure the default TCP/IP settings are used. In the Network control panel, select the TCP/IP-> [*network adapter name*] in the installed Network Components list, then click Properties. The Obtain an IP address automatically setting should be selected in the IP Address tab. Every computer on your Windows 95 LAN should be configured this way.

Note: Chapter 8 "Setting Up Your Windows 95 LAN for Remote Access" explains this configuration process in more detail.

Configuring the Netopia

The Netopia So-Smart router can be configured using several different methods. One is to use the Windows 95 HyperTerminal program with the unit attached to a PC via the supplied RS-232 cable. This text-based approach uses a friendly text-based menu system to quickly walk you through the configuration. Or you can use the Smart Start program and your Web browser to configure the Netopia.

Using Smart Start and Your Web Browser to Configure the Netopia

The Netopia includes a simple program on the CD called Smart Start that lets you assign an IP address to the Netopia via your LAN. Once you set up the Netopia with its own IP address, you can use a Web browser or Telnet over your LAN to reconfigure the Netopia at any time. To use Smart Start, you need to use either a static or private IP address and a subnet mask IP address. For example, you can enter the private IP address 192.168.3.89 and subnet mask 255.255.255.240 in the Smart Start configuration dialog box (Figure 15.1). You'll also need to enter the serial number of your Netopia, which is located at the bottom of the unit. Once you submit these entries, you can use your Web browser to access and configure

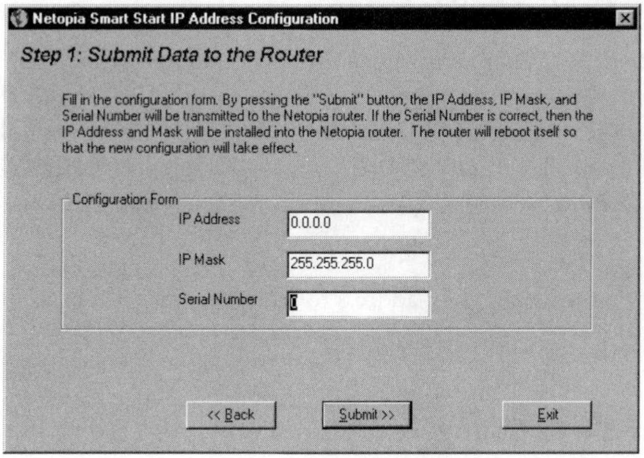

Figure 15.1 *The Smart Start dialog box for assigning the Netopia an IP address.*

Figure 15.2 The Netopia Router Home Page.

the Netopia. For example, entering 192.168.3.89 as a URL in your Web browser displays the Netopia Router Home Page (Figure 15.2).

Using Telnet to Configure the Netopia

The Telnet method of configuring the Netopia implements the same text-based menu system you use when you connect your PC to the Netopia via the Console (serial) port. But note, you cannot use Telnet to access the Netopia until you assign an IP address to the unit. To access the Netopia via Telnet, use the Windows 95 DOS window and enter

```
telnet [IP_Address]
```

where *IP_Address* is the assigned IP address for the Netopia. For example:

```
telnet 192.168.3.89.
```

Using the Console to Configure Netopia

Using the Smart Start program and your Web browser provides a graphical way to configure the Netopia, but the text-based menu system accessible from the Con-

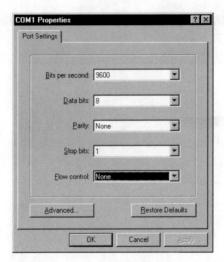

Figure 15.3 *The COM Properties dialog box.*

sole port is more straightforward. To initially configure using the Console method, you use the Windows 95 HyperTerminal program. The following steps explain how to create a HyperTerminal connection to the Netopia using the HyperTerminal program in Windows 95:

1. With the Netopia attached to your PC via the supplied RS-232 cable and turned on, choose Start|Accessories|HyperTerminal. The HyperTerminal window appears.

2. Double-click on the Hypertm icon. The Connection Description dialog box appears.

3. Type a name for your connection (such as Netopia Router), choose an icon, and click OK. The Phone Number dialog box appears.

4. In the Connect using list, choose the Direct to Com port for the serial port you're using to connect the PC to the Netopia; click OK. The COM Properties dialog box appears with the COM port number identified on the dialog box's title bar (Figure 15.3).

5. Change the Bits per second setting to 9600, and choose None for the Flow control setting. The Data bits, Parity, and Stop bits use the default values of 8, None, and 1, respectively.

6. Click OK. The HyperTerminal window appears. You're ready to configure the Netopia.

7. Choose File|Save to save your connection profile.

Figure 15.4 *The Main Menu screen is your starting point for configuring the Netopia.*

8. Press Ctrl+L. The Netopia ISDN Router's Main Menu screen (Figure 15.4) appears in the HyperTerminal window.

Using Easy Setup

The Netopia's Easy Setup item in the Main Menu is an easy-to-use tool that lets you configure the Netopia ISDN Router for connecting to the Internet. Easy Setup includes all the basic configuration options for the Netopia. You'll use your keyboard to navigate Netopia's configuration screens, enter and edit information, and make choices. Table 15.1 lists the keys to use for working with the Easy Setup menus as well as all the other menu screens.

ISDN Line Configuration

After selecting the Easy Setup item in the Main Menu and pressing Return, the ISDN Line Configuration screen appears (Figure 15.5). This is where you enter the ISDN set-up information. It consists of one pop-up menu and four editable fields.

Table 15.1 Navigation Keys for Netopia Configuration

To	Use These Keys
Move through selectable items in a screen or pop-up menu	Up, Down, Left, and Right Arrow
Execute an action, select an item, or open a pop-up menu of options for a selected item	Return, or Enter
Change a toggle value (Yes/No, On/Off)	Tab
Restore an entry or toggle value to its previous value.	Esc
Page up	PgUp
Page down	PgDn
Refresh the screen	Ctrl+L
Go to the topmost selectable item	<
Go to bottom right selectable item	>

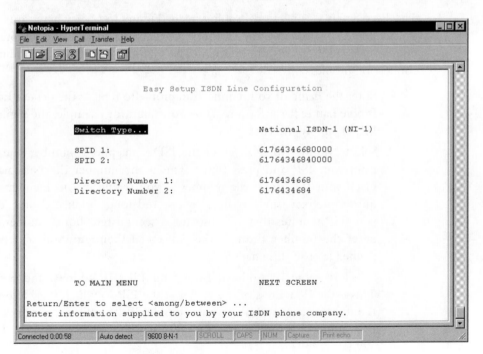

Figure 15.5 The ISDN Line Configuration Screen.

1. From the Switch Type pop-up menu, select the switch protocol your telephone company uses.

2. Select SPID 1, enter your primary ISDN SPID number, and press Enter. If you did not receive a SPID (AT&T 5ESS custom point-to-point switches have no SPID), skip this and the following step.

3. If you have a second SPID, select SPID 2 and enter the secondary SPID number the same way you did for SPID 1.

4. Select Directory Number 1, enter the primary directory number as you would dial it, and press Enter. Make sure you include any required prefixes (such as area, access, and long-distance dialing codes).

5. If you have a second directory number, select Directory Number 2 and enter the secondary directory number the same way you did for Directory Number 1.

6. Select NEXT SCREEN and press Enter. The Easy Setup Connection Profile screen appears.

Connection Profile Configuration

The Easy Setup Connection Profile screen (Figure 15.6) is where you configure the parameters that control the Netopia's connection to a specific remote destination, which in this case is the Internet. The Netopia supports a maximum of four connection profiles.

1. Enter the name of your connection profile to replace the default Easy Setup Profile name. It can be any name you want; for example, the name of your ISP, or simply Internet.

2. Select Number to Dial, enter the ISDN telephone number you received from your ISP, and press Enter. This is the number the Netopia dials to reach your ISP. Enter the number as you would dial it, including any required prefixes (such as area, access, and long-distance dialing codes). If your ISP requires that you also use a second telephone number, you can enter the number through the Advanced Configuration screens, as explained later in this chapter.

3. Select Remote IP Address, enter your ISP's IP address, and press Enter. This is the IP address of the router at the ISP to which the Netopia ISDN Router connects when using the profile. If your ISP account is a dynamic IP account, and the ISP has not given you the address, enter the IP address 127.0.0.2.

4. Select Remote IP Subnet, enter your ISP's subnet mask, and press Enter. This is the subnet mask for the IP address you entered in step 3. If your ISP

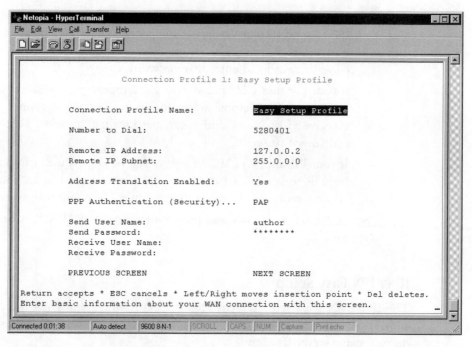

Figure 15.6 The Easy Setup Connection Profile screen.

account is a dynamic IP account, and the ISP has not given you the subnet mask address, enter 255.0.0.0.

5. Select Address Translation Enabled, toggle the setting to Yes by pressing the Tab key, and press Enter.

6. Select the PPP Authentication (Security) pop-up menu and choose the type of connection security your ISP told you to use (either PAP or CHAP). The default is PAP.

> If you choose PAP or CHAP, the items Send User Name, Send Password, Receive User Name, and Receive Password appear below the Authentication pop-up menu.

> If your ISP uses PAP, select Send User Name and enter the user name your ISP gave you to connect. Then select Send Password and enter the password.

> If your ISP uses CHAP, select Send Host Name and enter the user name your ISP gave you to connect. Then select Send Secret and enter the secret (CHAP term for password) your ISP gave you.

> If your ISP does not use PAP or CHAP, choose None.

If your ISP uses PAP and gave you a user name and password for the ISP to send to the Netopia Router when the router initiates a connection, select Receive User Name and enter that user name. Select Receive Password and enter that password.

If your ISP uses CHAP and gave you a user name and secret for the ISP to send to the Netopia when the router initiates a connection, select Receive Host Name and enter that user name. Select Receive Secret and enter that secret.

If your ISP uses CHAP, but you were not given a user name and secret, leave Receive Host Name and Receive Secret blank. You may encounter problems, however, when you try to connect to your ISP.

7. Select NEXT SCREEN and press Enter. The IP & IPX Easy Setup screen appears.

IP & IPX Easy Setup

The IP & IPX Easy Setup screen (Figure 15.7) is where you enter the Netopia IP address, IP address-serving information, the default gateway IP address, and the domain name server IP address.

1. Enter the private IP address 192.168.0.1 in the Ethernet IP Address setting. For the enabled NAT feature, the Ethernet IP address defaults to a specified address range for use within your LAN networks.

2. Use the default IP address 255.255.255.240 in the Ethernet IP Subnet Mask setting.

3. The Default Gateway IP Address defaults to the remote IP address you entered in the previous Connection Profile screen.

4. Select Domain Name Server IP Address, enter the IP address your ISP gave you for its DNS server, and press Enter.

5. Select the IP Address Serving, toggle it to On by pressing the Tab key, then press Enter. This enables the DHCP address-serving feature for the Netopia.

6. In the Number of Client IP Addresses setting, enter the number of available host addresses you want to allow Netopia ISDN Router to allocate to client computers on your network; press Enter. This number defaults to the balance of the subnet addresses above the Netopia ISDN Router's address, which is 13.

   If IP Address Serving is set to On, you can tell the Netopia ISDN Router where the set of allocated served IP addresses begins by select-

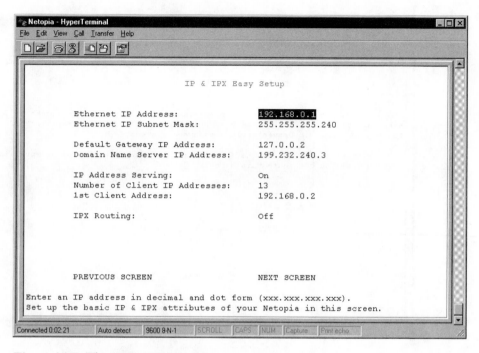

Figure 15.7 *The IP & IPX Easy Setup screen.*

ing 1st Client Address and entering the first IP address in the set. For Small Office Netopia ISDN Router models, this option is read-only and cannot be changed.

7. Select NEXT SCREEN and press Enter. The Easy Setup Security Configuration screen appears.

Easy Setup Security

The Easy Setup Security Configuration screen (Figure 15.8) lets you password-protect your Netopia ISDN Router. To do so, enter a user name and password in the Write Access Name and Write Access Password fields. These entries protect anyone else from gaining access to the Netopia to configure it. The user name and passwords may be up to 11 alphanumeric characters in length.

Enabling Easy Setup Configuration Selections

When you finish using Easy Setup you need to reset the Netopia ISDN Router for your new configuration settings to take effect. To reset the Netopia with your new Easy Setup Configuration changes, do the following:

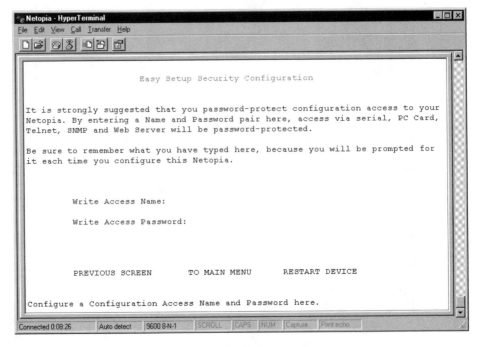

Figure 15.8 *The Easy Setup Security Configuration screen.*

1. In the Easy Setup Security Configuration screen, select RESTART DE-VICE and press Enter. A prompt asks you to confirm your choice.

2. Select CONTINUE and press Enter to reset the Netopia ISDN Router and have your selections take effect. The Netopia is reset and the Main Menu screen appears.

3. In the HyperTerminal window, choose File|Exit or press Alt+F4 to end the session. HyperTerminal displays a message box prompting you to confirm that you want to disconnect from the Netopia; click Yes.

At this point, you're ready to begin using the Netopia to connect to the Internet from any PC connected to your Windows 95 LAN.

Making Connections

Once the Netopia is set up, you're ready to access the Internet using any TCP/IP application. To surf the Web on any computer connected to the Netopia, simply double-click on the program icon. For example, clicking on the Internet Explorer or Netscape Navigator icon on your Windows 95 desktop automatically makes the

Internet connection and displays the specified starting page. ISDN connections via Ethernet take only a few seconds to complete instead of the 20 or more seconds it takes using Windows 95 Dial-Up Networking with a modem or ISDN adapter card or modem.

To use e-mail or network news, you need to configure your e-mail and network newsreader programs. This involves specifying the e-mail and network news server addresses supplied by your ISP. For each Internet user on your local LAN who wants a private e-mail address, you will need a separate e-mail account from your ISP. Generally, there is minimum charge of around $10 per e-mail account per month.

Reading the Netopia LEDs

The LEDs on the front of the Netopia let you monitor the status of your LAN, ISDN line, PC card, and power. Table 15.2 describes the functions of the Netopia LEDs.

A Tour of Netopia Configuration Screens

Beyond using the Easy Setup menu screens to configure the essential Netopia settings, there are a number of other menu screens for configuring a wide variety of features. The Main Menu is the starting point for all these menus. The following sections give you a quick tour of the options available from the Main Menu screen.

Advanced Configuration

The Advanced Configuration menu item displays the Advanced Configuration screen (Figure 15.9). This menu provides an extensive collection of configuration options, but the most commonly used are:

- *WAN (Wide Area Network) Setup.* Includes options for ISDN line configuration, managing connection profiles, and defining how the Netopia answers incoming calls.

- *Telephone Setup.* Lets you configure the Netopia's POTS ports for any analog devices you connect to the unit to share your ISDN line.

- *Network Protocols Setup.* Allows you to make changes to your IP and IPX configurations.

- *Scheduled Connections.* Enables you to configure the Netopia to automatically make connections at specified times.

Table 15.2 Status LEDs on the Netopia

LED	STATUS	FUNCTION
Receive (Ethernet)	Flashes yellow	Ethernet packets received by Netopia.
Link (Ethernet)	Solid green	Detection of Ethernet connection.
Transmit (Ethernet)	Flashes yellow	Ethernet packets being transmitted.
Collision (Ethernet)	Flashes red	Collision of Ethernet packets.
AUI (Ethernet)	Flashes yellow	Traffic received on AUI port.
Traffic (ISDN)	Flashes yellow	Packets in B1 and/or B2 channel.
Go (ISDN)	Solid green	Successful data connection in B1 and/or B2 channel.
	Blinking green	Successful analog connection for Phone 1 or Phone 2 port.
Ready (ISDN)	Flashes red	Not connected, not synchronized.
	Flashes green	Synchronized but no SPIDs have been registered.
	Solid red	All SPIDs failed to register.
	Solid green	At least one SPID has been registered.
PC Card	Solid green	PC card inserted into Netopia card slot.
	Solid red	PC card slot error.
	Off	PC card not inserted in card slot.
Power	Solid green	Normal operation.
	Solid red	System failure.
	Off	Netopia turned off or not receiving power.

Statistics, Utilities, Tests

The Statistics, Utilities, Tests screen (Figure 15.10) provides a variety of tools for checking the status of your connections, managing your connections, and performing diagnostics. The most commonly used configuration settings available from this screen are:

- *General Statistics.* Shows the status of your IP traffic as it passes through the Netopia; also displays WAN connection statistics.
- *Establish Connection.* Lets you manually establish a connection and check the results of the connection. The Disconnect option terminates a connection.
- *Ping.* Lets you check any host on the Internet to determine whether it's active.

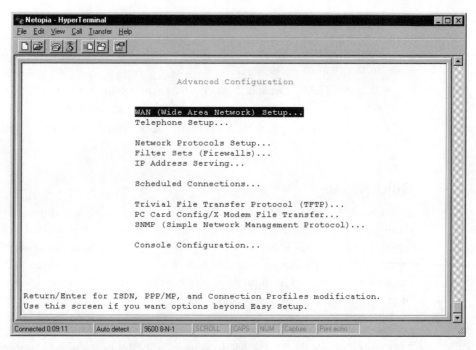

Figure 15.9 The Advanced Configuration screen.

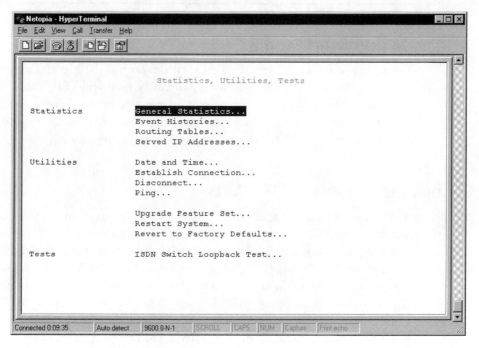

Figure 15.10 The Statistics, Utilities, Tests screen.

- *Restart System.* Lets you reset your Netopia to save any changes you've made in the current session.
- *Revert to Factory Defaults.* Lets you start your configuration process over by re-setting the Netopia to its original default factory settings.
- *ISDN Switch Loopback Test.* Lets you check your ISDN line to make sure it's working.

Quick Menus

The Quick Menu screen (Figure 15.11) is a shortcut to a number of important configuration screens. All these screens are also available via the other menu screens, but the Quick Menu screen puts them in one location. For example, all the Connection profile options listed in the Quick Menu screen are also available from the Advanced Configuration menu screen, but you have to go down the menu system several levels to access them.

TIP: You can use the Quick Menu screen for many of the most common Netopia configuration options.

Quick View and Security

The Quick View menu item displays a status report of the Netopia's current activities, including any connection profiles currently used and LED status. The Security menu item displays the Security Options screen that allows you to specify security parameters for the Netopia, including password settings for restricting remote access into the Netopia and for adding or removing users.

Configuring Netopia's POTS Ports

Analog devices such as telephones, fax machines, or modems can connect to the Netopia's two POTS ports at the back of the unit. These ports allow you to plug in the RJ-11 line from the device to the Netopia. You configure the POTS ports by choosing the Advanced Configuration item from the Main Menu screen; you next select Telephone Setup, which displays two menu items: Telephone Connection and Priority Ringing. Choose Telephone Setup to display the Telephone Connections screen (Figure 15.12).

This screen is divided into two categories, Inbound and Outbound. Inbound determines how an incoming voice call is directed through the Netopia. An in-

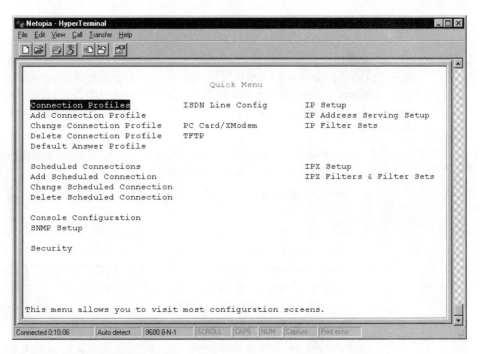

Figure 15.11 *The Quick Menu screen.*

Figure 15.12 *The Telephone Connections screen.*

coming call can enter via either of the two directory numbers, and can be routed to the phone jacks used internally by the router. Outbound controls the way calls from a given phone jack are sent from the Netopia. It directs which directory number and transmission service to use. To configure telephone connections, do the following:

1. For Inbound Directory Number 1 Connection, press Enter and choose one of the following selections from the pull-down list:

    Reject as Busy. Blocks calls, issuing a busy tone to the party trying to dial in.

    Phone 1. Directs calls out the Netopia ISDN Router's Phone 1 jack, ringing the phone or device plugged into that jack.

    Phone 2. Directs calls out the Netopia ISDN Router's Phone 2 jack, ringing the phone or device plugged into that jack.

    Phone 1 & Phone 2. Rings all devices connected to the Phone 1 and Phone 2 jacks.

    Router. Directs the incoming call, usually a data-over-voice call with a speech or 3.1-kHz service, internally for the router's use.

2. For Inbound Directory Number 2 Connection, press Enter and configure as described in step 1. If no number is entered for Directory Number 2 in the initial configuration, the option you select is stored but not used.

3. For Outbound Phone 1 Connection, press Enter and choose one of the following selections from the pull-down list:

    Blocked. Prevents outbound calls on that jack. Devices on that line hear a busy (reorder) signal. Inbound calls are still possible, depending on how the Netopia ISDN Router is configured in steps 1 and 2.

    Directory Number 1. Routes the outbound call out the number specified by Directory Number 1. This ensures that the call is made from the directory number you chose.

    Directory Number 2. Routes outbound calls out the number specified by Directory Number 2.

    Either. Routes outbound calls out either Directory Number 1 or Directory Number 2, depending on which is available, if either.

4. For Outbound Phone 1 Service Grade, press Enter and choose one of the following selections from the pull-down list:

    Speech. For typical speech-grade service used in telephone conversations.

    3.1-kHz Audio. For a higher grade of service that ensures better line conditions for data transfer, such as for facsimile machine or modem.

The 3.1-kHz service may not be available from the ISDN service provider, and there may be higher tariffs for its use. Check with your ISDN service provider about the availability of this service grade.

5. For Outbound Phone 2 Connection, press Enter and configure as described in step 3.

6. For Outbound Phone 2 Service Grade, press Enter and configure as described in step 4.

The Priority Ringing screen, which you access from the Advanced Configuration Screen under Telephone Services, allows a distinctive ring to be attached to up to 10 incoming caller IDs. To set up priority ringing, follow these steps:

1. For Caller ID, enter a telephone number sequence based on the following guidelines:

   The following characters are acceptable: 0 1 2 3 4 5 6 7 8 9 . ( ) / – ?. Other characters are invalid and cause the entire entry to be rejected.

   The question mark character represents a single-digit wild card. While matching the incoming caller ID with the priority ringing caller IDs, any digit is considered to be a match at the location where the ? appears. For example, the caller ID 415-555-111? matches incoming numbers 415-555-1112, 415-555-1113, and so on for priority ringing.

   The maximum entry length is 20 characters. Longer entries are rejected. Note, however, that telephone numbers consist of a maximum of 10 digits. For internal matching against an incoming call, the Netopia ISDN Router removes all characters that are not digits or wild cards.

2. For Ringing Tone, press Enter and select one of the ringing patterns listed.

3. To test a ringing pattern, highlight Preview Ring and press Enter. Select one of the ringing patterns listed. When one or more telephones are hooked up to either of the Phone 1 or Phone 2 jacks, the pattern rings briefly on the telephones not in use.

Fine-tuning Your Connection Profile

After establishing a profile using the Easy Setup option, you may want to make a few additional changes to fine-tune the Netopia. For example, you may want to change the default idle time setting from 300 seconds (five minutes) to less time. Or you may need to add a second ISDN number if your ISP requires you to dial a second number to use both B channels. The following sections explain how to make common changes to your connection profile.

Changing Initiate Call Type and Idle Time-out Settings

As you recall, some telephone companies charge a lower rate for analog calls than for digital data calls. The Netopia includes a toll-saver feature that "fools" the telephone company switch into treating a digital call as a voice call, which is billed at the lower POTS rate. Typically, local telephone companies allow unlimited call usage within the local calling area for a flat monthly rate. The data-over-voice feature allows data to be send at 56 Kbps instead of the ISDN 64-Kbps rate. Another toll-saving feature is Netopia's idle time-out, which lets you specify the amount of time your connection remains active after the last activity. The default is 300 seconds (five minutes), which you may want to change. To make these changes to your connection profile, do the following:

1. Choose Quick Menus from the Main Menu. The Quick Menu screen appears.
2. Select Change Connection Profile, select the profile you want to edit from the list, and press Enter.
3. Select Telco Options. The Telco Options dialog box appears.
4. To enable data over voice, select Initiate Data Service and press Enter. Next select Speech from the list and press Enter.
5. To change the idle time-out setting, select Idle Timeout (seconds) setting, enter the time in seconds, then press Enter.

Adding a Second ISDN Dial-Up Number

If your ISP uses two telephone numbers for an ISDN connection (one for each B channel) you can define a second ISDN number for Netopia.

1. Choose Quick Menus from the Main Menu screen.
2. Choose Change Connection Profile, select the profile you want, then press Enter.
3. Select Optional 2nd Number to Dial, enter the telephone number, and press Enter.

Changing B-Channel Usage and Compression

You can control how the Netopia uses the ISDN B channels to manage data communications traffic over ISDN. For example, you can specify that one or two B channels be used dynamically, depending on the volume of data being transferred.

1. Choose Quick Menus from the Main Menu screen.

2. Choose Change Connection Profile, select the profile you want, and press Enter.

3. Select PPP/MP Options and press Enter.

4. Select B-Channel Usage and press Enter. You can choose from one of the following four B-channel management settings:

> *Dynamic.* One or two B channels will be used, depending on traffic volume.

> *1 B Channel.* The Connection will use only one B channel.

> *2 B Channels.* Both B channels will be used for every connection.

> *2B, Preemptable.* Two B channels will be used but only one may be reallocated.

5. Select Data Compression. Choose from three compression options.

> None

> Ascend LZS

> Standard LZS

Upgrading Netopia Firmware

Farallon firmware updates, which become available periodically, are easy to make. Trivial File Transfer Protocol (TFTP) is a protocol used to transfer files between IP nodes. It is often used to transfer firmware and configuration information from an Internet server to a remote access device such as the Netopia. Before you use the TFTP facility in Netopia, you need to know the name of the firmware filename that you will be transferring. You can get this at the Farallon Web site, http://www.farallon.com. These firmware files use a .bin extension.

1. Make sure your Netopia is making a connection to the Internet.

2. Use Telnet or the HyperTerminal program to access the Netopia unit.

3. From the Main Menu, select the Advanced Configuration item and press Enter.

4. From the Advanced Configuration menu, select Trivial File Transfer Protocol (TFTP) and press Enter. The Trivial File Transfer Protocol (TFTP) screen appears (Figure 15.13).

5. Enter **tftp.farallon.com** in the TFTP Server Name field and Press Enter.

6. Enter the firmware filename in the Firmware File Name field and press Enter.

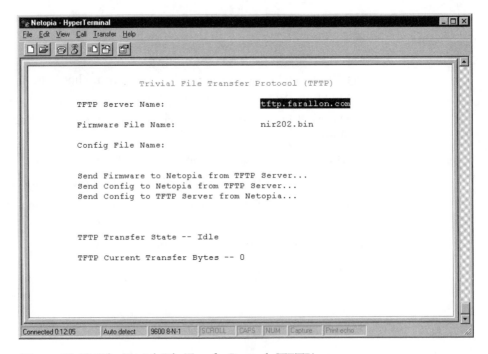

Figure 15.13 *The Trivial File Transfer Protocol (TFTP) screen.*

7. Select Send Firmware to Netopia from TFTP Server, and press Enter. A dialog box appears asking if you want to go ahead with the firmware upgrade.

8. Select CONTINUE to begin the download process. At the bottom of the screen, the TFTP Transfer State and TFTP Current Transfer Bytes show the status of the download. The system will reset at the end of the file transfer and put the new firmware into effect.

You're now ready to work with the new firmware upgrade using the standard connection options to the Netopia router.

What's Next

On to another ISDN router that includes DHCP and NAT capabilities, the Prestige 128 from ZyXEL. This router includes features comparable to those of the Netopia, and you set it up using a similar text-based menu system.

16 *The ZyXEL Prestige 128 ISDN Router*

The Prestige 128 from ZyXEL is a SOHO-friendly ISDN router that has all the cool features necessary to make a LAN-to-Internet connection a cost-effective option. This chapter lets you get behind the wheel of the Prestige 128 to see how it handles. Enjoy the ride.

About the Prestige 128

The Prestige 128 is a full-featured router with a street price of around $799, and is one of the best ISDN router values around. It includes a number of impressive features, including:

- *Single User Account (SUA).* Enables multiple users on a LAN to access the Internet simultaneously sharing a single-user ISDN Internet access account. The Prestige 128 includes a built-in DHCP server with NAT functionality to make this big cost-savings possible.

- *Data-over-voice support.* Allows data calls to be placed or answered using ISDN speech-grade capabilities instead of circuit-switched data-grade capabilities. In many areas, this feature enables Prestige 128 users to avoid paying higher ISDN per-minute charges.

- Firmware upgrades and configuration via software downloads from the ZyXEL Web site.

- Two analog ports to support analog devices (telephone, fax, and modem).

- IP and IPX routing support.

- Menu-driven configuration program for easy configuration and management.
- Access control management of Internet access for LAN users.
- Firewall filtering for controlled access to and from your LAN.
- Password protection for up to eight remote users connecting to your LAN, along with support for V.34 PPP over ISDN for remote access via 28.8-Kbps modems.

Getting Started with the Prestige 128

As is the case with other ISDN modems, there are standard requirements for getting your router working before you configure it. For the Prestige 128, you'll need to do the following:

- Order ISDN service and provision it for the Prestige 128.
- Order your ISDN Internet access account.
- Set up the Prestige 128 router by connecting it to your ISDN line, all your networked PCs, and any analog devices you want to share your ISDN line.
- Set up your Windows 95 LAN for dynamic IP addressing by configuring the Windows 95 TCP/IP properties for each PC.
- Set up the Windows 95 HyperTerminal program to configure the Prestige 128.

Ordering Your ISDN Service

The Prestige supports the Bellcore S Compatibility package ISDN Ordering Code as well as EZ-ISDN 1. The documentation includes the specific provisioning information in case your telephone company doesn't support either of these provisioning packages. You'll need the following information from the telephone company:

- ISDN switch type
- ISDN telephone numbers
- ISDN SPID numbers

Ordering Internet Service

The Prestige 128 will work with either a LAN access package that uses static IP addresses or a single-user Internet access account that uses dynamic IP addressing.

The single-user account based on dynamic IP addressing will be a lot cheaper than getting a LAN access package in which several static IP addresses are assigned. This is the option you'll probably use for affordable LAN-based Internet access. After you establish your Internet access account, you'll need the following information from your ISP:

- ISP's ISDN phone number
- ISP's IP gateway address, if any
- ISP's IP subnet mask, if any
- Authentication type (PAP or CHAP)
- Authentication name and password
- Domain Name Server (DNS) IP addresses
- Domain Name

Setting Up the Prestige 128

The Prestige 128's back panel has a connector labeled Terminal for attaching the router to a PC COM port. To make this connection, use one of the supplied cables. Connect one end of the supplied ISDN phone cable to the RJ-45 ISDN port labeled ISDN BRI on the back panel. Connect the other end of the ISDN phone cable to the ISDN wall jack. Connect the Prestige 128 to a hub using 10BaseT cabling. Plug any POTS devices into the RJ-11 ports.

If you have a choice, place the Prestige 128 in a location where you can view the LEDs on the front of the unit. This location will also need to be close to a power outlet and the incoming ISDN line. The LEDs on the front of the Prestige 128 provide valuable status information about your connection. Table 16.1 describes these functions.

Setting Up Your Windows 95 LAN for a Dynamic IP

With the Prestige 128 hardware installed, you're ready to move on to software installation. Before you configure the Prestige, make sure each Windows 95 PC on your LAN is properly configured. On the Windows 95 side of your LAN, make sure you have TCP/IP installed on each PC and bound to the network adapter card used for your TCP/IP connection to the Internet. For using the Prestige with a dynamic IP address Internet access account, make sure the default TCP/IP settings are used. In the Network control panel, select the TCP/IP-> [*network adapter name*] in the installed Network Components list, then click Properties. The Obtain an IP address automatically setting should be selected in the IP Address tab. Every computer on your Windows 95 LAN should be configured this way.

Table 16.1 The Prestige 128 Status LEDs

LED	FUNCTION
PWR	Indicates the power is on.
TST	Should be blinking if the Prestige is functioning properly.
ISDN: LNK	Indicates that the Prestige has an ISDN line connected to the WAN interface and that it has been successfully initialized.
ISDN B1 and B2	Indicates an active WAN session of that channel, or if the channel is making or receiving a call.
ETHERNET: LNK	Indicates the Prestige has been successfully connected to the LAN via the Ethernet interface.
ETHERNET: TX and RX	Blinking indicates there is data traffic over the LAN.
ETHERNET: COL	Indicates there are transmission collisions over the LAN.
PHONE: 1	Indicates an analog device is plugged into the phone port and is in use.
PHONE: 2	Indicates an analog device is plugged into the phone port and is in use.

Note: Chapter 8, "Setting Up Your Windows 95 LAN for Remote Access," explains this configuration process in more detail.

Setting Up the Windows 95 HyperTerminal Program

The Prestige can be configured using Telnet over your LAN or by connecting the unit to a PC via the supplied RS-232 cable and using the Windows 95 HyperTerminal program. You can use Telnet to configure your Prestige from anywhere on the local network after you initially configure it with an IP address. Use the DOS Telnet program in Windows 95.

The HyperTerminal approach uses a friendly and intuitive menu system that walks you through the configuration of Prestige 128. The following steps explain how to create a HyperTerminal connection to the Prestige 128 using the HyperTerminal program in Windows 95. Once you create the connection, you can save it to use again.

1. Choose Start|Programs|Accessories|HyperTerminal. The HyperTerminal window appears.

2. Double-click on the Hypertm icon. The Connection Description dialog box appears.

3. Type a name for your connection, select an icon, and then click OK. The Phone Number dialog box appears.

4. In the Connect using list, choose the Direct to Com port for the serial port you're using to connect the PC to the Prestige 128, then click OK. The COM Properties dialog box appears.

5. Change the Bits per second setting to 9600, and choose None for the Flow control setting. The Data bits, Parity, and Stop bits use the default values of 8, None, and 1, respectively.

6. Click OK. The HyperTerminal window appears. You're ready to configure the Prestige 128.

Configuring the Prestige 128

You configure the Prestige 128 using the System Management Terminal (SMT) interface, which is a text-based menu system. Getting to the SMT's Main Menu screen involves opening up the HyperTerminal window connected to your Prestige 128 and pressing Ctrl+L. A password prompt appears. Enter the default password 1234 and press Enter. The Prestige 128 main menu screen appears (Figure 16.1).

Note: The Prestige 128 has a system time-out security feature that automatically shuts down your configuration session if five minutes go by with no activity. If this happens during a configuration session, press any key to display the password prompt again.

Table 16.2 explains how to use the keyboard to work in the SMT interface. Fields displaying a question mark indicate that the information must be filled in before you can save the menu.

Getting Your Prestige Up and Running

The Getting Started menus in the Main Menu screen handle all the essential configuration options for getting your Prestige 128 up and running.

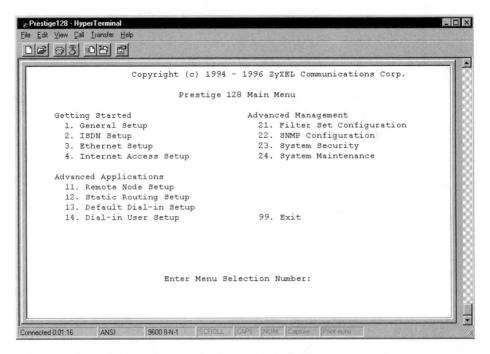

Figure 16.1 *The Prestige 128 SMT's Main Menu screen.*

Table 16.2 Keys Used in Configuring the Prestige 128

ACTION	DO THE FOLLOWING
Move forward to a submenu	Type in the menu number and press Enter.
Move backward to the previous menu	Press the Esc key.
Move the cursor	Use the Up and Down keys to move to the next or previous fields, respectively. Within a menu, press Enter or direction key to move to the next field.
Select an option from a list of choices	Press the Spacebar to cycle through the available choices.
Save your configuration	Press Enter with your cursor at the message. Press Enter to confirm or Esc to cancel. Saving the data on the screen in most cases will take you to the previous menu.

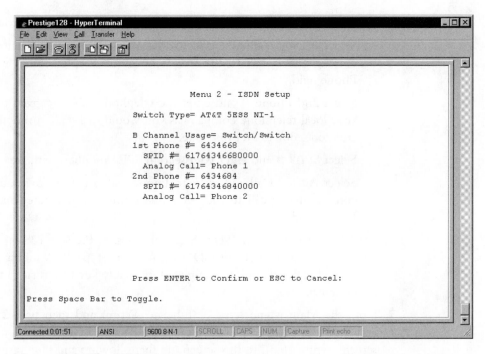

Figure 16.2 *The ISDN Setup screen.*

1. At the Enter Menu Selection Number prompt, type 1 (General Setup) and press Enter. The General Setup screen appears.

2. Enter a name for your system in the System Name field; optionally, add a location and contact name in the respective fields below the system name.

3. Make sure the Route IP setting is set to Yes. If it's set to No, use the Down arrow or Enter key to move to the setting, then press the Spacebar to cycle to Yes.

4. Press Enter until you return to the Main Menu screen.

5. In the Main Menu screen, type 2 (ISDN Setup) and press Enter. In the ISDN Setup screen (Figure 16.2) do the following:

   Select your ISDN Switch type.

   Select B Channel Usage. In most cases, this will be the default Switch/Switch entry. If you're using only one B channel, then select Switch/Unused.

   Select 1st Phone # and enter the telephone number given to you by your local telephone company as you would dial it. If you don't use an area code, don't enter one here.

Select SPID # and enter your first SPID number, with area code.

Select Analog Call and set it to Phone 1 if you want to route the incoming analog call to the telephone number you entered in the 1st Phone field.

Select 2nd Phone # and enter the telephone number given to you by your local telephone company as you would dial it. If you don't use an area code, don't enter one here.

Select SPID # and enter your second SPID number, with area code.

Select Analog Call and set it to Phone 1 if you want to route the incoming analog call to the telephone number you entered in the 2nd Phone field.

6. Press Enter to save your ISDN Setup changes. A Prestige 128 prompt asks you if you want to test the ISDN connection. Type Y. A loopback test is performed. After the test is completed, press any key to return to the Main Menu screen.

7. From the Main Menu, type **3** (Ethernet Setup) and then type **2** (DHCP and TCP/IP Setup) to display the DHCP and TCP/IP Ethernet Setup screen (Figure 16.3). In this screen, do the following and then return to the Main Menu:

Select DHCP; press the Spacebar to cycle through to the Server option. The two fields below the DHCP setting display default IP addresses used by the Prestige 128 for private IP addresses. The IP Address setting displays the private IP address used for the Prestige 128. This is the IP address you use to Telnet to the Prestige 128.

Enter the IP addresses of your ISP provider in the Primary DNS and secondary DNS Server fields.

8. In the Main Menu screen, type **4** (Internet Access Setup). The Internet Access Setup screen appears (Figure 16.4). Do the following and then return to the Main Menu screen:

Enter your ISP name and its host IP address, if you were given one.

Enter the ISDN telephone numbers provided by your ISP in the Pri Phone # and Sec Phone # fields.

Enter the user name and password for your Internet access account.

Make sure the Single User Account option is set to Yes. If not, select Single User Account and press the Spacebar to cycle to Yes. This enables the NAT feature of the Prestige 128. If you're using a static IP ac-

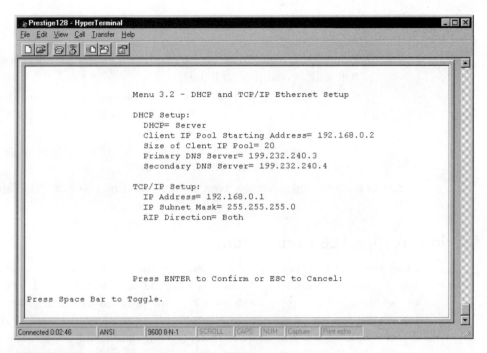

Figure 16.3 *The DHCP and TCP/IP Ethernet Setup screen.*

Figure 16.4 *The Internet Access Setup screen.*

count, enter your IP address in the IP Addr field. If you're using a dynamic IP account, enter 0.0.0.0.

Select Transfer Type under Telco Option and press the Spacebar to select the data rate for your ISDN line: 56K, 64K, or DOVBS. The DOVBS (Data Over Voice Bearer Service) tells the Prestige 128 to initiate the data call as an analog call, which can save you usage charges, depending on your telephone company.

9. In the Main menu screen, type **99** and press Enter to exit SMT interface.

Making Prestige 128 Connections

Once the Prestige is configured for basic operation, you're ready to access the Internet using any TCP/IP application. To surf the Web on any computer connected to the Prestige 128, simply double-click on the program icon. For example, clicking on the Internet Explorer or Netscape Navigator icon on your Windows 95 desktop automatically makes the Internet connection and displays the specified starting page. ISDN connections via Ethernet take only a few seconds to complete instead of the 20 or more it takes using Windows 95 Dial-Up Networking with a modem or ISDN adapter card or modem.

Remote Node Configuration

After creating your initial configuration of the Prestige 128, choosing 11 (Remote Node Setup) from the Main Menu screen lets you access your Remote Node Profile. From the Remote Node Setup screen, you select from a menu of profiles you've created. The names for the profiles are generated from the ISP's Name field in the Internet Access Setup screen. Typing the corresponding number for the profile displays the Remote Node Profile, which initially will be the one you created to get the Prestige up and running. Figure 16.5 shows a basic Remote Node Profile setup. It includes most of the settings you established using menus 1 through 4 in the Main Menu screen. You can change all these settings directly from the Remote Node Setup profile screen.

System Maintenance

Choosing 24 (System Maintenance) from the Main Menu screen displays a menu of tools for checking the status of your remote access activities and for performing diagnostics. The following describes the functions of these menu items:

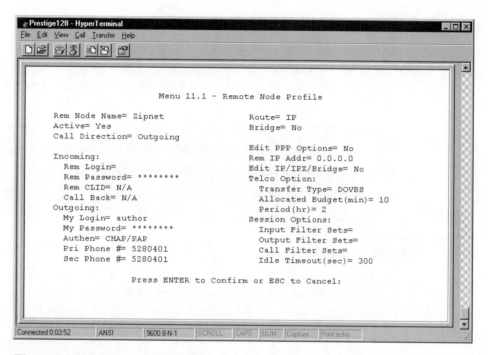

Figure 16.5 *A Remote Node Profile.*

- *System Status* displays a screen that monitors your ISDN line and network traffic.

- *Terminal Baud Rate* lets you change the baud rates for the RS–232 connection into the Prestige 128. The default is 9600 bps, but you can increase it to 38,400 bps.

- *Log and Trace* tools allow you to view the error logs and trace records for troubleshooting connections.

- *Diagnostic* includes controls for manually making and breaking connections and testing the status of your ISDN line and Internet connection.

- *Backup and Restore* let you back up your Prestige 128 configuration to a disk and restore a configuration from a disk back to the Prestige.

- *Software Update* enables you to install new firmware for the Prestige 128 from a PC connected via the RS–232 cable to the Prestige 128.

- *Command Interpreter Mode* allows you to diagnose, test, and configure the Prestige 128 using a specified set of commands.

- *Call Control* enables you to manage outgoing and incoming calls and the length of calls.

Common Prestige 128 Configuration Changes

In many cases, the basic settings of the Prestige 128 made using the menus in the Getting Started group may be all you want for remote access to the Internet. However, the following are some common configuration changes you may want to make:

- Change the password used to enter the SMT interface to configure the Prestige.
- Change the Idle Timer setting to reduce ISDN line usage charges.
- Set up Budget Management for managing connections.
- Change data transfer types.
- Save your configuration information to a file.

Changing the Password

Before you configured the Prestige 128, you had to enter the default password 1234 to access the SMT's Main Menu screen. You can change that password to something easier to remember. Here is how you change a password.

1. From the Main Menu screen, type **23** (System Security) and press Enter. The Systems Security screen appears.

2. Type **1** (Change Password) and press Enter to display the Change Password screen.

3. Enter the old password, **1234**, in the Old Password field.

4. Enter your new password in New Password field and then enter it again in the Retype to confirm field.

5. Press Enter twice to save the new password and return to the Main Menu screen.

Changing the Idle Timer

The default idle time out setting is 300 seconds (five minutes), which means the Prestige will stay connected even if there is no activity over the ISDN line for five minutes before automatically disconnecting the session. You may want to adjust this setting to around three minutes to reduce ISDN usage charges. Here is how to adjust the Prestige's Idle Timeout setting.

1. In the Main Menu, type **11** (Remote Node Setup) and press Enter. The Remote Node Setup screen appears. The name(s) listed in this screen came from the ISP field.

2. Type the corresponding number to the name of the remote node and press Enter. The Remote Node Profile screen appears (see Figure 16.5).

3. Move the cursor to the Idle Timeout (sec) setting and type in your replacement value in seconds. The range is 5 to 300 seconds.

4. Press Enter twice to save your Idle Timeout setting and return the Main Menu screen.

Setting Up Budget Management

The Budget Management feature provides a way to define a time limit for incoming and outgoing calls for a specific period of time. When this limit is reached, the call will be dropped and future outgoing calls will also fail. After each period, the total budget is reset. The default for the total budget is 0 minutes, and the period is 0 hours, which means budget control is not activated. Setting up budget management controls is done via the Remote Node Profile screen.

1. In the Main Menu, type **11** and press Enter. The Remote Node Setup screen appears. The name(s) listed in this screen came from the ISP field.

2. Type the corresponding number to the name of the remote node and press Enter. The Remote Node Profile screen appears (see Figure 16.5).

3. In the Allocated Budget (min) field, enter the number of minutes you grant a user with the time period you specify.

4. In the Period (hr) field, type in the number of hours you want to use to define a time period.

You can view all your Budget Management settings by doing the following:

1. In the Main Menu screen, type **24** (System Maintenance) and press Enter.

2. Type **9** (Call Control) and press Enter.

3. Type **3** (Budget Management) and press Enter. The Budget Management screen appears (see Figure 16.6)

Changing the Transfer Type

The default transfer rate used by the Prestige 128 is 64K for digital data calls, but you can change this setting if, for example, you want to use the data-over-voice feature to save on ISDN usage charges. Here's how to change the rate at which the Prestige sends data.

1. In the Main Menu screen, type **24** (System Maintenance) and press Enter.

2. Type **11** (Remote Node Setup) and press Enter. The Remote Node Setup screen appears.

3. Type the corresponding number for the remote node profile you want to change. The Remote Node Profile screen appears.

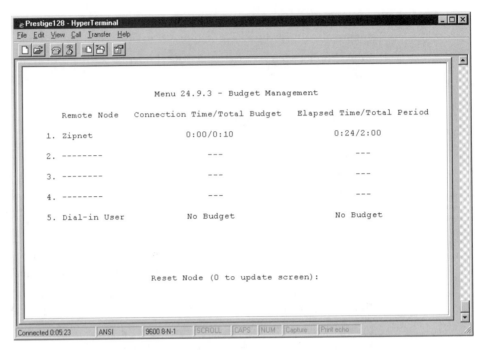

Figure 16.6 The Budget Management screen.

4. Navigate to the Transfer Type setting. Press the Spacebar to cycle through the following options.

64K. The default rate for digital data calls.

56K. Enables the Prestige to send digital data calls at the lower bandwidth for B channels that use in-band signaling.

DOVBS (Data Over Voice Bearer Service). Enables the call to be initiated as a voice call to save on ISDN usage costs in many telephone company service areas.

5. Press Enter until you return to the Main Menu screen.

Backing Up Your Configuration Information

Once you've invested some time in configuring the Prestige 128, you should save the configuration information to a back-up file in case your settings get corrupted. Here's how to back up your configuration settings, which you can restore to the Prestige 128 at any time.

1. In the Main Menu screen, type **24** (System Maintenance), and then type **5** (Backup Configuration).

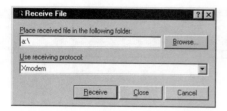

Figure 16.7 *The Receive File dialog box.*

2. Insert a disk in your disk drive.

3. Type **Y** and press Enter. The message Starting XMODEM download appears.

4. In the HyperTerminal screen, right-click and choose Receive File from the context menu. The Receive File dialog box appears (Figure 16.7).

5. Enter the path for your back-up file; for example **A:** for your disk drive.

6. Choose Xmodem from the Use receiving protocol list, and then click on the Receive button. The Receive Filename dialog box appears.

7. Enter a filename without an extension, then click OK. The file is downloaded to your diskette; the message Backup Configuration completed appears. OK appears in the HyperTerminal window.

8. Press any key to return to the System Maintenance menu.

Restoring a saved configuration file is done in a similar manner as saving a back-up file, but instead of choosing Receive File, you choose Send File from the HyperTerminal context menu. You type **6** (Restore Configuration) from the System Maintenance menu.

Using the Prestige as a Dial-In Server

The Prestige allows remote dial-in users to dial in and gain access to your LAN. This features enables users to have remote access capabilities with their Windows 95 PCs connected to the LAN. You can configure the Prestige 128 to receive calls from remote dial-in users. To do so, you use the Default Dial-in Setup screen to define the default dial-in parameters for dial-in callers. These settings affect incoming calls from all remote dial-in users.

1. In the Main Menu screen, type **13** (Default Dial-in Setup). The Default Dial-in Setup screen appears (Figure 16.8).

2. Many of the default setting are sufficient to use. The following are those you may want to customize for your remote access server needs:

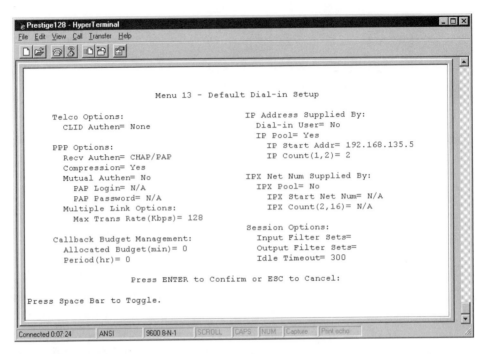

Figure 16.8 The Default Dial-in Setup screen.

Callback Budget Management. Use the Allocated Budget (min) field to define a budget of time for callbacks for all dial-in users. Use the Period (hr) field to set the time interval to reset the callback budget control.

Set the IP Address Supplied by Dial-in User to No. The IP Pool setting should be set to Yes. In the IP Start Addr field, define the first IP address in the pool. Use a private IP address as your starting point; for example, 192.168.135.5. Enter the number of IP addresses you want to add to the pool. The default 2 setting indicates the starting IP addresses of 192.168.135.5 and 192.168.135.6. You can choose 1 or 2, one for each B channel.

3. Press Enter until you return to the Main Menu screen. At this stage, you're ready to add individual remote dial-in users.

4. At the Main Menu, type **14** (Dial-in User Setup). The Dial-in User Setup screen appears (Figure 16.9). Notice there are eight fields for allowing that number of dial-in remote users.

5. Type **1** and press Enter. The Edit Dial-in User screen appears (Figure 16.10).

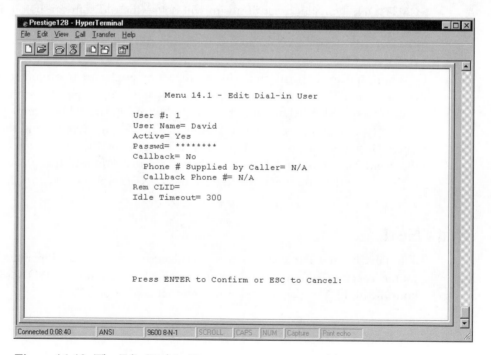

```
Prestige128 - HyperTerminal                                    _ □ ×
File  Edit  View  Call  Transfer  Help

 □ 🖆  🕾 🔏  🕮 🕙  🖻


                    Menu 14 - Dial-in User Setup

             1.  David
             2.  _____
             3.  _____
             4.  _____
             5.  _____
             6.  _____
             7.  _____
             8.  _____






                 Enter Menu Selection Number:


Connected 0:08:15   ANSI    9600 8-N-1   SCROLL  CAPS  NUM  Capture  Print echo
```

Figure 16.9 *The Dial-in User Setup screen.*

```
Prestige128 - HyperTerminal                                    _ □ ×
File  Edit  View  Call  Transfer  Help

 □ 🖆  🕾 🔏  🕮 🕙  🖻


                    Menu 14.1 - Edit Dial-in User

             User #: 1
             User Name= David
             Active= Yes
             Passwd= ********
             Callback= No
               Phone # Supplied by Caller= N/A
               Callback Phone #= N/A
             Rem CLID=
             Idle Timeout= 300






             Press ENTER to Confirm or ESC to Cancel:


Connected 0:08:40   ANSI    9600 8-N-1   SCROLL  CAPS  NUM  Capture  Print echo
```

Figure 16.10 *The Edit Dial-in User screen.*

6. Enter a descriptive user name in the User Name field and make sure the Active field is set to Yes.

7. Enter a password for the remote dial-in user.

8. Make sure the Callback setting is set to No.

9. Press Enter until you return to the Dial-in User Setup screen.

10. Repeat steps 5 through 9 for each additional dial-in user you want to set up. Start with 2 to set up the second user.

11. After configuring the last dial-in user, press Enter until you return to the Main Menu screen.

Updating Prestige 128 Firmware

The Prestige 128 allows you to update its firmware via a software transfer from your PC. But doing so is possible only through the RS-232 cable connection. You can't use Telnet to update the Prestige firmware.

• •

CAUTION: Updating your firmware will delete the old software before installing the new software.

___

You update the firmware with a procedure similar to that used to restore a configuration file, as explained earlier in this chapter. You type **24** (System Maintenance) in the Main Menu, and then **7** (Software Update). The Prestige prompts you to type **Y** and press Enter to continue. The Prestige reboots and the prompt Enter Debug Mode appears. Type **atur** at the prompt and press Enter. Then use the Send File command from the HyperTerminal window to upload the new firmware file that you downloaded from the ZyXEL Web site.

What's Next

The next chapter lets you surf the Internet using the Ascend Pipeline 75 ISDN router. Ascend Communications is the leading manufacturer of ISDN routers for both the SOHO market as well as for Internet service providers.

17 *Surfing the Pipeline*

Ascend Communications is the leader in ISDN routers for both the ISP server side and the end-user side of Internet connections. The Ascend Pipeline family of products includes a variety of ISDN routers designed for different remote access needs. The latest Pipelines include the SOHO-friendly DHCP and NAT features, although they are not as easy to set up as other SOHO ISDN routers. This chapter takes you through the basics of setting up the Ascend Pipeline 75 ISDN router.

The Ascend Product Line

The Ascend Communications Pipeline ISDN routers are considered the top of the line. They're typically more expensive and not as easy to configure as other ISDN routers, but using a Pipeline ensures reliable service. The majority of ISPs use the Ascend MAX family of routers, which are designed for the server side of Internet connections. The current members of the Pipeline family include:

- *Pipeline 25-Fx.* An Ethernet-to-ISDN bridge that supports four users. It includes an ISDN BRI port and two analog ports; it doesn't include IP routing or compression support.

- *Pipeline 25-Px.* A single-user Ethernet-to-ISDN IP router with two RJ-11 POTS ports.

- *Pipeline 50.* A IP/IPX protocol ISDN router with a BRI port but no POTS ports. Provides unlimited user LAN remote access and DHCP and NAT functionality.

- *Pipeline 75.* Includes the same features as the Pipeline 50 but with two POTS ports.

- *Pipeline 85.* Includes the same features as the Pipeline 75, with a four-port 10BaseT hub.
- *Pipeline 130.* Includes one BRI port and one frame relay or dedicated digital connection from 56K up to a T1 line.

Of all the Pipeline family routers, the Pipeline 50, 75, and 85 are the workhorses for the SOHO market. They include the right mix of features to get the most out of your LAN-to-WAN connection, including the DHCP and NAT functionality. Another nice thing about the Pipeline products is that the text-based menu system is fundamentally the same regardless of the Pipeline model you're using.

Ascend offers an integrated firewall product for its Pipeline router series called Ascend Secure Access Firewall. A firewall is typically a dedicated software application that performs dynamic monitoring of data packets to protect a local network from unauthorized users and traffic. The Ascend Secure Access Firewall is built into the Pipeline router as an add-on feature.

Note: At the time this book was written, Ascend had just added DHCP and NAT functionality to its product line. Ascend also had not released the Pipeline 85, which includes the four-port hub added to the Pipeline 75. Because the Pipeline 75 is this company's current staple for the SOHO market and incorporates the same configuration interface, I used it here to demonstrate how to work with Ascend's ISDN routers.

About the Pipeline 75

As noted, the Pipeline 75 includes DHCP and NAT functionality to enable you to use a single ISDN Internet access account. Unfortunately, the Ascend implementation of these features requires you to enter private IP addresses and TCP/IP configuration parameters in the TCP/IP Properties dialog box for every PC on your LAN.

• •

CAUTION: Ascend Communications sells the bulk of its ISDN routers to the technical market. Therefore, it has been slower to respond to the needs of the SOHO market by offering easy-to-use configuration software and incorporating other SOHO-friendly features such as true DHCP server functionality.

Getting Started with the Pipeline 75

As with other ISDN modems, there are standard requirements for getting your router working before you configure it. For the Pipeline 75, you need to do the following:

- Order ISDN service and provision it for the Pipeline 75.
- Order your ISDN Internet access account.
- Set up the Ascend 75 router by connecting it to your ISDN line, your LAN hub, and any analog devices you want to share your ISDN line.
- Set up the TCP/IP Properties for each PC on your Windows 95 LAN.
- Set up the Windows 95 HyperTerminal program to configure the Ascend 75.

Ordering Your ISDN Service

The Pipeline documentation includes the specific provisioning information for the Pipeline 75. If you're using the POTS ports, you'll need a multipoint configuration for your ISDN line, along with the following information from the telephone company:

- ISDN switch types
- ISDN telephone numbers
- ISDN SPID numbers

Ordering Internet Service

The Pipeline 75 will work with either a LAN access package that uses static IP addresses or a single-user Internet access account that uses dynamic IP addressing. The single-user account based on dynamic IP addressing will be a lot cheaper than getting a LAN access package in which several static IP addresses are assigned. This is the option you'll probably use for affordable LAN-based Internet access. After you establish your Internet access account, you'll need the following information from your ISP:

- ISP's ISDN phone number
- ISP's IP gateway address
- ISP's IP subnet mask
- Authentication type (PAP or CHAP)
- Authentication name and password

- Domain Name Server (DNS) IP addresses
- ISP Domain Name

Setting Up the Pipeline 75

Setting up Pipeline 75 is straightforward. Connect the Ethernet cable, the ISDN line, the terminal cable, and the power adapter.

1. Use the supplied RS-232 cable to attach the Pipeline to your PC's COM port. The Pipeline uses a DB9 connector, so it includes a DB9 male to DB25 female adapter if you need to convert a DB25 connector to a DB9 connector. Connect the nine-pin serial cable to the Terminal port on the back panel. You can also configure the Pipeline 75 using an RS-232 cable connected to a COM port and the Windows 95 HyperTerminal program.

2. Connect one end of the supplied ISDN phone cable to the RJ-45 ISDN port labeled ISDN BRI on the back panel; connect the other end of the ISDN phone cable to the ISDN wall jack.

3. Connect the Pipeline 75 to a hub using 10BaseT cabling. The Pipeline 75 includes the standard 10BaseT port for connecting the unit to your LAN hub. If you're connecting the Pipeline 75 via a hub for 10BaseT, use any RJ-45 Ethernet cables wired straight through—which means the same color wire goes to the same pin number on each end. If you are connecting the Pipeline directly to an Ethernet card for a single PC connection, use the special 10BaseT cable supplied with your Pipeline 75.

4. Plug any POTS devices into the RJ-11 ports.

5. Hook up the Pipeline 75 to the power supply. The Pipeline 75 has no power switch so the power always stays on.

If you have a choice, place the Pipeline 75 in a location where you can view the LEDs on the front of the unit. This location will also need to be close to a power outlet and the incoming ISDN line. The LEDs on the front of the Pipeline 75 provide valuable status information about your connection. Table 17.1 describes the functions of these LEDs.

Setting Up Your Windows 95 LAN for the Pipeline

The Pipeline handles the DHCP and NAT differently from other DHCP routers. To use the Pipeline's DHCP and NAT features, you must add an assigned private IP address to each TCP/IP stack on your Windows LAN and make sure each Windows 95 PC on your LAN is properly configured. First, confirm you have

Table 17.1 Pipeline 75 Status LEDs

LED	FUNCTION
PWR (Power)	Indicates the power is on.
Act (Activity)	Blinks when there are data packets transmitted or received via the Ethernet connection.
Col (Collision)	Blinks when there are collisions on the Ethernet interface.
WAN (BRI)	Off means there is an active BRI line but no connection. On means there is an active WAN session. Blinking means there is an error with the BRI connection.
Con (Condition)	Lights up when you connect the Pipeline to its power source; stays on while the condition of the unit is tested. Goes off when the test is complete.

TCP/IP installed on each PC and bound to the network adapter card used for your TCP/IP connection to the Internet.

You can use the private IP address 200.200.200.200 for your Pipeline; and use the private IP address 200.200.200.201 for the first PC, 200.200.200.202 for the second PC, 200.200.200.203 for the third PC, and so on. Use the subnet mask IP address of 255.255.255.0.

Here's how to configure your Windows 95 TCP/IP stacks to work with the Pipeline 75.

1. Open the Network Properties dialog box from the Windows 95 Control Panel.

2. In the Network dialog box, select the TCP/IP-> [*network adapter name*] in the installed Network Components list; click Properties.

3. In the TCP/IP Properties dialog box, take these actions.

   Select the Specify IP Address setting in the IP Address tab.

   Enter the first private IP address in the IP Address field; for example, 200.200.200.201.

   Enter the Subnet Mask IP address; for example, 255.255.255.0.

   Click on the Gateway tab, then enter the IP address of the Pipeline in the New gateway field; for example, 200.200.200.200.

   Click on the DNS Configuration tab and select Enable DNS. Enter your user name in the Host field and the domain name of your ISP in the Domain field. Enter the DNS server IP address in the DNS Server Search Order field and click on the Add button. If you have more than one DNS IP address, enter them.

4. After making your entries in the TCP/IP Properties dialog box, click OK twice and restart Windows 95.

5. Repeat steps 1 through 4 for each PC on your Windows 95 LAN.

Note: Chapter 8, "Setting Up Your Windows 95 LAN for Remote Access," explains this configuration process in more detail.

Setting Up the Windows 95 HyperTerminal Program

The best way to initially configure the Pipeline 75 is to use the Windows 95 HyperTerminal program with your PC connected to the Pipeline via the supplied RS-232 cable. The HyperTerminal approach uses a text-based menu system. The Pipeline configuration menus are not as easy to use as other ISDN router menu systems, but they get the job done.

After the Pipeline has been assigned its own IP address, you can access the configuration menus over your LAN via Telnet. You cannot use Telnet to perform the initial configuration of the Pipeline 75 because it requires an IP address, which you must enter as part of the initial configuration. Once the Pipeline has an assigned IP address, go to the Windows 95 MS-DOS prompt to display the DOS window, then enter:

```
telnet <IP address>
```

For example, if your Pipeline is assigned the IP address 200.200.200.200, then you enter

```
telnet 200.200.200.200
```

which then accesses the Pipeline's configuration menus.

The following steps explain how to create a HyperTerminal connection to the Pipeline 75 using the HyperTerminal program in Windows 95. Once you create the connection, you can save it to use again.

1. Choose Start|Accessories|HyperTerminal. The HyperTerminal window appears.

2. Double-click on the Hypertm icon. The Connection Description dialog box appears.

3. Type a name for your connection, choose an icon, and click OK. The Phone Number dialog box appears.

4. In the Connect using list, choose the Direct to Com port for the serial port you're using to connect the PC to the Pipeline 75; click OK. The COM Properties dialog box appears.

5. Change the Bits per second setting to 9600, and choose None for the Flow control setting. The Data bits, Parity, and Stop bits use the default values of 8, None, and 1, respectively.

6. Click OK. The HyperTerminal window appears. You're ready to configure the Pipeline 75.

The Pipeline Configurator

The Pipeline 75 includes a Java-based configuration program called the Configurator. At the time this book was written, the Configurator had not been updated to enable the configuration of the Pipeline 75's DHCP and NAT features. When the Configurator is updated, you should consider using it to configure your Pipeline 75. The Configurator is part of the CD that comes with the Ascend Pipeline 75. After installing the software, you double-click on the Pipeline Console icon in the Ascend Pipeline folder or choose Start | Programs | Ascend Pipeline | Pipeline Console. The Ascend Pipeline window appears (Figure 17.1).

Click on the QuickStart button. The QuickStart Pipeline Configuration window appears. This window provides a wizard to help you install the Pipeline 75 (Figure 17.2). Click on Start to begin the process.

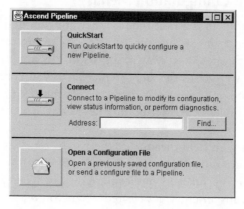

Figure 17.1 *The Ascend Pipeline window.*

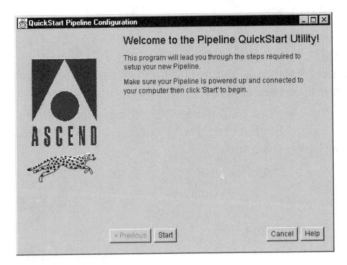

Figure 17.2 *The QuickStart Pipeline Configuration window.*

Configuring the Pipeline 75

To begin the Pipeline 75 configuration, launch the HyperTerminal program and then open the Ascend console screen. Press Ctrl+L to display the Main Edit menu (Figure 17.3). This menu contains a list of other menus, each of which can contain connection profiles and submenus. There are eight status windows to the right of the Edit menu.

Working with the Pipeline Configuration Menus

You traverse the configuration list in the Edit menu by selecting an item and then toggling through entries or entering strings of characters. The greater-than (>) symbol appears to the left of the item you're working with. On some items, you toggle by pressing Enter until you get to the right item. When you enter a string, square brackets ([ ]) appear, and you insert the characters within them. After you are finished, you press Enter. Table 17.2 describes the keys used for working with the Pipeline menus.

An N/A entry in a menu item field means that the parameter does not apply within the context of how some other parameters have been set in the profile. A blinking text cursor appears in the brackets, indicating you can start typing your entry. If the field already contains an entry, it's cleared when you type a character. To modify only a few characters of existing text, use the direction keys to position the cursor and then delete or overwrite the characters. To close the edit field and accept the entry, press Enter.

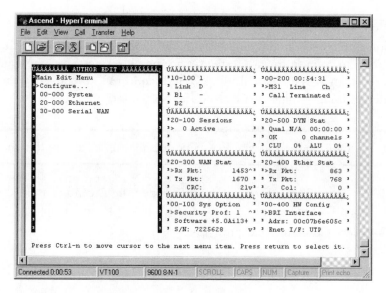

Figure 17.3 *The Pipeline Main Edit Menu.*

When you exit a profile, you are prompted to confirm that you want to save the changes. To do so, choose the Exit and Save options and press Enter, or press 2.

Table 17.2 Keys for Working with the Pipeline Menus

PRESS	TO
Ctrl+N, or the down arrow	Move to the next menu item.
Ctrl+P or the uparrow	Move to the previous menu item.
Enter	Select a menu item.
Tab	Move to the next window. A thick border surrounds the active window.
Backspace+Tab	Move to previous window.
Ctrl+V	Move to next page of the list.
Delete	Delete character under the cursor.
Backspace	Delete the character to the left of the cursor.
Ctrl+D	Open the DO menu.
Ctrl+L	Refresh the screen.

Setting Up the Basic Pipeline 75 IP Configuration

The following steps guide you through the basic configuration of the Ascend Pipeline 75 to connect to an Internet service provider's host machine using private IP addresses on your LAN and using DHCP and NAT to connect your LAN to the Internet using a single-user dial-up ISDN account.

Note: Configuring the Pipeline POTS ports is explained later in this chapter.

---

1. Using the HyperTerminal program, open the Ascend console screen. The Main Edit menu appears. If it doesn't, press Esc until it appears.

2. Select Configure and press Enter. The Configure menu appears (Figure 17.4).

3. In the Configure menu, do the following to configure your ISDN line settings:

    Select the Switch Type field and press Enter until you display the ISDN switch used by your telephone company for your ISDN line.

    Select the Chan Usage field and choose Switch/Switch.

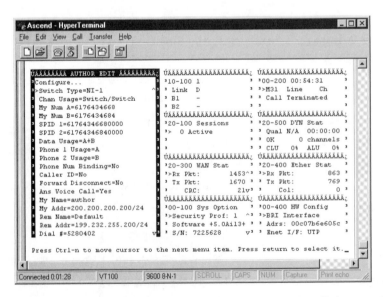

Figure 17.4 *The Configure menu is where you can enter all the essential Pipeline configurations.*

Select the My Num A field and enter the directory number of your first ISDN B channel.

Select the My Num B field and enter the directory number of your second ISDN B channel.

Select the SPID 1 field and enter the SPID assigned to the My Num A entry.

Select the SPID 2 field and enter the SPID assigned to the My Num B entry.

4. In the My Name field, enter your user name assigned by your ISP.

5. In the My Addr field, enter your private IP address for the Pipeline, which will be your gateway IP address. For example, enter 200.200.200.200.

6. In the Rem Name field enter a name for your ISP's server or any name you want to use to identify the remote server for this connection profile.

7. In the Rem Addr, enter the IP address of the ISP's remote host.

8. In the Dial # field, enter the phone number you dial to connect to your ISP.

9. Press the down arrow key to display the remaining Pipeline settings in the Configure menu (Figure 17.5).

10. Make sure the Route field displays the IP setting.

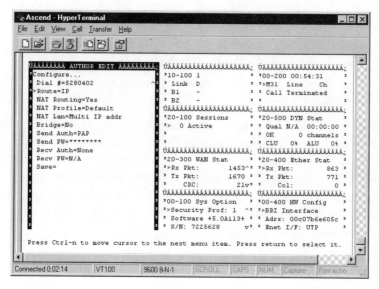

Figure 17.5 *Additional configuration options in the Configure menu.*

11. Select NAT Routing and choose Yes.

12. Select the NAT Profile and enter the name you entered in the Rem Name field.

13. Select the NAT Lan setting and choose Multi IP addr if you're using more than one PC on your Network.

14. Select the Send Auth field and choose Defines the authentication required on the remote network; for example, PAP or CHAP

15. Select Send PW and enter your login password for the ISP host.

16. Select Save and press Enter to save your changes.

After you configure the Pipeline 75's IP address using a terminal communications program, you can use Telnet to access it from a local or remote site. The Telnet method displays the same configuration menus as the terminal communications connection.

Configuring the POTS Ports

The Phone 1 Usage and Phone 2 Usage settings in the Main Edit Menu let you specify which directory number goes to which analog device, for example, to indicate that you want the fax machine to use the directory number in the My Num A or the My Num B field. You can choose one of the following settings:

- Choose A to route incoming calls to either the Phone 1 or Phone 2 port to use the directory number in the My Num A field.
- Choose B to route incoming calls to either the Phone 1 or Phone 2 port to use the directory number in the My Num B field.
- Choose None to prevent analog calls from being routed to the Phone 1 or Phone 2 jack.

In the Phone Num Binding field, a Yes entry means that an outgoing call will always be made on the directory number for the port to which the device is connected. If the B channel for that directory number is already in use, the call can't be made. A No entry means an outgoing call that would normally be made on a particular directory number can be made on the other directory number if the B channel for the first directory number is already in use and the B channel for the second directory number is free.

Setting Up Passwords

The Pipeline has three security levels, each of which is defined in a Security Profile. To see the list of Security Profiles, open the System menu in the Main Edit menu, select Security, and press Enter. When shipped from the factory, there are no password settings in place. Whenever the Pipeline is powered on, it activates the first Security Profile in this list, which is always named Default and always has no password. You may want to reset the privileges in the Default profile to restrict what can be done by anyone accessing the Pipeline configuration menus. Here's how.

1. Open the Default Security Profile and set the Operations privilege to No.
2. Assign a password to the Full Access Security Profile. Don't restrict privileges in the Full Access Profile.
3. Activate the Full Access Security Profile and proceed to configure the Pipeline. To activate the Full Access Security Profile, press Ctrl+D. A context-sensitive menu called a Do menu appears.
4. In the Do menu, press P or select Password. The list of Security Profiles will be displayed. Select Full Access and press Enter. The Pipeline prompts you for the profile's password.
5. Type the password and press Enter to accept it.

Note: The default password used for the Full Access Profile is *Ascend*.

What's Next

The next chapter takes you on your final ISDN router joyride with the Cisco 776. While Ascend is the leading ISDN router vendor, Cisco is the mother of all router manufacturers. The Cisco 776 represents Cisco's latest entry into the SOHO market.

PART
IV

Satellites, Cable
Modems, and xDSL

18 *Return of the Cisco 776 Kid*

C isco Systems is the world's leading router manufacturer, although in the ISDN router market the company is a relatively new player. However, its latest entries in the ISDN router market, which comprise the Cisco 770 series, are targeted directly to the needs of the SOHO market. This chapter explains working with the Cisco 776 ISDN router, which includes the full complement of SOHO-friendly features.

About the Cisco 770 Series

The Cisco 770 series of ISDN routers is the company's newest addition to its multiprotocol ISDN router products. Of the four models that make up the series—the 771, 772, 775, and the 776—the Cisco 772 and the 776 are designed for the North American market, which means they include the built-in NT1. The Cisco 772 doesn't include POTS ports; the 776 includes two. Other than the POTS difference, the 772 and 776 are similar devices. The 770 series includes three different configuration options:

- The Internet-ready feature set, which supports IP routing with no data compression and support for four LAN devices.
- The SOHO feature set, which supports both IP and IPX routing with compression for up to four LAN devices.
- The Remote Office feature set, which supports both IP and IPX routing with compression for up to 1,500 LAN devices.

The 770 series is similar to the Cisco 760 series but includes the following features not found in the 760 series:

357

- An integrated four-port Ethernet hub.
- A Call Connect/Disconnect switch on the front of the unit that allows you to manually make or connect data calls.
- ClickStart software, which allows users to configure the router using a Windows-based wizard that walks you through a simple configuration process for the 770 series.
- Two POTS ports. POTS telephone features include support for call waiting, cancel call waiting, call hold, call retrieve, three-way call conferencing, and call transfer.

The Cisco 772 and 776 support both the U interface and S/T interface, enabling you to connect an ISDN-based desktop video-conferencing system to the router. The Cisco 770 series supports dynamic IP addresses using DHCP and NAT; and Cisco adds an extension to NAT called PAT (Port and Address Translation). Using PAT, you can enable selected access to your LAN by specifying TCP/IP port numbers for particular types of data such as Web browsing, e-mail, or file transfer.

About the Cisco 776

Cisco Systems' 776 ISDN is the flagship router of the 770 series. It embodies state-of-the-art ISDN router technology with a powerful collection of SOHO-friendly features. The street price of the Cisco 776 is competitively priced at around $699. It includes the following key features.

- Easy configuration using a friendly, step-by-step Windows wizard program called ClickStart. You can also use a Web interface version of the configuration program:
- DHCP and NAT support that allows you to connect a LAN to the Internet via ISDN using a single-user access account. The Cisco 776 includes built-in DHCP server and NAT functionality to enable these big cost-saving features. You can also use the Cisco 776 as a static IP router.
- A handy Call Connect/Disconnect switch on the front of the unit for quickly making an ISDN connection or disconnection.
- Firmware upgrade and configuration via software downloads from the Cisco Web site.
- IP and IPX routing support.
- Built-in firewall filter for security. The preconfigured firewall blocks undesirable traffic originating from the Internet (for static IP connections). You can

also deploy more customized filters using the Cisco 776 extensive custom filtering capabilities.

- Two analog ports with advanced calling features for sharing your ISDN line with analog devices (telephone, fax, and modem). Support for call waiting, cancel call waiting, call hold, call retrieve, three-way call conferencing, and call transfer.

- An integrated four-port 10BaseT Ethernet hub; or you can connect the Cisco 776 to your existing hub.

- An S/T-interface port for adding an ISDN-ready device, such as a desktop video-conferencing system.

- PAT (Port and Address Translation) feature that enables specific data requests from the Internet to resources on the LAN; for example, Web browsing (HTTP) or file transfers (FTP).

- Data over voice, which allows data calls to be placed or answered using ISDN speech-grade capabilities instead of circuit-switched data-grade capabilities. In many areas, this feature enables Cisco 776 customers to avoid paying higher ISDN per-minute charges.

Getting Started with the Cisco 776

As is the case with other ISDN modems, you must meet some standard requirements for getting your router working before you can configure it. Here they are for the Cisco 776 router.

- Order ISDN service and provision it for the Cisco 776.
- Order your ISDN Internet access account.
- Set up your Windows 95 LAN for dynamic IP addressing by configuring the Windows 95's TCP/IP Properties for each PC.
- Set up the Cisco 776 router by connecting it to your ISDN line, all your networked PCs, and any analog devices you want to share your ISDN line.

Ordering Your ISDN Service

The Cisco 776 supports the Bellcore K Compatibility package ISDN Ordering Code or the Intel Blue for ProShare. The documentation includes the specific provisioning information in case your telephone company doesn't support either of these provisioning packages. You'll need ISDN switch type and ISDN SPID numbers. You don't need the ISDN telephone numbers, which are a subset of the SPIDs.

Ordering Internet Service

The Cisco 776 will work with either a LAN access package that uses static IP addresses or a single-user Internet access account that uses dynamic IP addressing. The single-user account based on dynamic IP addressing will be a lot cheaper than getting a LAN access package in which several static IP addresses are assigned. This is the option you'll probably use for affordable LAN-based Internet access. After you establish your Internet access account, you'll need the following information from your ISP:

- ISP's ISDN phone number
- ISP's IP gateway address, if any
- ISP's IP subnet mask, if any
- Authentication type (PAP or CHAP)
- Authentication name and password
- Domain Name Server (DNS) IP addresses
- Domain Name

Setting Up Your Windows 95 LAN for a Dynamic IP

With the Cisco 776 hardware installed, you're ready to move on to software installation. Before you configure the Cisco 776, make sure each Windows 95 PC on your LAN is properly configured. On the Windows 95 side of your LAN, confirm that you have TCP/IP installed on each PC and bound to the network adapter card used for your TCP/IP connection to the Internet. For using the Cisco 776 with a dynamic IP address Internet access account, verify that the default TCP/IP settings are used. In the Network control panel, select the TCP/IP–> [*network adapter name*] in the installed Network Components list, then click Properties. The Obtain an IP address automatically setting should be selected in the IP Address tab. Every computer on your Windows 95 LAN should be configured this way.

Note: Chapter 8, "Setting Up Your Windows 95 LAN for Remote Access," explains this configuration process in more detail.

Setting Up the Cisco 776 Hardware

Connecting the Cisco 776 to your LAN and ISDN line is easy—the router comes with a color-coded collection of cables. The following steps explain how to set up the Cisco 776:

1. Use the blue console cable to hook up the router to the PC you want to use to configure the 776. The cable connects to the Console port at the back of the 776 and a serial port on your PC.

2. Connect one end of the red ISDN U cable to the ISDN U port at the back of the unit and the other into the ISDN wall jack.

3. Connect any analog devices to the two ports labeled PHONE 1 and PHONE 2.

4. Do one of the following:

   Connect each PC's 10BaseT cable to an Ethernet port at the back of the 776.

   Connect the 776 to your existing hub using the yellow Ethernet cable provided.

5. Attach the power connector to the power connector port.

6. Turn on the power switch on the back of the unit.

Configuring the Cisco 776

Use the ClickStart Install program for Windows disk included in the Open Me First bag to initially configure the Cisco 776. The ClickStart program installs the Cisco Fast Step Setup program, which provides a friendly Windows 95 wizard to guide you through the configuration process. To install the ClickStart Install program, do the following.

1. Insert the ClickStart Install Program for Windows disk into your PC's A or B drive.

2. Choose Start|Run; enter **A:\SETUP** and click OK. Some temporary ClickStart files are copied to your hard disk, then the Welcome screen for the Cisco Fast Step Setup program appears.

3. Click on Next. The Choose Destination location page appears.

4. Click Next to use the default path for the Cisco Fast Step program installation.

5. In the Select Program Folder page, click Next to use the default folder name for Cisco Fast Step.

6. Click Next again to start copying files to your hard disk. After the files are copied, the Setup Complete page appears; click Finish. The installation of the Fast Step software is complete and the Fast Step welcome screen appears.

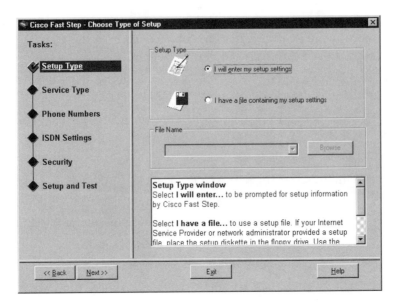

Figure 18.1 *The Choose Type of Setup page.*

Note: You can click on Yes, I want to review the ReadMe file now to display the readme text file in Notepad.

---

7. Click Next to display the Choose Type of Setup page (Figure 18.1).

8. Select I will enter my setup settings in the Setup Type group, and click Next.

9. In the Select Services page (Figure 18.2), select Internet Service Provider only, then click Next.

10. In the Router Connection Type page (Figure 18.3), select the Direct connection to the router using the config cable setting.

11. Click Next twice. The Fast Setup program connects to the router and the Phone Numbers page appears.

12. Enter the dial-up numbers for connecting to your ISP and click Next.

13. In the ISDN Settings page (Figure 18.4), do the following:

    Select the telephone company switch type used for your ISDN connection from the Switch Type drop-down list.

    Enter your first SPID number in the SPID1 field.

    Enter your second SPID number in the SPID2 field.

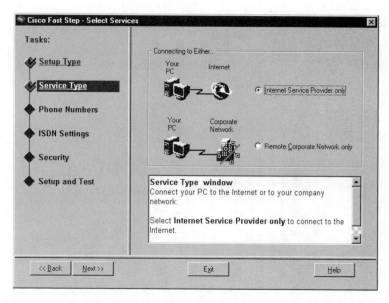

Figure 18.2 *The Select Services page.*

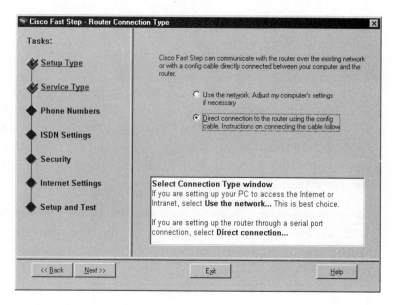

Figure 18.3 *The Router Connection Type page.*

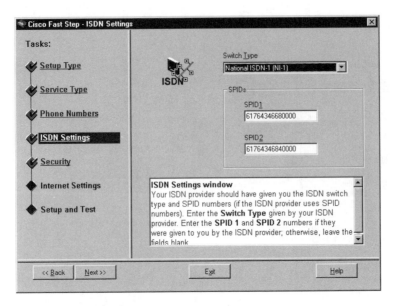

Figure 18.4 *The ISDN Settings page.*

14. Click Next. Fast Setup tests your ISDN connection and then displays the Security page.

15. In the Security page, enter your login user name and password for accessing the Internet via your ISP's host; click Next.

16. In the Domain Name Server Settings page, enter your ISP's DNS server IP addresses; click Next.

17. In the Additional Remote Network Setting page (Figure 18.5), enter the IP address of the ISP's WAN gateway in the WAN field and enter the subnet mask. If your ISP provided no IP address, enter 0 in the settings boxes.

18. Click Next. The Setup and Test page appears (Figure 18.6). The connection is made and the successfully connected page appears. You're now connected and can use any TCP/IP program.

TIP: You can open the Setup program again at any time by choosing Start|Programs|Cisco Fast Step|Setup for 700 Series, which displays the wizard again.

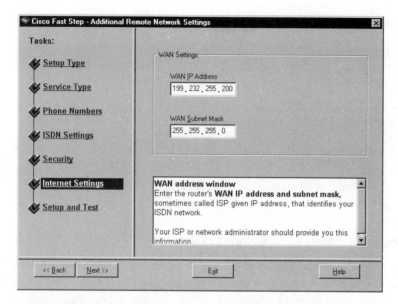

Figure 18.5 The Additional Remote Network Settings page.

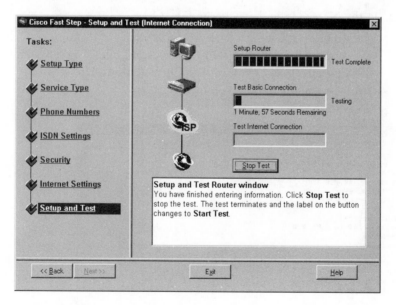

Figure 18.6 The Setup and Test page.

IP Routing Settings

When you select the Internet Service Provider only setting in the Service Type page, the Cisco Fast Step program configures IP routing using DHCP and NAT. It assigns the following IP addresses.

- The router's IP address is set to 10.0.0.1, which is the default gateway for your network.
- The DHCP address pool starts at 10.0.0.3; the subnet mask is set to 255.255.255.0 for all the computers on your LAN.
- The default profile is initially configured with the blank IP address of 0.0.0.0. This instructs the 776 to obtain an IP address from the ISP router.

Manually Editing Your Configuration

A configuration text file saved as setup.cfg in the C:\Program Files\Cisco Systems\Fast Step ISDN\ folder stores the settings you've established using the Cisco Fast Step configuration program. This text file can be opened and edited using the Windows 95 Notepad text editor.

1. Choose Start|Programs|Accessories|Notepad.

2. In the Notepad window, choose File|Open.

3. In the Open dialog box, choose the All Files (*.*) option in the Files of type drop-down list; navigate to C:\Program Files\Cisco Systems\Fast Step ISDN\setup.cfg and click on the Open button. The setup.cfg file appears in the Notepad window (Figure 18.7).

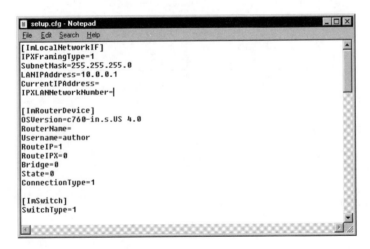

Figure 18.7 *The setup.cfg appears as a text file in the Notepad window.*

On opening the setup.cfg file, you can edit in Notepad. Changes are made in the same way you edit a system.ini and win.ini files in Windows 95.

Making Cisco 776 Connections

Once the Cisco 776 is set up, you're ready to access the Internet using any TCP/IP application. To surf the Web on any computer connected to the Cisco 776, simply double-click on the program icon. For example, clicking on the Internet Explorer or Netscape Navigator icon on your Windows 95 desktop automatically makes the Internet connection and displays the specified starting page. ISDN connections via Ethernet take only a few seconds to complete instead of the 20 or more it takes using Windows 95 Dial-Up Networking with a modem or ISDN adapter card or modem.

You can terminate your ISDN connection by closing the TCP/IP application, which uses the time-out setting; or you can press the Call button on the front of the 776 to terminate the call immediately.

To use e-mail or network news, you need to configure your e-mail and network newsreader programs. This involves specifying the e-mail and network news server addresses supplied by your ISP. For each user on your local LAN who wants a private e-mail address, you will need a separate e-mail account from your ISP, for which there is usually a minimal charge of around $10 per e-mail account per month.

Reading the Cisco 776 LEDs

The LEDs on the front of the Cisco 776 let you monitor the status of your LAN, ISDN line, analog devices, and power. Table 18.1 describes these functions.

Monitoring Your Connections

Choose Start | Programs | Cisco Fast Step | Monitor for 700 Series to display the Cisco 700 Series Monitor dialog box (Figure 18.8). This dialog box lets you track the status of your ISDN line connections. The Line Usage Summary group box shows the total number of hours and minutes of channel usage. Totals are shown for the following entries:

Today	12:01 A.M. through the current time
This Week	Sunday 12:01 A.M. through the current time
This Month	First of the month 12:01 A.M. through the current time
Last Month	First through the end of the month

Table 18.1 Cisco 776 LED Functions

LED	FUNCTION
RDY	Indicates the router's operating status. On when power is supplied to the router and when the router completes its self-test procedure and begins operating.
NT1	On (unblinking) indicates that the internal NT1 and the ISDN switch have synchronized over the ISDN line. Blinking (five blinks per second) indicates that the internal NT1 is attempting to synchronize with the telephone switch. Blinking (one blink per second) indicates that the internal NT1 is attempting to synchronize with the ISDN terminal device(s).
LINE	On (unblinking) indicates synchronization between the NT1 S interface and the ISDN terminal device(s).
LAN	Lights when packets are sent to or received from the Ethernet within the last minute.
LAN RXD	Blinks when packets are received from the LAN via Ethernet.
LAN TXD	Blinks when packets are sent to the LAN via Ethernet.
LK1 LK2 LK3 LK4	Hub port status indicators. On when there is a connection on the respective link. Blinks (one blink per 1.5 seconds) when there is a problem with the link.
CH1	Blinks when a call is being connected on the first ISDN B channel. After the call is established, the LED remains on without blinking.
CH1 RXD	Blinks when packets are received from the first ISDN B channel.
CH1 TXD	Blinks when packets are sent on the first ISDN B channel.
CH2	Blinks when a call is being connected on the second ISDN B channel. When the call is established, the LED remains on without blinking.
CH2 RXD	Blinks when packets are received from the second ISDN B channel.
CH2 TXD	Blinks when packets are sent on the second ISDN B channel.
PH1 PH2	Blinks when the corresponding basic telephone service line is off the hook. Blinks in the following patterns when entering DTMF commands for the corresponding basic telephone service port on the router: Blinks on and off twice per second for two seconds if the command is entered correctly. Blinks on and off once per second for four seconds if the command is entered incorrectly.

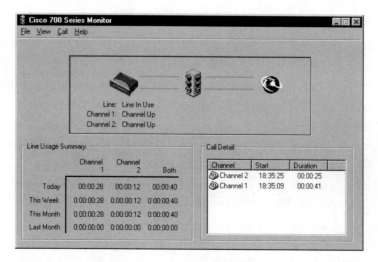

Figure 18.8 *The Cisco 700 Series Monitor dialog box.*

The Call Detail list box shows each call, the line it was made on, when it started, and the hours and minutes of its duration. The scrolling list box also shows all calls made in the last 60 days sorted by the time of the call.

Note: You can't run the Cisco Fast Step configuration program with the Monitor. Choosing the Fast Step program with the Monitor on displays a message stating that Fast Step Setup cannot be run. Click OK. Then right-click on the Monitor icon on the Windows 95 taskbar, choose Suspend Monitor, and click Yes to shut off the Monitor. Then choose Start|Programs|Cisco Fast Step|Setup for 700 Series, which displays the setup wizard.

Beyond the Basic 776 Configuration

As you've seen, the Cisco Fast Step Setup program, which provides a friendly Windows 95 wizard to guide you through the configuration process, will get you up and running for remote access. However, there is a storehouse of other configuration options that are accessible only by using a command line. To make configuration changes at the system command level, you use the Windows 95 HyperTerminal program. Once you connect to the 776 via HyperTerminal, you can perform hundreds of configuration operations using Cisco 700 Series Command Reference documentation that's included with the Cisco 776.

Using HyperTerminal to Configure the Cisco 776

The process necessary to access the Cisco 776 using the Console method via the Windows 95 HyperTerminal program is detailed in the following steps:

1. With the Cisco 776 attached to your PC via the supplied RS-232 cable and turned on, Choose Start|Accessories|HyperTerminal. The HyperTerminal window appears.

2. Double-click on the Hypertm icon. The Connection Description dialog box appears.

3. Type a name for your connection (such as Cisco 776), choose an icon, and click OK. The Phone Numbers dialog box appears.

4. In the Connect using list, choose the Direct to Com port for the serial port you're using to connect the PC to the Cisco 776; click OK. The COM Properties dialog box appears.

5. Change the Bits per second setting to 9600, and choose None for the Flow control setting. The Data bits, Parity, and Stop bits use the default values of 8, None, and 1, respectively.

6. Click OK. The HyperTerminal window appears. You're ready to configure the Cisco 776.

7. Choose File|Save to save your connection profile.

Working with Commands

Once you're connected to the Cisco via HyperTerminal, you face a blank screen until you press Enter, which displays a system prompt, such as author>, which is the name of the router. This router name was set up when you specified your user name for your ISP using the Cisco Fast Step Security page. At the system prompt, you can enter a variety of system management commands, some of which are listed in Table 18.2. Note that the bold characters are the actual command characters you enter at the system prompt.

Note: For a complete command listing with instructions, use the Cisco 776's Command Reference Guide or the handy Quick Reference Cards for essential configuration settings.

Table 18.2 Cisco 776 Command Sampler

COMMAND	DESCRIPTION
show	Displays the router's configuration and the status of both B channels.
show **co**nfig **all**	Displays all the configuration parameter settings.
help	Displays the list of commands and the syntax for each command.
version	Displays the firmware release version used by your Cisco 776.
show **se**curity **all**	Displays the Cisco 776's router security configurations.
set **pa**ssword **sy**stem	Sets a password for access to the Cisco 776 for changing the configuration.
set **sp**eed **vo**ice	Sets outgoing data communications to voice over data.
set <B channel> **time**out <*number of seconds*>	Configures the amount of time each B channel will remain idle before disconnecting. The default setting is Off. For example, to set the idle time to 300 seconds for the first B channel, enter: **se**t **1 time**out **300**
show **dh**cp **co**nfig	Displays the Cisco 776's DHCP configuration.

What's Next

You've been through the ISDN gauntlet. Now it's time to break into the higher-bandwidth options of satellite, cable modems, and DSL. The next chapter looks at the extraterrestrial option for high-speed Internet access including a hands-on satellite service flight check. Having a satellite dish in your yard is a lot better than a pair of pink plastic Flamingos.

19 *Dishing Out Bandwidth via Satellite*

One of the few high-bandwidth technologies almost universally available right now is satellite-based data communications. This extraterrestrial high-bandwidth option is still in its infancy but it holds promise as an extension to terrestrial high-speed data communications. There are a number of big satellite plans in the works but most will not see action until the year 2000 to 2002. One exception is DirecPC from Hughes Network Systems, which is available today. This chapter leads you on a hands-on journey through setting up and using the extraterrestrial DirecPC system for Internet access.

Looking Up to the Sky for Internet Access

High-bandwidth options such as ISDN, cable, or DSL are great only if you happen to live in an area where they are available. Unfortunately, much of the United States is devoid of high-speed bandwidth options outside the larger metropolitan areas. For anyone living in rural areas, satellite-based data communications may be the only viable high-speed option beyond POTS.

Satellite-based data communication is for those who want to live, work, and play beyond the tether of terrestrial systems. They leapfrog over land-based systems by broadcasting their signals over a large landmass from 23,000 miles above the earth. In this way, satellite service can be made available throughout the United States. All you have to do is point a satellite disk (also called an antenna) to the sky for access.

The Internet access via satellite market is a subset of the home satellite TV market, and satellite-based TV communications are already in full swing. Several companies already offer TV systems to compete with land-based cable TV operators. These systems include DirecTV from Hughes Network Systems, Dish Network and EchoStar from EchoStar Communications, and others. In the very near future, most of these satellite TV systems will allow you to use a single satellite dish for both television and Internet access. Already, the prices for customer equipment, including the dish and PC or TV interface devices, have fallen to a few hundred dollars from several thousand dollars just a few years ago.

Satellite technology has rapidly improved in terms of power, bandwidth capacity, and satellite life spans to enable data communications at more affordable rates. Satellite used to cost $150 to $250 million to manufacture. Today, the cost of building more powerful satellites is $12 to $15 million. Satellite company representatives assert that satellites can cost-effectively deliver blanket coverage to provide broadband services in areas outside metropolitan regions, where other carriers are less likely to focus their efforts. Satellites provide a wireless complement to the terrestrial network; they will not replace it. While the future promises more satellite options and bandwidth for Internet access, this option will continue to be a premium service costing more than most land-based remote access technologies.

Between 1998 and 2000, a number of global satellite networks will be deployed. These multibillion-dollar projects will launch hundreds of satellites. From the standpoint of remote access, the following are some that promise to deliver Internet access at more reasonable prices.

- The Teledesic Corporation, which is backed by Bill Gates (Microsoft) and Craig McCaw (McCaw Cellular Communications) has the most promising systems for remote access, because it's designed from the ground up to deliver Internet access for fixed locations.

- Hughes Network's SpaceWay system will enable easier and more powerful Internet access service capabilities than today's DirecPC system. SpaceWay's two-way digital dishes will cost less than $1,000 and could be in service by 1999.

- The Alcatel-Alsthom and Loral Space and Communications satellite system called Skybridge will be based on 64 low-orbiting satellites and is expected to begin operating in 2001.

- The Motorola satellite system called Celestri will be a $12.9 billion global satellite network system for voice, data, and video communications.

Still, with all that promise, satellite-based data communications technology has warts. For one thing, you have to purchase and install the equipment, including a satellite dish. Satellite communications also suffer from a phenomenon called *satellite delay*, a consequence of getting data up and down 22,300 miles. This takes nearly a half second, more than twice the transcontinental delay through today's Internet.

Workings of a Satellite System

Satellite communication systems transmit signals from Earth-based transceivers (transmitter/receiver) to space satellites. These satellites are placed in *geostationary orbits,* where they travel 22,300 miles above the Earth's equator, the distance at which the satellite's period of rotation matches the Earth's and the satellite always remains in the same spot over the Earth. These satellites are referred to as GEOs (geostationary orbit satellites), which are primarily LEOs (low-Earth-orbit satellites). Ground station transceivers are then aimed at the satellite and multiplexed signals containing hundreds of channels are transmitted over microwave beams to and from the satellite.

Transmissions to satellites are called *uplinks,* and transmissions to ground stations are called *downlinks.* Satellite antennas range in size from 18 inches to 33 feet in diameter; the size depends on transmission requirements. End-user TV and Internet satellite dishes typically are 18 to 24 inches in diameter. The next generation of consumer satellite dishes will be VSAT (very small aperture terminal) dishes that support two-way communications. Today's satellite-based TV systems are based on Ku-band technology, which is a one-way broadcast technology. The next generation of satellite technology will use Ka-band technology that supports two-way and higher bandwidth data communications capacity.

Teledesic Project

Teledesic Corporation is a joint venture between Bill Gates and Craig McCaw, whose plan it is to build an Internet-in-the-sky system using up to 840 low-orbiting satellites. This system proposes to offer broadband bandwidth-on-demand services ranging from 16 Kbps to 2.048 Mbps. These satellites will be linked to terrestrial telecommunications systems via high-capacity ground stations. However, they will also form an independent system of their own, using high-speed inter-satellite links between each satellite and eight of its neighbors. This nonhierarchical *geodesic mesh* will be highly tolerant of faults, local congestion, and the disruption of downlinks.

The $9 billion Teledesic project will consist of interlinked geostationary satellites that will target areas just outside of metropolitan areas, as well as high-end telecommuters with broadband satellite-based services. Teledesic is not focusing on serving mobile customers; however, the project is designed to provide services to fixed locations. Boeing, the plane manufacturer, is the prime contractor for building the satellite system. Already, Teledesic has all its frequency and U.S. construction and operating licenses in place. The satellites are scheduled to go up in the years 2000 and 2001. This system will be able to provide the equivalent of 20,000 simultaneous T1 lines. Since this is a shared capacity, it will be able to support up to two million users.

SpaceWay

Hughes Communications' SpaceWay system will expand the capabilities of satellite communications beyond its current DirecPC system. Hughes will first launch two geostationary satellites above North America and Asia. Europe and Latin America will be added later. The HS702 is the geostationary satellite through which Space-Way bits will flow. Four pairs of HS702s costing $3 billion will cover the world.

SpaceWay will be able to reach those consumers and businesses that don't have access to ADSL, cable modems, or direct fiber connections. It will offer Internet access directly to businesses and homes via geostationary satellites. SpaceWay uplinks will come in three flavors: Using a 26-inch dish, the SpaceWay uplink will send data at 384 Kbps; using a 47-inch dish, the uplink will support 1.5 Mbps; and using an 11-foot dish, the uplink will support up to 6 Mbps. SpaceWay intends to offer high-speed services for between $30 and $40 a month for the end-user bandwidth options.

Satellite Access to the Internet with DirecPC

Broadcast satellites like those used for digital television have plenty of bandwidth, but they deliver it one way. Hughes Network Systems uses a few tricks to make *one-way broadcast satellite* imitate a two-way personal Internet connection. With DirecPC Internet service, subscribers send data requests over the Internet via a modem over their regular telephone lines to the Hughes satellite control center, which sends the information to the satellite. The satellite sends the response of a command to the user.

Each subscriber's connection downstream is 400 Kbps, which is more than three times the speed of ISDN. However, the upstream capability is only as good as an Internet connection over terrestrial connections. For Web surfing and file

---

Note: The Hughes satellite that delivers the DirecPC service is in geostationary orbit around the Equator. If your line of sight to the south is obstructed, it will inhibit your DirecPC service. If you are unsure about the suitability of your location for DirecPC, call DirecPC at 1-800-886-4947 to verify that you can use the service.

---

downloads, the satellite option works well because most information is coming from the Internet down to your system. The satellite option doesn't work for interactive applications such as Net phones or video conferencing.

The DirecPC system has some disadvantages that you should know about, because they limit its appeal, particularly if you have other remote access options available.

- DirecPC uses an ISA adapter card that interfaces to your PC. Unfortunately, the DirecPC system doesn't allow you to have any other network adapter cards installed on your system. The result is that the PC you use for the DirecPC must be a standalone.

- The DirecPC Internet service can get expensive because its fees are based on usage, which fluctuate based on the time period you use the system and the amount of data being sent down to you.

- In most cases, you'll need a professional to install your satellite dish; this costs extra, too.

- You must have another Internet access account for your modem connection.

The DirecPC system requires a satellite dish separate from the one used by Hughes DirecTV service. This means that if you want both services, you'll need two satellite dishes. In the future, DirecPC does plan to release a dish that delivers both high-speed Internet access and DirecTV programming. The new combined TV and Internet access system will be named DirecDuo. One cable from the satellite dish will go to a box on your TV and the other will plug into the DirecPC adapter card.

Note: The bottom line on whether to use the DirecPC system is availability and pricing of other remote access options in your area. DirecPC should be used only if there are no other comparable remote access options available in your area, or if the terrestrial high-bandwidth options are more expensive.

How the DirecPC System Works

DirecPC is an asymmetrical system. You send your request for URLs through your modem. That request is then routed to the appropriate Web server via the DirecPC Network Operations Center (NOC). The high-bandwidth information you requested (graphics, video, etc.) is then sent back to the NOC, beamed to a Hughes satellite, and then directly to your home at up to 400 Kbps. For example, to download a 5-MB file from a remote server, you first start the DirecPC Navigator application, which uses the Turbo Internet service to connect via modem to your ISP. Once the connection to the Internet has been made, you request the file you want from the remote site's server. When your request is sent, a return address header that contains your computer's address is automatically attached. This address tells the remote server where to send the file you've requested. At this point, the DirecPC software jumps in. It intercepts the request for the file before it leaves your computer and adds another address header to the request. This new address is the address of the DirecPC NOC.

When the DirecPC NOC receives the request, it forwards it to the remote site's server. When the remote server sends your file, it sends it to the operations center, instead of to your computer. When the operations center receives your file, it transmits the file to the DirecPC satellite in space. A satellite transponder receives the signal and in turn beams it back to Earth, where it is received by your satellite antenna. The signal goes from the antenna to the DirecPC adapter installed in your computer. Figure 19.1 shows the schematic for satellite-based Internet access using the DirecPC system.

When you purchase the DirecPC Personal Edition, you get a 16-bit ISA card. Once installed, this card connects via coaxial cable to the DirecPC 21 elliptical satellite dish mounted outside your home. The satellite hardware, combined with the DirecPC Personal Edition software and a modem ISP account, delivers your Internet access.

You can use your existing ISP with DirecPC. You can also keep your current e-mail address. If you don't have an ISP, when you register your DirecPC Personal Edition, DirecPC can provide you with an ISP account. But note that DirecPC does not support direct connections to online services such as AOL, CompuServe, and Prodigy.

To install and use the DirecPC, you'll need the following:

- An unobstructed line of sight to the south from your home or office.
- PC with a Pentium processor.
- Windows 95. In fact, this is the only OS that DirecPC supports.
- At least 16 MB of RAM and 20 MB of hard disk space.
- A modem (9,600 bps or higher).
- An Internet service provider (monthly cost not included in service price from DirecPC).

The Cost of DirecPC

The DirecPC system hardware itself doesn't cost that much when compared to other remote access options. The list price for the DirecPC Personal Edition is

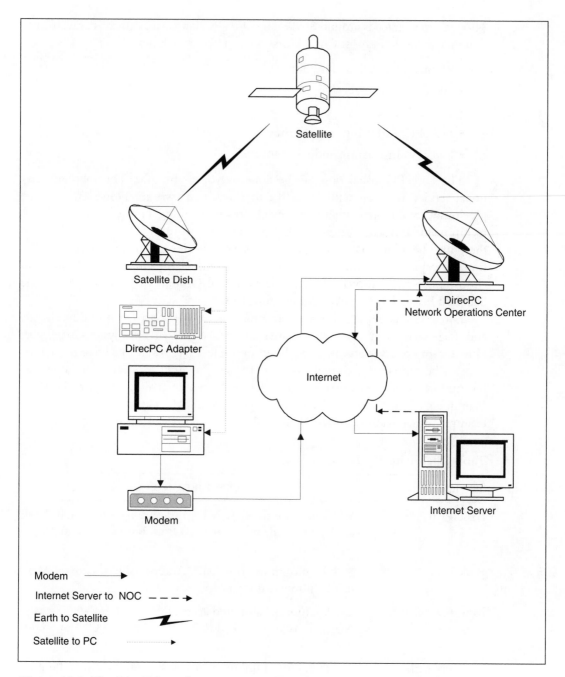

Figure 19.1 *The DirecPC satellite system using a combination of a modem for upstream access and satellite for downstream data.*

$499; its street price is around $399. The DirecPC Personal Edition is available nationwide and sold in most CompUSA stores. The kit includes:

- 21-inch elliptical satellite dish
- 100 feet of coaxial cable
- 16-bit ISA card
- DirecPC Turbo Internet software
- DirecPC Installation and User Manual

The DirecPC installation can be done by you or by using Dictaphone, a national service working with DirecPC, to install your system. However, as noted previously, setting up a satellite dish can be tricky, so using a professional installer is recommended. Installation using Dictaphone will cost from $99 to $199, although there may be additional fees depending on your location and for custom installation, as explained in the next section. If you install the dish yourself, you can choose from two hardware kits: the Basic Install-Ground Mount for $99, or the Standard Install-Roof or Wall Mount for $149.

DirecPC charges a one-time activation fee of $49.95, a flat monthly charge, and usage charges. It's the usage charges that make the DirecPC system expensive. DirecPC offers a variety of plans, listed in Table 19.1, based on different factors, such as the time of day or night you use the service and the amount of data moving upstream and downstream. While 60 or 80 cents per megabyte for the Basic Plan doesn't sound like much, these charges can quickly add up to big bucks. For example, downloading a 10-MB file will cost either $6 or $8 depending on the

Table 19.1 DirecPC Monthly Plans

SERVICE PLAN	DESCRIPTION
Basic Plan	$9.95 per month; $.60/MB from 6:00 P.M.–6:00 A.M. M–F, all day on weekends; $.80/MB from 6:00 A.M.–6:00 P.M. M–F.
Bulk Plan	$24.95/month up to 64 MB. Additional blocks of 64 MB can be purchased for $24.95 each.
Moon Surfer Plan	$39.95/month unlimited access from 6:00 P.M.–6:00 A.M. M–F; all day on weekends. $.80/MB from 6:00 A.M.–6:00 P.M. M–F.
Sun Surfer Plan	$129.95/month unlimited access from 6:00 A.M.–6:00 P.M. M–F; $.60/MB from 6:00 P.M.–6:00 A.M. M–F; all day on weekends.

time of day you download the file. And downloading graphics and multimedia files from Web sites is more expensive.

One other expense is, of course, an Internet access account for your dial-up modem part of the connection. As noted, you can continue to use the Internet service provider where you already have an account; or you can sign up for Internet service through DirecPC, in which case, the cost is in addition to your satellite connection.

Installing the DirecPC System

Installing the DirecPC system is a multistep process. As explained earlier, you can opt to have a professional do the whole thing for you, or you can do the PC side and have the installer set up the antenna. You may find that the best option is to install the DirecPC adapter card and DirecPC navigator software on your PC and then use an installer to set up your satellite dish. Whichever route you take, these are the basic steps for installing the DirecPC system.

1. Install the DirecPC adapter card.
2. Set up the DirecPC Navigator software.
3. Install and align the satellite dish.

Using Dictaphone to Install Your DirecPC Dish

The DirecPC package consists of two major hardware components, the ISA adapter card and the satellite dish antenna, which is installed in your backyard, on your roof, or on a building structure. You'll most likely install the ISA adapter card yourself but you may want to use DirecPC's Dictaphone installation service to set up the satellite dish. Using a DirecPC installation service will cost from $99 to $190, depending on your installation needs. The following are the three available installation packages and prices. Once you decide on the option you want, call 1-800-886-4947 to schedule the installation.

- *The Basic Install option.* Includes setting up your satellite dish and nothing else. This entails mounting a ground-level antenna only; one point of entry into your home; and up to a 50-foot cable run from the satellite dish to the wall plate. ISA adapter card installation is not included. The cost of this installation is $99 plus tax (where applicable). Additional cables and optional labor are charged separately.

- *The Standard Install package.* Includes a roof or wall antenna mount only; one point of entry into your home; and up to a 100-foot cable run from the satellite dish to the wall plate. ISA card installation is not included. The cost of this installation is $149 plus tax (where applicable). Additional cables and optional labor are charged separately.

- *The Premium Install package.* Includes a roof or wall antenna mount and ISA card installation into your PC; one point of entry into your home; and up to a 100-foot cable run from the satellite dish to the wall plate. The price of this package is $199 plus tax (where applicable). Additional cables and optional labor are charged separately.

All three of these installation packages include the alignment of your satellite dish to make it operational. If you choose the Basic Install or Standard Install package, you'll need to install the ISA card and software *before* the installer arrives so it is ready for the satellite alignment procedure. Installing your DirecPC adapter card and the DirecPC Navigation software also registers your system with DirecPC, which means that as soon as your satellite dish is installed, you'll be able to use it. The Premium Install package includes setting up everything you need to get up and running.

More involved satellite dish installations are considered custom installations, which are charged at $89 an hour, plus any materials. (For example, installing a satellite dish on top of a large apartment building.) Furthermore, a mileage charge may be added if you live more than 35 miles from the center of a major metropolitan area, so when you call to schedule an appointment, be sure to ask if you are within the standard installation area.

Note: If you want to install the satellite dish yourself, check local zoning codes, covenants, and other restrictions. Some communities prohibit installing satellite antennas or place limits on their mounting height. The DirecPC kit includes the Antenna Installation Guide, which provides detailed instructions.

Installing the DirecPC Adapter Card

As you have no doubt figured out from the preceding sections, the DirecPC adapter card is an ISA card you install into your PC. The card includes a coaxial cable connector for attaching the cable between the satellite dish and the DirecPC 21 elliptical satellite dish. After you install your DirecPC adapter card, you can then install and configure the DirecPC Navigator software. The satellite dish doesn't have to be installed before you install the DirecPC adapter card. The following steps explain how to perform this procedure:

1. Switch off your PC and all peripheral devices and unplug the power cord from the outlet. Touch a metal surface on your computer to ground yourself to discharge any static electricity.

2. Remove the cover from your computer. (Refer to the documentation that came with your computer for the procedure.)

3. Locate a free 16-bit ISA expansion slot inside your computer; remove the screw from the metal plate covering the slot you have chosen, and then remove the cover plate from the slot.

4. Verify that all of the DIP switches on the DirecPC adapter are set to Off (the default settings). The DIP switch is the set of tiny toggle switches mounted on the adapter card. Use the tip of a pen or a small screwdriver to flip a switch to the off position. The Off position allows the DirecPC adapter card's I/O and IRQ settings to be controlled by software.

5. Install the DirecPC adapter into the slot. Be careful not to damage the cable connector. Align your adapter's slot connector with the ISA expansion slot, and firmly press on the adapter until it is fully seated into the slot.

6. Secure the adapter to the expansion slot with the screw you removed from the cover plate. This screw, which secures the DirecPC adapter to the PC chassis, must be completely tightened to provide continuous bonding between the DirecPC adapter and the PC chassis.

7. Install the computer cover, plug the AC power cord into the power outlet, and turn on your PC. You're ready to begin installing the DirecPC Navigator software.

Setting Up the DirecPC Navigator Software

The DirecPC Navigator program is the software manager for operating your DirecPC connections. Installing the DirecPC Navigator software not only sets up the DirecPC adapter card, it also registers your system with the DirecPC registration server via a modem connection.

Note: If you encounter any problems during installation, DirecPC offers technical support 7 days a week, 24 hours a day, at 1-800-347-3272.

Getting Started

Before you can install the DirecPC Navigator software, you must do the following:

- Make sure all network components in your Network Properties dialog box are removed, except for TCP/IP and Dial-Up Adapter. The DirecPC Navigator software will not properly install with any network adapter cards and other protocols installed on your PC. After the Navigator software is installed, the entries in the Network Properties dialog box should read as follows:
  - Dial-Up Adapter
  - HNS DirecPC NDIS Driver
  - TCP/IP ->HNS DirecPC NDIS 3 Driver
- Make sure you have a modem set up in Windows 95. As part of the DirecPC Navigator software setup, the Auto Setup program dials the DirecPC registration server to register your system and establish your satellite service.
- Turn off any virus-detection program you may be using. Some of these programs interfere with the DirecPC software installation.
- Gather the following information about your existing ISP modem account:
  - PPP login name and password
  - Any IP addresses assigned to you for modem connections
  - ISP phone number

DirecPC Turbo Internet is compatible with most dial-up Internet service providers that use the PPP protocol, support either standard PAP or CHAP options for password login protection, and do not require certain types of scripting prior to starting the PPP protocol.

Installing the DirecPC Navigator Software

Installing the DirecPC Navigator configures your PC for the DirecPC adapter card and Windows 95 TCP/IP properties. As part of the installation process, your DirecPC system is registered online automatically, and your Internet access account information for DirecPC is downloaded. This information is in turn used by the DirecPC Setup program to configure your PC for DirecPC communications.

Note: During the installation process, the DirecPC's Auto Setup program downloads your TCP/IP configuration parameters from the registration server and saves them in a file named paramrsp.acm located in the DirecPC bin directory. The file is formatted as a .ini text file. You can use the Notepad to open the file and print it out to check your assigned IP addresses and other connection information.

Here are the steps for installing the DirecPC Navigator software.

1. Start Microsoft Windows 95 and insert the DirecPC Personal Edition CD into the drive.

2. Choose Start|Run, and type **[*drive*]:\SETUP**, where [*drive*] is the name of the drive into which you inserted the CD-ROM (for example, D:\SETUP).

3. Click on the OK button.

The Setup program prompts you to specify the modem and modem settings for making the online registration connection for DirecPC. Next you're prompted to fill out a registration form, which you do once using the Online Registration dialog box. You must fill out this information in order to register your DirecPC system and download the necessary configuration information.

- Your name and billing address.
- Installation information, if different from your billing address. This information is used to provide you with the satellite dish coordinates.
- Credit card information: card number and expiration date.
- The Turbo Internet option you want. Basic Plan, Bulk Plan, Moon Surfer Plan, or Combination 1 Package (Moon Surfer plus Bulk Plan).
- Your e-mail address.

Once you've completed your registration form, make sure your modem is turned on, then click Next. The DirecPC Navigator program connects to the DirecPC Registration server, uploads your information, and downloads your configuration information. Following the online registration, the Internet Service Provider Information dialog box appears, where you enter information about your modem-based ISP. Enter your login name and ISP telephone number, then click Next.

The Auto Setup program installs Microsoft TCP/IP (if it's not already installed) on your system and makes entries in your TCP/IP Properties dialog box using the information it downloaded from the registration server. The Auto Setup program sets your Windows 95 TCP/IP stack as follows:

- Activates the Specify an IP address setting.
- Enters your assigned IP address from DirecPC in the IP Address field; enters a subnet mask IP address.
- Enters an IP address in the Installed gateways field.
- Activates the Enable DNS setting in the DNS Configuration page; enters a host and domain name and a DNS server IP address.

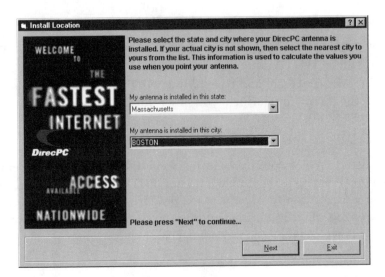

Figure 19.2 *The Install Location dialog box.*

The Auto Setup program prompts you to install Internet Explorer and/or Netscape Navigator from the DirecPC Personal Edition software CD, if you don't have a Web browser already installed. If you do, you will need to configure the DirecPC Navigator to work with the Web browser and any other TCP/IP applications, as explained later in "Before Running an Application."

After the TCP/IP settings are in place on your system, the Install Location dialog box appears (Figure 19.2). This dialog box is for determining the coordinates for setting up your satellite dish. Choose the state and city you're located in and click Next. The Antenna Pointing dialog box appears (shown later in Figure 19.9), which displays the azimuth, elevation, and polarization values for your location. A loud beep sounds to aid in making these alignments, as explained later in this chapter. Write the displayed settings down to use for aligning your satellite dish. These values will be used whether you or an installer sets up your satellite dish.

Note: If you had a professional install your DirecPC antenna, it will already be aligned with these values.

Using the DirecPC Navigator

The DirecPC Navigator is the command center for interacting with your satellite, modem connections, and your TCP/IP applications. The DirecPC folder includes

Figure 19.3 *The DirecPC Navigator window.*

the Antenna Pointing, the Auto Setup, and the DirecPC Help programs, as well as the DirecPC Navigator program. The following sections explain how to use the Navigator to manage your Internet connections and its applications.

Tour of the DirecPC Navigator

Once the DirecPC software is installed on your system, the DirecPC Navigator icon appears on your desktop. Double-click on this icon to launch the DirecPC Navigator window (Figure 19.3). Or you can choose Start|Programs|DirecPC |DirecPC Navigator to open the Navigator window.

The menu bar includes the following menus and menu items:

- The File menu includes the Exit command to end your Navigator session.

- The View menu includes commands to view or hide the Viewer, to review the status of your current DirecPC services, and to return to the content home page.

- The Start menu lists the applications managed by the Navigator. You can start up any of these applications by choosing them from this menu.

- The Options menu grants access to system management options for applications and services, and lets you control the size of the toolbar icons.

- The Help menu points you to help information.

The primary role of the DirecPC Navigator toolbar is to provide quick access to your TCP/IP applications that have been added to the Navigator for satellite connections. Each program you add to the Navigator appears as a button with the program's icon displayed. Other buttons on the toolbar let you hide or display the Viewer, go to the content home page, or access the DirecPC context help system.

The Viewer is the scrolling window that displays DirecPC Web pages that are periodically downloaded automatically via satellite for DirecPC customers. You can hide the Viewer by clicking on the Toggle Toolbar Size button (the first button on the toolbar). Clicking on the button again displays the Viewer.

The Status bar displays the modem status (colored circle), satellite signal status (colored rectangle), and key encryption status (key symbol) icons. Table 19.2 describes what the different colors signify.

Before Running an Application

If you installed Internet Explorer or Netscape Navigator from the DirecPC Personal Edition CD, then you can use these programs immediately from the DirecPC Navigator toolbar by clicking on the appropriate button. If your TCP/IP applications were in place when you installed the DirecPC Navigator, then you must add them to the Navigator to enable the satellite linkup to work with the specific application. (Adding applications into the Navigator is explained later in "Managing Internet Applications.") You also need to add the IP address of the

Table 19.2 The DirecPC Navigator Status Indicators

STATUS INDICATOR	COLOR	SIGNIFIES
Modem	Red	Not connected
	Yellow	Connecting/disconnecting
	Green	Connected
	Blue	Suspended
Satellite Signal	Red	Bad signal
	Yellow	Marginal signal
	Green	Normal signal
Access Keys	Red	Need update of encryption key
	Yellow	Update of encryption key in progress
	Green	Up-to-date encryption key

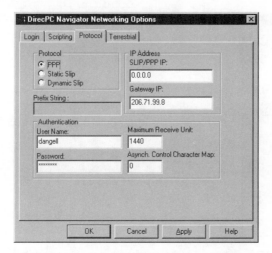

Figure 19.4 *The Navigator Networking Options dialog box.*

DirecPC gateway to the Networking Options dialog box in the DirecPC Navigator. Here's how.

1. Choose Start|Run and enter **winipcfg**; click OK. The IP Configuration window appears. Note the IP address in the Default Gateway field. You'll use this IP address in configuring the PC Direct Navigator for making your connections.

2. In the DirecPC Navigator window, choose Options|Networking. The Navigator Networking Options dialog box appears (Figure 19.4).

3. Click on the Protocol tab.

4. In the Gateway IP field, enter the IP address that you got from the IP Configuration window; click OK.

Managing Internet Applications

Any TCP/IP applications (such as Web browser, FTP, or e-mail) you plan to use with your satellite connection must be added to the DirecPC Navigator before you can use them. To add an installed application to the DirecPC Navigator, do the following:

1. Choose Options|Toolbar Buttons. The Change Applications in Toolbar dialog box appears (Figure 19.5).

2. Click on the Add button. The Add/Edit Application in Toolbar dialog box appears (Figure 19.6).

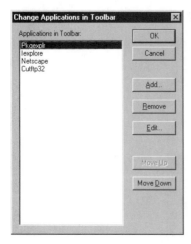

Figure 19.5 *The Change Applications in Toolbar dialog box.*

3. Enter the name for the menu item in the Menu text field.

4. Enter the path and program filename in the Command field; or click on the Browse button and navigate to the program.

5. If you want the program to start up automatically whenever you open the DirecPC Navigator, check the Start automatically when DirecPC Navigator starts box.

6. Click OK. A message box appears asking if you want to save your changes to the toolbar; click Yes.

Each program you add to the DirecPC Navigator appears as a button on the toolbar or in the Start menu. You can remove or edit any entry by choosing Op-

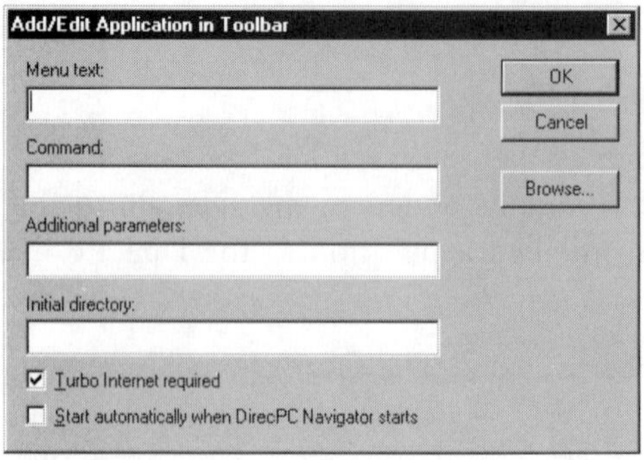

Figure 19.6 *The Add/Edit Application in Toolbar dialog box.*

tions | Toolbar to display the Change Applications in Toolbar dialog box (Figure 19.5). Select the application you want to remove or edit and click on the Remove or Edit button. The Move Up and Move Down buttons let you rearrange the positions of your icons on the toolbar.

Making Connections with DirecPC Navigator

Running applications is easy, once they're set up to work with the DirecPC Navigator. You simply click on the application's button on the toolbar in the DirecPC Navigator window. For example, to open Internet Explorer, you would click on the button displaying the browser's logo. The modem connection is made for an Internet linkup to the Hughes satellite system. When the terrestrial connection is made, the Internet Explorer window appears and the data streams down from the satellite to display the Web page. Figure 19.7 shows the default DirecPC home page as it appears in Netscape Navigator after the connection is made. When you exit Internet Explorer, both the modem and satellite connections are quickly terminated.

You can use the Turbo Internet to access the Internet through your browser, or you can use the Package Delivery service. The Turbo Internet service provides

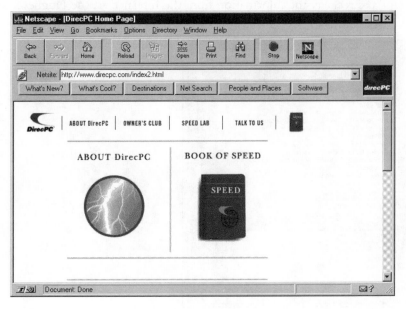

Figure 19.7 *The DirecPC home page in the Netscape Navigator window means your satellite connection is fully operational.*

the high-speed (up to 400-Kbps) connection. Turbo Internet also supports all Internet capabilities that your ISP offers. The Package Delivery service provides high-speed (up to 3-Mbps) access to digital information, such as software applications, computer-based training, multimedia, and electronic documents. You can select software or other digital objects from an online catalog. The selections are then broadcast to your computer via satellite.

Note: You cannot use the Turbo Internet and Package Delivery Services at the same time. If you are using your Internet browser and want to use the Package Delivery service, you must first exit from the browser.

Choosing View|DirecPC Navigator Status in the Navigator window displays the Event Log and Statistics dialog box (Figure 19.8). This dialog box allows you to view system messages about the status of active connections and drivers.

Managing Networking Services

The Turbo Internet service included with the DirecPC Personal Edition sends information from your PC to the Internet via a modem-based Internet access account and receives the information from the Internet via the Hughes satellite. The

Figure 19.8 *The Event Log and Statistics dialog box.*

DirecPC system automatically manages the phone line connection so that it's in use only when needed by DirecPC.

In the event you experience problems either accessing or receiving Internet information, you can use the Navigator Networking Options dialog box (see Figure 19.4) to make changes. To access this dialog box, choose Options|Networking. The following describes the four tabs in this dialog box:

- The Login tab displays the modem settings for your ISP connection, including the ISP phone number and inactivity timer.

- The Scripting tab lets you create scripts for logging into ISP systems that require login scripts to make a connection.

- The Protocol tab displays your assigned IP address, the gateway IP address for your ISP, login user name and password, and protocol options.

- The Terrestrial tab displays options for specifying satellite or terrestrial links for each application. The settings in this tab are useful for controlling which tool uses which connection option. For example, you may want your e-mail, which is text-based, to be both sent and received via your modem connection and not via the satellite.

Antenna Alignment and Signal Strength

The process of accurately pointing the antenna reflector at the satellite is called *alignment*. Accurately aligning the dish to the satellite is critical to the operation of the DirecPC system. When the reflector is pointed directly at the satellite, the adapter receives a strong signal. If the reflector is not positioned properly, the signal may be weak, causing errors during data transfers.

If you hire a professional to install your satellite dish, you won't need to worry about alignment because that is part of any installation service. In most cases, you won't have to make any alignment adjustments later either, although some satellite dishes do fall out of alignment for various reasons; for example, the dish's line of sight to the satellite might become blocked, or the structure to which the dish is attached might shift.

You can check the status of your satellite signal by following these steps in the DirecPC Navigator Antenna Pointing program.

1. Choose Start|Programs|DirecPC|Antenna Pointing. The Install Location dialog box appears (Figure 19.2).

2. Select your state from the My antenna is installed in this state drop-down list.

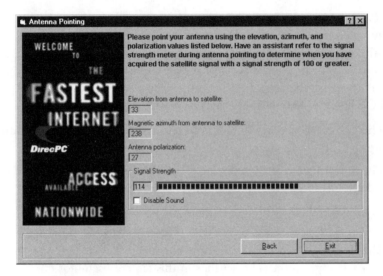

Figure 19.9 *The Antenna Pointing dialog box lets you check out the strength of your satellite signal under various conditions.*

3. Select your community from the My antenna is installed in this city drop-down list.

4. Click Next. The Antenna Pointing dialog box appears (Figure 19.9); you will hear a beep, which is used to help align the satellite dish if it needs to be adjusted. You can turn off the beep by clicking on the Disable Sound check box.

The Signal Strength horizontal indicator displays a number indicating signal strength. The optimal signal rate is between 114 and 120. Signal quality worsens during inclement weather because of atmospheric conditions. When it is cloudy or raining, the rate can dip down to the 90 to 100 range. Signal strengths in the 60 to 80 range can cause transmission problems.

Physically aligning the DirecPC dish involves adjusting the disk mount. To do so, you loosen and tighten the bolts to adjust the polarization, azimuth, and elevation settings you got from DirecPC or from your installer. The azimuth and elevation values are calculated and displayed by the Antenna Pointing software; or you can get them from DirecPC technical support. The azimuth and elevation angles are the trajectory coordinates for setting up your satellite dish so it's pointed directly at the satellite and receiving a strong signal. These values are often accurate enough to enable you to align the satellite. However, a variety of factors, such as power lines or large buildings, may reduce the likelihood that you can align the satellite properly using just the calculated values, which is why you are better off having a professional installer set up and align your satellite dish.

Performing an alignment procedure can be a one- or two-person task depending on how far the PC is from the antenna. If the antenna is close enough for the person aiming the antenna to hear the computer speaker (or if you can connect a remote speaker to the PC and place the speaker next to the antenna), you can use the aforementioned beeps generated by the PC as a reference. Otherwise, it is probably best to have a second person watch the computer monitor as it displays the signal strength meter information. That person can provide feedback to the person aiming the antenna as to how well the signal is being received.

The antenna alignment procedure involves standing behind the dish reflector (the satellite dish) and slowly moving the dish as you hone in on the strongest audio signal emanating from your PC, which measures the signal strength. To obtain maximum signal strength after a strong signal has been detected, rotate the antenna reflector slowly through the strong signal range (left and right as necessary) and position the reflector direction in the center of the strong range. Fine-tune the signal strength by adjusting (raising or lowering) the elevation adjusting screw to point the antenna reflector to the middle of the signal strength range.

What's Next

Now that you have been exposed to extraterrestrial Internet access, it's time to come back down to Earth and check out the high-bandwidth Internet access service being delivered by the cable TV companies. Cable modem service offers an impressive bandwidth value—if you can get it. It's time to see what's on cable.

20 *What's on Cable*

Cable modem service is a bandwidth bargain. Internet access via your cable company can deliver T1 line speeds downstream for around $39.95 a month! The speed is exhilarating, when you consider that a 10-Mbps file can be downloaded in 54 seconds. Unfortunately, cable modem service still is not widely available; you're more likely to live in a community that doesn't have cable modem service than one that does. However, if the cable companies get their act together, cable-based Internet access promises to be the bandwidth of choice for the SOHO market. This chapter looks at what's on cable for remote access.

Is Cable Modem Service in Your Future?

As I pointed out in the beginning of the book the second largest high-speed public network in the United States is the cable television system. The cable industry has been wiring America for the last 25 years, and its coaxial cable now reaches 90 percent of American homes. Cable companies have a huge source of untapped bandwidth; and exploiting this bandwidth for the Internet is touted as the single greatest opportunity for universal, high-speed digital communications. The combined pool of millions of high-bandwidth cable lines exceeds any capacity the telephone companies have to offer.

But in addition to an availability problem, the cable industry has financial, technical, customer service, and self-perception problems. Many cable operators they see themselves as one-way entertainment companies, not common carriers of data communications. On the technical front, only about 15 percent to 25 percent of cable systems can handle the two-way communications required for the higher-bandwidth connections. Upgrading these systems is expensive for an industry that carries a large debt already.

On the service front, the cable industry suffers from a history of poor and unreliable customer service, worse even than the telephone companies. Programming outages are still common experiences for cable TV customers. In addition, huge capital demands are being made on cable companies to build a new Internet access infrastructure, at the same time it is facing competition from deregulation and satellite television services.

Adding to the cable industry's woes is its fragmented structure and the growing competition from satellite-based TV. The cable industry is a mixture of a large number of small cable operators and several large cable companies. And unlike telephone company prices and service, which are regulated on a state-by-state basis, cable service is regulated on a community-by-community basis. This means each town and city determines cable service options and pricing through negotiations between local governments and the cable companies. The result is a protracted approval process for new cable-based services.

In spite of the current state of the cable industry, the cable companies have a window of opportunity through which to deploy their cable modem service before the telephone companies begin deploying xDSL technology, which begins in 1998. The cable option is an exciting prospect for the SOHO market because it delivers high bandwidth at consumer prices, which may help keep the telephone companies in check in terms of their pricing of xDSL service.

Furthermore, regardless of all the uncertainty, cable modem service is a bandwidth bargain. Cable modem service for Internet access typically costs in the range of $30 to $60 a month. Included in that cost is the use of the cable modem (property of the cable operator), and a standard PPP Internet access account. Installation costs between $99 to $150. The cable industry delivers its bandwidth using the Internet-friendly, flat-rate pricing that includes unlimited Internet access.

Comparing the cost of cable service to POTS for Internet access highlights the value of cable modem service. In the Boston area, a basic POTS line from NYNEX costs around $25 a month with a set-up charge of $37.50 (for home service), whereas dial-up Internet access accounts cost around $12.95 to $19.95 a month. And don't forget the cost of the modem. So already a basic POTS account costs around $40 a month compared to $49.95. For an extra $9.95 a month, you get the bandwidth power of a T1 line.

What you get in terms of data communications speed depends on your local cable system. The newer cable systems are using a technology called *hybrid fiber coaxial* that enables two-way data communications over cable lines. Cable modem service over these systems can deliver data upstream at rates between 512 Kbps to 10 Mbps, and downstream between 2 Mbps and 30 Mbps. The typical configuration for two-way cable modem service is 1.54 Mbps downstream and 300 Kbps upstream. Of course, there are throughput issues that affect the actual data transmission speed at any given time.

Although only 15 percent to 25 percent of cable systems have been upgraded with the new two-way cable infrastructure, the cable industry is planning to spend $14 billion to upgrade their one-way networks over the next few years. Converting to digital fiber service, required for Internet access, will cost around $250 per home.

A real-world example of a two-way cable modem service is MediaOne (formerly Continental Cablevision), which offers an Internet service called MediaOne Express. The service costs $39.95 a month for a single PC, which includes the cable modem and an unlimited-use Internet access account. If you have a network adapter card for connecting to the cable modem, the installation costs $99; otherwise, the installation cost is $149. MediaOne runs periodic promotions to waive the installation fee. The MediaOne Express service delivers up to 1.5 Mbps downstream and 300 Kbps upstream. By the end of 1997, MediaOne plans to deliver MediaOne Express service to nearly 60 communities in Massachusetts and New Hampshire. Its system will pass by 500,000 homes.

Getting higher bandwidth out of a cable system doesn't require two-way technology, however. Cable modem technology is also available for using one-way systems in combination with a POTS line to deliver downstream data speeds of between 500 Kbps to over 1 Mbps.

Cable modems, usually external boxes (although there are some internal adapter cards), are used as the interface between your PC and the cable service for Internet access. External cable modems connect to your PC via a standard network adapter card. True to the way the cable television business works, cable modems are owned by the cable company and leased to the customer for a monthly fee, much the same way you're charged for the cable TV box.

Cable modem service, too, has its share of problems. A cable modem is a shared connectivity medium, which means you share the trunk line capacity with several hundred to a few thousand homes in a network neighborhood. Right now, with only a few users taking advantage of this service, connections are always speedy, but in the future when every house in your neighborhood is using cable modems, the network has the potential to become seriously bottlenecked. The use of neighborhood networks based on Ethernet provides quick access, but also creates security risks for any PC connected to the cable system networks; each PC on the neighborhood network is open to other users on the network. Finally, because cable companies are new to the Internet access business, they lack some services considered essential by many businesses, including domain names and LAN connections.

Meet the Cable Companies

As noted, the structure of the cable industry is on a community-by-community basis. Each cable system serving a specific town or city is a franchised service; small and large cable operators own these cable franchises. Within the cable industry there are several large cable companies that dominate the cable service market. The companies include:

- *TCI (Tele-Communications Inc.) with 14 million subscribers.* TCI has 12.5 percent of its infrastructure upgraded for Internet access. The company offers a cable modem service called @Home.

- *Time Warner with 11.5 million subscribers.* Time Warner has 40 percent of its infrastructure upgraded for Internet access, and offers an Internet service called Road Runner.

- *MediaOne (formerly Continental Cablevision) with 4.2 million subscribers.* MediaOne has 10 percent to 15 percent of its infrastructure upgraded for Internet access. The MediaOne cable modem service is called MediaOne Express. US West, the regional telephone company serving 13 western states, owns MediaOne.

- *Cox Cable with 3.3 million subscribers.* Cox has 20 percent of its infrastructure upgraded for Internet access. The company offers a cable modem service also called @Home.

- *Comcast Cable with 4.3 million customers.* Comcast is offering Comcast@Home Internet service.

@Home is a partnership among TCI, Comcast, and Cox Communications. @Home deployment by Comcast includes communities in Florida, Maryland, Michigan, and New Jersey. Cox Communications has deployed @Home service in Arizona, California, and Nebraska. TCI has deployed @Home service in California, Connecticut, Illinois, and Washington.

How Cable Modem Service Works

The cable system has its own architecture and lingo. Understanding the fundamentals of how the cable system operates is helpful for determining what you can and can't do with cable service.

Cable System Architecture

The basic cable TV system uses coaxial cable to deliver its video signal. Cable *drops*, which are the segments of cable that run from the street or the telephone

---

Note: The cable network system doesn't reach anywhere near the number of business locations as it does residential areas. Because of this discrepancy, cable modem service better serves the home-office segment of the SOHO market. Cable commuters and Internet-dependent home-office workers will benefit the most from cable service.

---

pole to your home connect the main cable line at places called *taps*. These taps send the video signal to the cable headend, which connects the cable television network with dishes that receive both satellite and traditional broadcast TV signals.

This traditional architecture for cable TV service is primarily a one-way broadcast model. The television signals are sent from the cable operator's headend to cable TV users via the coaxial cable that goes into a cable box and then to the TV set. This is a one-way system because cable TV users aren't sending back anything. Figure 20.1 shows the topology of a one-way cable modem system. These systems are inherently asymmetric, which means they offer more bandwidth for downstream traffic and less bandwidth for upstream traffic. The upstream channel is located in the middle of the amateur radio and short-wave broadcast range, which is extremely sensitive to RF interference.

For cable operators to offer two-way Internet access via cable would require the rebuilding of their networks and cable infrastructures. This new infrastructure would include a hybrid fiber/coaxial (HFC) distribution network, dedicated network servers, strategically placed routers, and high-speed backbones. Recent advances in technology have permitted cable operators to cost-effectively push fiber optics deeper and deeper into the cable system, upgrading the wiring out on the street in such a way as to vastly improve signal quality and reliability. This process also allows for reliable two-way data transmission.

The HFC system subdivides a cable system into neighborhood networks. Cable drops connect to the main fiber optic line at places called *nodes*. The typical cable systems node serves between 500 to 2,500 homes. This creates several independent cable subsystems within a cable system for a given community. HFC results in less noise and cleaner signals, and breaks up the system into several smaller systems, which eliminates a single point of failure. In the case of MediaOne service in Massachusetts, each node can support up to 600 users. When capacity exceeds that number, a new node is added.

Your computer is connected to the Internet over the same cable system that delivers your CATV service. Although your cable video service (to your TV) and your Internet access enter and leave your home over a shared wire, the two services are completely independent of each other, and use of one has no effect on the other. Computers are connected to the cable system using the same coaxial cable that car-

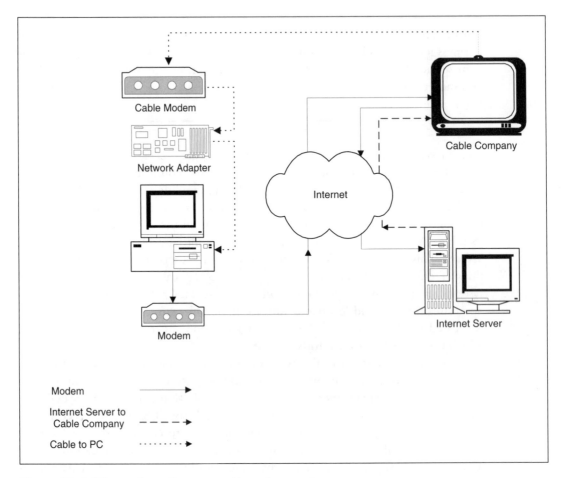

Figure 20.1 *The topology of one-way cable modem service.*

ries more traditional video signals, and data bits are modulated onto a single channel, directly alongside video services. Using one channel in either direction, data runs between your home and the cable headend. Servers for e-mail, newsgroups and Web-site caching are located within the cable system's fiber network, offering speed and reliability that far exceeds the Internet at large. Figure 20.2 shows the topology of a two-way cable modem system used for Internet access.

Making the cable-to-PC connection requires a cable modem to modulate and demodulate the cable signal into a data stream. Cable modems also include features such as tuners to separate the data signal from the rest of the broadcast, networking management capabilities, and encryption features. Each cable modem has an Eth-

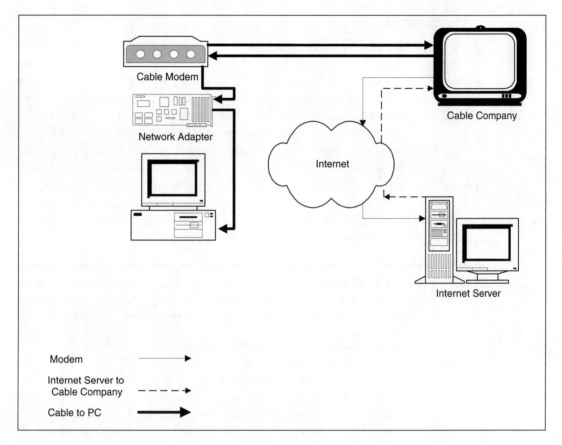

Figure 20.2 *The topology for two-way cable modem service.*

ernet port that connects to the computer (or network) on one side and to the cable connection on the other side. You install an Ethernet adapter in the PC, connect it to the cable modem's Ethernet port via a standard RJ-45 connector (10BaseT cabling), and then you configure your Windows 95 PC with the Microsoft TCP/IP stack in the Network control panel. As far as your PC is concerned, it's hooked directly to the Internet via an Ethernet cable.

As mentioned, cable modem service is also available for one-way cable systems. These systems use a POTS modem to send commands upstream to the headend. The downstream data from the Internet is sent via the cable system at cable modem speeds of 500 Kbps to 1.2 Kbps. These systems aren't as elegant and don't support the higher speeds of two-way systems, but they deliver Internet access at speeds that are more than four times that of ISDN.

Cable Modems

Using the word modem to describe a cable device may be a little misleading in that it conjures up an image of a typical telephone dial-up modem. A cable modem does modulate and demodulate signals, but the similarity ends there because cable modems are an order of magnitude more complicated than their telephone counterparts. Cable modems are part modem, part tuner, part encryption/decryption device, part bridge/router, part network interface adapter, and part Ethernet hub.

Cable modems are currently selling in the $500 range but prices are expected to drop quickly to around $200 as manufacturing volumes pick up, standards emerge, and chip set designs are locked in. During the next one to two years, the consumer will not be able to buy cable modems in the retail computer distribution channel. Instead, they will lease the modems from the cable companies as they do the cable converter boxes today.

Note: According to Dataquest, cable modem shipments are expected to increase from 43,000 units in 1996 to over 500,000 units in 1999.

Cable modems come in two flavors, depending on whether the cable operator is using a one-way system or has upgraded to a two-way system. For one-way systems, the cable modem sends the upstream data via a 28.8-Kbps modem. The downstream data from the Internet comes in at cable modem speeds of between 500 Kbps to 1 Mbps. This asymmetric rate imbalance can work for Internet access only where text commands are sent via the modem and all the bandwidth-demanding multimedia megabytes are coming down to your PC via the cable connection.

The Hayes ULTRA Cable System is a PC adapter card that works in one-way systems. It has a built-in 28.8-Kbps modem for the upstream and 4 to 5 Mbps downstream. Hayes is selling this as a complete system for cable operators with end-user adapter cards and headend equipment. The cards sell for $179 for cable operators.

In two-way cable systems, the cable modem sends and receives data over the cable system to enable greater bandwidth capabilities. These cable modems can deliver data upstream at rates between 512 Kbps to 10 Mbps and downstream at 2 Mbps to 30 Mbps. Few PCs will be capable of connecting at such high speeds, so the more realistic number is 3 to 10 Mbps. In the upstream direction, speeds can be up to 10 Mbps. However, most modems will probably be in the range of 200 Kbps and 2 Mbps.

Bay Networks (LANCity) and Motorola (CyberSURFR) are currently the dominant cable modem manufacturers, although there are a number of other cable

Table 20.1 Sampler of Cable Modems and Speeds

Cable Modem/Company	Downstream Capacity	Upstream Capacity
CyberSURFR (Motorola)	10 Mbps	768 Kbps
LCP LANCity (Bay Networks)	10 Mbps	10 Mbps
Remote Link Adapter (Hybrid Networks)	30 Mbps	512 Kbps
P545 (Phasecom)	2.048 Mbps	2.048 Mbps
HomeWorks Universal (Zenith Network Systems)	4 Mbps or 500 Kbps	4 Mbps or 500 Kbps
DataXcellerator (Scientific Atlanta)	1.2 Mbps	28.8 Kbps
ULTRA (Hayes Microcomputer)	5 Mbps	28.8 Kbps

modem vendors. However, a shake-out of cable modem vendors has already reduced the field somewhat. Hewlett-Packard, IBM, and Intel have cut their losses and exited the cable modem business. Table 20.1 provides a sampling of currently available cable modem products and their speed capacities.

Cable Service Throughput

Cable modem speeds vary widely and don't reflect actual throughput. A number of factors determine the speed of the data as it goes from the cable company's servers to your PC. A cable modem may be able to deliver up to 30 Mbps over the network, but the device with the slowest throughput along the way determines the effective speed. The PC bus or the video display for a Pentium will receive data in excess of 4 Mbps. A cable system can deliver up 10 Mbps to a computer through the 10BaseT Ethernet interface, depending on the cable modem used. The upstream bandwidth from the PC to the cable system ranges from 1 to 3 Mbps.

The biggest threat to cable modem data throughput comes from the cable network architecture itself. Cable modem services use a shared Ethernet-based networking medium. Clusters of 500 to 2,500 homes share a node connected by fiber optics. As these neighborhood networks support larger numbers of active users, the volume of traffic may overwhelm the system, which means everyone's data transmission rates will drop. Cable modem service is not a guaranteed bandwidth, so it will fluctuate. However, the architecture of the hybrid fiber coaxial (HFC) system allows for more capacity to be added.

If ISDN is any indicator, it won't be the cable modems causing problems in the future for cable service. It will be how fast the cable companies can convert their one-way systems to full-blown two-way systems. In the case of ISDN, the computer industry delivered some very cool hardware only to see the telephone companies not deploy it or charge too much for ISDN service.

The Persistent Connection

Cable service provides a persistent connection, which means there is no dial-up process; your cable connection always ready and waiting. The untapped potential of the persistent connection goes well beyond convenience. Office 97 and Windows 97 or 98, depending on when it's released, are built around the persistent connection. Both of these Microsoft products integrate the Web into the mechanics of working in Windows and Office programs.

Note: Chapter 9 explains the new features of Windows 95 and the Internet Explorer 4.0 suite of Internet tools designed for persistent connections.

The downside of the persistent connection is security. As noted, the cable network is a public network that uses Ethernet as the basis for creating neighborhood networks. This shared bus architecture makes every Windows PC connected to it open to others, unless all the sharing features of Windows 95 are shut off. In time, however, cable modem service providers will be adding fixes to eliminate this problem. Already, MediaOne introduced a data packet filtering system that eliminates this security flaw.

Standards and Cable Labs

Cable Television Laboratories (Cable Labs), the research and development arm of the cable industry, has been actively pursuing standards for cable modems to enable interoperable, high-speed cable modems. Cable Labs is behind the Data Over Cable System Interface Specification (DOCSIS), a set of standards for interoperable cable modems. Implementation of this standard will drive the price of cable modems from around $400 to $200 or less.

Beyond modem standards, Cable Labs is also working on standards covering several areas: the connection to the subscriber's PC, the consumer radio-frequency interface, the cable network connection to the home, the interface between the router and the cable headend, and the interface from the headend to the Internet. Cable Labs is also is researching digital compression technology.

The Cable Modem-to-PC Connection

Again, the method used for connecting a cable modem to the PC is via Ethernet, to handle the capacity of cable data communications. The typical external cable modem connects to your PC via a network adapter card and 10BaseT cabling. An internal cable modem adapter card appears as a network adapter to your PC.

The current crop of cable modems support only one PC. They do this by recognizing TCP/IP traffic from the PC with the network adapter card, which has the unique MAC (media access control) layer address that the cable modem knows about. As you'll learn later in this chapter, the short-circuit system is a hassle if you're running a Windows 95 LAN.

To use cable modem service, you must be using a PC running Windows 95, and have at least a 486 DX/50 processor. Ideally, you should have a fast Pentium with lots of memory, a big and fast hard disk, and a fast video card so your screen redraws at a rate that keeps up with the download.

MediaOne Express Cable Service

MediaOne (formerly Continental Cablevision), already introduced as one of the big four cable companies, offers cable modem service in the Boston area. By the end of 1997, MediaOne plans to deliver MediaOne Express service to nearly 60 communities in Massachusetts and New Hampshire, to pass by 500,000 homes. It also promises to provide one free Internet access connection to every school in every community it serves.

The MediaOne Express service delivers up to 1.5 Mbps downstream and 300 Kbps upstream using the Bay Networks LANCity cable modem over a two-way system. The MediaOne Express package includes the cable modem, an Internet access account, and free technical support. The basic installation for a customer without a network adapter card is $149. If the customer has a network adapter card, the installation is $99. The network adapter card supplied by MediaOne costs an additional $49 for a 3Com EtherLink III ISA card or a 3Com PCMCIA card for a laptop. The monthly charge for a current MediaOne cable TV customer is $49.95 a month; for people without cable TV service, the cost is $59.95 a month. This monthly charge is added to the cable TV bill.

Note: MediaOne Express is moving to correct and enhance its package by including new features such as multiple e-mail accounts, remote hosting, non-Internet remote access, custom domain names, and a LAN version.

Cable Modem Service Installation

When you order cable modem service, probably two installers will come, one to work on the computer side of the system, the other to handle the cabling requirements. The cable installer will run the cable to where your computer is located, regardless of where your television is located, neatly tacking it down along its path.

The installer setting up your PC will ask you some basic questions about your computer system from a checklist, and then install an Ethernet card if you need one and set up a customized version of Netscape Navigator—although you can use any Web browser or TCP/IP client application you want. The installer will connect the Ethernet 10BaseT cable from the PC to the back of the modem. The coaxial cable from the cable system also connects to the back of the modem.

When the installation is complete, the installer will walk you through the setup. You'll sign the service agreement, a work order, and a form that says the installer didn't mess up your computer system.

A Tale of Two Installations

When I ordered cable modem service (MediaOne), I already had ISDN service, which had been installed by my local telephone company, NYNEX. The installation of the ISDN line compared to the installation of cable modem service, which went as described in the preceding section, was as different as night and day. For starters, it took me approximately three weeks to figure out the provisioning of my ISDN line and to get NYNEX out to my premises to install the line. NYNEX charged me $190 to install the line, which they brought only to the network box; there was an additional charge of $65 to bring the ISDN line to my office. To get Internet access, I had to pay an another monthly fee for an ISDN account of around $20, plus the usage charges of the ISDN line, which run anywhere from $40 to $90 a month. Certainly, cable modem service was a bargain compared to ISDN from NYNEX; but what really struck me was the difference in the customer service.

Diary of a New Cable Modem User

My first cable modem connection experience was exhilarating: screens flashed and files downloaded at lightening speeds. I downloaded a 15 MB file in 94 seconds flat. I listened to sound clips and viewed video clips with wild abandon. But I also quickly discovered who was running slow servers or not keeping up with the demand at the server end.

On day 2 of my cable adventures, I had a problem connecting to the Internet. I called the 800-number for customer service. Within a few minutes, a tech support person walked me through procedures to isolate the problem. It turned out that the cable modem had to be rebooted, which required unplugging the modem's power and then plugging it in again—there was no switch on the modem. I ran into a few more glitches, including an Internet service disruption and a cable system failure.

The Bay Network's LANCity modems (the brand I use) include two green LEDs located on the front panel that let you know the status of your cable service connection. One LED indicates the power is on and the other indicates the cable connection is alive and well. Both need to be shining a steady green to stay linked. Another set of two LEDs flicker when data is being transferred.

Cable Modem Service Restrictions

The MediaOne subscriber agreement forbids the use of your cable modem connection for handling a busy Web site or other server that creates a lot of data traffic between your site and the Internet. MediaOne reserves the right to disconnect or reclassify the service to an unspecified commercial grade for failure to comply with any portion of its contract. To quote the MediaOne service agreement:

> Excessive data transfer may interfere with the experience of other users. You agree not to interfere with the use of the equipment or services by other Customers or disrupt the Continental backbone network nodes or network services. Violation of any part of this section is grounds for immediate termination of this Agreement and your continued purchase of the Service, or reclassification to a commercial grade of service, at Continental's discretion.

Another MediaOne Express service restriction is that only one PC can have access to the cable modem. This is done by configuring the cable modem to accept TCP/IP packets from a specified network adapter card, the one in the PC used for remote access via the cable modem. The cable modem looks for the unique MAC layer address of the Ethernet card; for example, a MAC address might be 00-80-AE-00-00-01.

If you modify the software or hardware supplied by MediaOne Express and that disrupts your service, thus requiring a visit to your home for repair or correction, MediaOne will charge you for the visit at some unspecified rate. If upon termination of the agreement, your modem is not returned to MediaOne in good condition, you can be charged $650 for its replacement.

Making Connections

MediaOne Express installs a modified version of the Netscape Navigator; the default page is the MediaOne Express home page. You can change this and any other settings in Netscape Navigator. MediaOne also sets up the Netscape Navigator e-

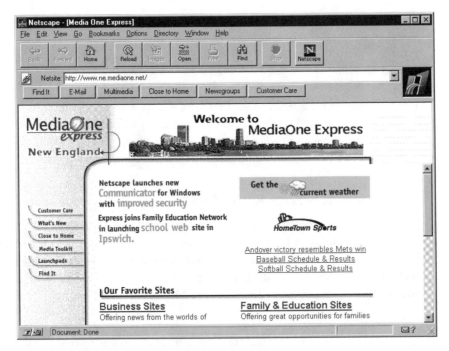

Figure 20.3 *The MediaOne Express home page as viewed from the customized Netscape Navigator.*

mail to work with your assigned e-mail account. You can only use this e-mail address, not one with your own domain name. However, if you have an e-mail account at another site on the Internet you can access it and use it via your MediaOne Express service.

Because the cable modem works at the Ethernet level, your Internet connections are seamless and fast. You can use any TCP/IP application, and it works without any configuration beyond the initial TCP/IP properties setup done by the installer. Double-clicking on any application instantly connects you to the Internet. Figure 20.3 shows the Netscape Navigator with the MediaOne home page.

Windows 95 and Cable Modems

The Bay Networks LANCity modem acts as a DHCP server for the PC you have connected. The MediaOne Express cable modem service assigns a specific IP address for the LANCity modem as well as other settings, such as gateway and DNS server IP addresses.

You can always check out the assigned IP address for your current session by using the winipcfg program. To open the winipcfg program to display the IP Configuration window, choose Start|Run, enter **winipcfg**, and click OK. The IP field displays your IP address for the current session.

Because the LANCity modem acts as a single-user DHCP server, the Microsoft TCP/IP stack in Windows 95 retains the default settings that enable your PC to act as a DHCP server. The cable modem connects to your PC using an Ethernet card and the Microsoft TCP/IP stack bound to the card. Selecting the *TCP/IP->Network Adapter Card* in the Network Components list and clicking on the Properties button displays these DHCP enable settings.

- In the IP Address tab, the Obtain an IP Address automatically is selected.

- In the DNS Configuration tab, the Disable DNS setting is selected. This means that your computer in not identified using the Domain Name System (DNS).

- In the Gateway tab, no gateway IP address is used in the New gateway setting.

- In the WINS Configuration tab, the Disable WINS Resolution setting is selected. The Windows Internet Naming Service (WINS) enables you to use programs that require the NetBIOS protocol.

Watch Out for the Big Security Hole

Because cable modem service is based on Ethernet, every PC connected to a cable modem is a workstation on the neighborhood network that supports hundreds of homes in your area. This is why only the TCP/IP protocol can be bound to your Ethernet card attached to your cable modem and the Windows 95 File and Print Sharing functions must be turned off. If they are not, your shared resources appear as a shared resource on all the other users' Windows 95 PCs on your neighborhood node. If you have a shared hard drive without a password, any of the several hundred users on your network will have complete access to all the programs and files on your hard drive. Your shared drives will appear as icons in the Network Neighborhood windows of any other cable modem users connected to your node.

Not all cable modem services have this security problem. MediaOne Express service recently added new features to its cable modem system to prevent other users from having access to your PC if you leave Windows 95 File and Print Sharing features turned on.

Note: Microsoft has compiled a document of security tips for users connected to the Internet via cable modems, available at the Microsoft Web site (www.microsoft.com). Also, make sure you have the Windows 95 Service Pack 1 installed on your system for added Internet security.

Again, make sure your Windows 95 File and Print Sharing features are turned off whenever the cable modem is attached to your system. You can check your File and Print Sharing status by clicking on the File and Print Sharing button in the Network Properties dialog box (the Network applet in the Control Panel). In the File and Print Sharing dialog box, uncheck the settings I want to be able to give others access to my files and I want to be able to allow others to print to my printer(s).

Note: You can use passwords for restricting access to shared resources in Windows 95, but it increases your odds of a security breech.

The One-PC-One-Cable-Modem Limitation

Cable modem service is currently sold as a single PC connection option, not as a shared LAN-to-Internet connection. The cable modems are configured to recognize TCP/IP traffic coming only from a specified Ethernet card using its unique MAC address. Moreover, because you can't bind any Windows 95 file- or print-sharing features to the Ethernet card used by the cable modem, you can't have the PC connected to a Windows 95 LAN.

Note: MediaOne Express has received a number of complaints about this lack of LAN support and has responded by starting trials for a LAN-based cable modem service that will be priced higher than the single PC cable modem service.

There are a couple of workarounds to this limitation that allow your PC to participate in your local area network, although none of them is perfect. Furthermore, these solutions won't allow you to share your cable modem service.

The first method is a temporary reboot of your network adapter card bindings and the connection of the Ethernet 10BaseT cable from your PC to your LAN hub. You'll need to activate the File and Print Sharing feature and reboot your system. When you want to return to your cable modem service, you must remove File and Print Sharing from the Network Properties, reconnect the cable modem to your PC via the 10BaseT cable, and then reboot your system.

The other method involves adding a second network adapter card to your PC and configuring it with only File and Print Sharing. Here's how.

1. Make sure your PC is shut down and the power is turned off before you install your NIC.

2. Remove the case to your PC. Each computer manufacturer has a different case design, but in general, you will remove four to eight screws from the back side of the computer case, then slide the case away from the chassis.

3. Remove the back panel cover to reveal the free slot you want to use for the NIC.

4. Insert the NIC into the empty card slot (ISA, VESA, or PCI bus slot). Make sure you have the card aligned properly and insert it firmly but carefully.

5. Insert the retaining screw into the mounting flange on top of the card to secure the card to the computer case.

6. Restart your PC and Windows.

If it's a Plug-and-Play network adapter card, Windows 95 will automatically detect the card and display a dialog box prompting you for the network driver. Once the card is installed, open the Network Properties dialog box to add the File and Print sharing binding to your new network card. Make sure that Windows did not bind the TCP/IP protocol to the second Ethernet card you plan to use. Verify that only the NetBEUI protocol component is available for your second network adapter card.

To change any binding for a network adapter, select the network adapter driver from the Network Components list in the Network window, then click on Properties. Click on the Binding tab, which displays all the network protocols available on your system and bound to the network adapter. If the protocol has a check mark in the check box alongside the protocol name, it's bound to the network card. Make sure only the NetBEUI protocol has a check mark next to it. Click OK twice, and restart your system.

What's Next

There's one more significant high-bandwidth technology that may be able to deliver cable-modemlike speeds; it's called Digital Subscriber Line (DSL). These services, intended to be rolled out by the telephone companies between 1998 and 1999, could be another high-bandwidth option for the SOHO market. The next chapter introduces you to this telephone company service.

21   *High-Speed Connections via DSL*

Digital Subscriber Line (DSL) is a family of high-bandwidth technologies emanating from the telephone companies. The telecommunications industry is positioning DSL as high-speed Internet access technology to rival cable modem service. But don't run out to buy DSL, because it's not available. DSL service will most likely be deployed in meaningful numbers between 1998 to 1999. Still, DSL is an important remote access technology that bears watching. This chapter introduces you to this promising high-bandwidth option.

The DSL Option

As cable operators begin deploying cable modem service to compete in the Internet access game, local telephone companies are scrambling to find their own high-speed remote access game plan. Spearheading this effort by the Regional Bell Operating Companies (RBOCs) is Digital Subscriber Line technology. DSL technologies targeted at the SOHO market can deliver downstream data communications at speeds ranging from 128 Kbps to 6 Mbps and upstream at 16 Kbps to 640 Kbps.

What's different about DSL service compared to other telephone company offerings for the SOHO market—most notably ISDN—is that it's a dedicated connection, not a dial-up service. Consequently, DSL service probably will be sold as a flat-rate service instead of a usage-based service.

DSL started out as a technology that would give telephone companies a way to compete with cable TV by delivering both television and phone service via standard twisted-pair telephone lines. Originally, DSL was intended to allow the telephone companies to deliver interactive TV, called video-on-demand (VOD), to the mass market. But the telephone companies backed away from this plan because demand for VOD never materialized. However, another demand did, which was, surprise, Internet access. The telephone companies dusted off their DSL technology and repackaged it for Internet access.

DSL emerged from efforts by Bellcore in the late 1980s, the former research arm of the RBOCs. It was developed as a technique using DSL modems at either end of a phone line to filter out the incessant background noise or interference on copper wires to allow clearer connections. The term DSL doesn't refer to the telephone line, but to the modems that convert a regular POTS line into a high-speed digital pipe.

DSL offers the RBOCs the ability to tap the potential of hundreds of millions of installed copper loops. Telephone companies recognize that DSL technology is a vehicle by which they can generate new revenues from their huge extant copper wiring infrastructure, which connects all the telephone company subscribers to the central office. Because DSL can leverage these POTS lines for high-speed data communications with minimal changes to the telephone switching system, it means DSL service can be deployed faster with fewer financial risks for the RBOCs. DSL will play a crucial role over the next 10 years, as telephone companies try to extend the life of their huge infrastructure of twisted-pair copper wiring used for connecting telephone subscribers to central offices. By doing so, the telephone companies buy the time they need to build their next generation of broadband services centered on fiber optics.

The DSL system is an end-to-end connectivity solution that bypasses the existing switching infrastructure. Consequently, DSL technology doesn't require upgrades to the central office switching facilities, an expensive and time-consuming process that was one of the main reasons for ISDN's slow deployment. DSL service uses modems at the customer's premises and DSL access multiplexors (DSLAMS) at the central offices. DSLAMS are hubs that split DSL's digital signal away from the analog voice circuit, and thus the telephone company's switching equipment. Telephone companies can add DSL capabilities as demand warrants. In contrast, to make a central office ISDN-ready, telephone companies had to add software upgrades to their digital switches, which cost anywhere from $200,000 to $500,000.

While DSL technology holds great promise, it also has a number of problems and presents some unanswered questions. By most estimates, 60 percent to 70 percent of the U.S. population live close enough to a telephone company central office to take advantage of the more popular DSL technologies, which have a distance limitation of 12,000 to 18,000 feet; 20 percent of public-switched networks can't handle DSL because they've been conditioned with repeaters, which must be removed to enable DSL. Another big issue for DSL deployment is price. In the long run, the expected price points for DSL service targeted at the mass market range from \$50 to \$200. However, early deployments of DSL technologies are being priced at hundreds of dollars per month.

Another concern about DSL is that it may be long on hardware alternatives but short on service options. While most RBOCs have publicly announced big rollouts of DSL service, whether they will deliver a service that is affordable and targeted to the needs of the SOHO market is unknown. If ISDN is any indicator of the telephone companies' past performance in delivering higher-bandwidth solutions, the doubts are well founded. However, because of the differences in how xDSL technology is being delivered, compared to ISDN, the telephone companies may be able to deliver xDSL in a reasonable time frame. Other concerns center on the fact that the RBOCs may not deploy DSL technologies quickly for fear of cannibalizing their profitable T1 and second analog line services.

Note: Because DSL is made up a several different technologies, you often see the term xDSL. The x is a placeholder for the full collection of Digital Subscriber Line services.

DSL Flavors

Almost an entire page of new acronyms have been coined based on DSL technology. DSL includes several bandwidth configuration options defined by the following acronyms:

- ADSL (Asymmetric Digital Subscriber Line)
- RADSL (Rate-Adaptive Digital Subscriber Line)
- IDSL (ISDN Digital Subscriber Line)
- SDSL (Symmetrical Digital Subscriber Line)
- HDSL (high-data-rate Digital Subscriber Line)
- VDSL (very-high-data-rate Digital Subscriber Line)

Each of these technologies has different capabilities and configurations. The most likely DSL candidates being touted for SOHO connectivity are ADSL, RADSL, IDSL, and SDSL.

ADSL

Asymmetric Digital Subscriber Line (can deliver more than 6 Mbps downstream and up to 640 Kbps upstream, and new ADSL modem technology can achieve downstream rates of up to 9 Mbps. ADSL does this on any existing telephone lines without loop conditioning to distances up to 12,000 feet from the central office to the subscriber. It's estimated that approximately 80 percent of telephone lines are ADSL-compatible.

An ADSL circuit connects an ADSL modem on each end of a twisted-pair telephone line, creating three information channels—a high-speed downstream channel, a medium-speed duplex channel that can support 640 Kbps both ways, and a POTS channel. The POTS channel is split off from the digital modem by filters, thus guaranteeing uninterrupted POTS, even if ADSL fails. Analog devices such as fax machines and telephones can coexist with ADSL lines because a portion of the wire frequency has been reserved for an analog line. ADSL users will have both a standard analog phone jack and a digital line for hybrid devices.

To create multiple channels, ADSL modems divide the available bandwidth of a telephone line in one of two ways—*frequency division multiplexing* (FDM) or *echo cancellation*. FDM assigns one band for upstream data and another band for downstream data. The downstream path is then divided by *time division multiplexing* (TDM) into one or more high-speed channels and one or more low-speed channels.

Because ADSL includes support for POTS, as well as a number of other features that make it a good candidate for the SOHO market, it's the DSL technology that is getting the most attention. Dataquest predicts the base of Asynchronous Digital Subscriber Lines to growth from 18,000 in 1996 to more than 3.1 million by the year 2000. Dataquest sees ADSL-related equipment sales rising from $36 million in 1996 to $1.4 billion by the year 2000. Semiconductor companies have introduced ADSL transceiver chip sets that are already being widely used in market trials. As these chip sets improve in performance and fall in price, ADSL modems will become affordable.

RADSL

Rate-adaptive Asymmetric Digital Subscriber Line is the rate-adaptive variation of ADSL. The greatest benefit of this technology is its flexibility; RADSL allows the service provider to adjust the bandwidth of the DSL link to fit the need of the application and to account for the line length and quality. Through network management, the service provider can predefine the bandwidth or enable it to be self-adjusting. This feature is particularly attractive to telephone companies because it means they can charge different rates for different bandwidths. Additionally, RADSL extends the possible distance from the subscriber to the central exchange office, thus increasing the percentage of homes served by DSL services.

RADSL, like ADSL, will relieve some of the congestion on voice networks, as it also supports POTS. This allows network providers to route data to the data networks and voice to the circuit-switched networks, versus both voice and data going through the circuit-switched network, as is currently done with analog modems and ISDN services.

Pacific Bell is using RADSL for its DSL service. Using RADSL allows the company to roll out its FastTrak ADSL service with two different configurations based on the same technology. One offering will be an asymmetrical product with 1.5 Mbps downstream and 384 Kbps upstream. The other bandwidth option will be a symmetrical package that supports 384 Kbps downstream and upstream. The symmetrical package is targeted at the SOHO market, and will include Internet access for an estimated cost of under $200.

IDSL

ISDN Digital Subscriber Line is a dedicated cousin of dial-up ISDN service currently offered by the telephone companies. It delivers 128 Kbps of bandwidth like ISDN, but like all DSL technologies, it does it without integrating into the expensive telephone company-switching infrastructure. IDSL connections go directly to the data network, enabling RBOCs to conserve switch resources and avoid network congestion. This allows them to offer a flat-rate ISDN service to their subscribers, because IDSL calls do not require central office switch and voice infrastructure resources. The beauty of using IDSL from the end-users' perspective is that they can use their extant ISDN equipment, which is affordable and easy-to-use high-bandwidth technology.

Unfortunately, early announcements of IDSL service releases indicate that the pricing, while attractive compared to dial-up ISDN service, is still beyond the reach of many SOHO sites. UUNET, the world's largest provider of Internet services, is deploying IDSL service nationally, but at a cost of well over $1,000 a month for a mere 128 Kbps!

Interprise Networking services, the data networking arm of US West Communications, is offering IDSL service using pricing based on an individual case basis. It's estimated that the service may cost around $175 per month, including Internet access. Ascend Communications, the leading maker of ISDN routers, is supplying the IDSL routers used for Interprise's IDSL service. These routers have a similar interface to Ascend's ISDN cousins.

SDSL

Symmetric Digital Subscriber Line provides symmetric (bidirectional) high-speed, variable-rate communications at ranges from 160 Kbps to 2,084 Mbps. SDSL will not reach much beyond 10,000 feet, a distance over which ADSL achieves rates above 6 Mbps. SDSL has a similar capacity to HDSL technology, but with an important advantage: It's suitable for individual subscriber premises, which are often equipped with only a single telephone line.

SDSL can be packaged in lower-bandwidth configurations to offer a more affordable dedicated connection. For example, HarvardNet, an ISP in the Boston area offers SDSL service starting at 128 Kbps for $299. This dedicated connection can be upgraded to 384 Kbps or 768 Kbps without new equipment.

HDSL and VDSL

High-bit-rate Digital Subscriber Line service has been around for a few years. It's deployed as a direct replacement for traditional T1 service, which was expensive and required lengthy implementation times because it required adding line conditioning and repeaters to improve the quality of the telephone line. HDSL transports data at a full-duplex T1 rate of 1.544 Mbps across existing twisted-pair lines but requires the use of two separate telephone lines. This high-performance technology is the quickest and most cost-effective option to deploy T1 lines, which is why it has become very popular in the T1 line marketplace. HDSL provides T1 line rates over telephone lines of up to 12,000 feet in length between the telephone company's central office and the customer site.

Over time, ADSL and SDSL may replace HDSL. However, T1 service using HDSL technology has become very profitable for telephone companies. As a result, some telephone companies take a dim view of pricing ADSL as a SOHO product because it can deliver the same capacity on the downstream as a T1 line that costs an average of $1,500 a month.

Very-high-bit-rate Digital Subscriber Line (VDSL) is an asymmetrical technology that can only be leveraged very close to the central office. The closer the customer is to the central exchange office, the higher the data rate. For example, at 1,000 feet from the CO, the downstream rate can reach up to 52 Mbps; at 3,000 feet, a subscriber may attain data rates up 26 Mbps; and at 5,000 feet away from the central office, a subscriber can get a data rate of 13 Mbps.

DSL Technology Issues

ADSL and RADSL are being positioned as the mainstay bandwidth warriors for the telephone companies as they prepare to do battle with cable companies. Early tariff services will only be available selectively for the first year or two, while telephone companies equip central offices with access network hardware.

Although DSL technology bypasses the existing telephone-switching infrastructure, it still requires a new infrastructure. However, by not having to upgrade or modify the vast telephone-switching infrastructure to support DSL, the lead time is reduced to considerably less than the several years it takes telephone companies to make wide-scale changes to their switching systems. Telephone companies must add DSL servers at their CO facilities to accommodate new DSL capacity as demand rises.

The term for twisted-pair wiring without any switching services is *dry pair*. Proponents of DSL technologies make it sound as if you simply hook up any twisted-pair cable with DSL modems and get high-speed data communications. In reality, it's more complicated. Moreover, there are still unresolved standards and pricing issues. Consequently, DSL should be regarded as an incomplete bandwidth product.

Competing ADSL Versions

There are two competing ADSL technologies on the market today for ADSL, each with its proponents and detractors. AT&T's Paradyne subsidiary developed the CAP (Carrierless Amplitude and Modulation) as a modulation scheme for ADSL. Amati Communications (which developed the DMT technology) and a number of other DSLAM and DSL modem vendors are championing the DMT (Discrete MultiTone) modulation scheme.

CAP describes a process in which incoming data modulates a single carrier that is then transmitted down a telephone line. The carrier itself is suppressed before transmission (it contains no information, and can be reconstructed at the receiver); hence, the adjective carrierless. DMT describes a version of multicarrier modulation in which incoming data is collected and then distributed over a large number of small individual carriers. DMT creates these channels using a digital technique known as Discrete Fast-Fourier Transform.

Practically speaking, the difference between ADSL modulation schemes may not significantly slow ADSL deployment, because phone companies will pick the standard for they want for their infrastructure, and customers will use the ADSL modems supplied by the telephone companies, much the way cable modems are supplied by the cable companies. That said, here are some details regarding these two schemes to consider.

The American National Standards Institute (ANSI) adopted an ADSL standard based on the DMT architecture. Currently, CAP adapters are considerably cheaper than DMT alternatives. They are available in production quantities and are functioning well in trials. US West and Bell Atlantic are running their technical trials on FlexCAP adapters from Westell, while GTE is testing CAP and DMT adapters.

DMT prototype transceivers have proven to have high transmission speeds, simplicity, reliability, and good line noise characteristics. DMT appears to be faster than CAP at distances both close to and farther from the central switch. DMT also seems to be more robust, capable of handling shortcomings in the phone network. DMT can operate over a wider range of line conditions and support longer wire lengths. All in all, however, the two specifications aren't that far apart.

AT&T's Paradyne division designed ADSL transceivers using CAP technology in 1994, and it licenses its technology to manufacturers. Westell claims its FlexCAP adapters have a more than 90 percent share of units being tested, but it has begun to manufacture DMT adapters. Paradyne is the only manufacturer of CAP chip sets, whereas there are a number of DMT chip suppliers. Microsoft announced it would develop software built on Windows NT to allow phone companies to provide ADSL networks based on Westell's FlexCAP device. At this stage in the evolution of DSL modems, it looks as though both CAP and DMT may be supported.

ATM over DSL versus PPP over DSL

Asynchronous Transfer Mode (ATM) is a cell-switched, connection-oriented, full-duplex, point-to-point protocol that dedicates bandwidth to each computer on a network. It uses asynchronous time division multiplexing (TDM) to control the flow of information over a network. ATM is an industrial-strength networking protocol that operates at bandwidths ranging from 25 Mbps to 622 Mbps, although most use the de facto standard of 155 Mbps. ATM is designed to integrate LAN, WAN, voice, video, and data communication functions into a single uniform protocol and design.

Packet-switching systems don't perform well for real-time, two-way traffic, such as interactive video, because it's designed to handle data bursts as opposed to steady data streams. ATM overcomes this limitation by using cells, which are fixed-length packets, rather than variable-length packets. ATM does not employ a shared-bandwidth medium but instead creates virtual connections for each computer on a network.

ATM was designed for public telecommunications systems and large-scale enterprise networks. RBOCs and large corporations prefer a form of DSL service called ATM over DSL. Making DSL work with the ATM infrastructure enables a DSL connection to support a wide variety of applications. Big companies are looking for multiple service over DSL for telecommuting, Internet access, and other data applications. Most ISPs, on the other hand, want PPP over DSL solution for Internet access. Currently, ATM over DSL and PPP over DSL are incompatible. To help resolve this battle, Microsoft, along with Alcatel, Cisco Systems, Fore Systems, U.S. Robotics, and Westel technologies, proposed an architecture that would use PPP over ATM over ADSL for interoperability between modems, routers, and DSLAMS.

DSL Modems

DSL modems achieve greater throughput by using digital signaling at the wire level intended to improve line quality, which is why they can't run over already provisioned lines or switches. One modem sits at the customer's site, and the other is in the phone company's nearest CO. At this stage of DSL development, end-to-end proprietary solutions are the order of the day because of the absence of interoperability standards. This means DSL modems and DSLAM products will most likely come from the same vendor. Fortunately, ADSL is a point-to-point medium, so interoperability concerns are minimized.

From a subscriber's perspective, DSL modem connections are completely transparent. Initial ADSL modems are likely to be similar to ISDN routers, offering an analog port for a phone or fax and an Ethernet connection to plug into a PC or hub. Already there are a number of DSL modem vendors, many of which will be unfamiliar to PC users because they're telecommunications equipment suppliers. However, there are a growing number of well-known PC communications companies entering the DSL modem arena, including U.S. Robotics and Hayes. U.S. Robotics is selling a DSL modem solution called VIPER-DSL. Hayes Microcomputer is collaborating with Alcatel to deliver ADSL modems designed for the SOHO market. These new modems will support Microsoft's Plug-and-Play. The Alcatel/Hayes products will provide up to 8 Mbps downstream and a maximum of approximately 640 Kbps upstream, built around DMT modulation scheme.

Leading DSL modem vendors include Westell, which manufactures the Flex-Cap2 RADSL modem; and Alcatel Alsthom, which is a large French telecommunications company. Alcatel has been awarded the prime contract to provide DSL modems for four RBOCs, including Ameritech, Bell South, SBC, and Pacific Bell. PairGain Technologies is the DSL market leader; it manufactures a family of DSL modems for ADSL, RADSL, and HDSL. Ascend Communications is supplying IDSL routers for US West's IDSL service. These are similar to Ascend's popular Pipeline series of ISDN routers. Other players in the DSL modem field include Cisco Systems, Motorola, and Amati Communications.

DSL and SOHO Remote Access

The greatest potential drawback of DSL service is not the technology but the gatekeepers, which are the telephone companies. The RBOCs have been and continue to be strong monopolies in their respective service areas. They move slowly, and traditionally haven't been SOHO-friendly in the delivery of bandwidth at affordable prices. The following sections explore the issues that will impact positively and negatively the deployment of DSL service for the SOHO market.

Can the Telcos Deliver DSL Competitively?

Most RBOCs have publicly announced major rollouts of DSL service. Whether they will deliver affordable services packaged for the needs of the SOHO market remains to be seen. ISDN service is a good example of how telephone companies can interfere with a bandwidth product intended for the mass market. Nevertheless, because of the differences in how DSL technology is delivered compared to ISDN, the telephone companies may be able to deliver DSL within a reasonable time frame and at an affordable price.

One positive development since ISDN is the emergence of cable companies as high-speed Internet access providers, a topic that was discussed in the previous chapter. Certainly, cable modem service has its own problems, but cable companies represent a potentially serious challenge to the telephone company monopoly on bandwidth. The cable companies are already deploying high-speed Internet access at SOHO-friendly prices. This challenges the telephone companies to do the same.

While proponents of DSL point out the lack of cable modem deployment, they should realize that DSL deployment will be an equally lengthy process. It is not as simple as DSL vendors would have you believe; infrastructure must be added to facilitate the use of copper wires, for one thing. Furthermore, DSL service could mimic the ISDN marketplace; that is, long on hardware alternatives but short on service options. ISDN equipment vendors took a leading role in making ISDN hardware service better and less expensive, but many RBOCs delivery of the service was so poor or expensive that many SOHO users lacked real access to the technology.

Finally, RBOCs promise to provide ADSL service at $50 to $200 a month may not hold up. The RBOCs have high cost structures, which is how they justify their tariff filings. Consequently, they may not be able to or want to offer inexpensive DSL services, especially if those services cannibalize their profitable T1 and second analog line services.

Competitive Local Exchange Carriers

A potentially positive factor in the deployment of DSL service at more affordable prices comes from provisions in the Telecommunications Act of 1996. A key provision of this legislation was to enable other service providers, such as ISPs, to buy bulk telecommunications services from RBOCs at discounted prices and then re-sell them. Companies buying telecommunication services from incumbent telephone companies are defined in the Telecommunications Act as competitive local exchange carriers, or CLECs. In this way, an ISP can buy telephone lines in bulk from the RBOCs and then publish its own state's public utility commission for DSL service. Incumbent carriers must also provide CLECs room for their equipment in central offices. How much impact this option will have in creating competition for the RBOCs in delivering DSL service remains unknown. RBOCs will undoubtedly make this process as difficult as possible for CLECs.

DSL Tariffs

In telephone industry lingo, prices are called tariffs—a term that implies a monopolistic pricing structure. Tariffs are filed in each of the 50 states by way of public utility commissions (PUCs) or similar agencies. These governmental agencies are chartered to look after the public interest within the recognized monopoly power of essential utilities. However, many of these state regulatory agencies are political organizations that are more telephone company-friendly than consumer-friendly.

DSL tariffs are undefined at this point, and they could range from around $50 (as for ISDN dial-up service) to around $1,500 (as for T1 line service) a month. Moreover, once telephone companies decide what to charge, DSL will face a tariff process that could take years.

While RBOCs may not have to replace the copper wiring, they will want to recoup their investments in configuring each CO to support DSL. Telephone companies are also unsure how to bill for DSL service. Traditionally, telephone companies have been usage-based bandwidth providers for the mass market. Consequently, they haven't quite figured out how to bill for DSL Internet access because it's a dedicated service that doesn't fit the usage-pricing model.

Pacific Bell's Bellwether FasTrak ADSL Service

Pacific Bell was an early leader in adopting ISDN service and deploying it to the SOHO market. The huge California market is a major battleground for the cable versus telephone bandwidth war. There, the cable forces are TCI and Cox Cable with @Home. Therefore, this market has a huge impact on remote access. Take note of these statistics.

- By the year 2000, over 42 million Internet and online subscribers in the United States will be Californians.
- Thirty-five percent of worldwide Internet traffic originates or terminates in California.
- Thirty percent of North American domain names are registered in California.
- Fifty-one percent of California small businesses use some kind of online services.

Pacific Bell plans to roll out DSL in mid-1998 by introducing two RADSL packages called FastTrak ADSL. The RADSL package designed for the SOHO market will provide a symmetrical connection at 384 Kbps for both upstream and downstream. The other package will deliver an asymmetrical service with 1.5 Mbps downstream to the subscriber and 384 Kbps upstream to the network. These RADSL offerings will use the Discrete MultiTone (DMT) modulation scheme and will allow both data and voice service. Pacific Bell, learning from its ISDN deployment experience, will also package a total Internet access solution for the SOHO market. Pacific Bell along with Ameritech, Bell South, and SBC is part of the Joint Procurement Consortium, which selected Alcatel as the sole source vendor for the initial DSLAMS and DSL modems deployments.

Your DSL Game Plan

The bottom line on DSL service is, keep your eye on it but don't expect it to be a serious candidate for your remote access needs in the near term. Optimistic deployment projections of late 1997 and early 1998 are not likely to materialize. Most DSL watchers predict deployment between mid-1998 and 1999. Even then, expect to see a confusing assortment of DSL options offered by different telephone companies, with correspondingly complex tariffs. Different telephone companies will embrace DSL with varying degrees of enthusiasm. Some will try to deliver a DSL service that is the right mix of bandwidth and price to make it an attractive option for the SOHO market. Others will offer no meaningful DSL service for the SOHO market.

One other important source for DSL service availability could be the ISPs in your area. If they get through the RBOC maze to become competitive local exchange carriers (CLECs), they may offer some reasonable DSL service. Again, for now, the best strategy is to take a wait-and-see approach, and in the meantime, try to work with 56-Kbps modems, ISDN, or cable modem service.

What's Next

This is the end of the line. All that's left are the appendixes, which include a comprehensive guide to remote access resources, including applications, utilities, hardware, and more, as well as detailed information on the software included on the CD. And don't forget to check out the Glossary if some of these new terms have left you acronym-befuddled.

PART
V

Appendixes

Appendix S

A *Windows 95 Remote Access Resources*

A cornucopia of remote access products and resources are available for Windows 95. This appendix lists remote access hardware, applications, and services. It also explains additional remote access software options, such as desktop video conferencing and Net phones.

ISDN

ISDN Remote Access Devices

ISDN remote access devices come in two flavors: the single-user ISDN modems (internal and external) and ISDN routers.

COMPANY	PRODUCT
3Com Corporation Voice: 800-638-3266 or 408-764-5000 Fax: 408-764-5000 Web: www.3com.com	3Com Impact IQ (external ISDN modem) Office Connect 535 (router)
ADTRAN Voice: 800-827-0807 Fax: 205-971-8699 Web: www.adtran.com	Express XRT (external ISDN modem) Express RT (external ISDN modem)

COMPANY	PRODUCT
Alpha Telecom Voice: 205-881-8743 Fax: 205-880-9720	CyberJet (internal ISDN modem)
Angia Communications Voice: 801-371-0488 Fax: 801-373-9847 Web: www.angia.com	I-Bahn PCMCIA card
Ascend Communications, Inc. Voice: 800-621-9578 or 510-769-6001 Fax: 510-814-2300 Web: www.ascend.com	Pipeline series of ISDN routers: Pipeline 25-Fx Pipeline 25-Px Pipeline 50 Pipeline 75 Pipeline 85 Pipeline 130
Cardinal Technologies Voice: 717-293-3000 Web: www.cardtech.com/	Cardinal IDC 100i
Chase Research, Inc. Voice: 800-242-7387 Fax: 615-872-0700 Web: www.chaser.com	NetChaser ISDN-TA 460K
Cisco Systems, Inc. Voice: 408-526-4000 Fax: 408-526-4100 Web: www.cisco.com	Cisco 760 and 770 Series (routers)
Diamond Multimedia Systems, Inc. Voice: 408-325-7000 Fax: 408-325-7070 Web: www.diamondmm.com	Supra NetCommander ISDN modem
Eicon Technology Voice: 214-239-3200 Fax: 214-239-3304 Web: www.eicon.com	DIVA PCMCIA DIVA Pro (internal ISDN modem)

COMPANY	PRODUCT
Farallon Computing, Inc. Voice: 510-814-5000 Fax: 510-814-5023 Web: www.farallon.com	Netopia So-Smart Router (model 635) Netopia ISDN Modem (external) Netopia ISDN PC Card (PCMCIA)
Flow Point Corporation Voice: 888-867-4736 or 408-364-8300 Fax: 408-364-8301 Web:www.flowpoint	Flow Point 128
ISDNet, Inc. Voice: 408-260-3080 Fax: 408-260-3090 Web: www.isdnnet.com	ISDNet NetRouter 1040 ISDNet NetRouter 1080 (includes hub)
Motorola Voice: 800-451-2369 Fax: 205-830-5657 Web: www.motorola.com	BitSURFR Pro EZ BitSURFR Pro ISA (internal ISDN modem)
Ramp Networks, Inc. Voice: 888-493-2726 or 408-988-5353 Fax: 408-988-5353 Web: www.rampnet.com	WebRamp Entré WebRamp IP
Shiva Corp. Voice: 800-847-4482 or 617-270-8300 Fax: 617-270-8599 Web: www.shiva.com	AccessPort (ISDN router)
Symplex Communications Voice: 313-995-1555 Fax: 313-995-1564 Web: www.symplex.com	Symplex RO-1 Gold
U.S. Robotics Voice: 847-982-5010 Web: www.usr.com	LANLinker ISDN Router Courier I Modem (external ISDN modem) Sportster ISDN 128K (internal ISDN modem)

COMPANY	PRODUCT
Zoom Telephonics Voice: 617-423-1072 Fax: 617-423-3923 Web: www.zoomtel.com	Zoom/ISDN Duo
ZyXEL Communications Voice: 714-693-0808 Fax: 714-693-8811 Web: www.zyxel.com	Prestige 128 (Router) Omni TA 128 Elite 2864I

ISDN Service Providers

All ISDN service is delivered and billed by your telephone company. Most telephone companies have Web sites and ISDN customer service centers that can give you information about getting ISDN service and how much it's going to cost you.

TELEPHONE COMPANY	INFORMATION SOURCE
Ameritech	24-hour voice and fax-back system: 800-832-6328 Home ISDN service: 800-419-5400 Business ISDN service: 800-417-9888 Web: www.ameritech.com/
Bell Atlantic	ISDN InfoSpeed Solutions Center: 800-204-7332 Small businesses: 800-843-2255 TeleProducts: 800-221-0845 Web: www.bell-atl.com/
BellSouth	ISDN individual line service: 800-858-9413 Web: www.bell.bellsouth/
GTE	24-hour, menu-driven voice and fax-back system: 800-888-8799 Voice: 214-718-5608 Web: www.gte.com/

TELEPHONE COMPANY	INFORMATION SOURCE
NYNEX New England	24-hour, menu-driven voice and fax-back system: 800-438-4736 ISDN Service Center: 800-650-4736 Web: www.nynex.com/
NYNEX New York	24-hour, menu-driven voice and fax-back system: 800-438-4736 Voice: 914-644-5152 Web: www.nynex.com/
Pacific Bell	24-hour voice and fax-back system: 800-995-0345 ISDN Service Center: 800-472-4736 Web: www.pacbell.com/
Southwestern Bell Corporation (SBC)	Austin: 800-792-4736 Dallas: 214-268-1403 South Houston: 713-567-4300 North Houston: 713-537-3930 ISDN DigiLine Service: 800-792-4736, x500 Web: www.sbc.com/
US West	24-hour voice and fax-back system: 800-728-4929 Voice: 800-246-5226 Web: www.uswest.com/

56K Modems and Routers

There are a number of 56K modems and modem multiplexor/router products. Just remember that there are two competing 56K modem technologies (x2 and K56flex) that are incompatible, so you need to make sure the server side of your connection uses the x2 and K56flex technology.

COMPANY	PRODUCT
Best Data Products Voice: 818-773-9600 Fax: 818-773-9619	Smart One 56X External Smart One 56F Internal

COMPANY	PRODUCT
Boca Research Voice: 561-997-6227 Web: www.bocaresearch.com	MACH 2 56K
Cardinal Technologies Voice: 717-293-3000 Web: www.cardtech.com/	Connecta 56K
Diamond Multimedia Systems, Inc. Voice: 408-325-7000 Fax: 408-325-7070 Web: www.diamondmm.com	SupraExpress 56K
Global Village Communication Voice: 800-736-4821 Web: www.globalvillage.com	TelePort 56K x2
Hayes Microcomputer Products Voice: 770-441-1617 Web: www.hayes.com	ACCURA 56K
Motorola Fax: 205-830-5657 Web: www.motorola.com	ModemSURFR 56K VoiceSURFR 56K
Ramp Networks, Inc. Voice: 888-493-2726 or 408-988-5353 Fax: 408-988-5353 Web: www.rampnet.com	WebRamp M3 (modem router/multiplexer)
U.S. Robotics Voice: 800-877-2677 or 847-982-5010 Web: www.usr.com	Courier V.Everything LANLinker Dual Analog (Modem Router)
Zoom Telephonics Voice: 617-423-1072 Fax: 617-423-3923 Web: www.zoomtel.com	Zoom/FaxModem 56K (internal) Zoom/FaxModem 56K (external)

Cable Resources

The following lists the large cable companies offering cable modem service and other resources for finding more information on cable modem service.

COMPANY/ORGANIZATION	DESCRIPTION
@Home Voice: 888-780-4663 Web: www.home.net	Partnership of TCI, Cox, and Comcast.
Cable Datacom News Web: CableDatacomNews.com	Online news about cable modem service.
Cable Television Laboratories Web: www.cablelabs.com	R&D arm of cable companies.
Comcast Voice: 888-793-9800 Web: www.comcastonline.com	Cable company offering @Home Internet access service.
Cox Communications Web: www.cox.com	Cable company offering Cox@Home Network Internet access service.
MediaOne Voice: 800-665-5501 Web: www.mediaone.com	Cable company offering MediaOne Express Internet access service.
TCI (Tele-Communications Inc.) Web: www.tci.com	Cable company offering @Home Internet access service.
Time Warner Cable	Cable company offering Road Runner Internet access service.

DSL Resources

Getting information about DSL service from telephone companies is difficult. Consequently, there are a limited number of resources available for finding more information on this topic.

COMPANY/ORGANIZATION	FUNCTION
ADSL Forum Web: www.adsl.com	DSL industry trade group.
Alcatel Telecom Web: www.alcatel.com	DSL equipment manufacturer. Supplying systems for Ameritech, Bell South, Pacific Bell, and SBC Communications.
Amati Communications Web: www.amati.com	DSL equipment manufacturer.
Ameritech Web: www.ameritech.com	Telephone company in DSL trials.
Ascend Communications Web: www.ascend.com	Making IDSL (ISDN Digital Subscriber Line) routers for US West.
Bell Atlantic Web: www.bell–atl.com	Telephone company in DSL trials.
GTE Web: www.get.com	Telephone company in DSL trials.
Motorola Web: www.mot.com	DSL equipment manufacturer.
Pacific Bell Web: www.pacbell.com	Telephone company offering FasTrak ADSL services in 1998.
PairGain Technologies Web: www.pairgain.com	DSL equipment manufacturer. DSL modems used by US West.
TeleChoice Web: www.telechoice.com	DSL information and consulting services.
U.S. Robotics Web: www.usr.com	DSL equipment manufacturer.
US West Web: www.uswest.com	Telephone company in DSL trials.

COMPANY/ORGANIZATION	FUNCTION
Westell Technologies Web: www.westell.com	DSL equipment manufacturer.
Microsoft SUPERCOMM '97 Web: www.microsoft.com/isp /supercomm/	Explains the ADSL interoperability collaboration to standardize ADSL service.

LAN Hardware

COMPANY	PRODUCT
LINKSYS Voice: 800-546-5797 Fax: 714-261-8868 Web: www.linksys.com	Network adapter cards, hubs, printer-sharing devices.
Axis Communications Voice: 800-444-AXIS or 617-938-1188 Fax: 617-938-6161 Web: www.axis.com	Printer and storage-sharing devices.
3Com Corporation Voice: 800-638-3266 or 408-764-5000 Fax: 408-764-5000 Web: http://www.3com.com	Network adapter cards and hubs.
Intel Corporation Web: www.intel.com	Network adapter cards.
Kingston Technologies Voice: 800-337-7032 or 714-435-2600 Fax: 714-435-2699 Web: www.kingston.com	Network adapter cards and hubs.

Windows 95 Technical Support

Technical support for Windows 95 is available from Microsoft at no charge for the first 90 days, and the 90-day clock doesn't start ticking until you make your first call. The technical support number is 206-637-7098. Call-in hours are weekdays 6:00 A.M. to 6:00 P.M. (Pacific Standard Time).

After the 90-day free support expires, you can get support from Microsoft on a per-session basis. Calling 900-555-2000 costs $2 per minute, with a $35 maximum. You are not charged for the time spent on hold. The charges are added to your telephone bill.

TIP: The Microsoft Web site (www.microsoft.com) is a primary source for Windows 95 support. It includes lots of free software for downloading, as well as Service Packs.

TCP/IP Remote Access Applications

The essential TCP/IP applications for most remote access connections include a Web browser, e-mail, FTP, and network newsreader programs. If you're doing file transfers over the Internet, you need an FTP client and possibly an FTP server. Although you can use a Web browser for file transfer, using an FTP program that includes a simple FTP server and client program may be easier to deal with than setting up a Web server.

Web Browsers

COMPANY	PRODUCT
Microsoft Corporation Web: www.microsoft.com	Internet Explorer 4.0
Netscape Communications Web: home.netscape.com	Netscape Communicator

E-mail

COMPANY	PRODUCT
Microsoft Corporation Web: www.microsoft.com	Outlook Express, which comes with Internet Explorer.
Netscape Communications Web: www.netscape.com	Messenger, which comes with Netscape Communicator.
Qualcomm Voice: 800-238-3672 Web: www.qualcomm.com	EudoraLite Eudora Pro

FTP

COMPANY	PRODUCT
Nico Mak Computing Web: http://www.cuteftp.com	CuteFTP (client FTP program)
Ipswitch Voice: 617-676-5700 Fax: 617-676-5710 Web: http://www.ipswitch.com	WS_FTP Pro (client FTP program)
Texas Imperial Software Voice: 512-257-2578 Fax: 512-378-3246 Web: www.wftpd.com	WFTPD (FTP server and client program)

Newsreaders

COMPANY	PRODUCT
Forte Voice: 619-431-6496 Fax: 619-431-6497 Web: www.forteinc.com	Free Agent Agent

COMPANY	PRODUCT
Microsoft Corporation Web: www.microsoft.com	Outlook Express, which comes with Internet Explorer.
Netscape Communications Web: www.netscape.com	Collabra Newsreader, which comes with Netscape Navigator.

Remote Control Software

Remote control software is a way to access data or applications stored on a PC or a network from another PC over a data communication link. Remote control enables a remote client PC to take over another PC (called a host) via an analog dial-up, LAN, or Internet connection. The remote client takes control of the host PC's CPU, screen, and keyboard, and runs applications on the host or transfers files between the host and client. Since the host does most of the processing, remote control is great for accessing applications and services that your remote client lacks the power or local storage to run.

Remote control over the Internet via TCP/IP enables users to access their office computers from local ISP accounts anywhere in the world, saving on long-distance charges. In order to connect to another PC over the Internet, you must know its IP address, and the computer must be connected to the Internet.

COMPANY	PRODUCT
Stac, Inc. Voice: 619-794-3741 Web: www.stac.com	ReachOut
Farallon Computing, Inc. Voice: 510-814-5000 Fax: 510-814-5023 Web: www.farallon.com	Timbuktu Pro
Microcom Voice: 800-822-8224 or 617-551-1000 Fax: 617-551-1021 Web: www.microcom.com	Carbon 32 Copy

COMPANY	PRODUCT
Symantec Corporation Voice: 800-441-7234 or 408-253-9600 Fax: 408-253-3968 Web: www.symantec.com	Norton pcAnywhere
Artisoft, Inc. Voice: 800-846-9726 Fax: 520-670-7101 Web: www.artisoft.com	InSync CoSession Remote
Traveling Software Voice: 800-343-8080 Fax: 206-485-6786 Web: www.travsoft.com	LapLink for Windows 95
Avalan Technology Voice: 800-441-2281 Fax: 508-429-3179 Web: www.avalan.com	Remotely Possible

Net Phones

Net phones let you carry on voice conferences over the Internet. To make a Net phone call, you launch a Net phone program, then dial up a PC using an IP address. If the receiving party is logged on with the same Net phone software you're using, his or her Net phone rings. You're sending the digital data representing your voice over a network.

Note: The potential of Net phones to circumvent long-distance rates is a big element of their appeal. Feeling threatened, a group of long-distance carriers, acting through their trade group, the America Carriers Telecommunication Association (ACTA), has asked the government to stop the technology before it has a chance to develop. The Federal Communications Commission is conducting hearings on ACTA's petition. Currently, there are no restrictions on Net phone use, although the technology imposes plenty of its own.

Regular phones let you and the person you call speak as if you were in the same room; the Internet can't guarantee that kind of responsive, high-quality service. The digitizing process may fail, resulting in *dropouts*, which are audio gaps in the conversation. Net phone quality is limited by the amount of data that can be pumped across the Internet. Consequently, the typical 28.8-Kbps modem, for example, is easily overwhelmed by a Net phone call.

You may need to add components to your computer system before you can use Net phones. Most programs require a sound card, speakers, and microphone. The microphone acts as your mouthpiece and the speakers as your receiver. The sound card translates digital input into analog output, and vice versa.

COMPANY	PRODUCT
Intel Corporation Voice: 800-628-8686 Web: www.intel.com	Internet Video Phone (voice and video)
VocalTec Voice: 201-768-9400 Fax: 201-768-8893 Web: www.vocaltec.com	Internet Phone for Windows with Video Internet Phone for Windows
FreeTel Communications Voice: 800-838-0490 Web: www.freetel.com	FreeTel FreeTel+ FreeTel Personal Edition
Microsoft Corporation Web: www.microsoft.com	NetMeeting (voice and video)
Netscape Communications Web: www.netscape.com	CoolTalk (voice and video)
NetSpeak Corp. Voice: 561-997-4001 Web: www.netspeak.com	WebPhone
Third Planet Publishing Voice: 972-733-3005 Fax: 972-380-8712 Web: www.digiphone.com	DigiPhone DigiPhone Deluxe

COMPANY	PRODUCT
Voxware Voice: 609-514-4100 Fax: 609-514-4101 Web: www.voxware.com	TeleVox VoxChat

Net Faxing

Sending faxes over the Internet is growing in popularity. Web fax technology is in its infancy, so currently there are just a few choices: NetCentric's FaxStorm, FaxSav's FaxSave for Internet Suite, and Symantec's WinFax Pro. Both products are available for free download and don't require any additional hardware or phone lines to send faxes. Both charge 15 cents per page for domestic faxes and varying rates for international faxes.

COMPANY	PRODUCT
NetCentric Voice: 617-720-5200 Web: www.netcentric.com	FaxStorm
FaxSav Voice: 800-909-0040 Web: www.faxsav.com	FaxSave for Internet Suite
Symantec Corporation Voice: 800-441-7234 Web: www.symantec.com	WinFax Pro. Includes NetCentric's FaxStorm

Groupware

Groupware, or collaborative software, such as Microsoft Exchange or Lotus Notes, can dramatically narrow the distances between people, but they're usually too expensive and complicated to operate for the SOHO market because they require dedicated Internet servers. A new genre of groupware software and services is emerging that is targeted at the need of the SOHO market for inexpensive collaboration tools.

Netopia Virtual Office

One software product designed for the SOHO market is Farallon's Netopia Virtual Office. Netopia Virtual Office begins by creating your personal Web page using images of familiar office metaphors, such as an inbox/outbox, messaging, conferencing, and chat. Using passwords, you choose which features to put under lock and key. You can chat in real time with colleagues who are in their virtual offices; or several participants in different locations can huddle over a Power Point presentation, marking it up in real time on their computer screens. In addition to making standard Internet capabilities easier to use (from e-mail to FTP), Netopia Virtual Office adds value with the real-time remote communications capabilities of Farallon's Timbuktu software. With Timbuktu, you can operate a remote computer from another computer far away.

> **Netopia Virtual Office**
> Farallon Computing, Inc.
> Voice: 510-814-5000
> Fax: 510-814-5023
> Web: www.farallon.com

Netscape Virtual Office

Netscape Communications and Concentric Network Corporation have created a new groupware service called Netscape Virtual Office that provides a private Internet-based server that geographically dispersed people can use as a central collaboration site. This private Intranet service allows a small business to set up a full-featured, secure Internet site with support for a variety of services, including HTML documents, e-mail, discussion forums, and project collaboration tools. The service charges a monthly service for each user. At the time this book was written, Netscape and Concentric had not finalized the cost of the service. Concentric is providing the groupware hosting services for the Virtual Office.

> **Netscape Virtual Office**
> Concentric Network Corporation
> Voice: 800-939-4262
> Fax: 408-342-2810
> Web: www.concentric.net

Desktop Video Conferencing

Of all the remote access applications, desktop video conferencing (DVC) is the most exciting—but also the most bandwidth-demanding. It adds interactive visual and audio elements to your remote access communications. Desktop video-conferencing systems support both one-on-one conferences as well as group meetings. Desktop video conferencing over higher-bandwidth technologies can be a useful option for many activities where a face-to-face meeting is important.

PC-based video-conferencing systems are available for use via a 56K (POTS), ISDN or other telecommunications or cable connection, as well as over LANs and the Internet. Many of these video-conferencing systems work on multiple networks, while others work only on the POTS or ISDN public-switched telephone network. Internet-only DVC systems are considerably less expensive than the systems that support dial-up, LAN, and Internet video conferencing. These systems rely on your remote access device to make the video-conferencing connection.

The basic video-conferencing kit can be assembled from individual components or by purchasing complete systems, which include the following:

- A video/audio card that includes ports for connecting the video camera and audio devices (microphone, headphones, speakers).

- A small digital color video camera: It typically mounts on top of your monitor or has its own stand.

- Video-conferencing software that includes data compression software, as well as a collection of collaborative computing tools. These tools enable you to display and share applications such as Word97 or Excel97; illustrate points or develop ideas using a whiteboard feature; video and audio adjustments; address books for making automatic connections; and file-transfer programs for uploading and downloading files.

- For POTS or ISDN video conferencing, the kits typically include an analog modem or ISDN terminal adapter. ISDN systems use an S/T-interface (RJ-45) port for connecting to an NTI device.

Video-Conferencing Standards

Most video systems comply with the ITU (International Telephone Union) H.320 standard, which consists of a subset of other standards. The H.323 is the standard for desktop video conferencing over LANs, and H.324 is the standard for POTS connections.

Beyond the video conferencing element, much of the interaction during a conference involves reviewing and marking up documents, sharing information via files and applications, and exchanging faxes. The T120 standard, a general multimedia-conferencing standard covers these functions. Using this standard in desktop video-conferencing systems enables you to use whiteboard and application-sharing programs across different products. Like the H.320 standard, the T120 also includes a subset of other standards. For example, T127 establishes a way for video-conferencing users to execute simultaneous multipoint file transfers.

FPS and Resolution

The differences in the quality of desktop video-conferencing systems are a function of frames per second (fps) rate, resolution, and color bits per pixel. The higher the frame rate, resolution, and color bits, the better the quality of the video. *A frame is a single image within a video.* Frames per second is the number of pictures flashed in a second to give the image the illusion of motion, which begins at around 16 fps. Broadcast television presents a moving picture at 30 fps, which is based on the National Television Standards Committee (NTSC) standard. Most desktop video-conferencing systems deliver a video image at around 15 fps to 20 fps, although these rates continue to improve.

Resolution refers to the number of pixels your monitor and video adapter card can display. Because of the huge data demands made by video, having a video image the size of your PC's full screen is extremely demanding on a video adapter. Image sizes for most desktop video-conferencing system fit within windows that range from 160 ×120 to 320 × 240 pixels in size. (Pixel is short for picture elements, which are the little dots on the screen that light up in different colors to make pictures.) Standard video images measured in pixels are 160 × 120, 240 × 180, 320 × 240, and 640 × 480. Bits per pixel define the color depth of an image. The more bits supported, the better the color quality. Most of today's video adapter cards support 24-bit color.

Desktop Video Conferencing Systems

COMPANY	PRODUCT
Boca Research Voice: 561-997-6227 Fax: 561-994-5848 Web: www.bocaresearch.com	Video Phone Elite (POTS)
Connectix Corporation Voice: 415-571-5100 Fax: 415-571-5195 Web: www.connectix.com	Connectix Video Phone (Internet/POTS)

COMPANY	PRODUCT
Creative Labs Voice: 800-998-5227 Web: www.creativelabs.com	Share Vision PC-3000 (Internet/POTS)
Diamond Multimedia Voice: 800-727-8772 Fax: 360-604-1401 Web: www.diamondmm.com	Supra Video Phone Kit (Internet/POTS)
Intel Corporation Voice: 800-538-3373 Fax: 800-525-3019 Web: www.intel.com	ProShare Personal Video Conferencing System 200 (ISDN)
PictureTel Corporation Voice: 508-762-5000 Fax: 508-762-5245 Web: www.picturetel.com	PictureTel Live PCS200 (ISDN)
U.S. Robotics Voice: 800-342-5877 Fax: 847-676-7320 Web: www.usr.com	Big Picture Video Conference Kit (Internet/POTS)
VDO Voice: 415-846-7730 Fax: 415-846-7900 Web: www.vdo.net	VDO Internet Video Phone (Internet/POTS/ISDN)
White Pine Software Voice: 603-886-9050 Fax: 603-886-9051 Web: www.cuseeme.com	CU-SeeMe 3.0 (Internet/POTS/ISDN)
WINNOV Voice: 408-733-5922 Fax: 408-733-5922 Web: www.winnov.com	Videum Conference Pro (Internet)

Company	Product
PicturePhone Direct Voice: 800-810-9966 or 716-334-1577 Fax: 716-359-4999 Web: www.picturephone.com	Sells video conferencing systems and related products through mail order at discounted prices.

Antivirus Software

Viruses are everywhere on the Internet, and you need to protect your PC or LAN from the havoc they can wreak on your system. Fortunately, there are a number of good antivirus packages available.

Company	Product
Dr. Solomon's Software Voice: 888-377-6566 Web: www.solomon.com	Dr. Solomon's Anti-Virus
McAfee Associates Voice: 408-988-3832 Fax: 408-970-9727 Web: www.mcafee.com	McAfee VirusScan
Symantec Corporation Voice: 800-441-7234 Fax: 541-984-8020 Web: www.symantec.com	Norton AntiVirus
TouchStone Software Voice: 800-531-0450 Fax: 714-969-4444 Web: www.checkit.com	PC-cillin II

Compression Software

If you're moving data files across the Internet or any network, using compression software is essential for reducing uploading and downloading times.

COMPANY	PRODUCT
Canyon Software Voice: 415-453-9779 Fax: 415-453-6195 Web: http://www.canyonsw.com	Drag and Zip
Luckman Interactive Voice: 800-711-2676 Fax: 213-614-1929 Web: www.luckman.com	Micro Help Zip
Nico Mak Computing Voice: 800-242-4775 or 713-524-6394 Fax: 713-524-6398 Web: www.winzip.com	WinZip

Remote Access Utilities

There are a number of useful utilities to enhance your remote access activities. The following are a sampling of some useful programs. You can get free demo versions of these programs to try them out yourself.

Note: Some of these programs are available on this book's CD-ROM. See Appendix B, "What's on the CD-ROM."

Net.Medic

Net.Medic from VitalSigns Software lets you get a glimpse behind the scenes at the causes of poor Internet performance. Net.Medic allows users to monitor and diagnose the cause of slow response times from Web sites, whether they're caused at the client level, by the Internet service provider, the backbone, or the Web server. Net.Medic then recommends solutions and combats the problems via an Autocure feature. The Net.Medic dashboard offers a number of options for the Web surfer, including icons that illustrate a page's progress from site to desktop, and an index of retrieval times and delays. The product is bundled with U.S. Robotics x2 modems.

Net.Medic
Vital Signs
Voice: 408-980-8844
Fax: 408-980-8707
Web: www.vitalsigns.com

ISDN Accountant

ISDN accountant continuously monitors your ISDN router connections and usage time. Usually, for ISDN service, you are charged by usage so it's important to reduce connection time. Most ISDN routers don't include any software to monitor their usage. Moreover, the monthly telephone bill only lists the total connected minutes; it does not itemize each call with details such as date, time, and duration.

ISDN Accountant runs on your local Window 95 LAN and tracks your ISDN and Internet usage. It tracks who is using the Internet connection and detects if someone is overusing it. You can print reports from the monitoring data to provide you with a cost analysis over historical data. ISDN Accountant also alerts you to any unusual ISDN or excessive usage; tells you when the ISDN router is connected with no traffic; and reports on total daily ISDN usage.

ISDN Accountant
Kansmen Corp.
Voice: 408-263-9881
Fax: 408-263-9883
Web: http://www.kansmen.com

Dunce

Dunce is the demo version of Dunce Gold, which is a handy Windows 95 Dial-Up Networking utility. It provides a number of enhancements to the Dial-Up Networking facility.

- Lets you bypass the Connect to Dialog box.
- Reconnects you in the event of a disconnect.
- Expands the details on the Connect To dialog box.
- Enters your password in the Connect To dialog box.
- Runs and closes up to four applications automatically.
- Allows you to schedule connections at set times.
- Enables automatic pinging of a server to keep you online.

- Disconnects inactive feature.
- Logs connections.

Dunce and Dunce Gold
Vector Development
Voice: 913-539-6160
Web: www.vecdec.com

Internet Control Center

The Internet Control Center (ICC) is a handy program for anyone who is a regular Internet user. It automates connecting and disconnecting with your ISP via modem, monitors your connections, and enables one-touch application switching. You can run up to 12 Internet applications using the ICC toolbar to keep your desktop uncluttered. ICC also starts and closes the Microsoft Winsock.

Internet Control Center
UsefulWare Inc.
Voice: 770-424-2525
Fax: 770-242-2625
Web: www.usefulware.com

Security

Protecting your Internet communications and your PC or LAN from hackers is an important remote access undertaking. Each bandwidth option and corresponding remote access device provides varying levels of security for protecting your PC or LANs. For example, ISDN routers that use DHCP and NAT, along with filters, provide reasonable security against hackers accessing your LAN. Other bandwidth options, such as cable modem service aren't as secure.

Firewalls are software products that act as guards posted at incoming traffic to protect the local network from external threats from the Internet. A firewall disables certain packet-sharing network facilities to secure the local network. Traditionally, firewalls have been expensive and complex systems that were outside the reach of the SOHO market. Fortunately, affordable and easier-to-use firewalls should become more widely available to the SOHO market in the form of add–ons to remote access devices, such as ISDN routers. Ascend Communications, the leader in ISDN routers, offers an optional firewall package called Secure Access Firewall; it offers integrated security that works with the company's Pipeline series of ISDN routers.

Another firewall product for the SOHO market is McAfee's WebWall, which provides firewall protection for dial-up connections. The other area of security involves encryption to protect data communications over the Internet and other public telecommunication networks.

Company	Product
Ascend Communications, Inc. Voice: 800-621-9578 or 510-769-6001 Fax: 510-814-2300 Web: www.ascend.com	Secure Access Firewall for Pipeline ISDN routers.
McAfee Associates Voice: 408-988-3832 Fax: 408-970-9727 Web: www.mcafee.com	WebWall (firewall) NetCrypto (encryption)
Software Builders International Voice: 800-432-0025 or 770-541-1500 Fax: 770-541-1700 Web: www.netzip.com	PC Secure (personal firewall)
Pretty Good Privacy Voice: 602-994-0773 Fax: 415-572-1932 Web: www.pgp.com	PGP for Personal Privacy (encryption)

Establishing a Server Presence on the Internet

To establish a server presence on the Internet, you can take three paths. The first and usually the most expensive is to get a dedicated connection to the Internet and run a server on a powerful PC at your office. This option offers the flexibility in building your Internet server presence, but the high cost of dedicated connections to the Internet make this option out of reach for the SOHO market. The second path involves setting up an Internet server on a PC that you own and placing it at an Internet service provider's site to link it to the ISP's high-speed Internet connections. This option is more affordable than creating an in-house Internet server, but it can still be expensive, depending on the ISP.

The third path is the most affordable option, costing approximately $30 a month. You rent space on an Internet service provider's server to act as your Internet server. This service is often referred to as *Web hosting*. These services are widely available. Most ISPs as well as other companies offer these services. Typically, this type of account allows you to store up to 10 Mb of information and use a virtual domain name that makes the site appear as your own to Web users. These accounts can also include e-mail accounts and other support services. You connect to the site via the Internet and can upload files and Web documents as needed. The major limitation of this approach is that you may not be able to run programs in conjunction with your Internet site, such as a database.

Concentric Host Service

A good example of an Internet hosting service is ConcentricHost, offered by Concentric Network Corp (www.cnchost.com). Concentric offers three hosting packages.

- *ConcentricHost Home Office.* Includes five e-mail accounts, 5 MB of Web site storage, a Web site traffic allotment of 300 MB per month, and a dial-up Internet access account. It uses a customized subdomain name, such as www.mybusiness.cnc.com. This service cost $29.95 per month with a one-time $50 set-up fee.

- *ConcentricHost Small Business.* Includes five e-mail accounts, 10 MB of Web site storage, a Web site traffic allotment of 300 MB per month, and a dial-up Internet access account. This package supports full domain names so that your business can personalize its Web site using a registered domain name, such as www.mybusiness.com. This service cost $39.95 per month with a one-time $50 set-up fee.

- *ConcentricHost Premium.* Includes 10 e-mail boxes, 30 MB disk storage for Web site files and e-mail, a Web site traffic allotment of 1000 MB per month, dedicated IP addressing, and full domain name support. This service costs $59.95 per month with a one-time $100 set-up fee.

All three services provide easy-to-use Web publishing software, as well as tools for building and maintaining your Web site. You can add incremental services as needed, such as more Web site traffic allocation volume or storage space for Web files.

B *What's on the CD-ROM*

The CD-ROM accompanying this book includes a variety of handy remote access tools. All these programs enable you to test-drive a particular category of Windows 95 remote access software. I've made a special effort to offer a sampling of programs that will extend and enhance your Windows 95 remote access experience.

This appendix is also available as an HTML document (readme.htm) on the CD-ROM, which you can load in your Web browser. The readme document provides hyperlinks to all the software sites.

About the Software

There are three types of software on this CD-ROM: shareware, freeware, and demo or trial versions of commercial products. For shareware and commercial demo software, keep in mind that copyright laws apply to both and that the copyright holder retains all rights.

What Is Shareware?

Shareware is not a type of software, but a means of distributing software created by individuals or companies too small to make inroads into the more conventional retail distribution networks. The authors of shareware retain all rights to the software under copyright laws while still allowing free distribution. This gives the user the chance to freely obtain and try out software to see it if fits his or her needs. Shareware should not be confused with public domain or freeware software. If you continue to use shareware after trying it out, you are expected to register your use with the author and pay a registration fee. What you get in return depends on the author, but it may include a printed manual, free updates, telephone support, or other benefits.

What Is Freeware?

This CD-ROM also includes some software products known as freeware, or public domain software. These programs may be used free of charge, courtesy of public-spirited developers and contributors.

Demo Versions of Commercial Software

Most commercial software companies provide free or demo or trial versions of their programs on their Web sites. These packages may or may not include all the features of the commercial version, and they usually have a built-in time-out feature, which means that it expires 30 days after you install the software on your system.

General System Requirements

All the programs on this CD-ROM are Windows 95 programs, and most are 32-bit applications designed specifically to take advantage of the special features provided by Windows 95. General requirements for the software included on this CD-ROM typically include:

- Windows 95
- Pentium processor 75 MHz or higher
- 16 MB or higher of RAM
- 10 MB or more disk space
- Microsoft TCP/IP software with PPP or MPP
- Internet connection with 28.8 Kbps or better

Note: Each software program has its own unique requirements, which are usually noted in the accompanying readme.txt file.

Installing the Software

Installation instructions will vary depending on the type of file used for the software. There are two types of files on this CD-ROM.

FILE TYPE (FILENAME EXTENSION)	DESCRIPTION
.zip	Compressed files that must be uncompressed before executing the Setup program. You must use a file compression program to unzip these programs. Drag and Zip, a file compression program, is available on the CD-ROM.
.exe	Compressed self-extracting files, which means you can execute them as you would any Windows program. They unzip files and automatically run the Setup program.

To install software with the .exe extension, do the following:

1. Insert the CD-ROM in your CD-ROM drive.

2. Open the Windows Explorer.

3. Create a temporary directory for the program file you want to execute.

4. Navigate to your CD-ROM drive and copy the program file you want into the temporary directory.

5. Run the Setup program by choosing Start|Run; or double-click on the program file from the Windows Explorer and follow the instructions on your screen.

To install software with the .zip extension, do the following.

1. Insert the CD-ROM in your CD-ROM drive.

2. Open the Windows Explorer.

3. Create a temporary directory for the program file you want to execute.

4. Navigate to your CD-ROM drive and copy the program file you want into the temporary directory.

5. Unzip the program using a compression program. You can use the Drag and Zip program, which is included on the CD-ROM as your file compression program.

6. Run the Setup program by choosing Start|Run; or double-click on the program file from the Windows Explorer and follow the instructions on your screen.

Programs on the CD-ROM

The following programs are included on the *Windows Remote Access Toolkit* companion CD-ROM. They represent a varied sampling of important remote access and LAN management tools. The program filename is noted below the description of the software.

Note: The software on this CD-ROM were the latest versions at the time this book was written. Before installing any of these programs, you may want to check the software company's Web site for any new versions.

Adobe Acrobat Reader

The Adobe Acrobat Reader 3.0 allows you to view, navigate, and print PDF files that are created using Adobe Acrobat and Acrobat Capture software. The PDF format is widely used on the Internet as the preferred format for software user guides and other documentation.

Adobe Systems Incorporated
Voice: 800-642-3623
Fax: 415-961-3769
Web: www.adobe.com

File: ar32e30.exe

CU-SeeMe

Cu-SeeMe 3.0 is the leading Internet (TCP/IP)-based video-conferencing software that allows you to collaborate with others using video, audio, and a whiteboard. It includes the following features.

- Multicasting support for LAN/WAN conferencing
- H.323 standards-based video codec (H.263) and whiteboard (T.120)
- Capability to view up to 12 participant windows simultaneously
- Caller ID support for incoming connections
- Motion JPEG (M-JPEG) video codec for higher-quality video over LANs, ISDN, or other high-bandwidth connections
- Support for Microsoft ActiveMovie

White Pine Software
Voice: 603-886-9050
Fax: 603-886-9051
Web: www.cuseeme.com

File: cu30.exe

Drag and Zip

Drag and Zip 95 (version 2.2) is a complete standalone or Windows Explorer plug-in file compression program. It includes these impressive capabilities.

- Zips and unzips files in the following formats: ZIP, LZH, GZ, and TAR.
- Works with Uunencoded, MIME and BinHex files.
- Makes Win 32 self-extracting files.
- Makes auto launch and password-protected self-extracting zip files.
- Scans zip files for viruses.
- Is compatible with Netscape Communicator and Internet Explorer.

Canyon Software
Voice: 415-453-9779
Fax: 415-453-6195
Web: www.canyonsw.com

File: dz95.exe

Dunce

Dunce (version 2.52) is the demo version of Dunce Gold. Dunce is a handy Windows 95 Dial-Up Networking utility that provides a number of enhancements to the Dial-Up Networking facility. It:

- Bypasses the Connect to Dialog box.
- Reconnects you in the event of a disconnect.
- Expands the details in the Connect To dialog box.
- Enters your password in the Connect To dialog box.
- Runs and closes up to four applications automatically.
- Allows you to schedule connections at set times.
- Enables automatic pinging of a server to keep you online.

- Disconnects an inactive feature.
- Logs connections.

Vector Development
Voice: 913-539-6160
Web: www.dunce.com

Files: dunce252.zip (program), duncehlp.exe (help file)

Free Agent

Free Agent (version 1.11) is the freeware version of Agent News & Mail Reader software. Agent provides a full complement of features for working with network news and e-mail. The freeware version doesn't include all the bells and whistles of the Agent News & Mail Reader, some of which are listed here.

- Multitasking support
- Kill and watch filters
- Cross-post management features
- Ability to launch URLs from messages
- Support for MIME attachments and the MAPI e-mail protocol
- Full e-mail functionality
- Spelling checker
- Customizable toolbar
- Full offline working capabilities to save on connection charges

Forte, Inc.
Voice: 760-431-6400
Fax: 760-431-6465
Web: www.forteinc.com

File: fa32-111.exe

Internet Control Center

The Internet Control Center 32 (version 4.0) is a handy program that automates connecting and disconnecting with your ISP via modem and monitors your connections. You can run up to 12 Internet applications using the ICC toolbar to keep your desktop uncluttered and enable one-touch application switching. ICC also starts and closes the Microsoft Winsock.

UsefulWare Inc.
Voice: 770-424-2525
Fax: 770-242-2626
Web: www.usefulware.com

File: icc32-40.exe

ISDN Accountant

ISDN Accountant (version 1.0) continuously monitors your ISDN router connections and usage time. Because most ISDN service is billed on a usage basis, it's important to efficiently manage your connection times for LAN-based connections. ISDN Accountant runs on your local Window 95 LAN and tracks your ISDN and Internet usage. It tracks who is using the Internet connection and detects when someone is overusing it. You can print reports from the monitoring data to provide you with a cost analysis over historical data. ISDN Accountant also alerts you to any unusual or excessive usage; it informs you when the ISDN router is connected with no traffic and provides reports on total daily ISDN usage.

Kansmen Corp.
Voice: 408-263-9881
Fax: 408-263-9883
Web: http://www.kansmen.com

File: isdneval.zip

LittleBrother

LittleBrother (version 1.5) is a Windows 95 application that allows your company to manage and measure Internet activities so that you can control unproductive uses of your LAN-to-Internet connection. LittleBrother includes the following features.

- Defines specific Internet activities as productive, unproductive, or neutral. Unproductive sites can include newsgroups, network games, and other distractions.

- Blocks unproductive sites on the Internet and identifies who is spending productive and unproductive hours on the Internet.

- Assigns Internet/intranet access to users according to their needs.

- Provides auditing of Internet activities, such as who is using it, how it is being used, how long it has been used, and whether the use is regarded as productive.

- Provides capacity planning statistics on how your network and Internet resources are used.
- Provides automatic alarms for excessive usage.
- Generates reports based on a variety of variables.

Kansmen Corp.
Voice: 800-200-9811 or 408-263-9881
Fax: 408-263-9883
Web: http://www.kansmen.com

File: klbeval.exe

Netopia Virtual Office

Farallon's Netopia Virtual Office is a Web-based Groupware product designed for the SOHO market. Netopia Virtual Office begins by creating your personal Web page using familiar office metaphors such as an inbox/outbox, messaging, conferencing, and chat. Using passwords, you choose which features to put under lock and key. You can chat in real time with colleagues who are in their virtual offices; or several participants in different locations can huddle over a PowerPoint presentation, marking it up in real time on their computer screens. In addition to making standard Internet capabilities (from e-mail to FTP) easier to use, Netopia Virtual Office adds value to the real-time remote communications capabilities of Farallon's Timbuktu remote control software.

Farallon Communications, Inc.
Voice: 510-814-5000
Fax: 510-814-5023
Web: www.farallon.com

File: nvolle.exe

ReachOut Passport

ReachOut Passport is an Internet-based remote control software package. It includes a host version of the program that resides on the computer you want to take control of via the Internet. On the client side (called a remote viewer), ReachOut Passport comes as a plug-in for Netscape Navigator and as an ActiveX Control for Microsoft Internet Explorer. Together, these programs allow you to take control of any desktop connected to the Internet.

Note: You must use the serial number 1033-0259-6742-6858 to install ReachOut Passport.

Stac
Voice: 800-522-7822
Fax: 619-794-3741
Web: www.stac.com

Files: roppeval.exe (program), roppm.exe (documentation)

WFTPD

WFTPD (version 2.34) is a shareware version of WFTPD Pro, a Windows 95 FTP server software package that allows remote users to connect to your PC and use FTP over the Internet to transfer files. WFTD has the following capabilities:

- Individual enable and disable feature for anonymous access, uploads, and downloads.
- Configurable messages displayed to user at login and logoff.
- Access control based on user name/password and user's host/network address
- Assignable rights based on a directory-by-directory basis.
- Automatic resumption of interrupted transfers.
- Configurable maximum number of connected users and time-out on idle connections.
- Management of connected users.

Texas Imperial Software
Voice: 512-257-2578
Fax: 512-378-3246
Web: www.wftpd.com

File: 32wfd234.zip

What's Up

What's Up (version 2.13) is a high-performance, low-cost network monitoring tool designed to give LAN administrators the ability to monitor any networked device in real time. What's Up checks the status of any server, hub, router, printer, or desktop with an IP address. It also allows you to monitor any Internet server. What's Up provides desktop alarm, digital beeper, alphanumeric pager, and e-mail notification; and its graphical network mapping and monitoring capabilities provide up-to-the minute management of a network. You can create a graphical map of your network and then connect it to real-time monitoring services.

Ipswitch, Inc.
Voice: 617-676-5700
Fax: 617-676-5710
Web: www.ipswitch.com

File: whatsup.zip

WS_FTP

WS_FTP (the Limited Edition of WS_FTP Pro) is the world's most popular Windows 95 FTP client program. With WS_FTP, you can connect to any remote system that has a valid Internet address and an FTP server, browse through directories and files, and transfer files between the two systems. WS_FTP includes the following features:

- Automated connections for frequently accessed remote sites
- Convenient drag-and-drop capabilities for simplifying file transfer tasks
- Support for firewalls
- Support for over 30 different remote file systems
- Automatic saving of host configurations

Ipswitch, Inc.
Voice: 617-676-5700
Fax: 617-676-5710
Web: www.ipswitch.com

Files: wsftppro.zip (program) ws_ftp.pdf (user guide;
     use Adobe Acrobat to read)

User Assistance and Information

The software accompanying this book is provided as-is, without warranty or support of any kind. Should you require basic installation assistance, or if your media is defective, please call John Wiley & Sons' product support number at 212-850-6194 weekdays between 9:00 A.M. and 4:00 P.M. Eastern Standard Time, or contact us via e-mail at wprtusw@wiley.com.

To place additional orders or request information about other Wiley products, please call 800-879-4539.

Glossary

56-Kbps modem The latest generation of analog modems that can reach speeds of up to 56 Kbps under ideal telephone line conditions. The enhanced speed is accomplished by eliminating one of the two digital-to-analog conversions that occur during modem communications. The two competing 56K technologies are x2 and K56flex.

ADSL (Asymmetric Digital Subscriber Line) A high-speed digital communication technology that can deliver up to 9 Mbps downstream and 640 Kbps upstream over standard telephone lines.

analog communications The method of voice transmission used in today's telephone networks. This technology converts voice to electrical signals and amplifies them so that thet can be sent over long distances. An analog-based data transmission is at the bottom of the telecommunications bandwidth pyramid.

asymmetric communications One data channel supports a larger data communications capacity than the other channel, which means data traveling in one direction moves faster than data moving in the opposite direction.

asynchronous communications The form of data communications that transmits data one bit at a time with start and stop bits added. This is the method used for data communications over POTS using modems.

AT&T 5ESS The leading telephone switch used by RBOCs, made by AT&T. For ISDN service, these switches use Custom or NI-1 software.

ATM (Asynchronous Transfer Mode) A cell-switched, full-duplex protocol for industrial-strength networks that operate at bandwidths ranging from 25 Mbps to 622 Mbps. ATM is designed to integrate LAN, WAN, voice, video, and data communication functions into a single uniform protocol.

B channel (bearer channel)   The communications channel used for delivering data or voice communications over ISDN. Each B channel supports up to 64 Kbps. The standard ISDN BRI connection includes two B channels.

bandwidth   The amount of data that can flow through a channel. The greater the bandwidth, the more data that can travel at one time.

bearer services   A communication connection's capability to carry voice, circuit, or packet data.

Bellcore (Bell Communications Research)   The former research arm of the regional telephone companies. Bellcore played a leading role in developing DSL technologies and ISDN standards.

Bellcore compatibility packages   A standardized method used for ordering ISDN service, developed by Bellcore.

binding   A process that defines the relationship between a network adapter card and network protocols used in conjunction with that network adapter card. For example, you bind the TCP/IP protocol to a network adapter card that connects to a LAN-based remote access device to enable that PC to connect to the Internet.

BONDING (bandwidth on demand interoperability group)   The combining of two or more B channels to form a single channel with a bandwidth greater than 64 Kbps. Most ISDN devices support bonding.

bps (bits per second)   The basic unit of measurement for data transmission speed over a data communications link.

BRI (basic rate interface)   The standard interface to ISDN that includes two B (bearer) channels and one D (data) channel.

bridge   A device that connects two networks of a similar type into a single, larger network.

broadband   High-speed bandwidth technologies that allow combined transmission of data, voice, and video using several streams of data.

bus topology   A local area network topology based on 10Base2 coaxial cabling, which uses a single cable routed through a work area with PCs connected anywhere along on the line. Each computer is connected via a BNC T connector, and each end is terminated with a small terminator piece. This LAN topology is being replaced by the star topology, which uses 10BaseT cabling.

cable drop   The segment of cable that runs from the street or the telephone pole to a home or office. The cable drop connects the home or office to the neighborhood network.

cable modem   A device for using cable service for data communications. A cable modem can transfer data at speeds up to 10 Mbps downstream.

CAP (Carrierless Amplitude Phase Modulation)   A modulation scheme used for asymmetric digital subscriber lines (ADSL). CAP describes a process by which incoming data modulates a single channel that is then transmitted down a telephone line. CAP is one of the two competing modulation schemes used for ADSL; the other scheme is DMT.

CATV (community antenna TV)   The original term used for early cable television service, which used a single powerful antenna for servicing an entire community.

channel   Any pathway used for data transmission. A communications channel is a logical device defined separately from the cabling that actually delivers the data communications link. Each channel is an independent unit that can transfer data concurrently with other channels; for example, an ISDN line includes three channels: two bearer channels, and one data channel. Each B channel can support data transmissions of up to 64 Kbps, for a combined capacity of 128 Kbps.

CHAP (Challenge Handshake Authentication Protocol)   A security protocol that arranges an exchange of random numbers between computers. The machine receiving a number from the first computer performs calculations on that number using a previously agreed-upon string of characters as a secret encryption key.

circuit switching   A form of communications in which an information transmission path between two devices is routed through one or more switches. The path is assigned for the duration of a call.

circuit-switched service   Used as the basis for most telephone communications. POTS (plain old telephone service) and ISDN are circuit-switched services, which means that the communications pathway remains fixed for the duration of the call and is not available to other users.

CLEC (competitive local exchange carrier)   A company that buys telecommunications services from an incumbent telephone company at a discount to resell to customers. The Telecommunications Act of 1996 allowed CLECs as a way to bring competition into local telephone service.

client/server computing   The foundation for networking, in which one computer acts as the host or server and the other computer acts as a client. In the case of remote access, your PC acts as the client computer that connects to a server.

cloud   A commonly used term that defines any large network, such as the public-switched network or the Internet.

CO (central office)   The facility housing the local telephone switches that handle all the telephone system's call-routing and other functions. The CO is the telephone company side of the local loop that connects all telephone subscribers to the telephone network.

codec (coder/decoder)   Hardware that transforms analog data into a digital data form and converts digital data back to analog form. Used in a wide variety of remote access applications.

common carrier   A regulated telecommunications company that provides services for public use.

compression   A process for reducing the number of bits required to transmit information over a data communications link.

CPE (customer premises equipment)   A telco term used to describe equipment used at the customer's premises. In the United States, CPE includes any devices that connect to the telephone line, which the customer must purchase (or lease), install, and maintain.

crossover cable   A special 10BaseT cable in which one pair of the eight wires is crossed. These cables are used to connect a network device, such as a router, directly to a single PC via a network adapter card.

CSD (circuit-switched data)   An ISDN circuit-switched call for digital data communications in which a transmission path between two users is assigned for the duration of a call. A provisioning option for each B channel.

CSV (circuit-switched voice)   An ISDN circuit-switched call for digital voice in which the transmission path between two users is assigned for the duration of a call. A provisioning option for each B channel.

CSV/CSD (alternate circuit-switched voice/circuit-switched data)   An ISDN B-channel configuration that allows either circuit-switched voice or circuit-switched data communications. A provisioning option for each B channel.

D channel   Data channel. The separate channel for out-of-band signaling between the user and the ISDN network.

demarcation point   The point at the customer premises where the line from the telephone company meets the premises' wiring. From the demarcation point, the end user is responsible for the wiring.

desktop video conferencing   A PC-based video-conferencing system that allows people to conduct video conferencing in real time from their desks via a LAN, WAN, or the Internet.

DHCP (Dynamic Host Configuration Protocol)   Set of rules that allow IP addresses, subnet masks, and default gateway addresses to be assigned to workstations on an as-needed basis. DHCP removes the requirement that individual workstations must have static IP addresses.

Dial-Up Networking   A Windows 95 facility for connecting computers via analog and ISDN modems. It enables connecting computers using the same networking protocols to allow remote access communications.

distributed workplace   Any decentralized workplace that is linked by a wide area network system or the Internet.

DMS-100   A telephone switch made by Nortel. For ISDN service, these switches use proprietary or NI-1 software.

DMT (Discrete MultiTone)   A modulation system used for asymmetric digital subscriber lines (ADSL). DMT describes a version of multicarrier modulation in which incoming data is collected and then distributed over a large number of small individual channels. DMT is one of the two competing modulation schemes for ADSL; the other is CAP.

DN (directory number)   Telephone numbers for ISDN. A BRI line can have up to eight directory numbers, depending on the switch type used by the telephone company.

Domain Name System (DNS)   The text-based addressing or naming structure used as a friendlier interface to IP addresses. Domain names have a hierarchical structure delineated by dots (periods). The order of levels in a domain name always proceeds from the most specific to the most general when viewed from left to right.

downstream   Data traffic moving from the remote network to the local network or computer; for example, data moving from a server on the Internet down to a PC via a data communications link.

driver   A program that controls a hardware device and communicates with operating systems and applications; for example, a network adapter card driver interfaces between the network card and Windows 95.

DSL (Digital Subscriber Line)   A family of high-speed data communication technologies that work over standard twisted-pair wires running between the telephone company central offices and subscribers. The devices at each end of the local loop enable the higher data communications capacity.

DSL modem   The device that enables standard telephone wiring to deliver high-speed data communications. One modem sits at the customer site and the other in the telephone company's central office.

DSLAMS (digital subscriber line access multiplexors)   The devices at the telephone company's central office for connecting customers using DSL modems.

dynamic bandwidth allocation   A key feature of ISDN remote access devices that allows automatic adjustment of the number of B channels in use depending on the volume of data being sent or received. Automatically adjusting bandwidth up or down based on your data volume means you use only what you need.

dynamic IP addressing   A process by which an IP address is assigned by a DHCP server to the client for the current session only. After the session ends, the IP address returns to a pool of IP addresses available for new callers.

enterprise network   A large geographically dispersed internetwork under the jurisdiction of a large organization. It typically includes several different types of networks and computer systems from different vendors.

Ethernet   The local area network protocol used in most PC networks. Most Ethernet networks support data transmission speeds up to 10 Mbps.

EZ-ISDN   A standardized set of ISDN line configurations developed by the North American ISDN User's Forum (NIUF) to make ordering of ISDN service easier.

FCC (Federal Communications Commission)   The United States government agency responsible for regulating the telecommunications industry at the federal level. The FCC is also in charge of carrying out the mandate of the Telecommunications Act of 1996.

fiber optics   A new generation of telecommunication wiring that uses light beams sent through thin strands of glass or other transparent materials. Fiber optics can transmit large amounts of data.

fractional T1   A subset of bandwidth from a T1 line, which has a capacity of 1.54 Mbps. A fractional T1 line can use any combination of the 24 channels of 64 Kbps available in a T1 line.

frame relay   A high-speed, dedicated packet-switching service offered by the telephone companies that can deliver data communications at up to 1.54 Mbps. Frame relay is used by large corporations to build fast network connections over public switching facilities.

full duplex   The bidirectional communication capability in which transmissions travel in both directions simultaneously.

functional devices   A classification of ISDN operational functions used to describe which tasks the different components of an ISDN configuration perform. For example, the Network Termination 1 function defines the NTI device that presents your premises as a node on the ISDN network.

GEO (geostationary orbit satellite)   A satellite that travels in an orbit 22,300 miles above the Earth's equator, where the satellite's period of rotation matches the earth's rotation. The result is that the satellite always remains in the same spot over the Earth.

half duplex   Data transmission that takes place in only one direction at a time.

HDSL (high-data-rate Digital Subscriber Line)   A high-speed digital communication technology that can deliver up 1.54 Mbps in both directions over two standard telephone lines. HDSL is widely used for dedicated T1 lines.

headend   The cable operator's facility for its TV and Internet access operations. For Internet access, the headend is the terminus for upstream data communications from cable modems and the conduit for downstream data communications from the Internet.

HFC (hybrid fiber coaxial)   A new cable distribution system that connects fiber optics to neighborhood network nodes for the delivery of two-way Internet access cable service. A typical node serves 500 to 2,500 homes. Cable systems that use this system can offer two-way Internet access services via cable modems.

hub   A central network device that joins 10BaseT cables from PCs into a star configuration. A typical hub for a small network has 5 to 10 10BaseT (RJ-45 ports) for connecting PCs via network adapters and other devices into a network.

IDSL (ISDN digital subscriber line)   A dedicated line version of the Integrated Services Digital Network service, which is already offered by telephone companies as a dial-up service. Delivers data at 128 Kbps in both directions over a dedicated connection.

IEC (interexchange carrier)   The telephone company that provides telephone service outside the local telephone companies. For example, AT&T and MCI are interexchange carriers. Also referred to as IXCs.

IEEE 803.2   The protocol that defines an Ethernet network at the physical layer of network signaling and cabling.

in-band signaling   Network signaling that is carried in the same channel as the bearer traffic. In analog telephone communications, the same circuits used to carry voice are used to transmit the signal for the telephone network.

interface   A specification that defines the protocols used at a particular reference point in a network. The basic rate interface (BRI) refers to an access interface to ISDN.

internetworking   Data communications across different network operating systems.

InterNIC (Internet Network Information Center)   The organization in charge of domain name registration and other services for the Internet.

interoperable   Two devices are interoperable when they can work together, which is the result of standardization of protocols.

IP (Internet Protocol)   The internetworking protocol that forms the basis of the Internet and IP addresses.

IPX (Internet Packet Exchange)   Novell's NetWare internetworking protocols.

IRQ (interrupt request)   The internal electrical signals used by a device within a PC to indicate when the device needs access to the CPU.

ISDN (Integrated Services Digital Network)   The digital telecommunications service offered by telephone companies that delivers data communications via standard POTS lines at a speed of 128 Kbps.

ISP (Internet service provider)   A company offering data communication connections to the Internet. There are thousands of ISPs in all sizes, from national to regional and local providers.

ITU (International Telephone Union)   A United Nations organization that specifies telecommunications standards.

IXC (interexchange carrier)   Long-distance telecommunications carrier, such as AT&T, MCI, and Sprint. These telephone companies use local exchange carrier switches as gateways for calls into their long-distance networks. Also referred to as IECs.

K56flex   The 56K modem technology developed by Rockwell and Lucent and supported by most PC modem vendors. K56flex is one of two competing 56K modem technologies; the other is x2.

Kbps (kilobits per second)   Unit of measurement in thousands of bits per second for data transmission.

LAN (local area network)   A group of computers and other devices linked via a network operating system and Ethernet media.

LATA (local access and transport area)   Local exchange carriers (RBOCs) provide service within a LATA. Typically, a LATA comprises multiple area codes. In most cases, RBOCs are prohibited from offering telecommunication services between LATAs.

LEC (local exchange carrier)   The local telephone company. An LEC is also called an RBOC (Regional Bell Operating Company).

local exchange area   A geographical area in which a single, uniform set of tariffs for telephone service is in place. A call between any two points in an exchange area is considered a local call.

local loop   The pair of copper wires that connects the end user to the telephone company's central office, which is the gateway to the global telephone network.

logical channels   The three channels of a BRI connection, which are defined not as three physically separate wires but as three separate ISDN system channels.

MAC (media access control layer)   A protocol layer that controls access to a specific network adapter card.

Mbps (million bits per second)   A measurement for high-speed data transmission used in LANs and other high-speed digital communication links.

Microsoft ISDN Accelerator Pack   Free software that enables ISDN connections via the Windows 95 Dial-Up Networking facility. It supports Multilink PPP, which allows an ISDN adapter to bond two B channels together for 128 Kbps of bandwidth.

modem (modulator/demodulator)   A device used to send data over analog telephone lines. It converts digital signals to analog signals at the sending end and converts analog signals to digital signals at the receiving end.

MPPP (Multilink Point-to-Point Protocol)   The Point-to-Point Protocol for ISDN connections that allows use of both B channels for remote access to the Internet. MPPP also allows different remote access devices to communicate with each other. Also referred to as MP.

NAT (Network Address Translation)   Internet standard that allows a local network to use IP addresses not recognized by users outside the local network. NAT works in conjunction with DHCP to enable a Windows 95 LAN to connect to the Internet using a single-user account.

National ISDN   Defined by Bellcore, National ISDN 1 (NI-1) is an agreement among telephone companies and CPE vendors to jointly provide the first phase of standards-based ISDN. NI-1 is a collection of standards to allow CPE to work across different telephone company switches using the basic rate interface (BRI).

NDIS (network driver interface specification)   Provides a common set of rules for network adapter manufacturers and network operating system (NOS) developers to use for communications between the network adapter and the NOS. Most network adapters now ship with an NDIS driver. Developed by Microsoft.

NetBEUI (NetBIOS Extended User Interface)   Microsoft's implementation of NetBIOS. NetBEUI is used in Windows for Workgroups, Windows 95, Windows NT, and OS/2.

network interface box   The point at which the lines from the telephone company meet the wiring for your premises.

NIC (network interface card)   Provides the network interface to a PC via an adapter card.

node   A network junction in a data communications network, or a single device on a network such as a computer, network printer, or router.

NT1 (network termination 1)   Located at the end-user side of the ISDN connection, this functional device represents the termination of the ISDN system at the end-user's location. The NTI function is embedded in NTI and NTI Plus devices.

out-of-band signaling   Allows telephone network management signaling functions and other services to be sent over a separate channel rather than the bearer channel. ISDN uses out-of-band signaling via the D channel. Out-of-band signaling used in ISDN consists of messages rather than audio signals, as is the case with the touch-tone analog telephone system.

packet A grouping of bits into a formatted unit for transmitting across a network. The Internet is a packet-based network.

packet-switched service A service in which data is transmitted in packets through a network. Each packet has the ability to take a different route through the network. There is no predefined circuit, as is the case for circuit-switched service.

packet switching A data transmission method in which data is transferred by packets, or blocks of data. Packets are sent using a store-and-forward method across nodes in a network.

PAP (Password Authentication Protocol) A security protocol that establishes a two-way "handshake" to verify the identity of the two computers. PAP is not as secure as CHAP because passwords are sent in text format.

passband The frequency spectrum that determines the amount of data that can be transmitted through a channel. The passband determines the bandwidth of a channel.

PBX (private branch exchange) A telecommunications switch at a customer's premises that handles call management. The PBX connects to the telephone company via a dedicated, high-speed communications link to transport a large volume of traffic. Typically, PBX systems handle the internal telecommunications needs of large organizations.

PCM (pulse code modulation) The method used to convert analog audio to digitized audio.

PCMCIA (Personal Computer Memory Card International Association) The bus used for laptops, which implement credit-card-size cards that connect to external slots. Commonly referred to as PC cards, this system makes it easy for laptop users to change the hardware configuration of their machines. Common PCMCIA cards include modem and network adapters.

Ping A handy TCP/IP utility that allows a user to check whether a remote system is actively connected to the Internet by using the remote system's IP address. Ping acts as a sonar that bounces back status information.

Plug-and-Play A standard for simplifying installation of hardware devices in PCs running Windows 95. Windows 95 automatically detects Plug-and-Play-compatible devices attached to your system and uses software to configure IRQ and I/O settings instead of jumpers and switches.

point-to-multipoint connection A connection established between one device on one end and more than one device on the other end.

point-to-point connection   A connection established between two fixed points.

POP (point of presence)   A local access point for connecting to an Internet service provider. Your telecommunications charges are affected by your proximity to a POP.

port   An access point for data to enter, or a hardware receptacle on a network device for plugging in a connector.

POTS (plain old telephone service)   A term used for standard analog telecommunication.

PPP (Point-to-Point Protocol)   A communications protocol that allows a computer using TCP/IP to connect directly to the Internet. The new PPP/MP protocol is an improved version of this protocol for ISDN connection to the Internet.

PRI (primary rate interface)   An ISDN interface designed for high-volume data communications. PRI consists of 23 B channels at 64 Kbps each and 1 D channel at 64 Kbps.

protector block   The point at which the lines from the telephone company meet the lines from the network interface box at a customer's premises.

protocol   A set of rules that define how different computer systems and other devices interoperate with each other.

PSTN (public-switched telephone network)   Any telecommunications network that is available for public use. POTS and ISDN are part of the public-switched telephone network.

PUC (Public Utilities Commission)   A government agency at the state level that regulates telephone companies and other utilities. PUCs approve telephone company tariff filings, which affect how you're charged for telephone services. The FCC deals with similar regulatory functions at the federal level.

RADSL (Rate Adaptive Asymmetric Digital Subscriber Line)   The rate-adaptive version of ADSL (Asymmetric Digital Subscriber Line) service that enables the service provider to adjust the data transmission capabilities of ADSL, which can deliver up to 9 Mbps downstream and 640 Kbps upstream over standard telephone lines.

rate adaptation   A system that allows two pieces of data equipment operating at different data transmission rates to interoperate.

RBOC (Regional Bell Operating Company)   One of the large local exchange carriers that were created as a result of the breakup of AT&T. RBOCs provide telephone service within a specific region of the United States.

reference point   A specific point in the model that depicts how ISDN works. Each component of this model is identified using a reference point. For example, the U reference point defines the local loop of an ISDN connection. These reference points are also called interfaces, such as the U interface or the S/T interface.

remote access   A general term that refers to any computer-based data communications technology that connects a computer over a wide area network to a remote host.

repeater   Equipment used to amplify a signal to boost the range of the signal over longer distances.

RJ-11 connector   A modular connector used for four- or six-wire analog devices.

RJ-45 connector   A modular jack that can hold up to four pairs of wires. RJ-45 looks similar to an RJ-11 but is larger. ISDN connections use RJ-45 jacks at the S/T interface.

router   A hardware device that acts as a gateway among different types of networks to route data packets based on their protocols and addresses.

RS-232   An industry standard for serial communications connections.

S reference point   The ISDN reference point that represents where a CPE connects to a customer switching device, such as a PBX system.

S/T interface   Combines the ISDN reference points where a device connects to either an NTI or an NT2 functional device. Also called the S/T reference point.

SDSL (Symmetrical Digital Subscriber Line)   A high-speed digital communications technology that can deliver up 2 Mbps in both directions over standard telephone lines. SDSL can be packaged in a variety of bandwidth capacity configurations.

serial communication   The transmission of data one bit at a time over a single line. Serial communications can be synchronous or asynchronous.

SOHO (small office/home office)   A term applied to telecommuters and small offices located in homes or small-business locations and remotely connected to a corporate LAN or the Internet. These downsized workplaces are replacing traditional, large central office environments.

SPID (service profile identifier)   An alphanumeric string that uniquely identifies the service capabilities of an ISDN device. This identifier points to a particular location in the telephone company's central office switch memory where relevant details about the device are stored.

standard   A set of technical specifications used to establish uniformity in hardware and software.

star topology   A local area network topology based on 10BaseT cabling that connects from each PC to a network device called a hub. 10BaseT cabling uses RJ-45 connectors and wiring, which resembles standard telephone wiring used in business environments. This the most popular form of LAN topology.

static IP addressing   An assigned IP address used to connect to a TCP/IP network. The same IP number is used every time the connection is made.

subscriber loop   The pair of copper wires that connects the end user to the telephone network.

supplementary services   The collection of voice communications services available via ISDN. These services include call-management features such as call appearances, conference calling, and call forwarding.

switch   The equipment that connects users of a telecommunications network. Each subscriber has a dedicated loop to the nearest telephone switch. All of these switches have access to trunk lines for making calls beyond the local exchange area. A call from one user to another consists of a loop at each end of the connection, with switches and trunk lines used to route the connection between them.

symmetric communications   A transmission system in which both channels used in a data communications link have equal capacity for data transmission.

synchronous communications   A data transmission method in which data is transmitted in blocks separated by equal time intervals. This is a faster method of data communications than asynchronous, but both are serial communications.

T interface   The ISDN reference point that represents where an ISDN device connects to an NT1 functional device.

T1   The most widely used dedicated digital service from the telephone companies. T1 provides transmission rates of 1.54 Mbps. A T1 line can handle 24 voice or data channels at 64 Kbps each.

TA (terminal adapter)   The ISDN functional device that allows non-ISDN devices to work with ISDN. Any device that adapts a non-ISDN device for ISDN incorporates the TA function.

tariff   A rate and availability schedule for telecommunications services that must be filed with and approved by a regulatory body before it becomes effective. Tariffs also include general terms and conditions of service.

TCP/IP (Transmission Control Protocol and Internet Protocol)   The suite of networking protocols that enable disparate types of computers to communicate over the Internet.

TCP/IP stack   The software that allows a computer to communicate via TCP/IP. The Microsoft TCP/IP stack is included with Windows 95.

Telecommunications Act of 1996   Legislation passed by the U.S. Congress designed to provide users with more choices in service and pricing by opening the telecommunications industry to competition, especially at the local exchange carrier level.

telecommuters   Employees who work from home on a part- or full-time basis.

telephony   The marriage of computers and telecommunications.

throughput   An overall measurement of a communications link's performance. Throughput takes into account a variety of factors that inhibit the flow of data over a link. Such factors as total network traffic and switches slow down data transmission.

TLD (top-level domain)   The highest level in the hierarchy of the Domain Name System. These domains are commonly called organizational domains. They include .com, .edu, .gov, and others. The .com TDL is for businesses.

U interface   The reference point of an ISDN connection that includes the local loop wiring up to the NT1 functional device.

UART (universal asynchronous receiver/transmitter)   UART chips are the part of a PC's COM port that handles the communications between the CPU and the device attached to the COM port. Windows 95 supports the 16550A UART chip for higher bps rates.

upstream   Data moving from a PC or LAN to the remote network; for example, data moving from a PC via a data communications link to a server on the Internet.

VDSL (very high-bit-rate Digital Subscriber Line)   A high-speed digital communication technology that can deliver up 52 Mbps downstream for locations within 1,000 feet of the central office. Longer distances from the central office reduce the capacity. For example, at 5,000 feet from the central office, the data transmission rate drops to 13 Mbps.

virtual office   Any workplace outside the traditional office. Virtual implies the use of technology that enables information workers to re-create the support services of the traditional office.

VSAT (very small aperture terminal)   A satellite dish that supports two-way data communications.

WAN (wide area network)   A communication network that connects geographically dispersed sites.

whiteboard   Collaboration software typically bundled with desktop video-conferencing systems. It allows two remote users to share the same computer screen view just as people share a whiteboard in a meeting room.

winipcfg (Windows IP Configuration)   A Windows 95 utility that lets users view information about their TCP/IP and network adapter card settings.

WINS (Windows Internet Name Service)   The protocol that enables Windows 95 to work with a DHCP server. WINS handles routing information between a network device and the DHCP server after the IP address has been assigned.

WinSock   A program that conforms to a set of standards called the Windows Socket API (Application Programming Interface). A WinSock program controls the link between Microsoft Windows 95 software and a TCP/IP program.

x2   U.S. Robotics 56K modem technology. x2 is one of two competing 56K modem technologies; the other is K56flex.

Index

What's on the CD-ROM

The CD-ROM accompanying this book includes a variety of handy remote access tools. All these programs enable you to test-drive a particular category of Windows 95 remote access software. I've made a special effort to offer a sampling of programs that will extend and enhance your Windows 95 remote access experience.

Adobe Acrobat Reader

CU-SeeMe 3.0

Drag and Zip 95 (version 2.2)

Dunce (version 2.52)

Free Agent (version 1.11)

Internet Control Center 32 (version 4.0)

ISDN Accountant (version 1.0)

LittleBrother (version 1.5)

Netopia Virtual Office

ReachOut Passport

WFTPD (version 2.34)

What's Up (version 2.13)

WS_FTP (the Limited Edition of WS_FTP Pro).

CUSTOMER NOTE: IF THIS BOOK IS ACCOMPANIED BY SOFTWARE, PLEASE READ THE FOLLOWING BEFORE OPENING THE PACKAGE.

This software contains files to help you utilize the models described in the accompanying book. By opening the package, you are agreeing to be bound by the following agreement:

This software product is protected by copyright and all rights are reserved by the author, John Wiley & Sons, Inc., or their licensors. You are licensed to use this software as described in the software and the accompanying book. Copying the software for any other purpose may be a violation of the U.S. Copyright Law.

This software product is sold as is without warranty of any kind, either express or implied, including but not limited to the implied warranty of merchantability and fitness for a particular purpose. Neither Wiley nor its dealers or distributors assumes any liability for any alleged or actual damages arising from the use of or the inability to use this software. (Some states do not allow the exclusion of implied warranties, so the exclusion may not apply to you.)